GOVERNORS STATE UNIVERSITY LIBRARY

3 1611 00351 4491

S0-AQM-465

READING INSTRUCTION
FOR DIVERSE CLASSROOMS

GOVERNORS STATE UNIVERSITY
UNIVERSITY PARK
IL 60466

SOLVING PROBLEMS IN THE TEACHING OF LITERACY
Cathy Collins Block, Series Editor

Recent Volumes

Teaching New Literacies in Grades K–3:
Resources for 21st-Century Classrooms
Edited by Barbara Moss and Diane Lapp

Teaching New Literacies in Grades 4–6:
Resources for 21st-Century Classrooms
Edited by Barbara Moss and Diane Lapp

Teaching Reading:
Strategies and Resources for Grades K–6
Rachel L. McCormack and Susan Lee Pasquarelli

Comprehension Across the Curriculum:
Perspectives and Practices K–12
Edited by Kathy Ganske and Douglas Fisher

Best Practices in ELL Instruction
Edited by Guofang Li and Patricia A. Edwards

Responsive Guided Reading in Grades K–5:
Simplifying Small-Group Instruction
Jennifer Berne and Sophie C. Degener

Early Intervention for Reading Difficulties:
The Interactive Strategies Approach
Donna M. Scanlon, Kimberly L. Anderson, and Joan M. Sweeney

Matching Books and Readers:
Helping English Learners in Grades K–6
Nancy L. Hadaway and Terrell A. Young

Children's Literature in the Classroom:
Engaging Lifelong Readers
Diane M. Barone

Empowering Struggling Readers:
Practices for the Middle Grades
Leigh A. Hall, Leslie D. Burns, and Elizabeth Carr Edwards

Reading Instruction for Diverse Classrooms:
Research-Based, Culturally Responsive Practice
Ellen McIntyre, Nancy Hulan, and Vicky Layne

Reading Instruction for Diverse Classrooms

RESEARCH-BASED, CULTURALLY RESPONSIVE PRACTICE

Ellen McIntyre
Nancy Hulan
Vicky Layne

GOVERNORS STATE UNIVERSITY
UNIVERSITY PARK
IL 60466

THE GUILFORD PRESS
New York   London

LB
1573
.M3917
2011

© 2011 The Guilford Press
A Division of Guilford Publications, Inc.
72 Spring Street, New York, NY 10012
www.guilford.com

All rights reserved

No part of this book may be reproduced, translated, stored in a retrieval system,
or transmitted, in any form or by any means, electronic, mechanical, photocopying,
microfilming, recording, or otherwise, without written permission from the publisher.

Printed in the United States of America

This book is printed on acid-free paper.

Last digit is print number: 9   8   7   6   5   4   3   2   1

Library of Congress Cataloging-in-Publication Data

McIntyre, Ellen.
   Reading instruction for diverse classrooms : research-based, culturally responsive
practice / Ellen McIntyre, Nancy Hulan, Vicky Lane.
      p. cm. — (Solving problems in the teaching of literacy)
   Includes bibliographical references and index.
   ISBN 978-1-60918-053-9 (pbk. : alk. paper) — ISBN 978-1-60918-054-6 (hardcover :
alk. paper)
   1. Reading (Elementary)—United States.   2. Language arts (Elementary)—United
States.   3. Reading (Elementary)—Social aspects—United States.   4. Multicultural
education—United States.   5. Children—Books and reading—United
States.   I. Hulan, Nancy.   II Layne, Vicky.   III. Title.
   LB1573.M3917 2011
   372.41—dc22
                                                                                          2010041415

GOVERNORS STATE UNIVERSITY
UNIVERSITY PARK
IL 60466

About the Authors

Ellen McIntyre, EdD, is Professor and Department Head of Elementary Education at North Carolina State University, where she leads an innovative, rigorous teacher education program and teaches courses on literacy and diversity. Dr. McIntyre conducts research on teacher education, literacy instruction and student achievement, and the sociocultural factors that affect teaching and learning. Prior to her university work, she was a first-, second-, and sixth-grade teacher in an urban elementary school in Kentucky that served students of poverty. Her work has focused on classroom instruction and family involvement for students from populations who have historically struggled in school. Dr. McIntyre has published many books, including *Balanced Instruction: Strategies and Skills in Whole Language* (with Michael Pressley), *Reaching Out: A K–8 Resource for Connecting Families and Schools* (with Diane W. Kyle, Karen B. Miller, and Gayle H. Moore), *Bridging School and Home through Family Nights* (with Diane W. Kyle, Karen B. Miller, and Gayle H. Moore), and *Six Principles for Teaching English Language Learners in All Classrooms* (with Diane W. Kyle, Cheng-Ting Chen, Jayne Kraemer, and Johanna Parr). Her research has been published widely in such journals as *American Educational Research Journal*, *Reading Research Quarterly*, *Journal of Educational Research*, *Research in the Teaching of English*, *Reading and Writing Quarterly*, and *Journal of Literacy Research*, among others.

Nancy Hulan, MEd, is a PhD candidate in Curriculum and Instruction (Literacy Focus) at the University of Louisville in Louisville, Kentucky. She began her teaching career as a volunteer reading teacher at a girls' club for children living in poverty in Reynosa, Mexico, and has taught diverse populations of students as a Reading Resource teacher, a Title I teacher, and a second-grade teacher in Kentucky, Tennessee, and Las Vegas. In addition to working with students in kindergarten through fifth grade, Ms. Hulan has taught adult literacy and English language classes for adults. She has worked extensively with diverse populations, including English language learners and children of poverty. Her research includes investigations of student discussion patterns within the elementary classroom, instruction for linguistically and culturally diverse students, culturally responsive instruction and reading pedagogy, teachers' decision-making processes concerning literacy instruction, and teachers' use of children's literature (particularly multicultural literature) within classrooms. She has written articles on literacy teaching in the elementary classroom. *Reading Instruction for Diverse Classrooms* is her first book.

Vicky Layne, MAT, is the Literacy Coach at Engelhard Elementary School in Louisville, Kentucky, where she coaches a team of dedicated teachers, coordinates the schoolwide reading intervention program, conducts literacy professional development, teaches reading interventions to struggling readers, and co-teaches the school's "Talent Pool" program for advanced readers. She is finishing her "Rank I" certificate, which is 30 graduate credit hours beyond a master's degree, in Reading Education. Ms. Layne has taught all elementary grade levels and implemented the culturally responsive instruction model with diverse populations of students from kindergarten through fifth grade. She has conducted financial literacy workshops for elementary and middle school students in Kentucky and South Carolina and works with volunteer tutoring programs to promote literacy in the city of Louisville. *Reading Instruction for Diverse Classrooms* is her first published work.

Preface

Teachers want to be good at what they do. They want their students to be happy and to succeed academically. They work hard to take in the latest and greatest practices, and in doing so, they sift through new materials and professional books and attend teacher development sessions and graduate classes. Not surprisingly, some teachers become overwhelmed by mixed messages, seemingly different approaches they are expected to adopt, and exhaustive accountability measures. As we were writing this book, we were fully aware that our reading model might be perceived as yet another new thing that would have to be squeezed into an already packed curriculum.

And so we emphasize: *Our model of instruction includes teaching practices many teachers already do well.* It can include many of the material resources currently available in classrooms and schools. We are aware that some teachers practice *culturally responsive instruction.* That is, we realize most elementary teachers connect the curriculum to students' lives, have their students work in groups, work to maintain a rigorous curriculum with high expectations for all children, and use oral and written language strategies that match students' linguistic preferences and help students learn content across the curriculum. Also, many teachers already include books and other materials about kindness, responsibility, differences, and justice. Our model illustrates these principles while also highlighting how the subtle practices of encouraging student dialogue and allowing for more wait time and equitable turn taking enhances opportunities for learning. We weave in practices particularly useful for English language learners throughout the book. Our introductory chapters (Chapters 1–4) address these topics and set the foundation for the rest of the book.

We are also well aware that many teachers already structure reading instruction around the "big five" (phonemic awareness, phonics, vocabulary, fluency, and comprehension) advocated by the National Reading Panel (National Institute of Child Health and Human Development, 2000) and want the implementation of these components to be *research based.* In our book we suggest that teachers can and should implement these five reading components with instructional strategies that have been shown, in well-designed research studies, to actually improve instruction. Just teaching the big five is not enough. They must be taught in ways that have been shown to work with diverse populations of students. We carefully read the research to include only reading practices that have a research base, avoiding the inclusion of practices that are merely popular. We believe teachers should know the research that grounds their practice. Therefore, for each method chapter (Chapters 5–10) and in Chapters 13 and 14 (on family involvement and interventions, respectively), we summarize the findings of key studies that have been shown to be effective in improving students' reading achievement.

In Chapter 1, we describe principles for deciding what to do if research-based practice and culturally responsive instruction are at odds. Then, for each method chapter, we follow the research summary with a box of bulleted, easy-to-read "principles" for teaching that particular component of reading. We provide the rich descriptions of the research-based strategies with the standards for culturally responsive instruction in mind when it is feasible to weave the two perspectives together within one lesson. We use real examples from our classrooms or those we have observed in the research study that developed the model (McIntyre & Hulan, 2010). We conclude each chapter with a section highlighting how the instruction meets the needs of diverse populations of students. Our goal is to clarify the research, principles, and strategies of the model so that busy elementary teachers have access to the information in an easy-to-read format. We recognize that teachers want to know the research but lack the time to investigate these subjects in the way we have done for this book.

In Chapters 11 and 12, Nancy and Vicky, the classroom teachers who have authored this book, describe a week in their second- and fifth-grade classrooms, respectively. These rich, detailed descriptions of their teaching pull together the research-based literacy practices and standards for culturally responsive instruction into a practical, cohesive model of instruction. They illustrate the model by creating rigorous lessons that extend from students' background knowledge and allow for the children's different linguistic patterns. This model of instruction was designed to address the needs of all students, specifically the needs of the poor, of nonwhite cultural and ethnic groups, of those with less command of English, of those with less schooling, and of those who struggle with reading for other reasons, such as a disconnection between their worlds and school. This is the population of children in Nancy's and Vicky's classrooms.

What is different about this book is that we illustrate important and accepted research-based strategies and standards for culturally responsive instruction by blending these two different teaching orientations into a pragmatic model of instruction that focuses on tried-and-true reading strategies and new literacies for the 21st century. This book is future focused. *All* schools, not just urban classrooms or those in California, the Southwest, or Northeast, will include many immigrant children within the next decade. We are well aware of the rapidly changing demographics of classrooms. In 2010, 47% of 5-year-olds were nonwhite, mostly Hispanic, and that number will continue to increase. We are also well aware of the technological advances that have affected, and will continue to affect, teaching in U.S. classrooms. We welcome these changes because they are opportunities for more children to have access to increasingly sophisticated global information.

The pragmatic blending of multiple perspectives is the power of this book, but we will not claim it is easy to do every day. What we do know from research and our personal experiences is that when educators challenge students with high-quality, equitable instruction, students become engaged in school and literacy, and teachers begin to take notice. Once teachers see changes in children, they find it impossible to go back to teaching in traditional ways. We hope, through the instruction described in this book, that readers will become the teachers inspired to do the same.

ELLEN MCINTYRE
NANCY HULAN
VICKY LAYNE

Acknowledgments

We have loved writing this book together, but it would have been much more difficult, maybe impossible, to do it without the assistance of many collaborators. We would like to begin with the National Council of Teachers of English. This organization chose to fund the study that laid the foundation for this book. Without that support, Ellen McIntyre could not have led the teachers through the development and refinement of the instructional model presented in this book. We are also grateful to the late Michael Pressley, whose brilliant work inspired much of the work here and who generously connected us to Chris Jennison and Craig Thomas of The Guilford Press. We thank both Chris and Craig for their faith in us, for their encouragement and flexibility in getting the book done, and for pushing us to make this a better book. We also thank Tim Shanahan, whose excellent early review of the book helped us clarify our focus and purpose, as well as colleagues and research assistants at North Carolina State University—David Churchill, Barbara Copeland, Emmeline Aghapour, and Bradley Gregory—for their administrative and technical support during the writing of the book.

Our deepest appreciation goes to the many teachers who assisted with this book in some way, some allowing their teaching examples to be used, others assisting with technical aspects: Laura Beth Akers, JoAnn Archie, Mary Bell, Shelly Boulden, Karen Buckingham, Mary Ann Davis, Georgia Drury, Kris Gregory, Michael Ice, Tyler Jones, Ruth Lewis, Karen Loper, Carol Mills, Gayle Moore, Judy Sanders, Sarah Schuh, Gemma Wafzig, April Welch, and Susan Yusk. Personal gratitude goes to our greatest supporters: Ellen thanks Bill Morison. Nancy thanks Harper Hulan, Sandy and Bob Franklin, and Lynn and Henry Hulan. Vicky thanks God, and Stafford, Carole, Michelle, Diana, Adrian, and Charles Layne; Josephine and Ravi Buckner; and Louis Whitesides.

We acknowledge our students, who have challenged, questioned, amazed, and delighted us. Their rich cultural, linguistic, and historical backgrounds made our classrooms and lives more interesting and worthwhile. Finally, we want to thank the readers of this book, the elementary classroom teachers who have picked up yet another teacher professional book on reading instruction to learn what it takes to get all students in their classrooms to succeed at learning to read and to improve reading. It is teachers like you who positively affect the lives of young people, who encourage, inspire, care, and love their students and their work. We thank you for reading the book, but especially for doing the very challenging work you do.

Contents

1. Reading Instruction for Diverse Populations   1

Reading Instruction Past and Present: Theory and Approaches   2
Our Model: Research-Based, Culturally Responsive Reading Instruction   7
The Goal of Research-Based, Culturally Responsive Reading Instruction   17
Principles for Decision Making on Research-Based, Culturally Responsive Practice   17
Why This Book Now?   18
Cast of Characters   19

2. How Children Learn to Read   20

Theoretical Perspectives on Literacy Development   21
From Emergent to Conventional Literacy: Phases of Development   23
Reading Instruction That Matches Development   39

3. Children Who Struggle with Reading   40

Deficit Views of Children Who Struggle   41
So Why Do Some Children and Populations of Children Struggle with Reading?   42
Explanations for Group Differences   46
Schools and Teachers Affect Achievement Differences   48

4. Classroom Community and Discourse Practices in Research-Based, Culturally Responsive Classrooms   54

Creating a Culture of Care: The Class Meeting   55
The Reading Workshop: A Framework for Respectful, Rigorous Work   57
Dialogic Instruction: Using Talk to Learn   64
Attention to Language Differences   70

5. Word Study: Phonemic Awareness and Phonics   76

Research on Phonemic Awareness and Phonics   77
Principles for Teaching Phonemic Awareness and Phonics   81
Assessing Phonemic Awareness and Phonics   82
Strategies for Phonemic Awareness   86
Strategies for Phonics Instruction   88

Word Study Programs and Other Excellent Resources   94
Phonemic Awareness, Phonics, and Culturally Responsive Teaching   96

6. Fluency   97

Research on Fluency   98
Principles for Teaching Fluency   101
Assessing Fluency   101
Matching Texts to Readers   103
Strategies for Teaching Fluency   105
Fluency Instruction and Culturally Responsive Teaching   111

7. Comprehension   112

Research on Comprehension Instruction   114
Principles for Teaching Comprehension   117
Assessing Comprehension   118
Research-Based Comprehension Reading Strategies   119
Comprehension within Culturally Responsive Reading Instruction   132

8. More Comprehension Tools: 134
Vocabulary and the Instructional Conversation

Research on Vocabulary Learning and Instruction   136
Principles for Teaching Vocabulary   138
Assessing Vocabulary   138
Strategies for Teaching Vocabulary   139
The Instructional Conversation: Tool for Tackling Text   147
Vocabulary Instruction and Instructional Conversations
*   in Culturally Responsive Classrooms   152*

9. Writing   153

Research on Writing and Writing Instruction   154
Principles for Writing Instruction   158
The Writing Process: Nonlinear and Messy   159
Assessment of Writing   162
The Writing Workshop: Promises and Problems   164
Managing the Writing Workshop: Strategies in a Workshop Framework   174
Culturally Responsive Writing Instruction   176

10. New Literacies   177

Research on New Literacies   179
Principles for Teaching New Literacies   183
Assessment of New Literacies   184
Cool Tools: Strategies, Tools, and Activities with the Internet and ICTs   184
New Literacies and Culturally Responsive Instruction   191

11. Research-Based, Culturally Responsive Reading Instruction   192
in Second Grade

My Day Begins   192
Journal Writing: 9:10–9:25   193

Greeting: 9:25–9:35   194
Word Wall: 9:35–9:50   194
Shared Reading: 9:50–10:15   195
Word Work: 10:15–10:30   198
Guided Reading: 10:30–11:30   199
Learning Centers: Making Independent Work Time Meaningful   207
Writing   207
Research Projects   209
End-of-Day Thoughts   210
Research-Based, Culturally Responsive Instruction in Second Grade   214

12. Research-Based, Culturally Responsive Reading Instruction   216
in Fifth Grade

Morning Routines/Morning Meeting: 8:55–9:25   217
Shared Reading (Whole-Group Instruction): 9:25–9:50   220
Guided Reading (Small-Group Instruction and Literacy Stations):
 9:50–10:50   224
Word Work (Whole-Group Instruction/Conferences): 10:50–11:05   235
Writing Workshop (Whole-Group Instruction/Writing Conferences):
 11:05–11:45   236
Reflections   238
Research-Based, Culturally Responsive Instruction in Fifth Grade   239

13. Family Involvement   241

Research on Family Involvement   242
Principles for Family Involvement   244
Strategies for Involving Families   245

14. "What If My Students *Still* Need Help?":   253
Effective Reading Interventions

Why Children Still Struggle   254
Supplemental Instruction: The New Norm?   254
Response to Intervention   255
Research on Supplemental Reading Interventions   256
Principles for Reading Interventions   259
Effective Reading Interventions   260
Interventions and Research-Based, Culturally Responsive Teaching   264
Conclusion   265

Resources   267

References   275

Children's Literature Cited   291

Index   293

READING INSTRUCTION
FOR DIVERSE CLASSROOMS

CHAPTER 1

Reading Instruction for Diverse Populations

Teaching children to read might be an elementary teacher's most important goal and most challenging task. We know children will be limited throughout life unless they are proficient readers of a variety of texts. Children who read better do better in school, even in mathematics and science. Good readers acquire more knowledge about the world and are much more likely to attend college than children who do not read well. Good readers even enjoy better health and self-esteem. Few would disagree that reading is a top priority of elementary schools.

Consequently, many resources are dedicated to materials and professional development to help elementary teachers become better teachers of reading. Yet, while there is converging evidence on how children learn to read (Stanovich, 2000), there are competing perspectives on the most appropriate programs, materials, and methods for teaching reading, especially to children from populations who have historically struggled with reading. On this topic, the field of reading has a history of contentious debate. People care deeply about the issue.

We believe reading instruction should be based on the critical components of reading and the specific strategies that have been shown in well-designed studies to positively impact student learning. We also believe that with the increasing diversity of students in today's U.S. elementary classrooms, teachers must adopt instructional perspectives, attitudes, and strategies that attend specifically to the cultural and linguistic differences of their students in order to build on the skills and understandings children bring to school. Teachers must develop a firm understanding of why some children struggle with reading. Most children with reading difficulties lack phonological awareness and abilities (explained in detail in Chapter 5), and the factors that have contributed to these difficulties often have *sociocultural roots* (explained in detail in Chapter 3). Thus, materials and methods of reading must address the cognitive, instructional, motivational, and linguistic needs of the multiple and diverse populations we find in today's schools.

1

READING INSTRUCTION PAST AND PRESENT: THEORY AND APPROACHES

Teaching reading in today's elementary classrooms demands much of teachers. Teachers must understand literacy development, why some children struggle with learning to read and write, research-based instructional practices, the best uses of technology, new and classic children's literature, and where to find information on recent developments in the field. But just as important, excellent teachers of reading must know their students well. They must know their students' families and their students' out-of-school lives, backgrounds, passions, and struggles. Knowing students well can provide a source of information that can be harnessed for literacy instruction. Knowledge of students is a tool that, when combined with research evidence on effective instructional practices, becomes an indispensable aspect of effective literacy instruction. This book is designed to help teachers weave their understandings of learners with the experts' findings on best practices for culturally responsive, research-based reading instruction. To do this requires revisiting important movements in reading instruction of the past.

The Great Debate and the Reading Wars

The debate about how to teach children to read has been going on for more than 100 years. In the 19th century, people were drilled on letter recognition as one way to teach reading. In the early part of the 20th century, the whole-word method for teaching children to read came into vogue in response to research studies that showed that children learn words as easily as they learn letters and sounds (Huey, 1908), making the focus on whole words seem sensible. The whole-word method was prominent for decades, and new materials were produced to reflect the methodology. *Basal reading programs*, in which children read short texts that become longer and more challenging, became the model approach across the nation. Basal series provided procedures for the teacher to lead children through stories. The lessons usually included attention to new vocabulary, much repetition of words the children were expected to recognize, and simple instructional questions that assessed literal comprehension of the story. These basal readers were often filled with depictions of families that were not commonplace even then: white children and their parents who lived in suburban neighborhoods with the mother at home, two or three children, and a dog. Some of these basal approaches included phonics skills, but many did not.

In 1956, one influential book, *Why Johnny Can't Read* (Flesch, 1956), suggested that through the basal approach, thousands of children were not learning to read because they were not being taught "the code" or letter–sound relations, otherwise known as *phonics. Learning to Read: The Great Debate* (Chall, 1967) followed a decade later. This book summarized research findings on various reading instructional methods, favoring programs with a phonics focus. The field began to take notice, and publishers began to include phonics more extensively in their programs. Some programs with a heavy focus on phonics were referred to as *code-emphasis* approaches.

At the same time, reading researchers were using important information from the field of linguistics to understand what else children do as they read (Cambourne, 1988; Goodman, 1967; Goodman, Watson, & Burke, 1987; Wells, 1986). For example, children use multiple cues (the print, sentence grammar, and knowledge about the world or what is in the text) simultaneously to process print (Goodman, 1967). Many studies were showing readers as meaning makers (Cambourne, 1988; Harste, Woodward, & Burke, 1984; Wells, 1986), not children who simply "bark at print," a criticism of the code-emphasis approaches. The role of motivation and interest became important, and effective reading was seen as more than reading words (Westby, 2004). Studies in the United States, Australia, and New Zealand illustrated that meaning-based instruction using excellent literature instead of basal readers or skill sheets was becoming more popular with teachers and students. These classrooms were viewed by many as creating motivated, independent readers and writers. Instruction of this sort was termed *whole language*, and the movement changed reading instruction dramatically.

Whole Language

Whole-language classrooms focused instruction on meaning making using high-quality children's literature as the primary tool. Teachers often created *workshop*-like settings in which children had much choice in what they read. At the same time, the *writing process movement*, begun by Donald Graves (1983) and others, took hold and was aligned philosophically and theoretically with whole-language reading instruction. Skill instruction in these settings was controversial. Many educators claimed that children learned basic skills such as decoding through the focus on meaning-based instruction, rather than through explicit instruction modeled by the teacher and practiced often. In fact, some educators believed phonics and other skills did not need to be taught at all. Other reading educators were more hesitant about such claims. Despite the hesitation, whole-language instruction swept much of the nation in the 1980s, although the basal programs continued to be used by the majority.

The whole-language movement suffered many problems. There was little research evidence illustrating increased achievement when compared to the learning in other classrooms. There were vague messages about what makes excellent instruction and heated debate about the role of skills instruction. Many studies of whole-language instruction provided rich descriptions of interesting and lively classrooms, but few focused on student learning. Those that did concentrated only on a few children or teachers at a time, which meant that the findings could not be generalized for larger populations. These qualitative studies, while compelling, did not convince many educators or policymakers. Further, many whole-language supporters and researchers seemed to send mixed messages about the role of phonics in whole-language teaching. Some articles about reading instruction suggested that children did not need phonics, whereas others suggested that children learned phonics "naturally" in the context of reading.

The message about skills instruction frustrated and even angered some groups. In a now-famous series of articles, Lisa Delpit wrote two articles for the *Harvard Educational*

Review that deeply affected the thinking about whole-language instruction. The first article (Delpit, 1986), "Skills and Other Dilemmas of a Progressive Black Educator," told the story of Delpit's own journey from a skills-oriented teacher to a "progressive" (i.e., whole language, writing process) teacher educator, while quietly worrying about the effects of the progressive movement on the achievement of black children. After admitting her own guilt about following the movement, she questioned the movement's lack of attention to skills. She claimed that the writing process approach (and thus whole language) was focused almost exclusively on *fluency* or *voice*. She described how many black students were already fluent because of their cultural discourse practices of rap, rhyme, and metaphor but that they needed skills as basic as organization and punctuation in order to succeed in school. She suggested that the whole-language movement might be good for white students only, as it seemed to match the needs and discourse styles of that population.

The second article (Delpit, 1988) responded to the many people who wrote to Delpit about the first one (the letters both supported and challenged her) and was called "The Silenced Dialogue: Power and Pedagogy in Educating Other People's Children." It focused on the culture of power in classrooms and suggested that teachers must explicitly teach children who are not "of" the culture of power (e.g., students of color, speakers for whom English is not their first language, children with family history of low education or poverty) how to participate in the classroom. Delpit explains that in writing process and whole-language classrooms, some children are expected to know how to participate when they have not been *taught* how to participate. In the 1986 piece, Delpit described her students' responses to her whole-language teaching:

> My white students zoomed ahead. They worked hard at the learning stations. They did amazing things with books and writing. My black students played the games; they learned how to weave; and they threw the books around the learning stations. They practiced karate moves on the new carpets. (p. 13)

From her experiences, Delpit concluded that there is much value in the meaning-based, whole-language philosophy, but that teachers must be *explicit* in their teaching. They must be explicit about skills instruction, how to participate, and anything else students may need to know in order to succeed in school. She was not, however, inviting teachers to return to rote instruction on isolated skills. Hers was a call for teachers to attend to the cultural and linguistic needs of students.

During the same period (late 1980s and early 1990s), a plethora of studies was published that, taken together, illustrated unequivocally that phonological skill was essential to learning to read and that even adult poor readers suffered from lack of phonological skills (e.g., Adams, 1990). Additionally, many studies showed that although all children did not require direct or explicit instruction to learn these skills, many children did need it. Whole-language teaching, as attractive as it was, began to be viewed as part of the problem in reading rather than the solution.

The whole-language movement indeed suffered from a lack of explicit teaching. In 1992 Ellen (one of the authors of this book) witnessed the lack of teaching when she was invited to observe someone reputed to be an outstanding whole-language teacher. This teacher knew how to motivate, used exciting materials, asked just the right questions to get her students thinking, modeled her own enthusiasm for books, and so on. This teacher had set up an amazing environment full of rich literature and learning centers. During the teacher's *reading workshop*, Ellen noticed all of the above claims. Yet, she also noticed that during the entire morning, only *some* students approached the teacher with questions or comments about books. The teacher was expert in her interactions with those learners. Some students, however, never approached the teacher, and she did not approach them. The literacy "work" of the morning was to read books, and Ellen noticed that a good many students did read books. But some of the students only pretended to read. They quietly played the game as if they were participating, but they read nothing during the entire visit, similar to the black students in Delpit's class. Two of these students were male and the only black students in the class. This teacher was not racist and would likely have been as expert in assisting these young men as she was with the other students. Yet, because the classroom work was largely self-directed and students received help only when they asked, these two students and a few others received no help at all.

Although this lack of explicit teaching was documented and discussed by researchers, the whole-language movement thrived for a time because of all it offered. The movement has continued in one form or another in many teachers' classrooms, although some teachers have adapted their instruction to accommodate the extensive new evidence from studies on the role of phonological skills in reading. The term *whole language* fell out of favor with publishers in the mid-1990s and was replaced by other terms such as *balanced literacy*.

Balanced Literacy Approaches

Many teachers who had experienced whole-language teaching knew that the movement had made a difference to some children. At the same time, many also became aware that other children continued to struggle and that what those children needed was explicit instruction in skills, particularly phonics. More and more studies were published on the effectiveness of phonics and other skills in moving children to skilled reading acquisition. In 1990 Marilyn Adams published *Beginning to Read: Thinking and Learning about Print*, a summary of research on beginning reading that illustrated what children needed to know in order to learn to read, instructional practices that helped them get there, and the role of quality children's literature in early reading instruction. Researchers, teachers, and education leaders of all sorts were taking notice and advocating the inclusion of skills instruction within whole-language teaching.

Beginning in the mid-1990s, several books and articles on balanced instruction were published (McIntyre & Pressley, 1996; Reutzel, 1999; Spiegel, 1992, 1998; Weaver, 1998). But quite quickly, it became clear that the word *balance* meant different things to different people (Cowen, 2003; Fitzgerald, 1999; Moats, 2000; Spiegel, 1998). The field was certainly not settled on the issue of skills. And some research was beginning to show that teaching skills in the context of meaningful instruction (e.g., "embedded phonics") was not effective (Torgeson, 2002a). An additional problem with the concept of balanced reading instruction was that it was viewed as combining meaning-centered reading instruction with skills instruction. In many of the books and articles published on the topic at the time, the learner's background, history, culture, language, and family were not directly addressed. We return to this important point later.

Research-Based Reading Instruction

By the late 1990s, many in the field of literacy were advocating the explicit teaching of phonics in reading programs. Two additional reading panels published indisputable evidence about reading instruction that helped define the concept of research-based reading instruction. *The Prevention of Reading Difficulties in Young Children* (Snow, Burns, & Griffin, 1998) and *The Report of the National Reading Panel* (National Institute of Child Health and Human Development, 2000) shaped the reading instruction we find in many classrooms today.

The National Reading Panel (NRP) report, published in 2000, reported that five key areas must be addressed by the reading instruction in elementary classrooms: *phonemic awareness, phonics, fluency, comprehension,* and *vocabulary.* The report not only named these areas as the content to be taught in reading instruction, it also emphasized that the strategies teachers should use to teach these components be *research-based.* Because this term has also quickly gained many different meanings (as so often happens in education), we would like to be very clear about what we mean by *research-based.*

In education, there are many different kinds of research. In some studies researchers design experiments to compare the effects of two or more different approaches to teaching the same thing, being careful to control the many variables in classrooms (e.g., students' reading levels, backgrounds) so that the comparisons are valid. These experiments indicate that one approach is better than another at improving achievement on a particular skill or test. Shanahan (2002) would refer to the instruction that resulted in higher achievement gains in such studies as *research-proven.* These types of studies are considered by some researchers to be the most important because they include measures of student achievement. However, these studies might be limited in their explanations of why an approach or practice actually "worked."

In other types of studies, researchers strive to describe in rich detail some sort of instructional approach or strategy, at times documenting students' responses to the approach or strategy. These sorts of studies do not prove that one approach is more effective than another because different approaches are not compared, and often because achievement measures are not taken. These studies are highly valuable, though, because they often raise important questions or suggest *why* students might be disengaged or engaged in a lesson. Shanahan (2002) would call these sorts of studies *research-related* because the instruction described may have been based on related studies that have illustrated student learning.

Finally, there are instructional strategies and approaches that are adopted because there is a strong research base that supports the use of that strategy or approach. However, the original studies may have been conducted in very different contexts (e.g., with different populations, in different geographic regions, with different materials), thus making the adoption of the instructional approach only based on research but not proven by research. Shanahan (2002) calls these practices *research-based*.

The reading instructional strategies we advocate later in this book, such as reciprocal teaching, predicting, repeated reading, and many of the phonics strategies, have been shown in experimental studies to improve reading achievement (i.e., they are research-proven by the above definition). Some of the standards for culturally responsive instruction, such as dialogic instruction and use of wait time, are also research-proven. However, other practices that we advocate, such as providing choice in student work during the reading workshop or holding class meetings to allow for students to negotiate class rules, have not been researched in experimental studies and are merely related to what we know about human learning. This does not minimize their importance in any way, but rather demonstrates an ethical dilemma in educational research. Imagine a study comparing one teacher, who provides time each day for students to share their products and give and receive feedback, with another teacher who never allows students to share their work. Common sense suggests that children in the latter classroom would miss out on some positive and productive experiences, making the experiment unethical. This small component of a reading/writing workshop has not been examined in an experimental study with all variables controlled, nor should it be. Teachers' common sense about what is good for children should never be discarded. Still, educators should value and implement practices that have been proven to work or have a strong research base. We value both. Thus, we use the widely accepted term *research-based* to include all the practices that have been proven to raise student achievement or have a strong research base.

OUR MODEL: RESEARCH-BASED, CULTURALLY RESPONSIVE READING INSTRUCTION

The instructional model we present here seeks to take the very best features of past approaches and combine them with the promising essentials of instruction for the current century and future. This is not just the latest rendition of reading instruction, nor is it a haphazard conglomeration of a little of this and a little of that. It is a thoughtful instructional model that includes much of what many teachers already do, but with a focus on the individual and cultural needs of diverse populations of students. Specifically, we seek to provide elementary teachers with a guide for implementing *research-based reading instruction* through an approach that attends to the cultural and linguistic backgrounds of the students in their classrooms.

The Content of the Model: What to Teach

The reading instruction featured in this model is based on, and to some extent proven by, decades of research on what works in reading, most particularly the findings of the NRP, mentioned above. The model includes the NRP's five topic areas of an effective reading program—phonemic awareness, phonics, fluency, vocabulary, and comprehension—as well as topics that support reading (e.g., oral language, writing, new literacies). Each of the five components is addressed in a chapter later in this book. The model includes research-based strategies for teaching each of the above areas. For example, the phonemic awareness instruction advocated is systematic, daily, and explicit. Comprehension instruction includes routines and strategies shown by research to be effective, such as prediction, summarization, and reciprocal teaching (e.g., Farstrup & Samuels, 2002; Palinscar & Brown, 1984; Pressley, 2000).

In addition, the lessons and activities we describe specifically address diverse populations. In doing so, many lessons include multicultural literature and activities that connect children's background experiences with new texts and concepts. The literature used includes not only authors and characters of color or of distinct cultural groups (e.g., Appalachians), but it also, at times, includes books with topics of struggle and justice. Young children can begin to learn about justice by studying significant heroes in history, such as Ruby Bridges, Cesar Chavez, Ellen Ochoa, Barack Obama, or Mother Teresa; significant artists and performers whose work reflects an equity or justice theme, such as Maya Lin, Diego Rivera, or Jacob Lawrence; history from the perspective of people of color, such as Native Americans; and justice themes of bullying, stereotyping, racism, sexism, gender discrimination, prejudice toward particular groups (e.g., people with disabilities); the make-up of families; fairness, sharing, or kindness; differences; the environment; and taking a stand against injustice. The literature we share throughout the book includes authors of color such as Marie Bradby, Nikki Grimes, Pat Mora, Yoshika Uchida, and many more. We also provide a long list of favorite multicultural books in the Resources at the end of the book.

Importantly, our model of instruction proposes that teachers address such issues *at times* in their curriculum (not every lesson), complemented by other topics, genre, and content appropriate for the particular children in the group. Importantly, the primary focus of the book is on *expert reading instruction*. The book's simultaneous focus on diverse populations will open some teachers' eyes to what they may not have previously thought about—namely, how to attend to and adapt instruction to complement students' backgrounds, cultures, language patterns, and interests.

The Pedagogy of the Model: How to Teach

Pedagogy refers to the instructional strategies that make up the art or science of teaching. When teachers think about *how* a component of reading should be taught (the pedagogy), they must first consider the *research-based strategies* we know work for that component (phonemic awareness, phonics, fluency, comprehension, and vocabulary). These strategies are described in detail in Chapters 5–14 and come from multiple research reviews. Most instructional strategies are research-proven, whereas others are research-based (see, e.g., Adams, 1990; Allington, 2006, 2009; Beck, 2006; Cunningham, 2000; Farstrup & Samuels, 2002; Rasinski & Padak, 2000; Pearson, Barr, Kamil, & Mosenthal, 1984; Barr, Kamil, Mosenthal, & Pearson, 1991; Kamil, Mosenthal, Pearson, & Barr, 2000; Pressley, 1998, 2000).

Second, pedagogical standards and practices shown to be effective specifically with diverse populations of students, including English language learners, must be considered. We culled the research on instruction for many different populations of children (nonwhite and white with district cultural backgrounds, such as Appalachians) and found that most educators agree on a set of standards or principles for reaching diverse populations. Some of these educators refer to this practice as *culturally responsive instruction* (CRI), as we do in this book. Others refer to it as *culturally relevant pedagogy, equity pedagogy,* or *multicultural instruction.* This pedagogy not only includes instructional strategies but also attention to *classroom discourse,* the teacher–student and student–student interactions that are a vital part of instruction. (For research that provided the basis for these standards, see Almasi, O'Flahaven, & Arya, 2001; August & Shanahan, 2006b; Banks, 2003; Dalton, 2007; Echevarria, Vogt, & Short, 2004; Gay, 2000, 2002; Goldenberg, 1993; Grant & Sleeter, 2007; Irvine, 2006; Ladson-Billings, 1994; Moll & González 2003; Nieto, 1999; Shanahan & Beck, 2006; Tharp, Estrada, Dalton, & Yamauchi, 2000; Tharp & Gallimore, 1993.)

The instructional principles synthesized from the above studies comprise several themes. These principles or themes are enacted in classrooms that are respectful, uplifting, motivating, and challenging. Culturally responsive instruction is a perspective that permeates all a teacher does, rather than specific strategies. The following themes, though, are common principles advocated by all scholars on culturally responsive instruction:

- *Connecting curriculum to students' backgrounds* (finding out what students know and are interested in and using that knowledge to develop new understandings).
- *Building on students' home language or dialect* (allowing students' home languages and building from them to learn academic English).
- *Planning for dialogic instruction* (providing many opportunities for students to engage in academic conversation with peers and their teacher).
- *Maintaining a rigorous curriculum* (never allowing the curriculum to be watered down, but providing support so that students can engage in high-level thinking).
- *Attending to classroom discourse* (such as wait time, turn taking, types of questions asked, scaffolding students toward understanding).

These principles also reflect the extensive research conducted by the Center for Research on Education, Diversity, and Excellence (CREDE) at the University of California, Berkeley. Researchers associated with the center have conducted studies of many different populations of students in U.S. schools and have discerned patterns of what works with all students. The standards we adopt came, in part, from this work. As stated, these principles are meant to be implemented within a classroom culture of respect, care, and high expectations (Tharp et al., 2000).

Finally, most of this research also illustrates what Delpit argued for in the 1980s and what research-based instruction also shows: that excellent instruction for all children is *explicit.* That is, teachers must show and tell children how to do what they want them to do, from manipulating phonemes to connecting information across multiple texts. More about each of these areas and how they are woven together in this model of reading are described later.

In Figure 1.1, we summarize the primary aspects of the model. This model would be the *core reading program* in the classroom. (We identify interventions as supplemental programs later in the book.) The features of the instructional context in this core reading model are displayed across the top with arrows indicating that these features are meant to be woven throughout the instructional day, week, month, and year. They are the principles upon which the model can be implemented and are described in detail in Chapter 4. The four-quadrant diagram under the instructional context is our "hybrid" research-based, culturally responsive model. On the left are the features of the research-based instruction (the *content* of the model at the top and the *pedagogy* of the model at the bottom, with arrows connecting them). On the right are the principles for culturally responsive instruction, with the content on the top and the pedagogy on the bottom.

Some of these features overlap. For example, dialogic instruction has been shown in experimental studies to improve student achievement in reading (Tharp & Gallimore, 1993). Dialogic instruction is also shown in many qualitative studies to be culturally responsive (Goldenberg, 1993). Why is this feature culturally responsive? Because, done well, it can mean that instruction (1) connects to students' backgrounds, (2) allows for students' linguistic preferences, and (3) maintains high standards and rigor through high-level questioning and scaffolding. As you can see, all these CRI standards intersect.

Importantly for teachers, this model of instruction can be practiced with many of the materials already available in schools. Teachers might have to upgrade their collections of children's literature in order to have multiple copies of the sorts of books that will engage children. However, many published series of reading texts today include the sort of literature that we advocate in this book. In Chapters 11 and 12, Nancy and Vicky describe the published materials on which they rely to efficiently and effectively implement this model. Teachers need to be careful not to follow any guideline blindly without careful attention to the principles and research-based practices we describe in this model.

Blending Research-Based and Culturally Responsive Practice

In our instructional model, the reading research-based strategies and the culturally responsive standards can sometimes, but not always, be woven together in the same lessons. We return to this point later. For now, we illustrate these practices with examples from our own experience and that of several colleagues who implemented this model. We share the descriptions of the teachers (beyond Ellen, Nancy, and Vicky, the authors of this book who were described earlier) and students so that readers can see the diversity of the classrooms and thus more easily relate the practices to the model. Not all the classrooms were highly diverse racially or linguistically, although most of them were. However, all classrooms were diverse economically and culturally.

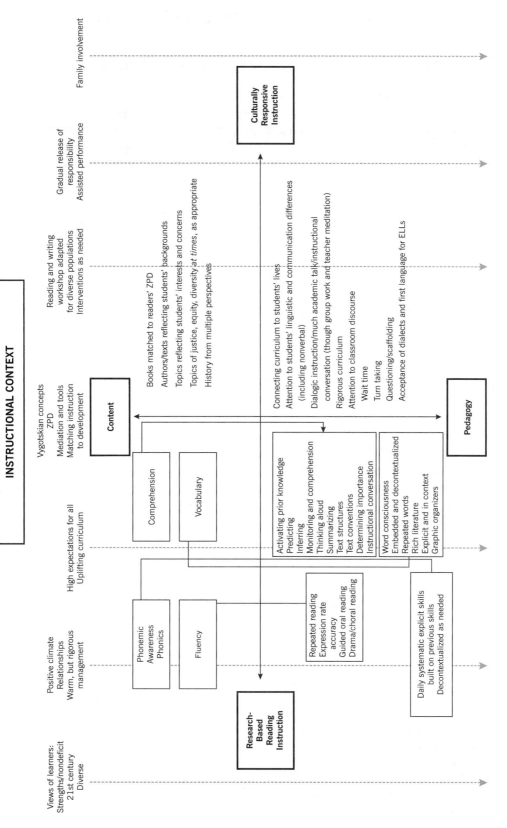

FIGURE 1.1. Model of research-based, culturally responsive instruction. ELLs, English language learners; ZPD, zone of proximal development.

VIGNETTE 1.1. DEVELOPING FLUENCY THROUGH CULTURALLY RESPONSIVE INSTRUCTION

Audrey is a white teacher of mostly black and ELL students in an urban school serving a largely multinational, multiracial population. She selects a poetic, repetitious text for fluency practice as part of an overall mini-unit study on civil rights. To conduct a lesson that is both research-based and culturally responsive, she reads a Nikki Giovanni poem aloud and engages the students in a deep discussion or instructional conversation (Goldenberg, 1993) on what the poet is communicating. She explicitly teaches the class how the poet selected the precise and concise words for the text. She has the students participate in repeated readings (Samuels, 2002), a common research-based strategy for developing fluency. Audrey follows the lesson by inviting students to respond to the poem through a product that connects the meaning of the poem to the experiences in their lives.

Connecting Curriculum to Students' Backgrounds for the Development of Fluency and Comprehension

If teachers get to know their students well, they can build curriculum from the students' backgrounds and interests. To implement this standard, teachers purposely connect instruction with students' backgrounds while assisting them in developing fluency, comprehension, and vocabulary skills. Two examples of how teachers have combined research-based practice with this particular culturally responsive strategy are presented in Vignette 1.1 and 1.2.

The research-based strategies in Vignette 1.1 include repeated reading and dialogic instruction. The standards for culturally responsive instruction in this lesson include connecting the lesson to students' backgrounds and interests, engaging the students in deep dialogue to help them understand, providing a safe way for children to participate (choral reading) that draws on their linguistic strengths rather than highlighting what

---

VIGNETTE 1.2. SYNTHESIS COMPREHENSION STRATEGY THROUGH CRI

Ellen is teaching a class of third graders, mostly white and black students, most of whom have Appalachian roots. Many in this group love baseball and baseball heroes. She chooses three different books on baseball heroes in an effort to connect with many of the students' interest in sports and to teach the students to synthesize information from multiple sources—a research-based strategy (Horowitz, 1985). In this strategy, the teacher draws out students' background information about baseball and invites them to make predictions for each text. She then reads aloud to the children, modeling taking notes and thinking aloud (Duke & Pearson, 2002) how she confirms her own predictions. From there, the students work in pairs to create Venn diagrams on the books, including how the three baseball heroes are similar and different. Finally, the children write short essays on the similarities between the ball players, drawing on the Venn diagrams for information to synthesize the books.

they might not be able to successfully do (e.g., read alone orally), and keeping instruction rigorous.

The example in Vignette 1.2 highlights different research-based strategies with the same standards for CRI. In this lesson, the teacher weaves together research-based strategies, such as prediction (Pearson & Johnson, 1978), synthesis (Horowitz, 1985), and "think-alouds" (Kucan & Beck, 1997), with standards for CRI: connecting to students' backgrounds, group work, and rigorous instruction with high expectations. The latter two standards are described in more detail below.

Building on Students' Home Language Patterns for the Development of Vocabulary "Word Consciousness"

Culturally responsive instruction involves attention to students' language and interaction patterns. In culturally responsive instruction teachers respect students' "home language" and communicate to students in culturally comfortable ways. Many scholars of CRI describe the different language patterns, including dialects, of various groups and the need for teachers to be sensitive and open-minded about language use, especially if the language is different from their own (Adger, Wolfram, & Christian, 2009; Dalton, 2007; Delpit, 1995). In the United States alone, language varies widely across different socioeconomic groups, cultural groups, and geographic regions. It differs in pronunciation, word usage, syntax or grammar, and in less obvious ways such as eye contact, gestures, and body language. For example, some children grow up in homes in which family members speak and react directly (e.g., "Shut the door!") with gestures and body language that communicate in ways that others may see as blunt, whereas others use less direct language (e.g., "What is the rule when we enter the house?"). No one style is better or worse than any other. They are merely different. That is the key: to see *differences* in language use as just that and not view differences as deficiencies. Most educators recommend that we attend closely to students' interaction styles and modify our own discourse at times to build on students' styles.

In Vignette 1.3, Vivette uses a linguistic form with which both she and many of her students are familiar. Because Vivette grew up in the community in which she

---

VIGNETTE 1.3. CALL AND RESPONSE TO TEACH SCIENCE VOCABULARY

In one highly diverse third-grade classroom in which 40% of students are African American (Foster & Peele, 2001), Vivette, an African American teacher, uses "call and response, a highly interactive African American communicative discourse style" (p. 33), think-alouds, and demonstration to teach high-level concepts in botany. The teacher asks a question, and the children and their teacher answer in unison. This process allows students who are unsure to listen to peers or their teacher and try out a response they may be unsure of. The teacher uses intonation and rhythm to convey the meanings of some of the words the students study, such as *entomologist*.

VIGNETTE 1.4. USING STUDENTS' DIALECTS TO TEACH STANDARD ENGLISH

Sarah taught in an urban Miami school serving African American children, all of whom spoke in African American English. Sarah allowed students to communicate in dialect but also took time every day to explicitly teach her first graders how to speak and write in "Standard English," a form of English generally accepted across the country (Wolfram & Ward, 2006). For example, if a student said, "Miss Schuh, we be needin' a new sharpener," Sarah would invite the child to say the same thing as if the child were speaking to the principal to request the new sharpener. She might write on the chalkboard:

> We *be needin'* a new sharpener.
> We *need* a new sharpener.

She would highlight the difference in print and speech and discuss with the children when and to whom each form of English is appropriately used.

---

teaches, she can draw on her knowledge of the community norms and linguistic patterns to engage her students. But like many other educational scholars and teachers of CRI (Gutiérrez, Baquedano-López, & Alvarez, 2001; Ladson-Billings, 1994; Lee, 1998), Vivette uses familiar language forms to "prod the students to articulate a deeper understanding through talking aloud about the process of problem solving or decision making, practices that may not have been part of their habitual or preferred repertoire" (Foster & Peele, 2001, p. 35). All teachers can learn these forms of participation by listening and learning from their students, reading about discourse styles, and being open-minded about language forms other than their own. The example of Sarah, a white teacher of all black students, is presented in Vignette 1.4.

We explain the meanings of phrases and concepts such as "Standard English" in Chapter 4. Some of these terms can be confusing, especially this one, because some linguists who study dialect don't really view any particular dialect as "standard." Later in this book, we illustrate how teachers can use other linguistic forms, such as call and response for fluency practices, think-alouds for comprehension work, demonstration for vocabulary instruction, and many other patterns of communication, which can draw students into the school curriculum, illustrating connections between the critical *content* of reading instruction and the *pedagogy* known to engage diverse populations of students.

Dialogic Instruction for Developing Comprehension

Educators advocating for CRI also emphasize group work and dialogic instruction as critical for engaging students who do not succeed in more traditional settings (Goldenberg, 1993; Lemke, 1990; Luxford & Smart, 2009; Tharp & Gallimore, 1993). Students learn from one another and therefore should have multiple opportunities to work in pairs and small groups. Students must also have opportunities to practice academic

Think–Pair–Share (Lyman, 1981) provides an opportunity for all students to participate in responding to a teacher's question rather than only one student at a time, as is done with traditional discourse. Students can "rehearse" answers to questions, which can increase the quality of their answers. They are nearly always willing to participate when they only have to respond to a peer. It provides a safe space for English language learners who may be struggling with expressing their views and ideas. It can work like this:

1. The teacher poses a high-level (Bloome & Greene, 1984) question on the theme of a book or concept the class is studying and asks the students to take a minute (usually not more) to *think* about the question.
2. Then the teacher invites the students to turn to someone seated nearby (or to use designated partners, if desired) and discuss the answers they formed in their minds. The children compare responses and add to or revise their own responses based on their peers' ideas. As a pair, they come up with one response.
3. After students talk briefly in pairs, the teacher calls for pairs to share their thinking with the rest of the class. This may lead to a larger instructional conversation or a listing of responses, depending on the goals of the lesson.

FIGURE 1.2. Strategies for talking to learn: Think–Pair–Share.

talk in these group settings with assistance from the teacher to clarify misconceptions or nudge students' thinking. Two common grouping practices that can be woven into research-based reading instruction follow. Details on how to build dialogic classrooms are described in Chapter 4. Strategies for conducting true instructional conversations (Goldenberg, 1993) are covered in Chapter 8.

Strategies for enhancing academic talk play major roles in maintaining high student engagement. But they must be conducted in ways that bolster confidence and emotional safety. The outdated raise-your-hand-if-you-know-the-answer method can intimidate students and deter them from being active participants. Instead, opportunities such as Think–Pair–Share (Figure 1.2) or Numbered Heads Together (Figure 1.3), which allow students time to think and respond in a safe environment, are more productive for student risk taking.

Spencer Kagan's (1994) Numbered Heads Together provides a format that gives students time to discuss ideas collegially and respond, based on their contribution to the group consensus.

1. Each student in a small group receives a number: 1, 2, 3, or 4.
2. The teacher poses an academic question or situation for discussion. Appropriate wait time follows. Individuals write their initial response.
3. The students "puts their heads together" and are given time to discuss the answer and come up with a response.
4. One number is called randomly and that student is responsible for sharing the group response.

The students' confidence is protected, and accountability during whole-group discussions is promoted.

FIGURE 1.3. Numbered Heads Together.

Rigorous Curriculum for Comprehension Development

Our reading instructional model favors a rigorous curriculum that focuses on high expectations, problem solving, an unwillingness to give up on any student, an advanced curriculum with regular feedback and celebration of progress, and uplifting curricular materials grounded in students' experiences. Examples of lessons that clearly push students' thinking are described throughout this book. The lessons are not intended merely to make students feel good; they are intended to get students to *move* in their development. In Vignette 1.5, Mara treats her diverse population of students as the highly intelligent and opinionated people that they are.

Attending to Classroom Discourse

In Chapter 4 we elaborate extensively on the role of classroom discourse and how it affects teaching and learning. We address instructional practices such as wait time, the amount of time a teacher waits after asking a question before calling on a student to respond. We also discuss how wait time affects what students produce. We illustrate patterns of turn taking, types of questions asked, and how teachers "scaffold" or lead students toward understandings. In Chapter 8 we elaborate on Mara's lesson, shown in Vignette 1.5, to illustrate how expert wait time, equitable turn taking, high-level questions, and expert teacher scaffolding during instructional conversations about topics important to the children are both research-based and culturally responsive. Indeed, the reading instructional model described in this book is built on the premise that when instruction is research-based, meaningful, challenging, collaborative, dialogic, and connected to the students' home and community experiences, students achieve more.

**VIGNETTE 1.5. READING BIOGRAPHIES AND DEBATING ON IMPORTANT TOPICS
IN THIRD GRADE**

Mara sits with her third-grade class in a circle on the floor. They have been discussing famous women in history during the week, and today they will talk about Maya Lin, the woman who was selected to create the Vietnam War Memorial. To enable this discussion, the class is reading the biography *Maya Lin: Linking People and Places* (2005) by Katherine Scraper. Mara begins by asking kids what they notice about the way the biography is written, asking them to compare Maya Lin's story to other biographies they have read. Students explain that this biography begins with an interesting and exciting story from Maya Lin's life, whereas other biographies they have read were written more chronologically, moving from birth to death. In this lesson, Mara guides the children through a heated discussion (illustrated in Chapter 8) that focuses on adult themes such as discrimination, race, and patriotism. Mara does not always agree with her students, and she respectfully tells them so.

THE GOAL OF RESEARCH-BASED, CULTURALLY RESPONSIVE READING INSTRUCTION

We have one goal for the implementation of the instruction described in this book: higher academic achievement for *all* learners. While few argue that reading instruction should be well grounded in research and that instruction should be connected to students' cultural backgrounds and ways of learning, there is less evidence for significantly higher achievement of students in culturally responsive classrooms as compared to more traditional settings. CRI has been criticized for a lack of attention to and evidence of student achievement. For example, educators have asked, "Sure, you've *engaged* the kids, but does this kind of teaching produce higher achievement?" and "How is this sort of teaching accomplished if the students don't have the basic skills to do them?" Our model of instruction is designed to assuage these criticisms. We believe that a focus on CRI does not have to be at odds with research-based reading instruction. We believe the two can and should mutually support one another. Our model includes some culturally responsive practices that are research-proven and research-based (see Tharp, 1989, for a review of research-proven, culturally responsive practices). Our model of instruction blends two theoretically different models of instruction. Indeed, both theories need one another.

PRINCIPLES FOR DECISION MAKING ON RESEARCH-BASED, CULTURALLY RESPONSIVE PRACTICE

The model can be implemented in a workshop environment with a well-established and positive classroom community, guided reading instruction, high-quality literacy centers, some choice in student work, writing instruction in which students write for authentic audiences as well as receive explicit instruction on cognitive writing skills, literacy across the curriculum, and family involvement. Many teachers reading this book will be well familiar with these components of excellent literacy instruction. Further, it matters what teachers think about the students in their class, their attitudes and demeanor toward them. This topic is addressed in Chapter 3.

What teachers say to the children and how it is said are additional critical features. Indeed, Chapters 4 and 8 focus on classroom discourse—the language in classrooms that can help or impede learning. Finally, the materials teachers use for reading instruction can also contribute to student engagement and learning, and this topic is addressed in several chapters. Is this instructional model all that different from what teachers already do? For some, the answer may be "Not so much," and they will simply want to tweak or refine their practices, choosing reading strategies that are research-based and not just popular or attending more closely to issues of culture or language. For others, the answer might be to start fresh; they may wish to throw out current materials, lesson plans, and beliefs altogether and begin to teach in a whole new way. For both groups, this book is an invaluable resource.

Finally, how do teachers decide when to use research-based strategies and when to use culturally responsive practices, especially if the two different philosophies contradict? The four teachers who participated in the research study on the development of the model (Mara, Audrey, Genna, and Jodi, featured in the book) and Nancy and Vicky, who also implemented the model, struggled at times with this question. Most had no difficulty finding research-based strategies. They knew that phonemic awareness and phonics must be taught directly, explicitly, and systematically (building from previous skills), and that strategies such as repeated reading, reciprocal teaching, and think-aloud procedures are advocated by reliable sources (e.g., Farstrup & Samuels, 2002; National Institute of Child Health and Human Development, 2000; research journals). They also found little difficulty weaving *some* research-based strategies with *some* CRI standards. For example, Mara taught her students how to summarize. She used a book that connected to her students' backgrounds; modeled the strategy through a think-aloud procedure; allowed her students to practice the strategy with a partner, speaking in their own dialects or their first languages; maintained rigor in the lesson through text choice and high-level questioning; and attended to wait time and turn taking during the lesson debriefing.

However, Mara struggled to weave phonics with CRI. Some phonics or word study programs (e.g., those we mention in Chapter 5) lend themselves to CRI more than others. The teachers in the study knew that they must follow the scope and sequence of their phonics programs to maintain the integrity of the instruction that was research-proven. The teachers seemed to know implicitly (and some explicitly) that to incorporate phonological instruction within some lessons was sometimes contrived and ill-conceived. Mara said that she taught phonics through hand claps and chants but admitted that her instruction in this area was nonsystematic and occasional, invalidating the definition of research-based for instruction on phonological understanding. In such instances, it is important that teachers follow the research-based procedures *as long as they see that their children are learning*. If teachers find that with some strategies or approaches, their students are not attending—are becoming bored, anxious, or disengaged—then they may be doing their students more harm than good. Again, careful observation and the common sense of teachers are still critically important.

WHY THIS BOOK NOW?

The diversity in U.S. classrooms has increased dramatically over the past few decades and will continue to do so for years. Teachers in all parts of the country—not just in the Southwest—and in all types of schools—not just urban—have large populations of English language learners. Many refugees from war-torn countries have children in our classrooms. Many diverse religious and cultural values are exhibited by our students. Teachers are scrambling to understand their students and to figure out how best to teach them.

This book describes how teachers can simultaneously address the five components of reading instruction, as outlined by the NRP report, while also meeting the specific needs of children of color, cultural and ethnic groups, the poor, those with less command of English, those with less schooling, and those who struggle with reading for other reasons. With the current push to teach from commercial programs and focus on the five components of reading as defined by the NRP, teachers have found it difficult to understand and/or implement responsive, equitable instruction while keeping to the mandates required by their school districts. Yet, the practical and moral imperative is to do both, and that is the purpose of this book.

CAST OF CHARACTERS

This book describes the research-based, culturally responsive reading model through the use of vivid examples from teachers who have successfully implemented it. The book is authored by a professor (Ellen) and two teachers (Nancy and Vicky). Ellen McIntyre was a first-, second-, and sixth-grade teacher in an urban elementary school serving students of poverty. Her body of work has focused on diverse populations of students in urban and rural settings. Nancy Hulan was a research assistant in the study that developed the model, and she also practiced this model for 2 school years before focusing full time on her doctoral work. The details of the study, including the teachers' struggles and successes of the model, are published elsewhere (McIntyre & Hulan, 2010). Vicky Layne took several graduate classes from Ellen, wherein she learned about the model and practiced it for many years. Examples of instruction also come from several additional teachers who have implemented the model, four of whom also participated in the research study (Mara, Jodi, Genna, Audrey). Other examples come from teachers with whom Ellen had previously worked or studied, and from whom she had learned. Finally, some examples are Ellen's, as she has conducted much professional development in schools where she directly teaches children while teachers observe and dissect her lessons. All teachers have given permission to use their examples in this book.

CHAPTER 2

How Children Learn to Read

We have all witnessed the adorable scenes of young children pretending to read to dolls or scribbling letter-like marks on a page and asking an adult, "What did I write?" Some adults, while seeing these behaviors as cute, discourage them because the children's productions are not accurate. However, scholars of *emergent literacy* (Sulzby & Teale, 1991; Teale & Sulzby, 1986) view such behaviors as critical milestones in children's literacy development. The term *emergent literacy* refers to the reading and writing behaviors that precede and develop into conventional literacy and includes all children do with print from birth until they read conventionally. Children are always in the process of becoming literate (Bissex, 1980; Clay, 1991; Sulzby, 1985). Emergent literacy researchers have noted patterns of behaviors, or benchmarks, through which most children move on their way to conventional reading and writing. Interestingly, researchers have also found that English language learners' developmental patterns parallel native English speakers (Amendum & Fitzgerald, 2010). Teachers must recognize these patterns in order to know what can be expected of most children and the best ways of assisting them in their development.

Over time, children move from emergent reading and writing behaviors to beginning reading and writing—what some have called "really reading" or "really writing" (Sulzby & Teale, 1991, p. 728). It is not always easy to recognize when children are *really* reading. You know it has happened when a child can pick up a text he or she has never seen before and comprehend it. The child applies all of his concepts about print and all of his skills with graphics, phonology, and sense making to comprehend something new. The reading of something new will sound halting and slow, but that is characteristic of *beginning reading*. When teachers of young children come to recognize the difference between emergent reading behaviors and beginning reading behaviors, they can appropriately support their students.

THEORETICAL PERSPECTIVES
ON LITERACY DEVELOPMENT

Studies of emergent and beginning reading come from multiple theoretical perspectives, primarily those referred to as cognitive (psychological) and those referred to as sociocultural. Cognitive theories are derived from the work of Piaget, and they help us understand what children are thinking and doing as they learn about print and problem solve the reading process. The sociocultural perspective is derived from the work of Vygotsky and helps us understand what happens between and among learners within their historical, social, and cultural contexts. Today, educators strive to understand literacy learning by combining the best of what we know from multiple perspectives (Purcell-Gates, Jacobson, & Degener, 2004; Tracey & Morrow, 2006; McCarthey, 2009). This chapter describes how children learn to read by drawing on these multiple perspectives.

The *context* of any reading situation is critical for understanding the reading process. The context is everything outside the mind of the reader—the teacher's words, the text read, the broader classroom setting, the school and district policies, the learner's prior experiences with text, her home and community environment, her cultural and language background, the larger national political movements, and more. Vygotsky illustrated that what happens inside the heads of learners is affected by the surrounding context. His work brought key concepts about learning to the forefront, providing educators with a vocabulary to discuss the very complex process of learning. We share some of these concepts below.

Mediation and Tools

Learning to read occurs in the context of children's history, culture, and environment, including their schooling and their instructional interactions within their schools. Children's minds do not simply develop naturally because they get older. They develop because of the assistance offered by more experienced peers or adults. Vygotsky used the word *mediate* to explain how something comes between the child and the child's progress in learning. Something *mediates* learning or helps it to happen. Vygotsky conducted a series of small-scale studies (although not designed in the manner in which many psychologists design them today) that examined learning, remembering, and generalizing words/concepts. Vygotsky referred to his own method as "experimental–developmental" (1978, p. 61), in that the experiments he conducted with learners provoked their development and thus illustrated it for analysis.

Vygotsky provoked development through the use of *tools*. Teachers use many tools to mediate young children's acquisition of literacy—books, paper, crayons, markers, graphic organizers, computers, and so on. He showed that when a child learns something, he uses tools to accomplish tasks, such as reading a passage. One cannot truly understand the learner or development without attention to the tools. The most important tool, however, is the speech in which learners engage with others and with themselves.

What a teacher, parent, or another child says to the reader can assist the reader through a text or with practice on a reading skill:

"Try it again."
"That word is *because*."
"Can you sound out that word?"
"What do you think the word over the door says?"
"Point to each word as you read."

These prompts are tools that assist the reader, and nothing can take the place of this sort of reading assistance.

Self-speech is also a critical tool. Adults and children use self-speech every day as they remind themselves of things, talk themselves through a task, or rehearse what they need to do or say in order to accomplish something. For example, when someone is learning a forehand in tennis, the self-talk might sound like, "Move to the ball, bend knees, racket back, swing high to low." Self-speech is not always evident in learners because it is often done in the mind. Yet the learner is using language to talk himself through something, and that self-talk is a primary tool for learning. It happens in learning to read too, as we shall see with some examples. In fact, teachers sometimes hear the audible speech of young readers as they self-talk their way through a text, using some of the prompts their teacher used earlier. "Point to the words," the reader might tell himself. Or, "Try it again." This sort of appropriation, or adoption, of the teacher's prompts illustrates another important Vygotskian concept: the zone of proximal development.

The Zone of Proximal Development

The use of tools in learning to read at school often occurs when the teacher is providing scaffolding (i.e., supporting in a skilled manner) in the learner's *zone of proximal development* (ZPD). Vygotsky (1978) defines the ZPD as

> the distance between the actual developmental level as determined by independent problem solving and the level of potential development as determined through problem solving under adult guidance or in collaboration with more capable peers. (p. 86)

This means that children learn best when what is taught to them is *just beyond* what they can do alone. They need the assistance of someone else. When they get that assistance, they are capable of accomplishing the task (e.g., reading a particular book, decoding two-syllable words) they could not accomplish alone. The next time they attempt the same task, they might be able to accomplish it alone. Vygotsky explains that what children can do with the assistance of others might be more indicative of their mental development than what they can do alone (1978, p. 85). This concept is critical for teachers. It means that the selection of tools (e.g., books), the task they ask children to engage in, and the type of scaffolding or support they provide for children makes a difference in what those children learn.

Why is understanding the ZPD important? For reading instruction, *it is vital*. First, understanding the ZPD affects assessment of children's progress in reading. While it is useful at times to assess children's independent or automatic skills (this is what is typically assessed in schools), that approach reveals only so much information and can be detrimental if teachers know only what children can do alone or cannot do at all. What is needed is knowledge of what children can do *with help*; this enables the teacher to make appropriate instructional decisions for the child. This point is further explored with examples.

FROM EMERGENT TO CONVENTIONAL LITERACY: PHASES OF DEVELOPMENT

Children's literacy development begins at birth and continues throughout life. As young children explore print and develop language, they become aware of how print works and the many uses for it (Yaden, Rowe, & MacGillivray, 2000; Sulzby & Teale, 1991; Teale & Sulzby, 1986). They learn that print means something. Initially, though, many children see all print (pictures, nonletter symbols, other graphics) as the same. Through interactions with others, they begin to differentiate between print and pictures; they begin to notice the shapes and forms that print takes, and they try them out in their writing attempts. They begin to "read" during this period of development by relying on the meaning, or *semantics*, of the text. Some children rely on what they know about how language works—the grammar or *syntax*—from years of talking and listening. Gradually the children begin to rely on print, or *graphophonic information*, to read (Barr, 1984; Biemiller, 1970; Clay, 1968; Ferreiro & Teberosky, 1983; Mason, 1984; Sulzby, 1985). When they begin to focus on print and understand that reading is a print-processing activity (Morris, 2008), they are moving from emergent to beginning reading. For most children, this shift occurs between the ages of 5 and 7, but for some children, it happens earlier or later. Importantly, reading development does *not* just happen "naturally." It occurs through interactions with others and often because of explicit teaching.

Phases of Reading Development

Children do some interesting things on their way to learning to read. Researchers who have studied children over months and years have documented patterns of behaviors that many, though not all, children exhibit on their way to learning to read. These patterns were observed as children repeatedly read their favorite storybooks (Bloome & Green, 1984; Heath, 1983; Sulzby, 1985; Yaden, Smolkin, & Conlin, 1989), read books in classrooms during independent reading time (Clay, 1968; Heibert, 1999; McIntyre,

1990), or completed tasks for researchers (Ferreiro & Teberosky, 1982; Ehri & Wilce, 1985; Sulzby & Teale, 1991). Many of these patterns will be familiar to readers who have spent time with preschoolers or primary-grade children. Importantly, the patterns overlap. Children do not move through one phase before the next. Children can be observed in behaviors in Phase 3 on one day and the next week illustrate behaviors in Phase 1. In general, though, the patterns correspond with development.

Phase 1: Reading Pictures with Oral-Like Language

Young children become interested in books and other texts early in their lives, especially if they know that these texts are a source of pleasure, information, or function to the important people in their lives. Thus, children will pick them up, look at them, and "read" the pictures. The language produced by children for some books sounds like talk, especially if they are reading it with someone else. In Figure 2.1, two young boys look at two different books together and "read" them with talk. What do these children know about reading? They already know a great deal, even though they are not reading in any conventional sense. They know that books are pleasurable and contain information that they want. They know how to hold a book and the direction the story reads (front to back, left page before right). They are emerging as readers.

Phase 2: Reading Pictures with Text-Like Language

If children hear books read to them, they begin to acquire a "written register" or knowledge of how written language differs from oral language (Purcell-Gates, 1988). Written language differs from oral language in many ways, and children notice this and begin to "read" in ways that sound much more like books. Their vocabulary becomes more sophisticated, their grammar more concise (e.g., adjectives in English come before nouns rather than after), and they begin to use story conventions such as "Once upon a time." Consider the examples in Figure 2.2 and see how the language the children use is different from the language used by children in Phase 1. In the first example, the girl is highly familiar with the book, reading it with many of the actual words of the text. In the second example, the boy is not familiar with his book, but reads it using written-like language so that it sounds like it could be a page in a story. These children know

The text says . . .	The child reads . . .
That very night in Max's room a forest grew.	"This house is in the woods." "Turn it to this part."
Their eyes were on Chewbacca. He was waving excitedly.	"Oh, yeah. That's Chewy." "Look at their eyes."

FIGURE 2.1. Emergent reading example: Reading pictures with oral-like language.

The text says . . .	The child reads . . .
I throw a stick, and he brings it back to me. He makes mistakes sometimes.	"If I throw a stick, he brings it back. Sometimes he makes mistakes."
That very night in Max's room a forest grew.	"In the morning the boy went to California."

FIGURE 2.2. Emergent reading example: Reading pictures with text-like language.

that language in books differs from oral language or conversation. They know that the syntax or grammar of written language is more formal and precise. This key insight will help children as they begin to predict words when they read the print in later phases of development. If a child has a written register, the child is much more likely to be able to predict words that would be appropriate for the story being read.

Phase 3: Reading the Text from Memory

These reading renditions are verbatim matches between the text and what the children read. Reading from memory is common for children who like to hear the same story over and over, especially books with highly repetitive text. The readings can be different, though. When we observe children closely, we see that at times they "read" with eyes only on pictures. At other times, they read from memory, but they track the print with their fingers, pointing to each word as they say it. Because children have the words memorized, they sometimes have to start over on a page if they "read" faster than they were able to track the print. These reading behaviors are critical for helping children develop important print concepts and for recognizing some words.

The child in the second example in Figure 2.3 can point to each word as she reads and has made a particularly important insight. She has learned the concept of *word*. As children develop oral language, they usually do not know when one word begins and another ends. "More milk" is probably one word to a 2-year-old. "Once upon on time" is "Onceuponatime" (one word) to many children. Because we do not speak with

The text says . . .	The child reads . . . and does . . .
The fox got on the bus. Then the bus went fast.	The child looks only at pictures and chants the words on each page, almost singing, "The fox got on the bus and the bus went fast!"
Over the river and through the wood, To grandfather's house we go.	The child sings slowly, as she points to each word in the book, "Over . . . the . . . river and through the woods . . . to grandfather's house we go."

FIGURE 2.3. Emergent reading example: Reading the text from memory.

spaces between our words, children initially do not "see" spaces between words in print. Eventually, though, through demonstration by others, children learn how to *voice–print match*, as shown by the child in the second example. Although she is still reading from memory (she may not recognize any of the words in isolation and she cannot decode yet), she has made a huge leap in her development.

Phase 4: Reading What You Know

This phase is fascinating to researchers but often causes puzzlement or dismay in teachers or parents. This is because some children go through a period in their reading development when they focus exclusively on words or word parts (sound–symbol relations) that they know automatically and seem to forget that texts are supposed to make sense! Some studies have shown that many children move through this stage despite differences in instruction (Biemiller, 1970; Ferreiro & Teberosky, 1983; Mason, 1984; McIntyre & Freppon, 1994; Sulzby, 1985). It is as if they have discovered that *real* reading is a print-processing activity (Morris, 2008), and they are working at reading as they might go about problem solving. In the examples in Figure 2.4, both children had previously read the books from memory, verbatim. Their readings sound like the children regressed in their development, but as we will discuss, this behavior actually shows a move toward conventional reading.

In the first example, the child seems to rely exclusively on the words he knows from sight. He seems to care little about sense making, although when he self-corrects in the fourth line, it is an indication that he knows that the sentence should sound like language. It's almost as if he is reading a list of sight words. He makes no attempt at sounding out words he doesn't know. This could be a signal to teachers that he needs explicit phonics instruction. We discuss this topic at length in Chapter 5.

The text says . . .	The child reads . . .
We will call our snowman Ned.	We will . . . snowman . . .
But first he has to have a head.	But . . . he head.
His head will have to have a hat.	To . . . a . . . hat.
His hat is on.	He . . . his hat is on.
Just look at that!	Just like at that.
He is so big.	He is so big.
He is so tall.	He is so tall.
He is the biggest man of all.	He is the . . . man of all.
Brown bear, brown bear, what do you see?	"Br . . . brrrrr . . . oun . . . oun . . . brown. Brown b—bear. Beer. Bear. Brown bear. Brown bear. W—hat. W—hat do you see?"

FIGURE 2.4. Emergent reading example: Reading what you know.

In the second example, the child reads a book he has previously memorized. Did he forget it? No! The child has come to understand that letters have corresponding sounds that make up words. He knows many of those sounds and is practicing them here. This phase often indicates that children are just becoming readers (usually in kindergarten and first grade in U.S. classrooms), a period in which much assistance is critical (Tharp & Gallimore, 1993). As stated, it is in this phase that phonics instruction becomes essential even for children who have acquired some skill at it, as this child has.

Phase 5: Beginning Reading

This is the phase when children begin to read conventionally, or *really* read. Teachers know that children are really reading when they can pick up a text they have never seen before and read it in a way that makes sense. When children use what they know about print (graphophonics), language (syntax), and the topic of the text and their world (semantics) simultaneously, they are really reading (Goodman, 1967; Clay, 1991; Ehri & Wilce, 1985; Mason, 1980, 1984; Stanovich, 2000; Sulzby, 1985). Beginning reading often sounds halting and can be quite slow, but observers can tell that the child is sense making. In the first example in Figure 2.5, the child decodes many words in each sentence and then rereads so that the text makes sense and she is motivated to read on. In the second example, the child reads slowly and haltingly, applying what she knows about phonics. When phonics does not work for her, she asks an adult to identify the problem word. She is using her resources to make sense of text and is motivated by the reading to continue.

Phase 6: Proficient Reading

Once children can read independently, they still need much assistance from others. They need to practice a lot, preferably monitored (or mediated) by a teacher. They need to read various genres (e.g., nonfiction, fiction, fables, poetry) in various formats (e.g., traditional books, magazines, Internet, visual texts) for multiple purposes, because

The text says . . .	The child reads . . .
In the morning James woke to see snow falling. He ran into the garden as fast as he could and started to make a snowman.	"In the /m— . . . /J- James/ . . . woke up . . . woke to see snow fl- fall . . . falling. He ran into the /gare . . . den/ . . . garden as fast as he . . . can, and state . . . start -ed to make a snowman."
There was once a shoemaker who worked hard and was honest.	(*very slowly*) "There was . . . /oh/ . . . once a shoe . . . maker who worked hard and was . . . /h- . . . / . . . (*asks researcher the word*) honest."

FIGURE 2.5. Beginning reading example.

The text says . . .	The child reads . . .
They have came by plane, by train, by car, and by bus. Some people have walked all the way to Washington from New York City. That's more than 230. One man has roller skated from Chicago.	They have came by plane, by train, by car, and by bus. Some people have walked home . . . all the way to Washington from New York City. That's more than 20 . . . 230 miles. (*Whoa!*) One man has rolled . . . roller skated . . . from Colorado. (*Child blurts, "That's better than walking!"*)

FIGURE 2.6. Proficient reading example.

becoming skilled readers means becoming adept at every kind of new type of text we want them to read. Some children will appear quite skilled in one context but struggle in others. For example, some children learn to read fiction quite easily but stumble through nonfiction because they are not used to the different structure of text. In the example in Figure 2.6, a third grader reads a text about the march on Washington. He makes miscues that indicate his easy comprehension, and he inserts comments as he reads.

These phases or patterns overlap, and each is not necessarily evident in every child because much of what children know is invisible to observers. The patterns described above, of course, are not the same for every child because children's social and cultural interactions are not the same. Children's prior experiences with reading, the quality of the scaffolding children receive, and the kinds of texts with which they interact are just some experiences that can affect their movement through the phases. Thus, some children will bypass some of the phases described above. Most important, as stated earlier, the children do not naturally move through these phases of reading simply because they grow older. Instead, their development is assisted by others.

Writing Development

Although the focus of this book is reading, it is important that teachers understand writing development in young children. Because writing development parallels reading development, teachers can learn much about reading development from what children put on paper or a computer. Sometimes children learn to write before they learn to read.

In the last few decades, we have learned much about how children become conventional writers through studies of young children's emergent writing. While children's drawings, scribbles, and letters strings were once thought to be merely play, today these constructions are viewed, like the reading productions illustrated above, as indicators of children's development toward conventional literacy (Bissex, 1980; Clay, 1975; Dyson, 1984, 1986; Harste et al., 1984; Teale & Sulzby, 1986). Some behaviors can be viewed as milestones or benchmarks. Children begin to show their understanding that print is different from oral language, just as they do in their pretend readings. Based on the work of emergent literacy scholars, teachers have learned that children tend to move through common phases of writing.

Phase 1: Scribbling

Children as young as 18 months have been observed scribbling on paper and then delivering the "message" to someone nearby. If the child asks, "What did I write?", it indicates that the child knows that print means something but does not yet know that there is a complex and precise structure to written language (Clay, 1975). Figure 2.7 is an example of a child's "writing" on his first day of kindergarten.

Phase 2: Controlled Scribbling

The more children are around others using written language with purpose and the more they observe the printed word, the more they see that print is controlled on a page. It looks a certain way. It is not all over the page as in Figure 2.7. In fact, in storybooks, print is separate from the picture. Figure 2.8 is an example of a child who "wrote" a story to go with the picture in his coloring book. Two other children have learned about letters and incorporate letter shapes into their texts (see Figures 2.9 and 2.10). These

FIGURE 2.7. Writing on the first day of kindergarten.

FIGURE 2.8. Controlled scribbling.

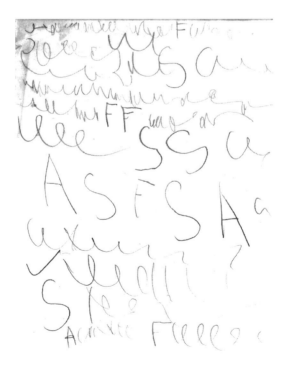

FIGURE 2.9. Controlled scribbling.

FIGURE 2.10. Controlled scribbling.

controlled scribbling examples came from preschoolers who wrote these texts at home. These children seem to know a bit more about how print looks in books than the child in the first example, who just scribbled, even though that child was older than the children who exhibit controlled scribbling. Why these differences might exist is the subject of Chapter 3.

Phase 3: Nonphonetic Letter Strings

After some instruction at preschool, kindergarten, or home, children learn that there is a correct way to make letters. They have moved beyond scribbling to writing by stringing letters together. Many children think that these strings of letters mean something because they look so much like print. It is also common for children to initially combine letters and numbers because they know that both mean something, but do not yet know their function. In Figure 2.11, Ellen observed a child write the letter string and then ask his father to read it. The father looked at the letters and said something like, "/Toyk-guk-oymk-puk/." The child scowled at his father, and the father shrugged at Ellen.

In the next example (Figure 2.12), a kindergartener named Justin wrote his name and then a string of letters for his story. Notice the letters he chooses; they are mostly from his name. Since children know that their name means something, they use this knowledge to write other text to complement their pictures.

In Figure 2.13, Sammy illustrates many concepts about writing: how numbers and words might be placed on a page, what a "graph" might look like, the length of a typical word, and (maybe) the beginning of sound–symbol correspondences, although it is too unclear to know for sure without asking the child to read his words.

FIGURE 2.11. Letter strings.

FIGURE 2.12. Letter strings.

FIGURE 2.13. Letter strings.

Phase 4: Writing the Known

After many interactions with parents, teachers, and peers and the children's explorations of print, children soon learn that letters must be sequenced in an exact order to mean something. Once they gain this insight, many children ask adults and older children to spell for them. The children may not yet know when one word stops and another begins in oral language and so might ask, "How do you spell *Onceuponatime*?" One 4-year-old asked "How do you spell *OldBill*?" of Bill's wife. A 5-year-old asked, "How do you spell *Thankyouforthegameboy*?" Some adults, aware that children can begin to compose on their own, encourage them to "write it the best they can." But many children initially resist inventing spellings. For some, it may be because they simply do not know the sound–symbol correspondences necessary to write on their own. Other children seem to be hung up on being accurate (which may be an aspect of personality or of an environment where accuracy is expected). Still, this period of *writing the known* is common in the early grades. If children stay in this period a long time, it may be an indication that they do not have the tools needed to *really* write.

Figures 2.14 and 2.15 are two examples of children writing what they know. In Figure 2.14, the child knows some words: *I* and *am*, and the concept of *sentence*. He even has a period after the first one! His additional words do not have sound–symbol correspondences for his intended message, but he clearly knows about how long words tend to be, and that they are made up of a variety of letters. In Figure 2.15, the child knows some words by heart—those that most children learn early in school (*I, like, love, see, dog, cat, mom, dad*). This child can create many sentences from these words and words she copies from around the classroom. But, of course, it is not *really* writing. Yet.

I am A Bg.

I am TK RB

I am R L a AB

FIGURE 2.14. Writing the known.

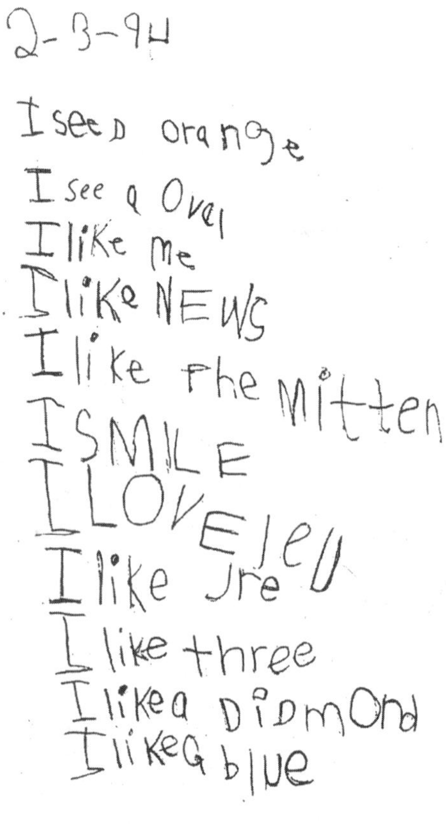

2-3-94

I seeD orange
I see a Oval
I like me
I like NEWS
I like the Mitten
I SMILE
I LOVE leU
I like Jre U
I like three
I like a DiDmOnd
I like a blue

FIGURE 2.15. Writing the known.

Phase 5: Invented Spelling

Children often produce writing before they read. In fact, some children write (encode) messages that adults can read (decode) but that the writers themselves cannot read back. Some children learn to read *through* writing; it is in the act of figuring out which letter–sound correspondences are needed for a message to others that some children learn to both encode and decode. In Figure 2.16, a student of Ellen illustrated the beginnings of sound–symbol knowledge with each word.

We refer to this phase in writing development as "invented spelling" (even though children invent spellings throughout childhood and beyond) and not "beginning writing" (even though the children *are* writing) because beginning writing includes reading the text to the teacher, which indicates the child's degree of sound–symbol matching and ability to decode the message.

Phase 6: Beginning Writing

Children are writing when they have enough "known words" and sound–symbol skills that they can write whatever they want to say and other people can read some or all of what is written. This period of writing can be quite fluent for some but still slow and laborious for others.

Figure 2.17 is also from one of Ellen's students in her combined first- and second-grade classroom. This child has plenty of known words and strong phonics knowledge, and it is easy to decode this message. The first line (cut off) says, "Yesterday my dad tuck [took]".

Once young writers can communicate a story about a major event such as the one above (a bicycle crash and hospital visit), teachers can begin to teach children about different genre, how to organize different texts, the role of word choice in good writing, and more. The children are ready to learn about the *craft* of writing (Fletcher & Portalupi,

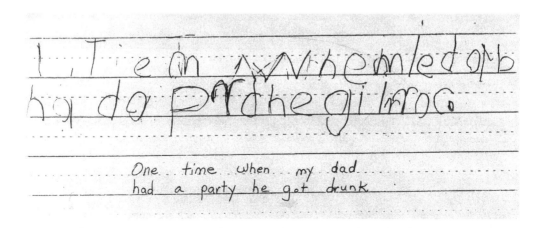

FIGURE 2.16. Beginnings of invented spelling.

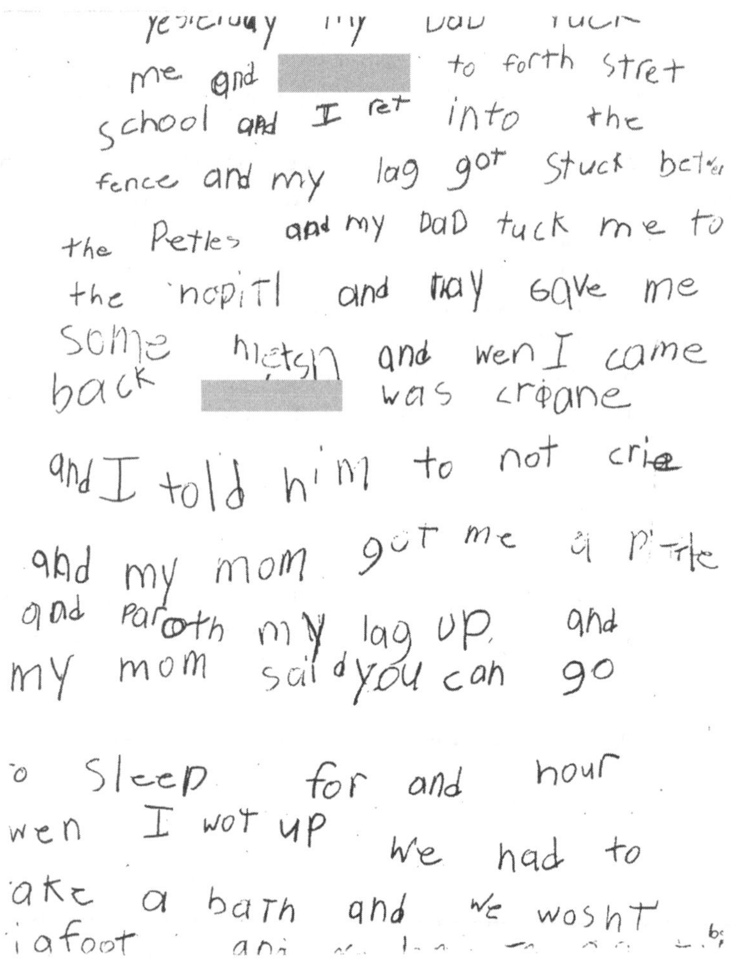

FIGURE 2.17. Beginning writing.

2007). Much of Chapter 9 is devoted to processes and strategies for research-based, culturally responsive writing instruction. An example of a child's writing of a nonfiction piece, at age 8, is shown in Figure 2.18.

The phases through which children move on their way to conventional writing parallel what they do as they learn to read. The phases do not map on to one another neatly, however. Instead, some children might be observed in multiple phases of reading development and do very little writing across several weeks. Other children learn to write first and only begin to tackle reading once they can decode some print. Still, understanding these phases is essential for knowing how to assist children in their efforts to acquire and perform these foundational skills. Below we provide the theoretical process for assisting children in their reading development. The details and strategies for how to help children learn to read and improve their reading are the topics of the rest of this book.

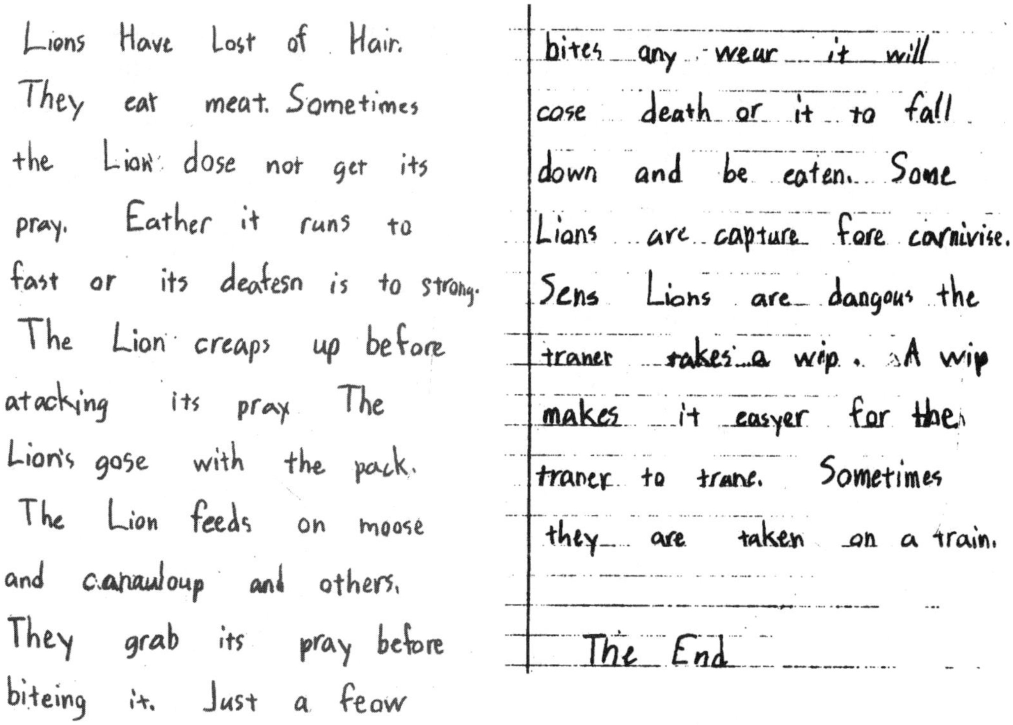

Lions Have Lost of Hair.
They eat meat. Sometimes
the Lion dose not get its
pray. Eather it runs to
fast or its deafesn is to strong.
The Lion creaps up before
atacking its pray The
Lion's gose with the pack.
The Lion feeds on moose
and c.anauloup and others.
They grab its pray before
biteing it. Just a feow

bites any wear it will
cose death or it to fall.
down and be eaten. Some
Lions are capture fore carnivise.
Sens Lions are dangous the
traner rakes a wip. A wip
makes it easyer for the
traner to trane. Sometimes
they are taken on a train.

The End

FIGURE 2.18. Nonfiction writing.

Assisted Performance and Reading Development

We often use the words *support* and *scaffold* to describe what a teacher, parent, or older child does to assist children in their reading development. Another useful term for help is *assisted performance* (Tharp & Gallimore, 1993). We use this term here because it emphasizes that assistance should be provided in ways that change the actual performance of the reader (or writer). Assisted performance is naturally provided in all cultures as children grow and learn in their early years; novices learn from experts as they work together on meaningful, purposeful tasks. This kind of teaching–learning situation is easily identified in homes and communities, such as when a parent or other adult teaches a child how to pack an overnight bag, tie a shoelace, play the piano, or do any other skill or task. This sort of assisted performance also occurs in classrooms during reading instruction. The process of learning to read, or learning a subskill of reading such as decoding or predicting the end of a story, occurs when the child interacts with others.

As an example of assisted performance, let us imagine a small group of first graders who are regularly exhibiting reading behaviors from Phase 3, reading from memory. The teacher selects a particular book that is short, predictable, and (hopefully) lively and interesting for the children. A very complex storybook would not be appropriate for these children in this lesson. The teacher's goal is to find a reading task that the children can do *with assistance*. First, the teacher reads the book aloud to the children, and they talk about the meaning and language of the book. The teacher reads the same book again and this time invites the children to join in chorally, reading some passages (building on their memory-reading skills). Afterward, the teacher explicitly teaches the children how to touch each word as they "read" each one (this skill is called *voice–print match*) for several pages of the book, modeling reading by phrases. Then the teacher helps each child in the group to perform the voice–print match strategy independently. The teacher provides coaching, questioning, and feedback for support.

If a child can already do voice–print match, then he or she does not need this lesson. But if a child cannot do it at all, even with lots of help from the teacher (and many preschoolers cannot), then the task is too difficult and a waste of time. If the children can successfully voice–print match with assistance, the teacher is teaching within the children's ZPD, just where she should be. Finally, the assistance the teacher provides (via coaching, questioning, feedback) is essential for moving the children forward. This book offers many strategies for helpful assisted performance.

Figure 2.19 depicts a child's movement through the ZPD in stages (Tharp & Gallimore, 1993). For example, in Stage 1, if the task is to read a particular text, the teacher or parent does most of the work, assisting the learner through demonstration and coreading (e.g., perhaps the teacher and child read a book together chorally). In Stage 2, the child attempts the same task with the same text, but on his or her own, using tools (e.g., self-talk and remembered strategies) for successfully reading the book. As the child self-assists, the teacher provides time for independent practice, monitoring the reading by observing the student carefully while the reader uses self-speech to take him- or herself through the task. If the child does not remain engaged, the teacher intervenes with strategies from Stage 1. Eventually the text becomes easy for the child, and he or she reads it automatically (Stage 3). Then, when a new task or new text (e.g. a more complex book) is introduced, the skill learned is deautomatized and the child needs assistance again.

Recursive loop			
Capacity developed			
Assistance by more capable others	Assistance by self	Internalization	Deautomatization
Parents | Teachers Experts | Peers Coaches			
Stage 1	Stage 2	Stage 3	Stage 4

FIGURE 2.19. Stages of the ZPD (Tharp & Gallimore, 1993).

READING INSTRUCTION THAT MATCHES DEVELOPMENT

On any given day, teachers know the text, the task or strategy, and the verbal assistance it might take to engage and assist their students within their ZPD. Teachers know when they must explicitly demonstrate or explain a concept or strategy and which subskills need daily systematic attention for particular children. This developmental instructional sequence is complex because it requires knowing what is going on inside the heads of the readers, where readers are in their development, and thus which kind of support is needed. From a sociocultural perspective, of course, it also requires knowing something about each child's history and culture, such as whether the child has observed reading in the home, how reading is perceived there, and who reads. It requires knowing something about the child's cultural language use, including speech patterns and participation structures, and the child's interests and attitudes. Teachers use this knowledge to plan the sequence of instruction and their interactions during the teaching episodes. The social–cultural–historical knowledge of the learners helps teachers determine their students' developmental levels and how best to assist them. This is a lot for teachers to know about their students. But many teachers across the nation are successful at using these tools simultaneously to help their students develop as readers. The purpose of this book is to show how it is done.

CHAPTER 3

Children Who Struggle with Reading

If you are a teacher or preparing to become one, you can probably identify the children you have taught or known who struggled with reading. You may have seen them "stuck" in one of the reading or writing phases described in Chapter 2. You may have taken additional time with these children, provided a specific intervention for them, or allowed an additional specialist to work with them. Perhaps there are particular materials you were expected to use for remediation. Still, you might not know why your students or the young people in your life struggle with reading or even how best to help them. Understanding why children might find reading frustrating could be the first tool in your repertoire of strategies for intervening in the struggle.

Many children in the United States struggle with learning to read or with reading some texts at various points in their lives. For some, it is a temporary period and for others, a lifetime of struggle. There are many reasons children struggle. For a few children, reading failure can be attributed to neurological or cognitive difficulties or disabilities caused at or before birth, by trauma, or from unknown causes. Many people assume reading difficulties are always the result of such causes. In fact, for most of the history of research on literacy, reading was defined primarily as a perceptual and/or cognitive process, and research on reading focused on the individual and what happens inside his or her head while reading. This *simple view* of reading (Pearson & Stevens, 1994) led to the general belief that a breakdown in the ability to read, in the conventional sense, resulted from something within the brain or mind of the reader.

However, the reasons many children struggle with reading are more complex and mysterious. Sometimes the difficulty involves multiple factors, some of which the child, family, or teacher has little control over (Shaywitz et al., 2000). Oftentimes though, the reasons are environmental. Today, many educators (e.g., Allington & McGill-Franzen, 2003; McIntyre, 2010) agree that for most children who struggle with reading, the reasons depend on each child's interactions with others in the context of his or her cultural and historical background—that is, factors outside the mind of the reader. This new view of reading—a *sociocultural view*—helps teachers and researchers understand the many complex variables that contribute to reading success or failure. Some of these variables are critical for understanding students. These explanations are addressed briefly, and later chapters address how teachers can mediate—or interrupt—environmental constraints faced by children who struggle with reading. But first, we address some common misconceptions about the role of the environment in literacy learning.

DEFICIT VIEWS OF CHILDREN WHO STRUGGLE

Many children who struggle with reading do not have health, neurological, or language difficulties. Nonetheless, they do not perform as well as others in classrooms or on tests of reading. Many happen to come from poor communities or are English language learners and form what is widely referred to today as the academic *achievement gap*. Unfortunately, many people—even many educators—mistakenly believe that these achievement differences indicate that poor or immigrant populations are inherently intellectually deficient. Other explanations suggest that children from poor or immigrant groups lack the proper experiences necessary to learn, suggesting that some people's experiences are more valuable than others (McIntyre, Hulan, & Maher, 2010). Some scholars have noted that some people believe that particular dialects are barriers to learning to read or indicators of ignorance (Adger, Wolfram, & Christian, 2007; Baugh, 2006; Purcell-Gates, 1996). Some citizens think that the families of struggling readers are themselves deficient parents and caretakers and perhaps cannot assist their children in learning. These *deficit views* of learners have prevailed, only recently being interrupted by some educators.

Today, most research disputes these deficit perspectives; each premise mentioned in the previous paragraph can be countered by many research studies and sometimes through common sense. Many studies have illustrated the intelligence of the children assumed to be deficient and that many teachers unwittingly underestimate what children know (Heath, 1994; Michaels, 1981; Moll, 1994; Stone, 2004; Rogoff, 2003). Some studies have shown how many children of color are misevaluated (Heath, 1994).

The view that children "lack experiences" is held by some people who believe that the experiences of some populations (often middle class, white, Christian, or a combination) are more valuable than the experiences of other populations (e.g., poor or working-class children, children of color, English language learners). However, different experiences, such as visiting an art museum or feeding cattle on a farm, are made relevant in school when the teacher makes them relevant. If teachers have students read books only about topics favored by the some groups, they may come to view children as lacking the prior knowledge needed to learn in school.

Further, many studies in the field of linguistics over the past several decades have shown that some dialects such as African American English or Appalachian English are not sloppily half-formed variations of English, but instead are well-developed and rule-governed language forms (Adger et al., 2007; Ogbu, 1988; Wolfram & Ward, 2006). Finally, the view that families do not care about education or are deficient caretakers is no more accurate for poor families or families of color than for wealthier or white populations (Kyle, McIntyre, Miller, & Moore, 2002; McIntyre, Kyle, & Rightmyer, 2005). Moll (1994) suggests that the rejection of deficit views—in particular, the view that some children are devoid of the proper experiences necessary for learning—is perhaps the most important construct that has governed a sociocultural view of learning.

SO WHY DO SOME CHILDREN AND POPULATIONS OF CHILDREN STRUGGLE WITH READING?

To understand why some individual children struggle with reading and why whole populations seem to struggle can be two separate questions. We address the *individual* first by looking at some environmental factors that may affect children's literacy acquisition or how well they develop as readers. Later we address *populations* of children in efforts to better understand and address group stereotypes and the many academic achievement gaps between groups of students.

Child and Family Variables

First, many children struggle with reading because they lack the necessary phonological awareness and skill (Adams, 1990; Stanovich, 2000). We address the remediation of this issue in Chapter 5. *Why* some children may lack these or other necessary skills, abilities, dispositions, and practices necessary for acquiring full literacy is the subject of this chapter.

With the emergence of sociocultural theory, educators have moved away from genetic, neurological, or perceptual explanations of reading success and failure as the only explanations for why children struggle. Instead, educators now recognize that many explanations lie primarily with factors related to, or embedded within, families' income levels or socioeconomic status (SES), although income in no way *causes* success or failure in literacy. Teachers of poor or working-class children might be able to predict the living conditions that affect children's access to literacy, but income should in no way be viewed as the cause of academic difficulties.

The reasons children may seem stuck in some of the reading and writing phases described in Chapter 2 are many. Three primary child and family factors that relate to achievement are shown in Figure 3.1 and described below. These factors show the complexity of the relationship between family income and school achievement.

First, there is *access to, or experiences with, print*. Children who come from poor or working-class families tend to have fewer print and print-related texts at home than children who come from families with more money (Lareau, 2000; Purcell-Gates, 1995; Teale, 1986). This makes sense, of course. Quality children's literature, computers, popular magazines, and hand-held gaming devices (yes, there is print material there!) are

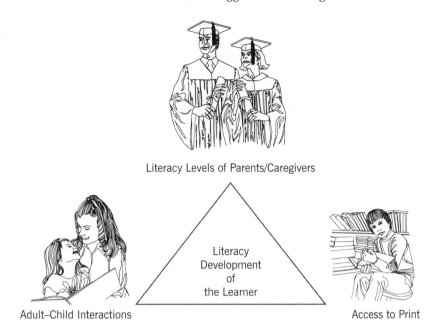

Literacy Levels of Parents/Caregivers

Literacy
Development
of
the Learner

Adult–Child Interactions   Access to Print

FIGURE 3.1. Factors affecting literacy development.

all expensive entertainment items. Families who struggle economically might be just as devoted to education as any family (and often are, as described later), but simply cannot afford the sorts of tools other families afford. Even if they do buy print-related items, if those items are not as attractive as the popular, expensive tools, the children are not as likely to use them and will favor nonprint activities. How children spend their out-of-school time makes a dramatic difference in their school achievement.

Second, as emphasized in Chapter 2, *adult–child interactions* are critical for children's development. Some children have parents or guardians who work more hours than those of some of their classmates, resulting in fewer interactions with adults during the day. We know from studies of language development (Hart & Risley, 1995; Heath, 1983; Wells, 1986) that adults who use adult vocabulary when talking with children help them develop stronger verbal and print skills. We also know that children who are read to at home also have an easier time achieving literacy skills (Purcell-Gates, 1988). Yet, when parents and guardians have to work many hours in order to pay bills or simply because they choose to, there is naturally less time devoted to these activities. While teachers should never use families' income to make assumptions about the time devoted to these activities, it is necessary for teachers to be ready to intervene when they suspect children may not have many print-related interactions at home. We address how this kind of intervention can be done throughout this book.

Finally, *literacy levels of adults in children's lives* are a key factor. Some students may be children of adults with low literacy themselves, thus increasing the risk of perpetuating the cycle of low literacy (Miller, 1995; Purcell-Gates, 1995). The cycle continues because some parents may not know how to assist their children, for example, by providing print-rich experiences. We are aware of no studies that have shown that parents with low literacy skills care less about literacy. In fact, in our experience (e.g., Kyle, McIntyre, Miller, & Moore, 2002), parents of low literacy care deeply that their children achieve more than they themselves have achieved. It is also important to recognize that the literacy levels of parents are less a factor in their children's achievement than what happens daily in the homes with respect to print-rich experiences (Aram & Levin, 2001; Lee & Bowen, 2006; Leseman & de Jong, 1998), as mentioned in Chapter 2. The factors closest to the child—literacy tools, activities, and interactions—most directly affect achievement, not the poverty or literacy levels of parents. Further, it appears that a *combination* of home literacy variables has more to do with achievement than any one factor alone (Aram & Levin, 2001; Lee & Bowen, 2006; Leseman & de Jong, 1998; Weinberger, 1996).

We do not assert that there are no parents who neglect their children's physical, academic, and emotional needs. Some parents, for whatever reason (e.g., drug addiction, illness) do not provide for their children in ways most members of our society believe that parents should. Often, but not always, these parents are poor. What is important to recognize is that income level itself does not *cause* low or high achievement and that many families of poverty care deeply about education and do what they can to provide for their children emotionally and physically. Specifically, we cannot *assume* that children of poverty have or do not have (1) access to print, (2) few interactions with adults around print, or (3) parents of low literacy. However, since poverty is a predictor of these factors, it may be important for teachers to assess these factors individually when questioning why a particular child might struggle with reading. There is much teachers can do to mediate, or interrupt, these factors that can either limit or promote children's literacy growth.

The Achievement Gap: Patterns across Individuals and Families

We have just emphasized the importance of *not* assuming characteristics of individuals or families based on perceived or real levels of income, race, cultural background, level of English proficiency, and so on. However, many studies have illustrated patterns of achievement by economic, racial, or cultural group (Miller, 1995). In general, across the nation, poor students tend to do less well in school than their middle-class counterparts. Also, in general, children of color (primarily African American and Hispanics) do less well in school than European Americans or Asian Americans. Indeed, when economic conditions are the same across groups, there is still an achievement gap by race. It is important to acknowledge this finding and not tiptoe around it by assuming that all gaps are caused by economic conditions. If we ignore this fact, we will continue to perpetuate it rather than seeking to understand how to interrupt it. Race is a touchy subject when we discuss achievement, no doubt. Consider Vignette 3.1. This scene is actually more complex than it appears here, and it took some unpacking for Ellen and the teacher candidate to understand what was going on. No Child Left Behind legislation requires that schools disaggregate student achievement data by race so that teachers, principals, and superintendents can see which groups of children are achieving and which are not.

VIGNETTE 3.1. UNPACKING RACISM AND TEACHING EXPECTATIONS

Ellen was supervising teacher candidates in the spring of 2009. Once a week, the candidates observed in classrooms, taught occasional lessons, or worked one on one with students under the mentoring of an experienced teacher. One day, a white female candidate came to Ellen distraught and asked to be moved to another classroom with a different mentor. The candidate told Ellen that she had witnessed a terrible, racist scene. The mentor teacher and two other teachers (all of whom were also white females) had invited the candidate to a gathering to discuss the achievement of the children in the class. In a private setting, the mentor teacher read a name from an index card, and the three teachers began to talk about how that child was doing in school. At one point, the teacher said, "Let's talk about the blacks." She read one child's name from a separate stack, and a chorus of laughter rose from the teachers, and comments were made such as "No way" and "Not on a prayer," meaning that the child would not succeed this academic year in this class. The teacher candidate was horrified. The teachers continued assessing the students in this way, at times making inappropriate comments for certain children.

Uncomfortable as this may be, it is a necessary step toward addressing achievement differences. The teachers in this district are required to discuss each child's progress and to attend to the progress of students by ethnic groups. This requirement is an attempt to expose what teachers and schools might be doing or not doing that impedes achievement for some children. In a sense, it is an effort to question whether instruction is culturally responsive to a given group.

Of course, in this case, laughing about the achievement of a child and assuming that the child will not succeed is abhorrent. The teacher candidate was right to be horrified and to perceive the scene as racist. In fact, one immediate reaction might be to wonder why the teacher would make such statements, since they reflect on *her* ability to teach. If there is "no way" a child will succeed, what is she, as the teacher, doing wrong? How should she change her instruction to ensure that the child *does* make it?

Still, it is critically important to discuss individual children's achievement for the purposes of figuring out why a child may be struggling and what can be done about it. Discussing achievement within the context of all sociocultural variables (e.g., race, class, culture, literacy level of parents) can help enlighten teachers and schools as to why some children struggle. Finding patterns for groups of children may indicate to teachers that they must adapt instruction to be more culturally responsive.

Of course, when schools find patterns of achievement by cultural groups, it may become all too easy to make the very assumptions we warn against: to hold a deficit view of some children without even knowing why. Such beliefs tend to stereotype or blame groups. That is one reason many researchers from different perspectives have worked to understand the factors that help explain these differences (Arzubiaga, Rueda, & Monzo, 2002; Marks, Cresswell, & Ainley, 2006; McCarthey, 2009; McGill-Franzen, 1987; Miller, 1995; Portes, 1999; Rueda & McIntyre, 2002; Turner & Edwards, 2009; van Steensel, 2006).

EXPLANATIONS FOR GROUP DIFFERENCES

The studies mentioned above show that the reasons for achievement gaps between groups are complex and have to do with *our country's history*. These reasons are also grounded in the *community cultural practices* of the populations from which the children come. They have to do with *school and teacher factors* that affect whole populations of children. These group factors intersect with the individual and family characteristics, making the reasons that some children struggle with literacy complex (see Figure 3.2).

Let's take *history* first. Much has been written about how major historical movements or events worldwide have affected literacy practices of particular groups and individuals (Brandt, 2001; Heath, 1991, 1994; Miller, 1995; Street, 1985). We know that in the United States, people of color have had less access to both education and income because of slavery, racist policies, as well as subtler forms of discrimination. Societal movements throughout our country's history have affected access in positive ways as well. For example, the removal of children from the workforce and their subsequent placement in schools raised literacy levels (Heath, 1994). People's interest in their own civil rights increased reading and writing for social purposes (Brandt, 2001). Studies also illuminated the power of community institutions, such as the black church, in raising literacy levels of its members. Heath (1994) described how desegregation affected the literacy practices of two young African American mothers in the mid-1980s during a time when they witnessed little overt political action as they struggled to keep jobs, feed their children, and move away from their communities. Indeed, any sizable increase in literacy levels for a population has depended upon changes in community organi-

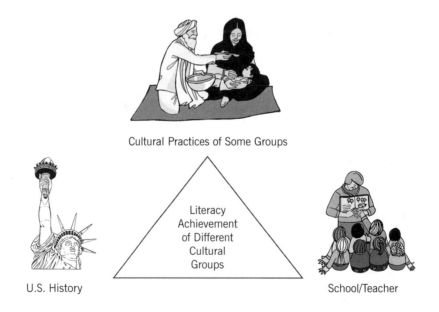

FIGURE 3.2. Literacy achievement of different cultural groups.

zations, such as churches, or changes in economic patterns, resulting in more leisure time—which, at least until the last few decades, meant more time for literacy (Brandt, 2001; Heath, 1994). While our country has made progress since the mid-20th century from severe racial discrimination and separate schools, it is far too soon to discount the effects of our nation's racial history on the literacy of some populations. It takes multiple generations for families to alleviate the effects of a lack of income and education (Miller, 1995). Further, family histories can change quickly, especially in eras of economic recession. Some studies that examined the effects of sociocultural variables on achievement neglected to assess literacy in homes and families over time, thus eliminating the crucial cultural–historical element.

The *cultural practices* mentioned above, such as access to print, literacy interactions, and literacy levels of families, form patterns identifiable by cultural and racial groups, often due to income levels across these groups rather than to race or ethnicity. Thus, if many of your Hispanic students do not seem to have many print texts in the home, it is not because Hispanic families do not care about literacy. It may be because, in general, Hispanic families in this country have less income than European American families. If many of your African American students seem to have few opportunities for extended talk with family members, it may not be because these families do not talk with their children; instead, it may be because the adults work two or three jobs in order to provide enough income for the family, thus limiting interaction time. Unfortunately, in this nation, these are common patterns.

Cultural practices of particular groups may also affect achievement. In one study, middle- and upper-middle-class African American students appeared, on the surface, to have every advantage the European American students in the wealthy suburban Ohio school district enjoyed. But the African American students were failing in school at disproportionate rates. In such circumstances, it is easy for outsiders to assume that the students were less capable than the European American students—that they were failing because they were less intelligent. They all had equal access, right? They had the same teachers and books. But in this study, the researcher (Ogbu, 2003) found several influences that went beyond race, income, or school variables to affect these students' achievement. These influences primarily involved cultural practices and identity. For instance, some of the students refused to become engaged with academic pursuits for fear of "acting white"; doing so implied the renouncing of African American identity and was greatly affected by peer pressure. The study also showed that while the parents of these students had high expectations for their children's school success, these parents were less involved in schools because they worked more hours (in order to live in the neighborhood) and monitored their children's homework and leisure practices less than the European American parents. The explanation for the students' relative lack of achievement is not meant to exonerate schools or to blame minority parents. Instead, it is intended to illustrate the complexity of factors that affect group achievement and the need to consider all the forces of history, family, and community that may affect school achievement.

SCHOOLS AND TEACHERS
AFFECT ACHIEVEMENT DIFFERENCES

Schools and teachers affect achievement differences too, of course. There have been many recent studies of how school and classroom environments affect reading and reading development. Sociocultural researchers are interested in how, when, why, and how much students learn in different classrooms and schools as explanations for why some children achieve more than others. Unfortunately, many studies have shown that some populations of children receive a very different education than others (Allington, 1977, 1983; Anyon, 1997; Finn, 1999; McDermott, 1977; Michaels, 1981; Rist, 1970), and the pattern is clear: Across the nation, instruction, materials, students' school experiences, and expertise of teachers are of lower quality in schools serving children of poverty than in schools serving middle-class kids. This does not mean that all teachers and schools serving poor kids are bad, of course; there are many examples to the contrary. Yet, this is and has been a national trend for a long time.

As we have said, many educators and noneducators attribute differences in achievement to the students themselves. And as we described earlier with respect to achievement differences, a child's history, family, and community do make a difference in how well the child performs in school. Yet, the studies above that examined school and teacher factors tell a different, additional story about why the achievement gaps persist. Often without knowing it or why, teachers in schools serving poor and working-class kids provide a lower quality of education. Let's examine what this looks like and why it might happen.

Schools in poor districts provide fewer high-quality materials; have older, more run-down buildings in which to house students; and have higher student–teacher ratios. Additionally, teachers in these schools are often beginning teachers who plan to leave these schools once they obtain experience. The turnover rate is very high, making the investment in professional development a challenge for school leaders. Individual teachers cannot do much about most of these factors, short of supporting school board members, politicians, and other civic leaders in making relevant policy changes. Yet, there are some factors teachers can directly affect. The first is the curriculum and instruction offered to the students. The second is the high or low expectations teachers have for particular students and how those expectations play out in classrooms.

Curricular and Instructional Differences

Schools serving poor and working-class students in this country commonly adopt basic skills models and packaged programs for reading instruction more often than schools serving middle-class students. These programs boast big gain scores on reading tests for struggling readers. Educators have made the case that "these kids" need this type of instruction. As suggested in Chapter 1, the argument is that if children lack "basic skills," then these programs are needed to raise those skill levels before moving on to more high-level skills.

There are problems with this assumption, as well meaning as it might be for some educators. Before we explain, we illustrate this flawed assumption with an example. One spring Ellen visited an urban school as part of a research study that was examining the relationship between early reading achievement and instructional practices. She was set to observe a second-grade class she had not visited previously. She sat with her laptop taking notes as the elementary teacher began her lesson. There were 12 students sitting in desks forming a semicircle around the teacher. They each had a basal reader, and each child had opened to a page with the text shown in Figure 3.3. The teacher enthusiastically encouraged the children to read. They were all cooperative, some to the point of docility. Ellen was stunned by the inane text. She looked at the students who sat cooperatively in their seats chanting the words. One African American male student sat slumped in his seat, politely chanting the words with the others. He and some of the others looked too old to be reading this material, and for a moment Ellen even wondered whether she was in the correct classroom for her research. She whispered to the instructional assistant standing nearby, "What grade is this?"

"Second," the assistant said.

When Ellen slowly nodded, the assistant proudly offered, "See that boy right there?" pointing to the African American male student Ellen had noticed earlier. Ellen nodded.

"He can read at a sixth-grade level."

"What's he doing here, then?" Ellen asked, alarmed.

She shrugged, "This is the top group," indicating that there was nothing she could do.

The *top* group? Ellen thought perhaps it was a remedial class for older students, and an inadequate one at that. This school used a direct instruction reading model, called SRA Reading Mastery, throughout the school, which served urban poor kids, most of whom were African American. At the time of this observation, this large urban school district had adopted this program for each of the schools serving mostly African American students in efforts to raise children's reading levels. These are the sorts of programs that some people advocate for *research-based reading instruction*. As described in Chapter 1, our own model of instruction, featured in this book, values research-based reading

---

The man was getting mad. He yelled, "Dog, stop reading that book and start playing ball."

She yelled, "I will not go into the hall, hall, hall, and I will not play ball, ball, ball."

The man was very mad now. He came into the room and got his coat. He said, "Well, I am going for a walk. Do you want to come with me?"

The dog said, "I will not do that, that, that, when I can sit here and get fat, fat, fat."

So, the tall man left and the dog went back to her book. She said, "I hate to walk, walk, walk, but I like to talk, talk, talk."

FIGURE 3.3. Direct instruction text excerpt. Excerpted from "The Dog Likes to Talk, Talk, Talk" in *SRA Reading Mastery Classic Edition* (2003).

instruction *when combined with features of culturally responsive instruction* that extend from sociocultural theory. What, then, is the problem?

Clearly, as in the case above, the direct instruction basal reader model works against some students, likely holding them back. It seems only to help students learn a few skills temporarily, never moving them toward the sort of analytical and critical thinking necessary for advanced reading. Many educators have even gone so far as to say that this instructional approach, and the many like it, are part of the *subtle mechanisms* (Finn, 1999) that keep poor kids less educated. They do little more than help kids acquire the "basics"—and probably do much more to keep bright kids disadvantaged.

Patrick Finn (1999) calls this kind of instruction "education for domestication" and "pretend school." Ann Dyson (1984) calls it "doing school." Janice Hale (2003) wrote, "Our children are being educated in schools that deliver the girls to public assistance and the boys to unemployment and incarceration" (p. 111). Clearly, this kind of teaching does not help students achieve beyond the most basic level of reading. Still, many claim that these programs are just what struggling readers need. Many who make these claims have good intentions. But what they often communicate is the longstanding problem we have in this country of holding low expectations for students of color, the poor, and students whose first language is not English. We address expectations in more detail shortly.

It is not just programs adopted for poor students that are problematic. Teachers also use different instructional strategies depending on the various populations they teach. In one famous study (Anyon, 1997), a researcher compared elementary instruction in different schools that served four different income groups: working class (e.g., children of unskilled workers), middle class (e.g., teachers, fire fighters), upper-middle class (e.g., doctors, TV executives), and elite (e.g., corporate executives). The researcher found that the children in the lower SES schools received more rote-type instruction focused on basic skills, whereas those in the higher SES schools received high-level thinking instruction. Children in schools serving working- and middle-class students were taught to follow rules, whereas those in professional and wealthy populations were taught to question authority, think beyond what is written in text, analyze data, and create new knowledge. A brief comparison of instructional practices is summarized in Figure 3.4.

Anyon's (1997) study was only one of many that illustrated this sort of curricular inequity across SES groups. One argument educators make for these differences is that many children in schools serving poor and working-class kids have not had access to much literacy (which may or may not be true, as we explained earlier) and thus need basic skills prior to high-level thinking. The argument is that struggling readers cannot do high-level thinking because they do not have the prerequisite skills. The other argument, as explained in Chapter 1, is that some of these programs have been shown to work, at least temporarily. Yet, a curriculum focused on basic skills arguably limits what students can learn by limiting access to high-quality instruction (Allington & McGill-Franzen, 2003; McGill-Franzen & Allington, 1991; Miller, 1995; McIntyre, 2010). We argue that this may be one of the contributing factors to school failure. It is important

Schools serving poor or working-class kids (parental jobs include nonsalaried, low-paying jobs or no jobs)	Schools serving *middle-class* kids (Parental jobs include police, firefighters, teachers, government workers)
• Totally teacher directed • Copying from the board • Lots of worksheets • Desks in rows • Punishment • Busywork • Student resistance • Behavior an issue • Isolated facts • Derogatory remarks made about students by teacher • Learning rules for writing • Reading materials old and low-level • Teachers feared by parents	• Heavy focus on textbooks • Getting the right answer the goal • Some choice in work • Reading the text and answering questions at the end of the chapter • Patriotism and holidays important • Following rules important • Cookie-cutter art
Schools serving *upper-middle class* kids (parental jobs include doctors, lawyers, engineers, some professors, bankers)	**Elite schools serving *wealthy* kids (parental jobs include financiers, politicians, entertainment, CEOs of companies)**
• Much choice in work • Group work • Workshop environment • Writing for authentic audiences • Creativity encouraged • Discussion of ideas • Discovery and experience valued • Current events • Students' opinions important • Student products: stories, essays, murals, crafts, graphs, film, etc. • Constant negotiation between teacher and student • Thinking valued • Doing good for the world prized • Questioning the status quo	• Rigorous curriculum • Reading the classics • Learning through conversation • Personal attention • Many controversial topics discussed • Teachers questioned by parents • Leading the world the goal • Reasoning and problem solving primary • Students ruled • Focus on excellence only

FIGURE 3.4. Patterns of instruction across social classes (Anyon, 1997).

for teachers and school leaders to constantly ask these two questions: Who is getting instruction focused only on the most basic skills? Who is getting instruction focused on analytical and critical reading? The question of who gets which kind of instruction is essential to any effort to work against these patterns.

Teachers' Expectations Matter

Obviously, progress has been made in educating children of poverty and students of color in this country. Today, with integration, affirmative action, detracking, and so on, efforts are being made to make educational opportunity more equal. However, there are still subtle mechanisms (Finn, 1999) in place that continue to sustain, or even promote, inequality in classrooms. One of those mechanisms is the expectations teachers hold for particular children in their classrooms.

Sadly, we now know that what teachers believe about students' backgrounds (even when those beliefs are not based on data) and the expectations they hold for their students affect the students' academic achievement, including reading, creating a self-fulfilling prophecy effect (Allington, 1977; Rist, 1970; Rothstein, 2002; Stanovich, 1986; Weinstein, 2004). Ray Rist (1970) conducted one of the most important sociological studies of teachers' expectations and the self-fulfilling prophecy. He observed regularly in an urban school serving all black students. The children came from different social classes, though, and more than half received public welfare funds. The kindergarten teacher received extensive information about each individual student prior to the start of the school year, including the child's zip code and whether he or she had attended preschool. The teacher grouped children at tables according to perceived similarities in expected performance. The children at Table 1 were well-dressed, verbal, and spoke in "Standard English." The children at Tables 2 and 3 were poor, spoke in African American dialect, were less verbal, and some had body odor. They were also darker in skin color than those at Table 1. The teacher allowed those at Table 1 to lead the pledge, pass out paper, and assist the teacher in other ways. During lessons, she gave the children at Table 1 more assistance, more scaffolding, and communicated to them that they were expected to do well. The teacher had low expectations for those at Tables 2 and 3 and told the researcher that those children had no idea what was going on in the classroom. Eventually, the children behaved in ways they were expected by their teacher and began even calling each other names like "dummy" and worse. The children at Table 1 internalized the disdain their teacher had for children at Tables 2 and 3 and began communicating similar sentiments to their classmates.

While we may not observe such dramatically classist and disturbing practices today, many well-meaning teachers believe that students of poverty cannot achieve as capably as middle-class students, largely due to their backgrounds, families, and life circumstances, and that they need to be remediated with basic skills (Delpit, 1986, 1988; Ferguson, 1998; Weinstein, 2004). Some teachers believe that poor students are in dire need of being rescued from their communities, families, and cultures (Finn, 1999; Lee, 2008; Marx, 2006). Expectations can be heard in educators' comments about particular student populations. We call this the "they" problem. We have heard such remarks as, "*They* need the structure," "*They* need phonics," "*They* don't have language," and "*They* need direct instruction." This problem extends to the families of the groups as well, such as, "*They* don't care about education," "*They* don't care about their kids," "*They* are never home," and "*They* spend all their extra money on videos" (McIntyre, Hulan, & Maher, 2010). These "overly deterministic pronouncements" (Lee, 2008, p. 275) reflect stereotypes of poor people and their children.

In a 4-year study of over 50 poor and working-class families, African American and European American (McIntyre, Kyle, et al., 2005; McIntyre, Kyle, Moore, Sweazy, &

Greer, 2001) researchers and teachers interviewed and visited families repeatedly. Not one family substantiated the truth of those statements. Unfortunately, educators have made those statements without talking with the families, sometimes without ever even meeting them. But, we know from extensive research that when teachers do hold these views about kids, they alter their interactions in subtle ways that communicate to the students that they do not expect them to achieve. This leads to the well-known phenomenon of the self-fulfilling prophecy.

A second prong of this expectations problem is the subtle (and sometimes not so subtle) racism white teachers have toward students of color. There is no doubt that racism has played a major role in school experiences and outcomes throughout the last century. Some Americans still believe in an innate cultural and intellectual inferiority of students of color (Herrnstein & Murray, 1994). Even well-meaning white people who do not think they hold prejudices, often do. Subtle feelings and behaviors are communicated to students, who in turn act on them. Teachers *do* treat children differently based on what they believe the children can achieve, and these actions affect student achievement (Ferguson, 1998; Weinsten, 2000). Rhona Weinstein (2004) describes her own Pygmalion experiments, such as when she took 10-year-old Eric (a nonreader) out of the bottom reading group, repositioned him in the middle group, and watched him learn to read, make friends, and become a confident school student. She also reports on a few large-scale studies that claimed similar results, particularly when they were conducted early in the school year when teachers have little prior knowledge of students.

However, Weinstein emphasizes that educating teachers about expectations may not be enough. Teachers must also change their actions. There are many studies on the ways in which teachers treat students differently based on their perceived achievement levels. In a summary of these findings, Ferguson (1998) claims that for low-performing students, teachers use less wait time; give students answers or call on someone else, rather than try to improve their answers by offering cues or rephrasing questions; accept inappropriate behavior or incorrect answers; criticize them more often for failure; praise them less often for success; fail to give feedback to their public responses; pay less attention to them; call on them less often with questions; seat them further from the teacher; demand less from low achievers (teach them less); make less use of their contributed ideas; not give them the benefit of the doubt in borderline cases; and generally have less friendly interaction with less smiling and eye contact. Who wants to be in a class like that?

We address the classroom discourse problems that create such inequitable instruction by providing teachers with detailed descriptions of instructional practices that counter the problems described above. In particular, Chapters 4 and 8 focus on teacher–student interactions that provide equitable instruction across students. It is a topic often left out of books on reading instruction, although it is critical for the success of all learners.

CHAPTER 4

Classroom Community and Discourse Practices in Research-Based, Culturally Responsive Classrooms

Successful teachers of all ages, types of students, and instructional contexts communicate care and respect for their students. No special instructional moves, research-based strategies, fancy technology, or deep content knowledge matter if the teacher does not create a culture of care and respect in the instructional setting. Peters (2006) says it well when he claims that it is impossible to teach a child unless you first capture and inspire that child. He says that a teacher must demonstrate care for every student, every day, and communicate that each is a valued, important human being. This sort of respect and care opens the learner's mind to what the teacher and environment have to offer.

Teaching is about relationships. Classrooms must be environments of trust if teachers are to demand the sort of high-level thinking we espouse in this book. When teachers push students to answer "How do you know that?", "What is your evidence?", "Can you explain your response?", and "Why do you think that?", the questions are interpreted as respectful, caring, even loving, *if* there is trust between teacher and students. The children learn that their teacher wants them to learn, expects them to think at high levels, and respects them as achievers. Even very young children can read these messages from their teachers. But it takes time and attention to develop this sort of environment.

So, before we share the nitty gritty of reading and writing instruction that is simultaneously research-based and culturally responsive (Chapters 5–10), we share our ideas about setting the stage for such an instructional model. In doing so, we elaborate on our main principles for culturally responsive instruction: (1) building curriculum from students' backgrounds, (2) building on students' home language or dialect, (3) group work and dialogic instruction, and (4) maintaining a rigorous curriculum. Throughout this book, these principles are captured and highlighted in individual lessons. However,

culturally responsive instruction must occur across the school day, across the school year, and across classrooms. Banks (2006) suggests that in order for culturally responsive instruction to truly affect learning, the whole *school* must be transformed. Thus, we elaborate on these key principles for affecting instruction across the school day and year, not just in literacy instruction.

CREATING A CULTURE OF CARE: THE CLASS MEETING

The Child Development Project is a professional development movement for elementary teachers focused on creating inclusive classroom learning communities that stimulate academic learning while also building values of fairness, kindness, and responsibility. This project, developed by the Developmental Studies Center (DSC) in Oakland, California, claims that children's ethical and social development are as important as their intellectual development. The center not only provides professional development on creating caring communities, it also provides rich children's literature on topics of kindness, fairness, responsibility, justice, and community. The school district in which Nancy and Vicky (authors of this book) teach adopted the Child Development Project more than a decade ago. Since then, the new school administrators have built on the project by adopting a "Care for Kids" (2009) initiative, and there is much professional development dedicated to these principles.

One book published by the DSC is called *Ways We Want Our Class to Be* (1996). This book is an excellent guide for how to create a community that fosters both kindness and learning, and it is similar to the *Morning Meeting* book (Krietel & Bechtel, 2002) used in the Care for Kids project. A key to creating the kind of classroom community described in these books is the implementation of *class meetings*. The class meeting is a forum for students and teacher to gather as a group and reflect, discuss issues, or make decisions about the ways they want their class to be (DSC, 1996). The goal is not to address problems, but to focus on learning and managing the classroom community. The meeting format provides an opportunity for students to talk through issues and participate in classroom decision making. The meeting builds a sense of belonging and responsibility and is a forum for teaching the norms of fairness, kindness, and responsibility. It is a safe place for students to discuss differences of opinions with their peers and their teachers and to try out new ideas within a supportive environment.

There are three kinds of meetings. The first is the "planning and decision-making meeting." Class members and teacher gather to discuss how they want to go about the day or week. Sometimes these meetings happen every day, as illustrated in Nancy's second-grade (Chapter 11) and Vicky's fifth-grade (Chapter 12) classrooms. In other classrooms, these meetings are held weekly or when the need arises. The second type of meeting is the "check-in meeting." The purpose of this meeting is to get together and reflect on "How are we doing?" or "What are we learning?" It can be used to ask "Is this the way we want our class to be?" These meetings can be used to celebrate successes, to discuss ongoing logistics of how the classroom works, to summarize what has been going on over a period of time, or to address a pattern of negative issues, but they should never be used to single out a person or incident that has been problematic. The third type of meeting is the "problem-solving and consciousness-raising meeting." This type of meeting might be used to raise students' awareness of another's point of view or to discuss how to treat each other in fairer, kinder, and more responsible ways. Topics are discussed in a climate of trust. Students work together toward solutions to problems in the classroom community.

As stated, all the ideas of the Child Development Project resonate with the standards for culturally responsive instruction. Teachers guide children toward getting to know one another and learning how to build consensus and make plans together. Teachers who use class meetings must establish ground rules, and the class members can decide them together. Typical ground rules for class meetings might be:

> One person speaks at a time.
> Listen to one another.
> Allow each other to disagree.
> No put-downs.
> No finger-pointing or blaming. (DSC, 1996, p. 24)

Nancy's rules for group work were (1) Treat people with respect; (2) Listen! (3) Use team work and help each other; (4) Try your best; and (5) Share materials and space. One class in the Child Development Project even added "No catching bees"! When children get to decide, we must be open to what is important to *them*. It may take a few sessions to decide fully on the ground rules, and they can be revisited as well. But they should be enforced. It may take just pointing to the rules as a reminder when a child violates a rule. It may take an individual conference with a child to discuss the importance of the rules or reviewing the rules before the meeting begins.

THE READING WORKSHOP: A FRAMEWORK FOR RESPECTFUL, RIGOROUS WORK

The reading workshop has been a popular instructional framework for elementary classrooms for some time. We believe it can provide an organizational scheme for the implementation of research-based, culturally responsive instruction, provided teachers insist on a caring environment and ensure that all children are engaged in rigorous, meaningful work that is research-based during the workshop period. Many teachers combine their reading workshop with their writing workshop. (We describe the writing workshop in Chapter 9.) Others keep them separate. The components of the workshop do not always need to take place in one uninterrupted block. Many teachers enjoy a read-aloud time right after lunch. Or, they begin the writing workshop after lunch because so many children have so much to write about after lunch and recess! Below we provide a general framework for the reading workshop by describing the common components. Then we highlight important reminders for teachers of diverse classrooms. Chapters 11 and 12 provide complete descriptions of literacy instruction in Nancy's and Vicky's second- and fifth-grade classrooms, respectively. The workshop environment is vividly portrayed in those chapters as they share their struggles, successes, and decision-making processes.

Components of the Reading Workshop

Many books have been written about the reading workshop, and there is no one correct model. The features described below do not necessarily need to occur every day or even every week. Deciding when to do what and how often should depend on the needs of the students. We provide a brief description of some key components here and elaborate on them throughout the rest of the book.

Shared Reading

Teachers sometimes use shared reading to segue from their class meeting to their reading workshop when literacy is taught in the mornings. Shared reading provides an opportunity for the teacher to share a book with the whole class and to give a research-based lesson on strategies or skills the whole group needs. With young children, teachers often use a "big book," an oversized book whose print is visible to a large group, although ordinary-sized books work too. These read-aloud sessions can be springboards for research-based lessons on connecting background knowledge to the text, predicting story content and confirming the predictions, making inferences, or summarizing the text. (All of these strategies are described in this book.) Shared reading can be a type of "mini-lesson" (below) or a time to simply share a book and discuss its meaning.

Mini-Lessons

Teachers often start their workshop period with a mini-lesson on a research-based skill or strategy they want the class to practice that day. It might be a lesson on what readers do when they come to words they do not know as they are reading. In such a lesson, the teacher might model and "think aloud" (described in Chapter 7) one or several strategies, such as how to read to the end of the sentence and make an educated guess of the word, how to decode the word based on word parts such as root words and affixes, how to ask a friend or look it up, or how to mark the page with a sticky note and figure out the word later (and keep on reading). Mini-lessons are demonstrations of how to do something; they can be lessons on how to read or write, or they can focus on management issues such as how to respond to someone else's writing. A mini-lesson might also focus on logistical concerns such as "How to choose a book just right for you." There are many examples of mini-lessons in this book, particularly in Chapter 9.

Word Work

Some teachers plan 10–15 minutes of word work during their reading workshop. This is a time to focus on phonics, spelling, and vocabulary. Many research-based lessons on these topics are provided in Chapters 5 and 8. Some teachers work these skill lessons into guided reading groups or have separate "word study groups" (Bear, Invernizzi, Templeton, & Johnston, 2004) to ensure that the lessons are part of an overall systematic plan for building on previously learned skills. Word work is one aspect of reading instruction that has a strong research base that should be followed closely.

Guided Reading Lessons

Guided reading lessons are the heart and soul of the workshop; they are when the research-based lessons on *how* to read happen. In these lessons, teachers guide children through the reading of a text (e.g., a piece of children's literature, something off the Internet, a magazine article, even a textbook). Sometimes the text may be on a topic that is closely aligned with the children's backgrounds and interests, or it may be written by an author who reflects the populations of the class. Just as often, the text used will be specifically appropriate for the teaching of reading conventions or particular strategies (e.g., a text with many extra features such as photos, captions, tables, and graphs). The teacher guides children through research-based lessons that may or may not link to the mini-lesson the teacher led earlier. For instance, if the teacher conducted a mini-lesson on how to summarize text, thinking out loud in front of students to illustrate the process, he or she might ask children during guided reading to practice this skill after the joint reading of a book, gradually releasing the responsibility of the task to the students, as described in Chapter 2. The various phonological, fluency, vocabulary, and comprehension skills that can be incorporated into guided reading lessons are found in Chapters 5–10, with vivid descriptions of the choices Nancy and Vicky make illustrated in Chapters 11 and 12.

Choice in Student Work

When some children are in guided reading groups with the teacher, what are the other children doing? In the reading workshop model, children are engaged in independent or collaborative work that is meaningful to them. Children should be provided with many resources for their work, including (ideally) multiple computers for Internet access and a rich diversity of children's literature. The students might work in learning centers or stations (below), as they do in Nancy's and Vicky's classrooms, or they might participate in spontaneous collaborations in which pairs or small groups of children come up with an idea for a project (e.g., develop a digital story about the history of the school to be shared with every classroom) and work together to accomplish the task. The important point is to explicitly teach children *how* to work together. This can be done in class meetings or mini-lessons.

In one first-grade classroom Ellen studied for a year, the teacher (Mary Ann) created a combined reading–writing workshop. After morning meetings, which contained a shared reading and mini-lesson, Mary Ann turned to her class, looked them in the eyes, and said, "What is your first work?" The children then thought about what they would do first.

One child raised her hand. "I am going to read *The Bear Came Over the Mountain*."

"OK," said Mary Ann with a grin, "but if you start singing, do so softly." The child smiled back at her teacher and got up from the group in search of the book.

"I am going to continue working on my catalogue," said one boy.

"OK, if you need references for what is in a catalogue, I have a few on my desk."

"I am just going to read a book I've never read before," said one proficient reader.

The decisions continued until all children were busily engaged in their work. Eventually, Mary Ann tapped several heads and indicated to the children they were to come with her for a small-group lesson.

Learning Centers or Stations

Many teachers establish learning centers or stations with specific activities at each, where groups of two to four children work together on tasks or projects. The activities often relate to specific strategies and skills that need practice or to the science and social studies topics the class is studying. Sometimes teachers allow children to work in any center of their choice. But often there are favorites, and teachers must work out a schedule.

Mathematics, Science, and Social Studies in Literacy Instruction

Because language is a tool for learning, we recommend weaving both oral and written language strategies into the content areas for maximum learning. When children write about how they solve problems in mathematics (shown in Chapter 9), they come to deepen their understandings about mathematical concepts. The same process works for learning any content. We want to emphasize, though, that while teachers should integrate literacy across the curriculum, we do *not* advocate replacing the teaching of mathematics, sciences, or social studies with books related to those disciplines. We believe in the reform-based mathematics instruction espoused by the National Council of Teachers of Mathematics (NCTM) and inquiry-based science and social studies espoused by the National Science Teachers Association (NSTA) and National Council of Social Studies (NCSS) and emphasize that teachers must give these subjects as much time as their district guidelines demand. Too often, mathematics and science are relegated to the end of the day, and in some classrooms, science is not taught at all. Too many elementary teachers in this country dislike mathematics and science and give these subjects less time and intensity than they deserve. This omission creates extremely inequitable opportunities for children who come from homes in which science and mathematics are not commonly discussed. The point of integrating literacy practices into the subjects is to enhance these subjects, not to replace them.

Sharing

One of the most important aspects of the workshop is the sharing time. Some teachers plan a sharing time each day, with a few children chosen to discuss how they spent their time, what they learned, and what recommendations they might make for their classmates. Some teachers plan special celebrations or sharing periods at the end of the week. These periods honor the ground rules of the class meeting.

The Read-Aloud

The read-aloud is a sacred time in many classrooms. This is the time for the class to sit back and thoroughly and deeply enjoy a book. It is not the time to teach lessons (the literature will have its own life lessons). It is the time to expose children to literature they cannot read themselves. The books might be historic, funny, sad, warm, or telling. The read-aloud can be followed by meaningful instructional conversations (described in this chapter and in Chapter 8) and are often a chance to discuss themes of justice, diversity, equity, or history. Just as often, though, the read-aloud can be a chance for the class to laugh uproariously together at a wonderfully funny book. We recommend daily read-alouds *in addition* to all the texts the students read for instructional purposes.

Choosing Multicultural Literature

The books teachers include in their lessons, advertise in their classrooms, and display on their walls let kids know what is valued that classroom. Many see these displays as unspoken but powerful forms of propaganda (McNair, 2003). Since children use the books they read to help shape and explore their understandings about the world, the role of selecting literature for the classroom is an important one. There is a "selective tradition" among teachers to favor books written by and depicting "white, middle-class, European-American male authors and subjects over works by and about women and other ethnicities or social classes" (Luke, Cook, & Luke, 1986, p. 209). Teachers tend to want to read the books they heard as children, perpetuating the problem of noninclusive literature in the classroom. These books can be good literature with powerful themes, but not literature that reflects the constantly shifting dynamics of today's schoolchildren.

It is important that teachers make their classroom libraries more inclusive by representing the diversity of the classroom and/or our society. Yokota (1993, p. 157) defines multicultural literature as "literature that represents any distinct cultural group through accurate portrayal and rich detail." Multicultural literature can be used to augment the curriculum and climate to make a classroom more inclusive (Young, Campbell, & Oda, 1995). Multicultural literature can serve as a source of reflection and affirmation on one's own life; it can also serve to teach about people who are different from the reader. Both help to make a classroom more welcoming and accepting of differences.

In the Resources of this book, we share a list of multicultural- and social-justice-themed books that we have found to be enjoyable and meaningful in the work of teaching reading within a research-based and culturally responsive frame. This is not an exhaustive list of good literature. It is merely a list of some of the titles we have used to engage students from a variety of cultural backgrounds. In our experience, a truly inclusive classroom library is constantly changing and growing in response to teachers' exploration of new and existing literature in libraries, on the Internet, and in other classrooms. Quality literature is continuously published, and is becoming more representative of the diversity in our society. We encourage you to become avid readers of children's literature, if you are not already. Nothing can match a teacher's pure excitement for a book in encouraging children to read. Vignette 4.1 shows Nancy's thinking about how she goes about selecting books for her diverse classroom.

VIGNETTE 4.1. NANCY'S THINKING ABOUT CHOOSING MULTICULTURAL TEXTS

My first step in analyzing a book is to take a picture walk, just like my kids. If it looks interesting, it might be to my students as well. I read the book, being attentive to accuracy and authenticity, interesting vocabulary, story structure, and reading strategies I can teach with the book (inferencing, predicting, etc.). For instance, I am naturally drawn to *The Secret Olivia Told Me* (Joy, 2007) because of the striking red, white, and black cover. It also shows on the cover that it has received the Coretta Scott King award, which honors books that encourage nonviolent social change. Another trait of the cover art that I like is the realistic depiction of African American girls. Many books that are written about diverse populations portray characters in unrealistic or negative ways and can, in fact, further racial stereotypes.

Most classrooms suffer from some sort of bullying or gossip. This book is a great way to show kids the problems that gossiping can cause. I keep a list in my plan book of books that I want to use for specific thematic purposes or skill lessons. So, when issues of gossip arise in my classroom, I'll choose this book. My list also includes possible reading strategies that might be the focus of lessons with this book. I take these from what I noticed when I read the book myself. In this book, a balloon in the pictures grows as the gossip spreads. I noticed when I was reading it that I was making predictions based on the events (her friend is going to be mad, the secret's going to spread, etc.), so the class could work on predicting while reading. This book would also be good for practicing summarizing, as it has a clear beginning, middle, and end, and clear cause-and-effect relationships.

When choosing multicultural literature for the classroom, teachers should be sure that the illustrations accurately and fairly depict the characters and setting. Look for authenticity of dialogue, details, cultural attitudes and perspectives, and illustrations. The historical and cultural information should be accurate. Teachers can get help from their students and family members in judging the authenticity of literature. Within quality multicultural literature the characters should have strong character traits and characterization, along with a strong plot. Many go in-depth into cultural issues, whereas others might skim the surface, introducing readers to a concept but not completely explaining it.

Some of the books we include in our list are folktales from various regions and cultures. The pictures and tales do not necessarily present an accurate depiction of the way people of those areas live, but they can help us learn something about the cultures or beliefs represented. It is up to the individual teacher to read literature before sharing it with children, and to be the mediator in cases in which books do not appropriately depict the peoples represented. Because it is very possible for teachers to create or reinforce stereotypes in children's minds, they need to look through the literature in their libraries and classrooms to make sure that they are sending positive, inclusive messages to their students.

Teachers should strive for a balance of ethnic and gender depictions across genres and should try to include literature that reflects a wide diversity of cultures. In recent years the publishing industry has been more responsive to this need, and positive, accurate multicultural literature is easier to find. Materials should be free of racist or sexist themes, words, or stereotypes. Kovarik (2004) suggests that we check the copyright date; books published before 1973 were often sexist, and diverse populations were inaccurately portrayed until the 1970s. This is not a perfect test, however. Keep in mind that one way stereotypes are passed on through the generations is through picture books.

Books that address topics of social justice, along with quality multicultural literature, should be a part of every classroom library and should be included within the curriculum and activities of the classroom. It is part of your role as a culturally responsive classroom teacher to create a climate of acceptance that includes positive, accurate, thought-provoking, and interesting literature. This type of climate can lead to rich discussions surrounding themes of social justice found within literature and the lives of students.

Gradual Release of Responsibility

The reading instructional model we present in this book is also built on the idea that real learning of complex mental tasks takes place gradually over time with the performance of authentic activities and the help of supportive teachers. This is why we emphasize a sequence of modeling and demonstration, followed by guided practice and then independent practice. The idea is that teachers gradually release the responsibility of learning to the children (Pearson & Gallagher, 1983). If we think of one simple children's book, such as *Brown Bear, Brown Bear, What Do You See?* by Bill Martin (1967), we can see how the gradual release of responsibility works:

First the teacher reads the book to the children.

Then the teacher reads the book again, inviting children to echo his or her lines.

Then the teacher reads the book a third time, inviting the children to chorally read with him or her. The teacher's voice fades when the children's voices are strong. When the children fumble, the teacher's voice gets louder.

Then, the teacher leaves the book in the workshop environment and encourages children to choose to read it with a partner.

Finally, the teacher sees the children reading the book independently. With some phonics and other skill lessons, the teacher begins to notice that the readers move away from memory reading to decoding the print.

Many skills are learned through this "apprenticeship model" (Brown, Collins, & Duguid, 1989) wherein teachers gradually see children doing what they once could only do with much assistance.

Diversity and the Workshop Approach

The workshop environment is one that has been questioned by some minority scholars. Recall the argument made by Delpit (1995), who worried that African American children may not be successful in such classrooms because they may not know how to interpret the unspoken rules of the format. We emphasize strongly that teachers must take actions to mitigate against any potential problems a workshop approach might foster. Primarily, teachers must find ways to observe students' processes and products and intervene if they are not achieving. If some children do not participate in meaningful, rigorous work during the workshop period, teachers can invite them to another guided reading lesson or provide a special (and engaging) assignment. Teachers must be careful not to fall into the trap described in Chapter 1, in which the teacher had a wonderful workshop but did not realize that some students were not reading or writing.

In most elementary classrooms today there will be a few, if not many, children for whom English is not their first or sole language. English language learners (ELLs), like all children, have varied experiences and skill levels with English. Many of the children born in the United States will speak fluent conversational English, while living in homes where adults speak something other than English. These lucky children who are growing up bilingual (or with multiple languages) are sometimes ironically and sadly viewed through the deficit lens we described in Chapter 3. As teachers, we must not assume that they understand English, especially the discipline-based academic language of science, mathematics, and social studies. ELLs need extra time and support. Some recent immigrants get this support through special classes (English as a second language [ESL], ELL) with specially trained teachers. But most ELLs are in regular classrooms full time and must be provided with accommodations by the teacher. In the reading workshop setting, it might be important to provide special materials or tasks for ELLs, depending on their needs. It may also mean that the teacher spends a few extra minutes with these children to give them the chance to share their views in both of their languages. We provide descriptions of how to assist ELLs in teacher-directed lessons later in this chapter.

DIALOGIC INSTRUCTION: USING TALK TO LEARN

Talk is the most powerful tool for learning. It is the foundation for relationships, verbal and emotional intelligence, and literacy learning (Fisher, 2009). Through dialogue children develop conceptual tools for thinking. As children talk *through* something, they come to know it; it is not the other way around (Tharp & Gallimore, 1993; Wells & Wells, 1989). As we noted in Chapter 1, most classrooms do not have the kind of creative dialogue or instructional conversation that bring students to new understandings. In traditional classroom discourse the teacher asks a question, a child responds, and the teacher evaluates the response (Cazden, 1988). This sort of classroom "discussion" encourages teachers to play the game "guess what is in the teacher's mind." When a class discussion includes children frantically waving their hands waiting to have their say, the children tend not to listen to one another and rarely, if ever, build on what another child contributed. This is not a conversation. It is not the kind of discourse that teaches.

Instead, dialogic classrooms are those in which talk is used to challenge thinking, to question one another and the texts, to explore what we know and are trying to know (Billings & Fitzgerald, 2002; Christoph & Nystrand, 2001). Dialogue happens when two or more people are listening to one another, sharing ideas, and taking account of different viewpoints. It involves taking risks because it is the differences in viewpoints that make dialogue so enriching (Fisher, 2009).

Learning to talk in these ways is a life skill that is critical for working with others, making points clearly, challenging others without offending, and, especially, listening to others. When talk is valued in classrooms, it creates democratic environments in which all students are given a voice to challenge, construct, and deconstruct the meanings around them. To assess the quality of their classroom talk, teachers can ask themselves the following questions about their classroom:

"Who does most of the talking?"
"What kind of talk is it?"
"Do the children respond to each other or just to me?"
"What types of questions do the students ask?"
"What types of questions do I ask?"
"What are the length and quality of children's responses?" (Luxford & Smart, 2009;
    McIntyre, Kyle, & Moore, 2006; McIntyre, 2007)

An assessment of the quality of classroom talk can lead teachers to improve the overall classroom discourse for all learners, even those who have historically contributed less to discussions.

Listening: A Key to Successful Classroom Talk

Children must listen in order to learn, and therefore teachers must teach children explicitly how to listen. We cannot assume that children will listen or that they know how to do so critically. We cannot assume that children will begin to listen merely because we say, "Now, listen here!" For some, it may take the practice of exercises to train the mind to listen and to hear. Many teachers create a signal for listening that is something other than their voice, something such as a bell, a special clap, or a song. Some teachers spend time early in the year teaching children to sit as still as possible and listen—to sounds they did not know existed. If a group can get up to a whole minute of intense listening, that is something! Fisher (2009) teaches children to "still the mind" by concentrating on one thing, eliminating distractions. He recommends having children breathe deeply and talk themselves into being calm. Many teachers have been trained in "active listening," which means to *think* about what is being said, not just to listen, and then discuss with others what was heard. All of these listening exercises pay off greatly as the year progresses and teachers do not have to repeatedly reteach procedures.

Teacher Questioning

Some questions invite dialogue, whereas others do not. Questions with yes–no or correct–incorrect responses do not encourage talk. Open questions, in contrast, encourage deep thinking and in-depth discussion. Examples include "What do you think about . . . ?", "How do you know . . . ?", "What would you think if . . . ?" The Greek philosopher Socrates taught through using increasingly complex and abstract questioning. Fisher (2009) posed several Socratic-type question prompts (see Figure 4.1). Two other excellent questioning activities mentioned by Fisher are described below.

Question of the Week

At the beginning of the day, the teacher poses a broad, open-ended question posted clearly in the room (e.g., "What happens to plants when they die?"). The question might be linked to the curriculum, or not, but it must require the children to do some deep thinking or researching before they can answer. The teacher may or may not decide to have students write responses. On Friday the class gets together in small groups to discuss their responses to the question. Then the teacher leads an instructional conversation (Goldenberg, 1993) on the question with the whole class (Fisher, 2009).

Question the World

Using a globe, children work in pairs to brainstorm questions to ask about the planet. The pairs share the questions with other pairs or in small groups. Then groups decide which question to discuss and share their answers with the whole class. Sample questions (Fisher, 2009, pp. 49–50) include:

"What are the most important problems we have to solve in the world?"
"Many people are dying of hunger in the world. How could we help them?"
"Many people are homeless. How should they be helped?"

Questions that seek clarification
"What is . . . ?"
"Can you explain that?"
"What does x mean?"
"Can you give me an example of . . . ?"
"Does anyone have a question to ask?"

Questions that probe reasons and evidence
"Why do you think that?"
"How do you know that?"
"What are your reasons?"
"Do you have evidence?"
"Can you give me an example/counterexample?"

Questions that explore alternative views
"Can you put it another way?"
"Is there another point of view?"
"What if someone were to suggest that?"
"What would someone who disagreed with you say?"
"What is the difference between those views/ideas?"

Questions that test implications and consequences
"What follows [or what can we work out] from what you say?"
"How does x differ from y?"
"What would be the consequences of that?"
"Is there a general rule for *hat*?"
"How could you test if it was true?"

Questions about the concept or key idea
"What is the concept or key idea?"
"How would you now define . . . ?"
"Where have we got to/who can summarize so far?"
"Are we any closer to answering the question/problem?"
"What do we still need to find out?"

FIGURE 4.1. Socratic questions for classroom learning. From Fisher (2009, p. 33). Copyright 2009 by Routledge. Reprinted with permission from Cengage Learning EMEA Ltd.

"How could the richer countries help people in the poorer countries? Should they? Why?"

"How might the problems of too much traffic on the roads be solved?"

Wait Time and Turn Taking

To take advantage of their excellent, open-ended questions that require thinking, teachers must also increase their "wait time" (Rowe, 1972) before accepting responses from students. Wait time is the period of silence following the teacher's question. In traditional classroom discourse, there is almost no wait time or up to only a second and a half. For some reason, we have been trained to think that good teaching is fast, with students' hands flying in the air during a rapid-fire question–answer period about some content. Teachers have been observed asking a question, choosing someone whose hand shoots up to respond, and then immediately choosing another to respond if the first child did not answer the question in the way the teacher expected. Again, this is an example of the "Guess what the teacher is thinking" type of classroom discourse, and it does not teach children anything.

Increasing the amount of wait time after posing questions can change the discourse in classrooms. Studies of wait time (Rowe, 1972; Tobin, 1987) show that when teachers practice waiting for at least 3 seconds before allowing responses, the quality of the responses increases dramatically; the responses are longer and more accurate. More children participate (not just those who automatically know the answer). Teachers begin to ask more thoughtful questions, and they help students (the thinkers) work through a response rather than giving up on them and moving to other students.

Increasing wait time is not always easy and must be practiced. Ellen has found that when her teacher preparation students analyze their own instruction by watching themselves on videotape, they are finally able to see the effects of wait time (or lack of it). Many teachers have to count silently, "One one-thousand, two one-thousand, three one-thousand" before they invite someone to respond. Many teachers also tell their students what they are doing and go as far as to say, "No hands up until I give you a signal. We are going to take *think time* first." Some questions are appropriate for a 3-second wait time, whereas others may need a 5-second wait time. Depending on the question, even a 30-second wait time might be appropriate. The idea is to teach children that this time is to be spent *thinking*.

It is also important for teachers to be quite deliberate about who they invite to respond after wait time. Studies have shown that in traditional classrooms, teachers unwittingly select boys more often than girls and white students more often than students of color. They choose verbal children over the quieter students and students who already know the answers more often than children who need the support and scaffolding to construct an understanding.

To mitigate against these negative patterns of classroom discourse, some teachers purposefully keep track of who has responded and who has not, perhaps by checking off names and not permitting those students to respond again until a certain number of other students has participated. This may seem contrived, and it may interrupt the natural flow of instructional conversations. Nevertheless, exercises like this might help teachers train themselves to foster more equitable turn taking. Eventually, when teachers can monitor their turn taking and observe who is left out, they may not need the check-off tools. Some teachers enlist the help of a literacy coach or peer to help with these observations.

Teacher Responses

After the children do some thinking and the teacher invites responses, it is now the teacher's turn to reply to the selected child's answer. Typically, what do we hear? "Good!"

"Right" "Yes!" Responses such as these might sound positive, but they often do more to confuse children. What was "good" about that response? What part was "right?" These exclamatory responses can also indicate to the child that his or her thinking can now stop. Instead, we recommend that teachers try to make more nonjudgmental responses that *encourage* rather than *praise*. Responses such as "OK . . . " or "Hmmm, what else?" encourage the learner to continue. Consider the following dialogue about a Chris Van Allsburg book between a teacher and student. (This is the gist of the conversation, not an exact transcript.)

TEACHER: What did you think of the book?

STUDENT: It was good.

TEACHER: In what way?

STUDENT: I like the story.

TEACHER: OK (*Waits, looking at the student and nodding.*)

STUDENT: (*after a 3-second pause*) Well, I liked how there was, like, a puzzle to the story, like a mystery. You didn't know how that boat got up there, and so that made it interesting.

TEACHER: OK, what else?

STUDENT: Well, at the end when the old man was walking away with his hurt leg, it made me want to read the story all over again.

TEACHER: Why?

STUDENT: Well, I started to think. That boy flew that boat a long time ago, and the story is the old man telling about the boy who flew the boat that crashed. So, the man is, maybe, the boy grown up. It's like what some writers do. They give you hints about what is going to happen.

TEACHER: Yes, many good writers do that. It is a writing technique called foreshadowing. . . .

In traditional classrooms, the teacher might have stopped with this child after the first, second, or even the third question. But it was her pushing with "What else?" and "Why?" that helped the child recognize, and the teacher make explicit, the literary technique of foreshadowing.

Strategies for Building Dialogic Skills

There are many strategies and exercises teachers can try for building dialogic skills in the classroom. We share some here. Also, in Chapter 8, we share tips for developing instructional conversations (Goldenberg, 1993; Tharp & Gallimore, 1993), defined as purposeful academic conversations around content. All of these skills help build the kind of respectful, rigorous classroom community that focuses on intellectual, social, and ethical development.

Talk Triangle

This activity, designed by Luxford and Smart (2009), is carried out in groups of three. One child takes the role of *speaker*, whose task is to talk extensively about a topic. The second role is that of the *questioner*, whose role is to ask the kind of questions that keeps the speaker going, adding detail and depth to the topic. The third role is that of the *observer*, who records the questions asked and assesses how well those questions brought out details from the speaker. Each child is given a role card that names the role and reminds him or her of what to do. A broad topic is then decided (e.g., "What was it probably like for an African American to live in the United States in the 1950s?"). After the conversation, the three assess the quality of the talk. The children then switch roles and (if they choose) begin with new questions.

Four Corners

Four Corners is a cooperative learning strategy that was developed by Kagan (1994) and has been used in a variety of iterations with many different age levels and subject areas. First, an issue, question, or topic is posed. Each corner of a room is assigned a stance on the issue. Students choose to stand in the corner that best aligns with their opinions or interests. When discussing an issue or piece of literature, this strategy can help teachers gauge students' opinions, interests, and understandings.

For instance, a classroom that has just read *Charlotte's Web* (White, 1952) can use Four Corners to explore characters' emotions and actions. The teacher would assign a character to each corner: corner 1—Charlotte; corner 2—Wilbur; corner 3—Fern; corner 4—Templeton. Students choose the character who interests them the most and get ready to explain why. Students then can work within their groups to complete character maps or make Venn diagram comparisons to famous real people or television characters. The questions or prompts could be written by the teacher beforehand or given on the spot (written on the board for students' reference). The groups work together to discuss and answer questions. The teacher moves from group to group and tries to scaffold further thinking and discussion. Groups can then present their findings to the rest of the class.

Another way to use Four Corners is to assign degree of agreement (or not) to the corners: corner 1—strongly agree; corner 2—agree; corner 3—disagree; and corner 4—strongly disagree. When students break into their corners, they have to hold critical discussions and give reasons for their choices. For example, a teacher could write on the board: "If someone calls a child a name, that person should be sent to the principal's office." Students break into groups based on their responses to the prompt. If they strongly disagree with the idea of a name caller being sent to the principal's office, then they go to the appropriate corner (4) and discuss their stance with their fellow group members. The teacher may have them write their reasons on a large piece of paper for the whole group to see or may have them discuss the topic using questions she has thoughtfully devised for them and written on chart paper. A debate could follow, involving the whole class. The prompt should involve some judgment, as the one above does. Some children may not think that name-calling is all that hurtful and may view it as teasing but not as bullying. Some may think that the problem should be handled in the classrooms. Others may think that the offender should be sent straight to the principal. It is with these controversial topics that children learn to think, decide, reflect, and use language to explain their thinking to others.

Numbered Heads Together

This strategy (Kagan, 1994), shared in Chapter 1, provides an opportunity for students to write their thoughts before collaborating. Each student in a small group receives a number: 1, 2, 3, or 4. The teacher poses a question or situation for discussion (e.g., "If there are poor people in the United States, should the United States give money to other countries in need, such as Haiti?"). Appropriate wait time follows. Individuals write their initial response. The group members "put their heads together" and are given time to share what they have written, discuss the answer, and come to consensus. One number is called randomly and that student is responsible for sharing the group's response. The students' confidence is protected, and accountability is promoted.

This strategy can be used for classroom community discussions as well. For example, the teacher and students brainstorm a list of rules for the classroom. Each group is given one of the rules and must explain why the rule should be followed by all members of the class. Students are assigned a number at their table and write their initial ideas. After an appropriate length of time for discussion, the teacher randomly chooses someone, for example, "Table 4, number 3." That student takes the lead and shares the group response. Because everyone in the group has collaborated, they have become accountable to one another. Any member of the class can be called upon, so everyone is compelled to pay attention. Also, children who do not normally respond in large groups have a ready answer to contribute.

ATTENTION TO LANGUAGE DIFFERENCES

How does a teacher manage to create a dialogic classroom community when so many of her students have "language differences"? The short answer to this question is to first recognize that everyone has language differences, including children whose families have been in the United States for many years. There is no one "correct" way to speak. Even dialects that sound very different to some people (e.g., African American English, Appalachian English, or Chicano English) are not incorrect or improper ways of speaking. These dialects are sophisticated, rule-governed, and valued by the members of the groups who use them. The growing English–Spanish combination of dialect is also a growing and rule-governed language form, not sloppy English. Linguists who study differences have found that *all* speakers are speakers of dialect, no matter how "standard" one person might sound compared to another.

Of course, there is a language of power (Delpit, 1995). In this country, that language is English, more specifically, a certain form of English in which grammar constructions are commonly accepted forms spoken by an educated class. Why should we care that our students learn to speak like another class of individuals? Many scholars wrestle with this question. If we must teach them "Standard English"—whatever that might mean (many linguistics suggest there is no one standard)—then does that not communicate to the students the deficiencies of their own dialects? These are tough questions. Yet, because our society does provide access or membership into groups based on perceived education (and language differences are a marker), we must find ways to teach our students about these differences and the features of the language of power. Details of these differences follow.

American Dialects: Language Variety That Brings Richness to the Classroom

Dialects of the United States are curious and fun, and many people love to talk about them. They are ever-changing, yet rule-governed. They are becoming *more* different from one another, despite the misconception that TV, radio, and the Internet have made everyone sound alike (Wolfram & Ward, 2006). Immigrants from Asia and Hispanic countries have affected English, and some dialects, such as African American Vernacular English (AAVE), also known as Ebonics, have become more distinct over time rather than less distinct. Dialects differ by geographic region, culture, ethnicity, and age of the speakers.

What are the features of a dialect? Linguists primarily study three language features. First, dialects are *lexical*, which means they have unique vocabulary. For example, a *boomer* is a type of squirrel found only in the Smokey Mountains, and a *dope* is a soft drink (or pop, soda) (Mallinson, Childs, Anderson, & Hutcheson, 2006). Second, dialects are *grammatical*; they have rule-governed forms of grammar that may be unfamiliar to nonspeakers of that dialect. The use of the verb *to be* is often a marker for AAVE, such as in the sentence, *He be leaving now.* Southerners often use the phrase *might could* to indicate a tentative suggestion of ability, such as in *I might could finish my homework before we go.* Finally, dialects have distinct *phonological* characteristics, or pronunciation. Southerners often pronounce *pin* and *pen* with the same vowel sound (like pin). Some New Englanders pronounce *car* as *cah* and *park* as *pahk*.

Southern American English (SAE) is the most widely recognized regional dialect of American English (Bailey & Tillery, 2006a). Many people in the South know the meanings of words such as *boomer, dope*, and *fetch.* They say *Y'all* and *I am fixin' to leave soon.* It is common to hear words like *hide* said as *hahd* or *mine* as *mahn.* Appalachian English has some of the same characteristics as SAE, but with additional variations, such as adding an *-s* to verbs that are singular in standard English. *The people goes.* Appalachian

English is also known for adding the *a-* prefix to words, such as in *He went a-hunting*. These Southern and Appalachian dialects have been around for almost 200 years and are complex and subtle. Yet, they are often perceived extremely negatively. Some view these dialects as incorrect, improper, and even ignorant. Thus, when people criticize the speakers of these dialects, it unfairly maligns whole groups of people and is "nothing more than a cover for a very ugly kind of prejudice" (Hazen & Fluhart, 2006, p. 18).

Another prevalent and highly criticized dialect is AAVE, or as many now call it, African American English (AAE). In 1996 a controversy erupted over Ebonics (as it was then called), as the Oakland, California school board passed a resolution declaring Ebonics the language of African Americans. African Americans and European Americans all over the country denounced the decision, and the school board had to rescind the resolution. But it got people talking and writing about dialect differences, and through this national conversation, many came to understand AAE as the complex, rich, and rule-governed dialect that it is. There are many lexical terms specific to the dialect, and AAE has such obvious pronunciations that often (not always) African Americans can be recognized on the phone. But it is the grammar that so disturbs people, especially the use of the verb *to be*, as in *He be staying home*. What is interesting is that this construction is complex and subtle in a way most people do not recognize (Baugh, 2006). That sentence does not mean just *He is staying home*; rather, it indicates a habitual situation, as in *He is staying home these days* (as in, he is not working, or he is ill). In any case, it is the role of the teacher to accept children's dialect differences, never allowing them to interrupt students' learning, while explicitly teaching the forms of English such as those found in most books that will allow them access to other discourse groups.

While SAE and AAE are the most recognized dialects in the United States, all people are speakers of dialects. The Texan dialect is distinct: Think of *dawg* for *dog*, and *warsh* for *wash*. Because of the Mexican influence, words such as *mesa* and *frijoles* are as commonly known as *table* and *beans* (Bailey & Tillery, 2006b). In New England, a *grinder* is a deli sandwich, and in most of New England, the words *cot* and *caught* and *stock* and *stalk* sound the same—but curiously, these words have distinct pronunciations in Providence, Rhode Island (Roberts, Nagy, & Boberg, 2006). In Philadelphia people say *Aur youse goin'?* for *Are you going?*, and they use grammatical constructions such as *Things are so expensive anymore* (Salvucci, 2006).

People in the Midwest often think they do not have dialects! Ellen grew up outside of Cincinnati and believed her own talk was the "norm," while others were speakers of dialects. She was in graduate school before she learned that not all people say, *Please?* to mean *Can you repeat that?* She did not know there were different pronunciations of *cot* and *caught* and *Don* and *dawn*. Ellen grew up saying, *I must warsh my clothes*, *drawling* for *drawing*, and *greazy* for *greasy*. (She still says *greazy*.) Many in the Midwest use the word *buckets* for pails and *blinds* for window shades (Flanigan, 2006).

Western states such as California and Oregon are influenced by the large Asian and Hispanic populations. There are also some recent characteristics of the Western states that many are now familiar with such as when statements sound like questions, such as *We cooked a great meal on Saturday?* (Conn, 2006). Chicano English, spoken in the

Southwest, combines features of Mexican Spanish with new lexical and grammatical constructs.

These wonderful variations in language can be explored and celebrated in the classroom. When teachers open their minds to learning from their students, they begin to see the brilliance in their students rather than nonexistent or mythical deficits. Also, language differences in no way interfere with learning to read. In the next chapter, we illustrate an unfortunate example of a child from Appalachia learning to read his first book while his teacher kept insisting he was reading incorrectly because of his pronunciation. Dialects only get in the way of learning to read if educators communicate to children that their dialect is wrong or if teachers underestimate students' abilities and understandings based on their dialects. Further, if teachers take the time to teach more universally accepted standard forms of English, at least with respect to grammatical constructions, they will be teaching children the language of power, when that form is appropriate to use, and why it is important to learn the differences. While there is no completely agreed-upon "standard" for Standard English, most would agree that the grammar of television newscasters is the expected grammar that must be learned for students to be accepted as a speaker of "Standard English." As we said, pronunciation and word usage, although still criticized, are less demonized than differences in grammar.

English Language Learners

The literacy instructional model presented in this book is designed to reach all learners in diverse classrooms. The model is based on research strategies and practices that have been shown to increase achievement of all learners, including the many students in our classrooms who are still learning English. Scholars of English language learners (ELLs) confirm the importance of the components of instruction we describe here (Li & Edwards, 2010; McCarthey, 2009). For instance, *Developing Literacy in Second-Language Learners: Report of the National Literacy Panel and Language Minority and Youth* (August & Shanahan, 2006b) emphasizes that ELLs need "enhanced teaching of what is good for native-language speakers" (p. 16)—which includes building on students' backgrounds, explicit and challenging discourse, active involvement of all students, scaffolded instruction, visual and graphic organizers, feedback to students, and opportunities for inquiry-based collaborative work.

Indeed, in a review of research on elementary literacy instruction for ELLs, Amendum and Fitzgerald (2010) suggest that what is good for native speakers is generally good for ELLs. Certainly the explicit teaching of phonemic awareness, phonics, vocabulary, comprehension, and writing benefits ELLs as it does native English speakers (Goldenberg, Rueda, & August, 2006). Also, children tend to mirror what they were taught (Fitzgerald, 1999; Fitzgerald & Noblit, 2000), and the developmental patterns of ELLs parallel native-language speakers' emergent literacy patterns, as we mentioned in Chapter 2. Amendum and Fitzgerald's review suggests that phonological awareness and understandings about word recognition developed in ways similar to development for native-language readers. They also reported on studies (e.g., Gersten & Jiménez, 1994) in which teachers used culturally responsive techniques and strategies to engage learners in more traditional lessons.

There are also models of instruction specifically targeted for ELLs that are closely aligned with the instructional model presented here. One example is the Sheltered Instruction Observation Protocol (SIOP), developed by researchers at the Center for Research on Education, Diversity, and Excellence (CREDE) mentioned in Chapter 1. These researchers have honored the research-based, culturally responsive instruction described here but have refined some aspects of instruction to specifically target the ELL population. *Sheltered instruction* is a means for making grade-level academic content (e.g., science, social studies, math) more accessible for ELLs while, at the same time, promoting their language and literacy development. In sheltered instruction, teachers adapt their language and teaching strategies in ways that make the content more comprehensible to students. For example, they use more movement, more visuals, and speak more slowly. The strategies they use include many of the research-based strategies that we include in this book (e.g., Duke & Pearson, 2002; Pressley, Woloshyn, & Associates, 1995).

The goal of SIOP is to guide teachers toward teaching content to all students while simultaneously assisting ELLs in developing literacy skills. The eight components of the model include:

1. *Preparation*, which includes writing and displaying both content and language objectives, choosing appropriate content concepts for the age group, identifying supplementary materials, adapting content for all levels of proficiency in English, and planning meaningful activities that integrate lesson contents.
2. *Building background*, which includes explicitly linking concepts to students' backgrounds and experiences, explicitly linking previously presented and new concepts, and emphasizing new vocabulary.
3. *Comprehensible input*, which includes using speech appropriate for students' level (rate, enunciation, simple sentence structure), clear explanations of academic tasks, and a variety of techniques to make concepts clear (modeling, visuals, gestures, body language).
4. *Strategies*, which include opportunities for students to use strategies (student problem solving, predicting, organizing, summarizing, categorizing, evaluating, self-monitoring), scaffolding techniques and understandings such as how much support to provide and when to relinquish support, and a variety of question types.
5. *Interaction*, which includes providing opportunities for academic talk, reduced group sizes for maximum language development, sufficient wait time, and ample opportunities for students to clarify key concepts.
6. *Practice/application*, which includes providing hands-on materials, authentic activities for applying content and skills, and opportunities for integrating all language skills (reading, writing, listening, speaking).

7. *Lesson delivery*, which includes high student engagement, appropriate pace, and addressing content and language objectives.
8. *Review/assessment*, which includes giving a comprehensive review of key vocabulary, giving a comprehensive review of key concepts, providing feedback, and conducting assessments of comprehension on all objectives.

We value all these components. We highlight the components of *building background knowledge* and *interaction* in our model, although we make reference to other SIOP components throughout the book.

This chapter has provided the overall classroom framework or structure that we believe enables the research-based, culturally responsive instruction described in this book. When teachers create a trusting workshop environment that provides opportunities for dialogic, creative, collaborative work and a time for explicit instruction on strategies and skills, children will be engaged and will achieve. We do not pretend that this sort of environment and all the strategies packed within it are easy to learn. But once the model is learned, teachers can sustain it because they begin to observe children taking responsibility for their own learning. This is our goal for research-based, culturally responsive instruction.

CHAPTER 5

Word Study

Phonemic Awareness and Phonics

A group of seven children and their teacher, JoAnn, a reading specialist in an urban school district, sit around a small table. Each child has a set of small laminated letters: *a, i, y, m, d, c, n, h, w*. JoAnn conducts a Making Words (Cunningham & Cunningham, 1992) lesson with these letters. She asks the group, "Can you use some of your letters to make the word *day*?" The children look at the letters and begin to manipulate them, softly vocalizing each letter sound. They choose the letters they think spell the word *day*, looking over at a classmate's words to be sure. Most children have the letters *d-a* for their words. Some have *d-a-y*. JoAnn encourages the children to look at their friends' words and make any corrections they wish. The children do, and those with *d-a* quickly recognize the word *day* and fix their spellings.

Then JoAnn asks the children, "Can you change one letter in that word to make *way*? The children work the problem, mouthing the sounds while looking at their letter options. JoAnn later asks, "How about *hay*?" "*May*?" Then she explains that there is not just one way to spell the sound /ay/; it can also be spelled *a-i* but only in the middle of some words with the /ay/ sound. JoAnn slowly pronounces *main* and *chain* as the children work to make the words using the laminated letters.

In Chapter 2, you learned that when a child pretends to read a favorite book by reciting memorized lines, it is an indication of an important developmental milestone and an illustration of the child's literacy skills, concepts, and strategies. You also learned that when the child's seemingly fluent emergent reading begins to sound choppy, slow, and halting, it may be an indication that the child understands that reading is a print-processing task (Morris, 2008) as well as a comprehension task. When children focus on print as they read (rather than just reading from memory), it may be just the right time in their development for explicit *phonics* instruction, connecting sounds to symbols. At this point, children should already have developed much phonemic awareness, which focuses only on sounds heard in oral words. These two areas—phonics and phonemic awareness—make up phonological instruction.

Phonological instruction encompasses all instruction that has to do with *sound*. Phonemic awareness and phonics are two critically important components to any reading program, and they are the topics of this chapter. It is extremely important for teachers to have an in-depth knowledge of how to address children's phonological needs. For children who do not struggle with reading because of sociocultural factors described in Chapter 3, the reasons for reading failure are usually related to how well they process sound–symbol relations (Torgeson, 2002b). To prevent more reading failure, teachers must address this critical area systematically and explicitly.

Phonemic awareness is the understanding that spoken words are made up of individual speech sounds called *phonemes*. *Phonics* is the instruction on the relationship of letters (graphemes) to sounds (phonemes). While a few children seem to learn these features of the alphabetic principle with little assisted performance, most children need explicit instruction on these skills combined with expert assistance from a teacher. As referenced in Chapter 2, Ehri (1991) has illustrated phases of development in learning to read words that reflect growing phonological knowledge. Instruction in this area that matches students' developmental levels is both research-based and culturally responsive.

This chapter begins with a review of some of the controversy surrounding phonics and what educators generally agree on today, including a review of research on the teaching of phonological skills. We provide general principles for teaching phonemic awareness and phonics, how to assess both, and specific research-based strategies that have been shown to increase student achievement. We also describe some models for *word study instruction*, which includes phonemic awareness and phonics, and we address the role that culture and language differences play in the learning of phonological skills for reading and writing.

RESEARCH ON PHONEMIC AWARENESS AND PHONICS

Although phonemic awareness has only recently received attention from educational researchers and policymakers, the teaching of phonics has been controversial for decades. A good part of the "reading wars" of the past few decades has focused on whether, how, how much, when, and what kind of phonics to teach children. Since reading is ultimately a meaning-making activity, many educators claimed that a focus on phonics instruction in elementary reading classrooms would produce children who overfocus on phonics, or "bark at print." Some were concerned that children would not see reading as a means for learning or pleasure, but only as a chore. Educators feared that children would lose their love of books if instruction focused on the tedious sub-skills of reading. The many exceptions to sound–symbol rules in the English language were cited as reasons to avoid teaching rules altogether, so as not to confuse children. It was also thought that children learned phonics *as* they read, not necessarily *before* they read, and thus that the time spent on phonics was wasted.

There is evidence that some children seem to disengage during phonics instruction in some classrooms (Powell, McIntyre, & Rightmyer, 2006; Wilson, Wiltz, & Lang, 2005). There may be many reasons for this disengagement. In some classrooms, the whole class is drilled on the same skill at the same time, quite naturally defying the concept of developmentally appropriate, or culturally responsive, practice. Since children in any given grade level typically vary widely in their development toward fluent reading, there is no way to teach children in their ZPD when teaching the whole class the same skill. Instruction must be *differentiated* to meet all students' needs. Further, some teaching of phonics was conducted in rote fashion and did not build on children's knowledge, making instruction boring and confusing. In some classrooms, instruction in phonics seemed arbitrary, sort of "hit or miss" (McIntyre, 1995). In other classrooms, it was the *teachers* who seemed bored and disengaged, and the children naturally followed suit. Mandatory teaching of these models seems to incite discontent in some teachers, who in turn exercise subtle as well as open acts of resistance (Samway & Pease-Alverez, 2005) or feel hopeless, frustrated, and drained (Shelton, 2005). Some consider their professional decision-making power to be undermined (Allington, 2002; Samway & Pease-Alverez, 2005; Shelton, 2005).

Despite these findings on the problems of some teaching of phonological skills, more and more well-designed studies have been published on "what works" for increasing early reading achievement for both native speakers of English and ELLs (Adams, 1990; Li & Edwards, 2010; Stanovich, 2000; Shanahan & Beck, 2006). As these studies were conducted on early reading, it became increasingly clear that *phonics and phonemic awareness are necessary components of reading instruction.* Many studies have shown indisputably that children who receive instruction on phonological skills learn the skills more than those who are merely exposed to literacy in others ways. Further, the instructional implications that resulted from these studies showed that instruction must be systematic, such that children build on previous skills learned. Thus the outstanding "Making Words" lesson JoAnn taught at the beginning of this chapter is only appropriate if it is part of a larger, ongoing plan of instruction that includes regular monitoring of student progress. We'll provide more about this later. We begin with a brief review of the findings on phonemic awareness.

Phonemic Awareness: Neglected but Essential

The report of the National Reading Panel (NRP; National Institute of Child Health and Human Development, 2000) included more than 50 studies on phonemic awareness. The authors of the report concluded that phonemic awareness is the best *predictor* of learning to read. This does not mean that phonemic awareness causes children to read. Indeed, some children learn phonemic awareness but do not become skilled readers. It does mean, however, that children who acquire phonemic awareness early and easily are also often children who read easily. It has become clear that phonemic awareness is critical. Unfortunately, it is still neglected in many early childhood and elementary classrooms.

The NRP report showed resoundingly that when children are taught phonemic skills, they learn those skills. Phonemic awareness and phonics are effective in helping children learn to read real words and *pseudowords*. Why would reading a pseudoword—for example, *blingwed*—be important? If children can read pretend words such as *blingwed*, we know that they are effectively decoding or processing the print and not relying solely on memory or the context of the sentence or passage—signs of poor readers (Stanovich, 2000). Not surprisingly, training in phonemic awareness also helps children with spelling. Studies show that high success in learning phonemic awareness, reading, or spelling involves children in the manipulation of phonemes, not just learning them by rote. Manipulation of phonemes requires several different skills, including segmenting (separating soundings), blending (bringing sounds together), and changing or deleting phonemes (e.g., remove the sound /s/ from the word *stop*). While some studies seem to favor some skills over others, it seems all phonemic awareness skills are important and affect the learning of the other skills (Blachman, 2000; Cunningham & Stanovich, 1998; Ehri, 1991; National Institute of Child Health and Human Development, 2000).

Some studies showed that *some* children can learn the necessary phonemic awareness skills through much exposure to books and word play (Adams, 1990; Cunningham & Cunningham, 2002). Cunningham and Cunningham claim, "whereas some studies show that phonemic awareness instruction facilitates learning to read and spell, other studies show that learning to read and spell enhances children's phonemic awareness skills" (2002, p. 124). The skills seem to be reciprocal. Still, other studies reviewed by the NRP indicate that some children do not learn the necessary skills through exposure to books and play; they need systematic, explicit instruction.

To be *explicit* means to directly point out relationships, such as saying to the children: "The words I say are made up of individual sounds. For example, when I say *book*, I am saying three different sounds, /b-oo-k/." *Systematic* means to teach in a way that builds on previous skills. Individual lessons must be part of a larger plan for helping children acquire the skills they need. The report also shows that children who scored highest on various phonemic awareness measures in the studies received instruction in *small groups*, even more than one-to-one instruction. A few studies highlighted the challenges faced by ELLs because they pronounce vowels differently, and some of the manipulations they are asked to perform do not work. This chapter describes teaching principles, strategies, and programs that are all research-based and address diverse populations of learners.

Phonics: Necessary but Not Sufficient

The findings included in the NRP (National Institute of Child Health and Human Development, 2000) report on phonics instruction are similar to the findings on phonemic awareness instruction. To learn to read, children must learn the relationships between the 44 speech sounds in the English language and the more than 100 spellings to represent them, and they must be able to apply this knowledge to new words they encounter in text.

The content of phonics instruction (*what* is taught) should correspond with children's development of word reading (Ehri, 1991) and children's developing orthography or spelling patterns (Read, 1981). We illustrate these patterns later in this chapter. As shown through research conducted by Read (1971), Henderson (1990), and Bear et al. (2004), the pattern of spelling development is clear. We can detect what children know by their errors. Studies of these spelling "errors" correspond with studies of reading development (Adams, 1990; Chall, 1983; Ehri, 1991; Juel, 1991). It is writing, though, that provides the window on children's development (Bear et al., 2004). Through an understanding of these stages of spelling development, teachers can determine the appropriate focus of phonics instruction for particular children.

Studies also show that the pedagogy, or *how* phonics is taught, also matters. *Synthetic phonics* instruction approaches begin by teaching children individual sounds for letters and then having them blend those letters together to make words (Cunningham & Cunningham, 2002). One example of a text written with the goal of having students apply synthetic phonics was shared in Chapter 3. Remember, "I will not do that, that, that, when I can sit here and get fat, fat, fat"? These programs can be useful for some children at some times (discussed below under "Decodable Text") and are favored by some researchers (e.g., Ehri, 1991). But many of the studies reviewed by the NRP have shown these programs to be less effective than approaches involving analytic phonics.

Using *analytic phonics*, children learn to decode by pattern and analogy, and they learn to separate the *onset* of a word from the rest of the word. The onset is the initial consonant of a word, such as /t/ in *tap*. The rest of the word, called the *rime*, includes the vowel sound and the final sound, /ap/. When children can separate the onset and rime, they can learn many new word families (i.e., words with the same rimes), such as they did in the example that opened this chapter. The children can then learn to categorize various sounds and spellings, a skill that can help them transfer knowledge to new words (Bear et al., 2004).

Finally, most studies show that children do not need to learn rules for sound–symbol correspondences. Children eventually learn to read words in chunks and use conditional rules for figuring out new words. For example, the *i* in *city* and the *e* in *cell* make the *c* say its /s/ sound, whereas the *a* in *cat* make the *c* says its /k/ sound. Most people show that they know these rules (without being able to say the rule) when they decode pseudowords such as *caltus* or *cimophot*.

Phonological Skills and Linguistic Differences

First grader Josh had just learned to read from memory a short book with a few sight words. The text said, "It will not go." ("It" was a tractor.) Josh pointed to each word and proudly read to his teacher in his strong Appalachian dialect, "/Hee-it will nat go./"

His teacher shook her head and said, "No. It's *It* will not go."

Josh nodded and read, "/Hee-it will nat go./"

The teacher again pointed and said, "*It*. The letter *I* says /iii/."

Josh, who seemed to hear the word *it* as exactly what he was saying, grew puzzled and tried again. His teacher helplessly told the researcher, "He just doesn't get it."

Many children from the Appalachian region of the United States pronounce the /h/ sound in front of words beginning with vowels. They often make one-syllable words sound like two-syllable words. Many African American children say /sistah/ for *sister*. Some people from the northern Midwestern states say something like /jab/ for *job*. Many Hispanics who are fluent English speakers still pronounce words with a dialect different from native speakers of all sorts. For example, they might pronounce *beat* as *bit*. Many children in the United States draw on multiple dialects they learn from home, school, community, and media to form their own pronunciations. As mentioned in the last chapter, teachers can and should accommodate students' language differences.

This makes teaching phonics even more challenging. The most important point for teachers to remember is that children's language patterns and dialects will not be a hindrance in learning to read unless the teacher allows them to be a hindrance. Josh successfully read that little book, but his teacher communicated to him that he was not reading and that something was definitely wrong. Nothing was wrong with Josh. Dialects are not a sign of ignorance, only of difference (Adger et al., 2009; Wolfram & Ward, 2006). It is important that teachers not underestimate children's knowledge or skills based on pronunciation differences.

Still, the language differences discussed in Chapter 4 can make the teaching of phonemic awareness and phonics harder. Speakers of various dialects pronounce vowel sounds differently, and it can confuse teachers if the sounds are different from what they expect. For example, if a teacher is expecting children to sort all words (sorting is an excellent teaching strategy) with the /a/ sound, some children may sort them differently if they pronounce *job* as /jab/. But teachers can work through these subtle differences by allowing them and by explicitly teaching phonemic awareness and phonics (Amendum & Fitzgerald, 2010; August & Shanahan, 2006a; Fitzgerald & Noblit, 2000; Linan-Thompson & Vaughn, 2007). So, if the child sees *job* and reads *jab*, it's OK. He or she will likely be consistent with all short -*o* words.

PRINCIPLES FOR TEACHING
PHONEMIC AWARENESS AND PHONICS

The principles for teaching phonemic awareness and phonics are the same, and they are derived from the many studies and reviews of studies on the instruction that has raised students' achievement in these areas and in reading. These important principles are presented in Figure 5.1.

- Children should spend most of their school language arts time reading and writing.
- Language play—exposure to books, songs, poetry, and chants—make learning phonemic awareness and phonics fun.
- Instruction should first assess what children already know (see the next section on assessment in this chapter).
- Lessons must be systematically delivered, not haphazard or "hit or miss."
- Phonemic awareness can be taught and learned at the same time or before phonics instruction.
- The daily instruction should build on the skills of yesterday's lesson.
- Instruction should often be conducted in small groups that match students' needs.
- Decodable text might be one tool for some children at some times in their reading practice, but there is little research base to claim it is essential for children or even positive. Use a variety of types of texts for reading practice.
- Look for what student use but confuse (Bear et al., 2004). This is a signal that they are ready to learn that skill.
- Use words kids *can* read and have them analyze them.
- Avoid rules, or at least avoid insisting that they learn the rules. If they do learn them, great. But it isn't necessary.
- Return to meaningful texts.

FIGURE 5.1. Principles for teaching phonemic awareness and phonics.

ASSESSING PHONEMIC AWARENESS AND PHONICS

Assessing children's phonemic awareness and phonics knowledge can take many forms, from traditional tests or assessments to analysis of students' spelling. Teachers can begin with careful observation and analysis of what children produce in the classroom. The strategies children use to read, whether they read from memory or attempt to process the print, and what they write when they are asked to truly communicate something, can provide telling information. Teachers can use the *stages of spelling orthography* described later to assess what their students know about sound–symbol relations, keeping in mind their dialects of accents. Teachers can use the reading and writing phases described in Chapter 2 as benchmarks for assessing students' development. From these authentic measures, teachers can then choose particular tests for a more fine-grained understanding of what students know. The important principles for assessment of phonemic awareness and phonics include:

- Use multiple classroom assessments to gain information from your students. What you observe and record while the children are engaged in authentic reading and writing behaviors may be your best clue to what children can do independently.
- Attend to students' linguistic differences when assessing these skills, as discussed earlier. Children may have good phonological skills but still pronounce sounds

differently than you do. As long as they begin to make the connections between sounds, symbols, and meanings, their pronunciations are not problematic!

- Your observations of children in small-group lessons with you or another adult will provide evidence of their ZPD. This evidence will guide you to the best instructional practices. When you discover what children can do *with help*, you are finding their developmental and instructional levels.
- Assess students informally and in a relaxed atmosphere. If you regularly take notes on what children do, they will not be intimidated when you document what they say and do during tasks or tests.
- Use the same scoring guides over several months to track progress. Keep samples of students' work to show growth to parents and guardians.

Bear et al. (2004), Ehri, Nunes, and Willows (2001) and Adams (1990) have outlined the most important phonemic awareness skills to be taught. Most of the studies indicate that phoneme segmentation and phoneme blending are the most important. Figure 5.2 is a tool all teachers can use.

The skills listed in Figure 5.2 can be used to assess children's level of phonemic awareness or to teach the skill. Adams (1990) recommends a general teaching progression from larger units of language to smaller units of language. For instance, children should be able to:

First, divide spoken sentences into words.
Then, divide words into syllables.
Then, divide syllables into onsets and rimes. (Adams says that this might be the key to unlocking phonemic awareness for many children.)
Then, divide onsets and rimes into phonemes and their corresponding letters.

How different that is from the old, traditional, "letter-of-the week" curriculum for kindergarteners! It is almost backward; children should have a lot more exposure to word manipulation before they are taught corresponding letters and sounds. The traditional approach might appear to "work" in some classrooms because some children already have the prerequisite knowledge, from preschool or home, that enables them to learn the letter of the week. It is important to remember, though, that many children need explicit instruction with syllables, onsets and rimes, and phonemes, along with their symbol correspondences.

Many tests of phonemic awareness can provide a quick, although not as thorough and accurate, assessment of children's knowledge and skills. For example, the Yopp–Singer Test of Phonemic Segmentation (Yopp, 1995) is a one-on-one administered test that asks children to segment phonemes from a list of 22 words. The children earn points if they correctly segment all sounds in a given word. There are many tests and tasks you can use to augment or support your classroom observation data (see Allington, 2006; Linan-Thompson & Vaughn, 2004).

Skill name	Definition	Prompts teachers can use
Phoneme isolation	Recognize the common sounds in words	"Tell me the first sound in *bell*." (/b/) "What is the second sound in *rose*?" (/ō/)
Phoneme identity	Recognize the common sound in different words	"Tell me sound that is the same in *penny, pit*, and *prize*." (/p/) "Do *pen* and *pipe* begin with the same sound?"
Phoneme categorization	Recognize the word with the odd sound from a sequence of words	"Which word does not belong: *song, party, sister*?" (*party*) "What word starts with a different sound: *bag, nine, beach, bike*?" (*nine*)
Phoneme segmentation	Break words into sounds by tapping out or counting sounds	"How many sounds do you hear in *ship*?" (/sh/ /i/ /p/) (three) "What sounds do you hear in the word *hot*?" (/h/ /o/ /t/)
Phoneme blending	Listen to a sequence of sounds and combine them to form a word	"What word is /b/ /oo/ /k/?" (*book*) "What word would you have if you put these sounds together: /s/, /a/, /t/?" (*sat*)
Phoneme deletion	Say the word that remains when a phoneme is removed	"What is the word *start* if you take off the /s/?" (*tart*) "What word would be left if the /k/ sound were taken away from *cat*?" (*at*) "What sound do you hear in *meat* that is missing in *eat*?" (/m/)
Phoneme substitution	Say a word with a new phoneme in place of an old one	I'm thinking of a word that rhymes with *cat*. It starts with /b/. The word is _____." (*bat*) "Say the word *pin*. Now say the word *pin* but instead of /p/ say /t/." (*tin*)

FIGURE 5.2. Assessing and teaching phonemic awareness.

The content of what should be taught should correspond with children's developing orthography (spelling) patterns. We illustrated phases in children's writing in Chapter 2. Interestingly, when children begin to use invented spelling and move through beginning writing, they exhibit more refined phases through their developing orthographic knowledge. As shown through research conducted by Read (1971), Henderson (1990), and Bear et al. (2004), the pattern of spelling development is clear. We can detect what children know by their errors. (See Figure 5.3.)

Look at a writing sample from one of Ellen's first graders, Jason, shown in Figure 5.4. See if you can categorize his spelling stage. What phonics does this child need? Jason knows some words automatically (*the, had, zoo*). He is missing some nasal sounds, such as the /n/ sound in *monkey*, but he seems to include it in *went*. Jason pronounces words such as *likes* as *lies*. He knows the sound–symbol correspondences for beginning and ending consonants, and he knows that vowels come in the middle of words (COIZ,

Spelling stage	What children know and do	Examples
Emergent	This encompasses the multiple phases covered in Chapter 2 when children are not yet writing conventionally.	Scribbles, controlled scribbling, letter strings
Letter name–alphabetic	When children use the name of letters to spell; Bear et al. (2004) specify early, middle, and late stages in this category, representing increasing sophistication.	LE for *Ellie* (early) LOP for *lump* (middle) BAKR for *baker* (late)
Within-word pattern	When children use their beginning knowledge of phonics (e.g., beginning sounds, short vowels) and words they know by heart from reading to spell. There are early, middle, and late stages for this period as well.	FLOTE for *float* (early) SPOLE for *spoil* (middle) CHUED for *chewed* (late)
Syllables and affixes	When children begin to grapple with multisyllabic words with prefixes and suffixes. There are early, middle, and late stages of this category as well.	SHOPING for *shopping* (early) DAMIGE for *damage* (middle) CONFEDENT for *confident* (late)
Derivational relations	When children (usually in middle school) use the meanings of words to figure out their spellings.	OPPISITION for *opposition*

FIGURE 5.3. Spelling stages and the knowledge they reveal.

I went to the zoo. I had fun today. 'Cause Little Jimmie decided he likes the monkeys. He's 2.

FIGURE 5.4. Invented spelling example.

DISADE). A few emergent writing skills and concepts are still there. He uses the numeral 2, and when he read the text aloud to Ellen, used the word *he* twice for "He likes" and "He's 2." He is in the letter-name stage, showing signs of early and middle knowledge of that phase. This window into Jason's development makes clear that he needs instruction on short- and long-vowel patterns. Jason, like many children, learned much phonics through the act of spelling inventively. Yet, he could have used more explicit, systematic instruction than he received. Indeed, how phonics ought to be taught was a focus of the NRP report. The following sections provide specific strategies for teaching phonemic awareness and phonics.

STRATEGIES FOR PHONEMIC AWARENESS

The following strategies for phonemic awareness teaching have been shown to be research-based and can be responsive to children's linguistic differences. If teachers build on what students already know, allow children to work in pairs and small groups, allow pronunciation differences based on dialect, conduct excellent discussions about how our language works, and keep the instruction appropriately rigorous, then these strategies will also be culturally responsive. It is important to remember, though, that the teaching of phonemic awareness must be systematic and not "hit or miss" in order to be both research-based and culturally responsive.

For ELLs, teachers should be consistent in their vocabulary use when they are explaining how to do something. For example, if a teacher is guiding children through a segmentation lesson, he or she might intentionally use the word *stretch* repeatedly, rather than using it the first time to explain what the children are to do with the words, and the next time using *separate*, and the third time saying *divide* (Linan-Thompson & Vaughn, 2004). The teacher should use as many visual prompts as possible and speak slowly and distinctly (Echevarria et al., 2004) while still communicating authentically, without a condescending or demeaning tone. This principle of the SIOP model, mentioned in the last chapter, is called *comprehensible input*. To provide comprehensible input, teachers find as many ways as possible—visually, tactilely, and verbally—to teach a skill. Finally, ELLs learn a great deal from others in the classroom, so pairing them with native speakers to conduct word study activities is often a good idea.

Picture Sorts of All Sorts

Sorting has become one of the most popular and research-based activities for learning both phonemic awareness and phonics. Children can sort by sound and later by spelling through both picture and word sorts. Sorting does not rely on rote memory. Instead, kids work with words they know and analyze their parts. They engage in decision making about how to sort words by their sounds and (later) by their spellings. Sorting is much more efficient and effective than rote drill on phonemic awareness skills or doing exercises in a phonics book. It is interesting and fun because the activities are hands-on and manipulative; children can work alone, in pairs, or in small groups. The activity builds on what children know. The following picture sorts, adapted from Bear et al. (2004), are good beginning exercises because they teach children how to sort.

Transportation Concept Sort
- The teacher reads aloud a short book on transportation, showing pictures.
- The teacher asks, "What do you notice about these pictures?" (Children respond.)
- The teacher asks, "If I were to sort the pictures—put them into two categories—what two groups could I make? Vehicles with wheels and vehicles with no _____?"
- The teacher leads the children into sorting the pictures.
- The teacher asks, "If I were to sort them into three groups, how might I sort them?"
- The children brainstorm ways to sort and then do some sorting in pairs.
- Groups of children share their responses.

Vowel Sounds
- The teacher says, "I have some pictures of many things [flag, tape]. The things either have the /a/ sound or /ay/ sound, either the short -a sound or the long -a sound. I want you to say the name of each picture aloud and put each card into one of the two groups."
- The teacher demonstrates with several cards.
- The teacher invites the students to work in pairs to practice.

Rhymes, Songs, Chants, and Poetry

Reading aloud nursery rhymes, poems, chants, raps, or Dr. Seuss books is one of the best ways to help children develop phonemic awareness. After reading one aloud a couple of times (and discussing the meaning), try reading only parts of it and allow the children to finish your sentences. For instance, you might say, "There was an old woman who lived in a shoe. She had so many children she didn't know what to _____." "She gave them some broth without any bread and spanked them all soundly and put them to _____."

Clapping Syllables

Another activity to help children attend to sounds in words is to have them clap out the number of syllables they hear. Teachers can demonstrate first how the names (first or last or both) of those they have been reading about, such as *Pat*, has a one-clap name. Others, such as *Lincoln, Martin, Roberts,* and *Rosa*, have two-clap names. *Obama* and *Confucius* have three-clap names, and *Sotomayor* has a four-clap name. They can then clap out each others' names. This lesson is appropriate no matter what dialect children speak.

Elkonin Boxes

Elkonin boxes (Elkonin, 1973) are boxes formed together in a horizontal line (see Figure 5.5). Each box represents a sound, so if teachers are working with four-sound words, such as *stop, flat*, or *shaker*, they would use four boxes. The boxes and markers are given to each child. The teacher explains that words can be divided into sounds. The teacher models how the word *stop* has four sounds, /s/, /t/, /o/, and /p/. As the teacher models the sounds, he or she moves a marker (such as an M&M) into each box. Then the teacher invites the children to participate by moving markers into boxes for each sound they hear in other four-sound words. If children in the early stages of letter-name writing, for example, spelling *Ellie* as "LE," were given an Elkonin box with three boxes and told that the word has three sounds and not two, they might slow down their word calling a bit to hear the /e/ sound. Again, students' orthographic knowledge, as shown through their writing, can provide excellent indicators for what you should be teaching them during word study. As is clear by this example, children hear syllables before they hear individual sounds. The teacher's role is to help the child move from hearing larger chunks of language (e.g., syllables) to smaller (e.g., individual sounds).

These are only a few of the many strategies for teaching phonemic awareness. The skills listed in Figure 5.2 should be your guide for what to teach. Bear et al. (2004) have an extremely comprehensive and developmental sequence for teaching all these skills.

STRATEGIES FOR PHONICS INSTRUCTION

In order for phonics instruction to be both research-based and culturally responsive to the particular children in a given classroom, with all their linguistic diversity, teachers must think about phonics practices in a variety of ways. Some practices emerge naturally out of reading and writing lessons and tasks and should be encouraged. Other practices are planned, explicit lessons targeted for groups of children with specific needs (as in the opening example of this chapter). Still others we describe involve the daily, systematic program instruction that build on skills in a sequential manner.

The following strategies for phonics teaching have been shown to be research-based and can be responsive to children's linguistic differences. As with phonemic awareness, if teachers build on what students already know, allow them to work in pairs and small groups, allow pronunciation differences based on dialect, conduct excellent discussions about how our language works, and keep the work rigorous for the particular children in

FIGURE 5.5. Elkonin boxes.

the lesson (not too easy), the following phonics strategies will be responsive to students' ways of learning without violating the integrity of the research-based principles.

Invented Spelling

One of the best tools for helping children acquire phonological and orthographic knowledge is allowing them to write, using sound–symbol relations they know and hear to invent the words they need to communicate. When children are in the act of deciding the letters to form words, they practice their phonological skills. The NRP (National Institute of Child Health and Human Development, 2000) report supports the encouragement of invented spelling.

Word Sorts

Most sorts described by Bear and his colleagues (2004) and Pinnell and Fountas (2003) are word sorts that invite manipulations of phonetic patterns. Word sorts allow kids to "compare, contrast, and sort words according to specific features" (Pinnell & Fountas, 2003, p. 155). There are two types of sorts: closed and open. In *closed sorts* the teacher defines the way students are to sort words. For example, the teacher might ask children to sort words from a list to find those with the /a/ sound (*cat, flat, sat*), or with the ending *all* (*call, ball, tall, small*) and those that do not. *Open sorts* invite students to sort words according to patterns that they discover in the words. For example, children might find that many of the words they are looking at include the same beginning sound or have three syllables. Sorts can be done individually, in pairs, or in groups. If the lesson includes group work and plenty of discussion with others and the teacher, it provides opportunities for teachers to practice cultural responsiveness within research-based lessons. Examples follow.

Word Families Sort (Short Vowel)

- This word sort works with both sound and spelling. Children first really listen to the words, then find their sound–symbol correspondences.
- The teacher says, "I have some words I am going to read. I want you to listen for the middle sound. If the middle sound is like /a/ in *tag*, put it in this group (show). If the middle sound is /i/, as in *fish*, put it here. If the middle sound is /o/, like *mop*, put it here."
- The teacher reads each word aloud and has students indicate into which group it goes.
- The teacher then has kids do the word sorts themselves as secondary practice.
- The teacher asks them, "What do you notice about how the words are spelled?"
- The teacher explains and models and then has the children practice with guidance and scaffolding. The teacher has the group consider both sound and pattern simultaneously to discover rules. When the sort is finished, the teacher has students read down the column of words to see patterns, explicitly stating what the groups have in common.

Spelling Sort

- The teacher writes two words on the chalkboard, such as *plain* and *plane*.
- The teacher tells children to make two columns and label them *plain* and *plane*. The teacher will read a word, and the children must put it into the correct column. He or she then proceeds to read the words: *main, pain, drain, wane, sane, chain, cane, gain, rain, stain, Shane, vain, grain.*
- The children decide on the spellings. This can lead to an excellent vocabulary lesson!

Word sorts are one of the best ways to prompt students to do the thinking necessary to see how the English language works. Today, it is easy to find ready-to-use lessons and materials for word sorts in the Bear et al. (2004) book or on websites for word sorts.

Making Words

Cunningham (Cunningham & Cunningham, 1992) describes a Making Words lesson using one of the many picture biographies of Rev. Martin Luther King, Jr. After reading and discussing the book, teachers can use the title to practice phonics skills. In any Making Words lesson, the teacher uses the letters from one six-letter word from the book to "make" many other words, with the goal of learning sound and spelling patterns of many words. In the case of *Martin*, Cunningham illustrates how teachers can use the letters of the title word (Martin) to lead students in manipulating the letters to make new words. For instance, the teacher guides the children to look at the letters: *a, i, m, n, r, t.* She makes a card with each individual letter on it so that the students can move the letters around. In some classrooms, teachers model the lessons in front of the whole class. In other lessons, teachers give each child in a small group a set of the six letters to manipulate individually. Once students are focused on these letters, the teacher asks, "Using some of these letters, show me you know how to make the word *am.*" From those six letters, the children choose the sounds they know to best predict which ones would spell *am.* From here, the teacher invites the children to change one letter in *am* to make *at.* She then invites them to add a letter to *at* to make *rat*, and so on, until the students have made the words *mat, man, tan, ran, ram, rim, trim, main, rain, train.* After the students have made all the words, they can begin to sort them by vowel sounds (*am, ram, tram; rim, trim*) or by consonant sounds, and so on. Making Words lessons take a bit of time to develop, but today teachers are lucky. Cunningham and her colleagues have created the lessons and even the tools for easy use (Cunningham, 1982, 2000).

Use the Words You Know

Use the Words You Know (Cunningham, 2000) is similar to Making Words. Students use the words they know to decode and spell many other words. The lesson begins with words the children already know. In Cunningham's example, the lesson is on transportation words, and so she uses *car, bike, van*, and *train*. The teacher reviews the vowel

car	bike	van	train

FIGURE 5.6. "Use words you know" chart.

sounds and spelling patterns of each of the four words. She puts the words in columns or gives students a chart like the one in Figure 5.6. Then the teacher says words with the same sound and spelling pattern as one of the four column words, such as *hike, brain, jar, pan*. The children must decide into which column the words go. Children will spontaneously offer words they think of: "Bar!" In the initial lesson, it is important to include only words with the same spelling patterns as the ones in the columns.

Vowel Types to Teach

The explicit instruction of vowel patterns can be insightful for children. The following vowel patterns can be embedded into word sort activities that help children discover the patterns. The patterns have real words with a few pseudowords thrown in for practice.

- CVC— when you have a consonant, vowel, consonant in a single syllable (*bed, chin, sudned*).
- CVCe—when you have a consonant, vowel, consonant, and a silent *e* in a single syllable. This letter grouping will usually make a long sound (*cave, wine, motewede*).
- VCCV—when you have a vowel, two consonants, vowel, the first vowel is usually short; if the word is one syllable, the middle letter is usually doubled (*robber, shopping, topped, filled, chilled, pobbed*).
- CVVC—when you have a consonant and two vowels, consonant. The vowel sound is almost always long (*nail, beak, poam*).
- CVV—when you have a consonant and two vowels, the vowel sound is almost always long (*hay, pie, smoat*).

Names

Use the children's names and their friends' and family members' names to build phonics knowledge. For example, if a child's name is Marcus, show him other names that begin like *Marcus* (especially names of people in the group or those he knows), such as *Mario,*

Mike, Malea, and *Mother.* Point out that his name ends with an *s,* and other names begin or end with that same sound, such as *Sam, Nicholas, Salma,* and *Charles.* You might even show names that have *s* in the middle of them, such as *Larissa, Jose,* and *Jasmine.* Children usually like working with names of people they know. A popular idea is to post the names on the classroom word wall so that students can continue to use these names as a reference.

Rhyming Books and Tongue Twisters

When you read books that rhyme, point out how the words are spelled similarly. When you read tongue twisters, point out how the words begin with the same sound and sometimes the same letters. Some children like to write or make up their own tongue twisters. Encourage this! You may want to model the process using one of the children's names.

High-Frequency Words

During each session, spend a few minutes on the list of high-frequency words in Figure 5.7. You may play a guessing game with the children to see if she can find the word you are thinking of. You might say:

   "It's in the first column."
   "It has four letters in it."
   "It begins with a *c.*"
   "It has a silent *e* at the end."
   "It finishes the sentence *I want you to* _____ *here.*"

Word Banks and Word Walls

Word banks and word walls are individual (banks) and class (wall) collections of words from which children can draw at any time. The words are used for practice of skills and just for reference when kids need to know a spelling. They are sometimes formed based on specific subject areas or can include only high-frequency words. Younger children need to have a word wall in their classroom that includes hard-to-spell high-frequency words that will help them with writing and reading those words correctly. Many games can be played with word banks and word walls. Practice with these words can be built into the morning ritual of a classroom, as described in Nancy's description of a typical morning in her classroom in Chapter 11. Some ideas include letting the class practice spelling words from the wall in different, fun ways, such as via mouse talk (whisper), robot, deep voice, or cheerleader.

   Cheerleader is performed as follows:

   WORD WIZARD: Give me a ____! (*Spells one letter at a time.*)
   OTHER KIDS: (*Repeat the letter that the Word Wizard said.*)

about	did	how	our	they're
after	do	I	out	thing
again	don't	in	over	this
all	down	is	people	to
am	eat	it	play	too
and	favorite	like	pretty	two
are	for	little	ride	up
at	friend	look	said	us
be	from	made	saw	very
because	fun	make	school	want
before	get	many	see	was
best	girl	me	she	we
big	give	more	sister	went
black	go	my	some	were
boy	good	new	talk	what
brother	had	nice	teacher	when
but	has	night	tell	where
can	have	know	that	who
can't	he	not	the	why
car	her	of	their	will
children	here	off	them	with
come	him	old	then	won't
could	his	on	there	you
day	house	other	they	your

FIGURE 5.7. High-frequency words (Cunningham and Allington, 1995).

(*They do this through the whole word. When finished:*)

WORD WIZARD: What's that word?

OTHER KIDS: (*Cheer the word.*)

Saluting sounds like the following:

WORD WIZARD: Sound off!

OTHER KIDS: What word?

WORD WIZARD: (*Says a word from the word wall.*)

OTHER KIDS: (*Spell the word, say it, and then say, "Yes sir [or ma'am]," as they salute.*)

In dribble and shoot, the Word Wizard points to the word. Students are standing and pretend to dribble for each letter as they say them aloud. When the word has been thoroughly spelled, kids pretend to shoot the ball and say the word at the same time.

Decodable Text

Decodable text is text that contains a proportion of words that have regular phonic relationships between letters and sounds; most regular patterns have one-to-one sound–letter correspondence. A decodable text might include something like "*The fat cat sat on a mat*" or "*Dan ran to the fan*," which includes the repeated /a/ pattern and a few high-frequency words. Reading such texts provides opportunities for students to practice and apply specific phonic pattern skills they have been taught within context. The use of decodable texts has both advocates (Ehri, 1991; Heibert, 1999) and opponents (Allington, 2006), and there are studies that both support and discourage their use. Most studies suggest that reading with decodable texts can be useful at some times for some purposes, but that overuse of them can be problematic. Decodable texts can be used in teacher or student-directed groups, mixed or same-ability groups, centers, with partners, or individually. They can be read chorally (all read at the same time while looking at the text), through echo reading (a teacher or leader reads and the students echo what was read), taking turns with partners, or individually. It is useful for students to receive immediate feedback and correction during practice with decodable text from a teacher or more knowledgeable peer. It might also be useful to reflect on the meaninglessness of the passage!

Rhyme Bingo

In this game, pictures (or words, depending on the level) are placed in the spaces of a bingo board. The teacher says words that rhyme with those words depicted on the board. Students must use their rhyme knowledge to make bingo. Before playing this game, the teacher should go over the pictures and tell kids what they are to diminish confusion. Like rhyme bingo, *rhyme memory* involves pictures of things that rhyme. A match might be one picture of a boy and another of a toy. The student with the most pairs at the end of the game wins.

WORD STUDY PROGRAMS
AND OTHER EXCELLENT RESOURCES

In an effort to emphasize that the teaching of phonemic awareness and phonics must be systematic, we recommend some of our favorite programs. These programs follow the principles outlined above for phonological instruction. They also provide assessment tools, teaching activities like those we described here, and a scope and sequence of activities that are aligned with developmental patterns. While many teachers can use the strategies named above to match instruction to learners, the following programs offer resources to make planning easier.

Words Their Way

Words Their Way (Bear et al., 2004) is a comprehensive word study model based on principles of Vygotskian theory important to a sociocultural approach to word development and reading. The authors emphasize the role of classroom interactions, pair and group work, and students' inductive thinking. Instruction is differentiated by groups of students based on their needs. Lessons help children perform tasks they would not be able to perform on their own. The lessons are all manipulative and fun, and the program comes with the necessary materials to download from a CD and laminate.

The program is based primarily on word sorting. The sorting gets increasingly complex as children learn new skills. The activities invite children to sort words by (1) sound, (2) spelling pattern, and (3) meaning (the spelling of words is also learned through understanding the meaning of those words—*composition* comes from *compose*). There are particular lessons for each of the stages of word knowledge we described earlier in this chapter. The authors suggest that phonics, vocabulary, and spelling instruction should be explicit, systematic, hands-on, with repeated practice, combined with fluency and comprehension instruction for a total instructional model, and differentiated within the class.

Phonics Lessons K–3

Phonics Lessons K-3 (Pinnell & Fountas, 2003) is based on a continuum that traces the development of word-solving skills through nine categories of learning: early literacy concepts, phonological and phonemic awareness, letter knowledge, letter–sound relationships, spelling patterns, high-frequency words, word meaning, word structure, and word-solving actions. The lessons are detailed and build on students' previously learned skills. Within each lesson is a section that describes what children should already know in order to participate. There are suggestions for working with ELLs, a list of materials needed, and an explanation of the instructional principle. The plan is clearly laid out with samples of charts needed during the lessons and step-by-step instructions for delivery. These can be tweaked, of course, depending on teaching style. After the principle is taught, students are given an opportunity to apply what they know while working individually, in partners, or in small groups.

In one sample lesson, a second-grade teacher begins by introducing rhyme. She teaches a song and reads a poem to demonstrate and point out the rhyme. Students are invited to contribute their suggestions for other words that might fit into the rhyming spots of the poem. Children eventually create books that reflect the poem and the skill learned in the lesson. The program includes assessments, games, templates for games and lessons, word cards for sorts, and a bibliography of books. The authors also include sample daily schedules.

PHONEMIC AWARENESS, PHONICS, AND CULTURALLY RESPONSIVE TEACHING

There is much research evidence that certain basic skills in reading, such as phonemic awareness and phonics, are learned before one can read for comprehension, search for information, make generalizations from reading, summarize, or synthesize information. Indeed, Stanovich (2000) claims that "the causal model [of reading]—phonological awareness facilitating decoding skills, which in turn determines word recognition ability, which in conjunction with listening comprehension determines reading comprehension— . . . has largely stood the test of time" (p. 61). There is a general developmental sequence to what children learn as they acquire the ability to read. However, there seems to be no guarantee that learning basic skills leads to more advanced skills in reading, making these skills *a necessary but not sufficient* part of a good reading curriculum.

The teaching of phonemic awareness and phonics must adhere to the principles of research-based teaching. For instance, instruction must be systematic and explicit. Teachers must directly explain how to participate in the lessons, why the skill is important, and what the students are expected to learn. Teachers must build lessons based on what students know and need. Fortunately, these principles are not in opposition to the principles for culturally responsive instruction. Teachers can still build curriculum that reflects some connection to students' lives by linking their word work to books they have read and discussed for meaning and content. They can build on students' home language patterns by allowing them to read in their dialects and pronounce words their way, as long as they learn the spelling–sound correspondences. Teachers can build in much group work and dialogic instruction that help children construct new understandings. And when teachers work to keep instruction within students' ZPD, they are providing appropriately rigorous instruction necessary for nudging kids into new developmental levels.

Importantly, though, the teachers in the research study who developed this model found that weaving research-based phonological instruction with culturally responsive instruction was the most difficult part. They wanted to follow the guidelines of the research and did so. Smart teachers! As we shared in Chapter 1, the teachers in the study knew that they must follow the scope and sequence of their phonics programs to maintain the integrity of the instruction that was research-proven. The teachers knew that to incorporate phonological instruction within some lessons was sometimes contrived and ill-conceived. As we suggested, it is important that teachers follow the research-based procedures *as long as they see that their children are learning*. If teachers find that with some strategies or approaches, their students are not attending—are becoming bored, anxious, or disengaged—then they may be doing their students more harm than good. Again, careful observation and the common sense of teachers are still critically important.

CHAPTER 6

Fluency

A group of second graders sit on a rug in their classroom facing their teacher, Nancy, as she holds up the book *Charlie Parker Played Be Bop* (Raschka, 1992). As she slowly displays the book's pictures to one side of the group and then the other, the song "Billie's Bounce" by Charlie Parker and Miles Davis plays in the background. After the song has played, Nancy begins to read the book aloud with a lyrical cadence, almost singing the lines. "Be bop. Fisk, fisk." She continues reading, and at the repetitive line "Charlie Parker plays . . . , " she puts her hand to her ear and the students say, "Be bop!" with the same expression their teacher demonstrated in the previous lines. Nancy is using the book to demonstrate and practice fluency with her students. In future lessons students will have the opportunity to read the lines with a partner and on their own, listening for the rate, accuracy, and expression in one another's renditions. Since this is a story written as poetry, it is introduced during the time of year when the students are working on poetry. Later in the day, during writing workshop, students will practice writing poetry with onomatopoeia, or sound words.

Nancy knows the importance of helping students develop fluency alongside their phonological and comprehension skills. She recognizes that books with rhyme and rhythm are excellent tools for developing fluency, and that choral reading and rereading are safe and productive strategies. Together the selected text, the research-based reading strategy of rereading, and the culturally responsive instructional strategies of choral reading and paired reading, all make this an excellent lesson for helping children develop fluency in reading.

What is fluency? Fluency is reading accurately, with appropriate speed and expression, while also comprehending what is read (Allington, 2009; LaBerge & Samuels, 1974; Samuels, 2002). Fluent readers accurately apply punctuation in sentences (e.g., pausing with commas, stopping briefly at periods), and when they read aloud, others can under-

stand. Fluent reading is highly related to word recognition. Fluent readers recognize words so quickly, they are often unaware that they are reading (Samuels, 2002).

Some children read so slowly and laboriously it is almost painful to listen to them. Often by the time they get to the end of a sentence accurately read, they cannot remember the first part of the sentence. Some children read slowly *and* make multiple mistakes in decoding words. Nonfluent reading greatly affects children's comprehension, and those who struggle may begin to view reading as a word attack exercise rather than an enjoyable, meaning-making activity. When children read painfully slowly, it is no fun, and unless they become more fluent, they will likely not choose to read as a leisure activity.

Of course, we know that all beginning readers read slowly. But some students are noticeably slower than others and need help acquiring fluency. As we know from previous chapters, the context of any reading situation affects the reading performance and plays an important part in assessing students' reading fluency. One critical aspect of the instructional context is the *text* (e.g., book, article, poem, Internet site). The fact that the text the child is reading has much to do with whether or not the child sounds fluent is addressed in this chapter. First, it is important to review what the research says about how children develop fluency.

RESEARCH ON FLUENCY

Strategies that promote better fluency in readers are grounded in studies that examined what children do in their minds as they read. Research illustrates a developmental sequence in how readers process chunks of print. For example, older, more experienced readers read larger chunks of texts (words and phrases) at a time, whereas younger, less experienced readers read in smaller chunks (letters and syllables). One study showed that second graders rely more on letter-by-letter processing while reading, whereas older students read entire words at a time (Samuels, LaBerge, & Bremer, 1978). These researchers found that beginning readers cannot simultaneously decode and comprehend. This finding has huge implications for the reading strategies teachers choose and the particular books selected for instruction. The latter is addressed below in the section on "Matching Readers with Books."

Younger, less fluent readers must practice to learn to read in larger chunks. It makes intuitive sense; practice of any skill will improve the skill. Theories on reading achievement of elementary school students emphasize the critical need for more reading practice for young children, especially children who struggle with reading. In particular, Stanovich's theory (1986) on individual differences in reading suggests that reading experiences and reading achievement have a reciprocal relationship; that is, experiences cause higher achievement. But also, higher achievement (better reading) causes children to have more experiences with text. Why not? Children choose to read because they are good at it. Although some claim that positive self-esteem, time spent reading, and good attitudes toward books increase reading achievement, Stanovich suggests that it works the other way: Better reading skill causes children to have positive self-esteem, good attitudes, and to do a lot of reading. It may be an interaction among these variables that is at work (Stanovich, 1986). In any case, those who are good readers usually become better readers, and those who begin school with few reading skills remain behind unless teachers intervene.

To become fluent readers, children need to practice reading and rereading whole texts, not isolated words. Yet in schools, the children who often need the most practice get the least. In one study, Allington (1984) found that first graders who were good readers read over 1,000 words in a week, compared to the poor readers in the same class who read as few as 16 words. He asked the now famous question, "If they don't read much, how are they ever gonna get good?" Indeed, the National Reading Panel (NRP) report (National Institute of Child Health and Human Development, 2000) indicates that the best readers read the most, and the poorest readers read the least. However, despite Stanovich's theory, the authors of the report caution that these studies do not imply causation; that is, more time spent reading in school has not been shown to necessarily *cause* better reading.

With the publication the NRP report, the relative value of independent reading time (also called SSR for sustained silent reading or DEAR for drop everything and read) as an instructional practice has come into question. These practices failed to produce a positive relationship between encouraging reading and either the amount of reading students did or their reading achievement. As stated earlier, though, the NRP report included only experimental studies, and the report neither recommends nor condemns SSR practices. Below we share studies that might provide some insight into why the NRP report cautions educators about classroom SSR practice.

One teacher research study (not included in the NRP) illustrates the conundrum of including SSR in the curriculum (Marshall, 2002). This sixth-grade teacher began with the question, "Are my students really reading during SSR?" She was frustrated by SSR because she perceived it as a waste of valuable time for some of her students because they were not actually reading during that time. She began to make changes in what students read, her accountability system, the schedule, and the time spent talking about the books to make the SSR period more productive. In this study, backed by the teacher's assessment, it appears that SSR is beneficial *if students are highly engaged*. One cannot assume that this is the case in all classrooms. Recall from Chapter 1, Ellen's visit to the whole-language teacher's classroom, in which some children soaked up the books while others only pretended to read.

Some studies of SSR show positive results. Cline and Kretke (1980) studied students who had been exposed to SSR practices through junior high school and compared these students to similar students who did not experience SSR. They found that the students who experienced SSR held positive attitudes toward reading, but did not achieve differently than students who did not participate in SSR. Taylor, Frye, and Maruyama (1990) had students in grades 5 and 6 record their time spent reading silently during their reading class and at home, keeping track of both assigned reading and reading for pleasure. Students averaged 15.8 minutes of reading during the 50-minute class and 15.0 minutes at home. Time spent reading during reading class contributed significantly to students' reading achievement. However, in these studies, the teacher did some kind of monitoring of reading; even the documentation of the amount of time spent reading affected the actual reading that was done. Thus, when reading was *mediated* by a teacher, improvement was shown—an idea to which we return. Importantly, teachers should find ways for children to practice reading during school hours that promote achievement.

Some studies have clear findings on effects of reading fluency. In one study by Samuels, Miller, and Eisenberg (1979, as cited in Samuels, 2002) college students attempted to read familiar mirror-image words (backward) to simulate what happens when beginning readers encounter words repeatedly. The results illustrated that when the words were first shown, the student read them letter by letter, similar to what beginning readers do. But when the words were familiar through repeated exposure, the students read them more holistically, at least in chunks. Thus, repeated exposure to the same words is important.

Indeed, a key strategy shown to help readers develop fluency is *repeated reading*. In one study, researchers wanted to see if using repeated readings with struggling sixth-grade readers would help them transfer reading skills to new texts. They found that the strategy worked when teachers kept at it over a 7-week period (Homan, Klesius, & Hite, 1993). Repeated readings have also been shown to increase fluency for third-grade students with learning disabilities (Sindelar, Monda, & O'Shea, 1990), to increase the general reading performance of second graders (Dowhower, 1987), and to improve third-graders' speed and word recognition (Rasinski, 1990; Taylor, Wade, & Yekovich, 1985). Why does repeated reading work? Schreiber (1980) suggests that the practice of repeated readings helps students discover the appropriate syntactic phrasing, or "parsing strategies," which are required for sense making when reading. In Vygotskian theory, this is an example of the construction of new understandings through a cognitive tool.

Further, repeated reading helps build sight word vocabulary. Building a sight word vocabulary is more difficult for ELLs than native speakers because ELLs are less familiar with the vocabulary and phonology of English (Calderon & Minaya-Rowe, 2003). There-fore, it is helpful for ELLs to learn or to be exposed to the oral and written version of words in English at the same time (Calderon & Minaya-Rowe, 2003). Allington (2009) warns, however, that too much repeated reading can begin to limit exposure to new words. Teachers must attend to particular students to see who needs more exposure to the same texts and who is ready for new texts. Shanahan and Beck (2006) lament the few well-designed studies of fluency instruction to promote the reading achievement of ELLs. However, the few studies they did analyze showed that fluency interventions help ELLs as much as they do native speakers.

Reitsma (2002) studied three different ways to improve the reading of first graders; (1) guided reading, which was "round robin" reading, in this case (when one student takes a turn to real orally while the other children are expected to follow along); (2) reading while listening to a tape-recorded story; and (3) independent reading with feed-back. Guided reading and independent reading were significantly more effective than reading while listening or the control group, indicating that *reading* improves reading, more so than listening. In a similar study, two kinds of reading practice—repeated read-ings and independent practice—were studied. Both were found to significantly improve reading performance of second graders (Dowhower, 1987).

The above studies have a common theme: The reading was *mediated* by the teacher in some way, which according to Vygotskian theory, would be necessary for children just acquiring reading concepts and skills. It makes sense to take children's developmen-tal levels into account when making instructional choices regarding the amount and type of opportunities offered for reading connected text. Thus, assessment of fluency, as with all components of reading, is important.

PRINCIPLES FOR TEACHING FLUENCY

Figure 6.1 outlines general principles for teaching fluency.

ASSESSING FLUENCY

Teachers usually have an ear for fluency and can spot a child who is reading too slowly for comprehension. Yet, to be sure that you are assessing fluency and not just whether a book is too difficult for a child, it is appropriate to make more formal assessments of children's fluency from time to time. It is also important to be discerning about assess-ments. After the NRP report was published, many materials and assessments focused on fluency, a reading component previously neglected. Not surprisingly, certain assess-ments and instructional practices became popular even though there was little research to support the product. We encourage teachers to refrain from blindly adopting prac-

- Assess children's fluency regularly.
- Demonstrate how to read fluently. Point out to children what is meant by fluency.
- Use repeated reading as a strategy for developing fluency.
- Have students practice a lot. Practice is the key to developing fluency.
- Choose texts that match children's independent reading levels for practice with fluency.
- Use a variety of texts to practice fluency.
- Be attentive to when students want to stop reading a given text.
- Use drama as a tool for fluency.
- For ELLs, provide many opportunities for joint or choral reading.
- Plan carefully for SSR. Teachers should be sure that children are *reading* during SSR time.
- Get kids hooked on favorite book series or topics. Lots of reading is the goal!

FIGURE 6.1. Principles for teaching fluency.

tices or tools because they are "hot" but instead to look at them carefully for appropriateness for their students. (See Allington, 2009, for more on problematic assessments of fluency.)

Running Records

A Running Record (Clay, 1985, 1991) is a time-honored, research-based assessment of reading that teachers can conduct with few materials. There are detailed descriptions of how to do running records, and many teachers learn to conduct them efficiently and effectively, gaining much information about their students as they do so. We encourage all teachers to spend time getting this worthy training. To summarize the process here, we use Allington's (2009) description of Running Records. The teacher selects a short text (1–3 minutes of reading) the child has not read but one that seems to be developmentally appropriate. The teacher invites the child to read the whole text, from start to finish, while the teacher notes the start and stopping time (to assess rate). The teacher has a copy of the text in front of him or her and records when the student makes an error or *miscue* (Goodman et al., 1987). If the reader correctly says the word, the teacher marks a check over the word. If the child misreads the words, the teacher marks a line over the word. If a reader omits a word, the teacher inserts an *o* over the word. If the reader inserts a word, the teacher indicates it with an insertion symbol. The page might look like this:

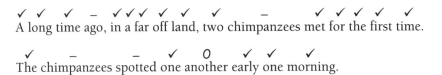

A long time ago, in a far off land, two chimpanzees met for the first time.

The chimpanzees spotted one another early one morning.

After the assessment, the teacher figures the accuracy rate by dividing the total number of words read correctly by the total number of words in the text. For example, in the text above, the student had a 21% error rate, or 79% accuracy level. But the word *chimpanzee* was stumbled over twice, which inflates this error rate a bit. (Most guides to Running Records suggest that teachers count a miscue only once, which would make this reader's accuracy level 83%.) To calculate reading rate (i.e., how many words per minute) divide the total time spent reading by the total number of words read to figure.

It is also critically important to consider the student when conducting Running Records. Just as teachers adapt instruction for certain students (certainly ELLs), they must adapt and accommodate assessments for some children. For example, pronunciation differences should not be considered "miscues." Also, there may be many instances when a child "reads" a word but does not understand its meaning. This is especially likely with ELLs, and teachers should be especially careful to listen for this when inviting the student to retell the story content. Also, some children will not identify a word because they have never encountered it before. For example, suppose a child comes upon the word *catastrophe*. A native speaker might not recognize it and might struggle with decoding it; this would be a miscue. But if you told the child what the word was, more than likely the native speaker would know what it means. But if an ELL came to a halt at that same word, it might be useful for the teacher to later tell the child the word and ask, "Do you know what that word means? Have you ever heard it?" It could be more a vocabulary need than a reading fluency problem.

It is important to keep accurate and regular records to track students' progress in fluency. Teachers should use both formal assessments, such as the Running Record, and informal assessments, such as observing and closely listening to a child read during instruction or independent practice time. Further, teachers should note whether the assessment was with "cold" material or with previously read material (Allington, 2009) because it makes a big difference. Although repeated reading is one of the most important instructional practices (see below), it may not be the best strategy for assessing readers. Keeping track of both cold and "warm" reading is important.

MATCHING TEXTS TO READERS

One of the biggest jobs teachers have is to select the texts for their students to read during instruction, independent reading time at school, and home leisure reading. Text selection is essential because books and other materials are the primary motivators of reading. Students read because they want to know what is inside that book, what the magazine can offer them, what information they can obtain from that website, and so on. Students read for both independent and social reasons, and so providing fun, funny, or fascinating texts that students can read successfully and *want* to read is a huge task.

Our reading model encourages teachers to select books for reading instruction that are culturally appropriate for the readers. This may mean that the book reflects the students—their language, interests, and culture. It may also mean that the book communicates an important message or historic event that reflects the diversity in classrooms today. It may mean that the text was written by people like the students. It is also important that students read about people who are different from themselves to learn valuable lessons about differences and similarities. This book provides titles of many books of this sort for reading instruction, read-alouds, and for classroom libraries.

As we stated earlier in this book, we do not mean to communicate that teachers should use *only* the culturally specific or justice-themed texts for the teaching of reading. While we would never promote or even condone the use of culturally insensitive books for reading (and there are still many out there), we also recognize that some books that seem culture-neutral can be excellent for reading instruction. For example, Denise Fleming's wonderful picture book *In the Tall, Tall Grass* (1995) is an excellent source for lessons on onset–rimes as well as fluency. It could be viewed as culture-neutral, although some may argue that Fleming's books are pro-environment, since they seem to celebrate nature. In any case, we advocate a wide variety of rich literature for reading instruction. Sometimes books will simply be *funny*. Texts that make children laugh could be your best tool for inviting readers to reread.

The other consideration for text selection is *text difficulty*. To assess whether certain texts are appropriately easy or challenging for their students, teachers need to think about multiple text features and whether a book is intended for instruction, practice, or independent reading. If the text is for practice, it should be familiar in topic and genre and easy for the child to read. Consider Figure 6.2. Of course, teachers can conduct lessons on the topic of the book to cultivate interest. They can read aloud varied genre to familiarize the child with how texts are structured. It is essential that teachers read aloud to students from a variety of genres to create interest and familiarity in both the topic and structure of the text. Consider a situation in which students have had little exposure to poetry; perhaps their previous teachers did not read poetry aloud to them. These students might read the poem as if it were prose and sound quite *dys*fluent in the process.

Sentence complexity and word difficulty are the two primary features of texts that determine how readable it is. Sentences that are longer and have more independent and dependent clauses are more complex than short, declarative sentences, making fluency

---

Topic: Is it interesting? Will it motivate?

Genre: Is the student familiar with reading this type of text?

Length: Will the length be tackled enthusiastically by the reader?

Sentence difficulty: Are the sentences simple enough for easy reading by this child?

Word difficulty: Will the reader be able decode easily so as not to interrupt fluency?

FIGURE 6.2. Assessing text difficulty.

and comprehension harder to achieve. Words that are new to the reader, are multisyllabic, or have unusual spelling patterns are more difficult to decode and thus harder to recognize. These are key features to attend to when choosing books for readers. There are some excellent sources on tools for determining the best match between readers and books (Brown, 1999; Mesmer, 2008). Most educators who write about text difficulty and reading instruction suggest the following: For independent reading time, children should practice with texts they find *easy*; these are books in which they can recognize 95%, or more, of the words. For reading instruction, children should be taught with texts in their ZPD, as described in Chapter 2; that is, the texts are those the students can read with assistance from the teacher. When choosing texts for reading instruction, the teacher must think about the backgrounds and interests of the readers, how much assistance he or she will provide, and the complexity of the books.

Many publishing companies now have "leveled" books that help teachers determine text difficulty. Their levels all differ, but if you find a company's system that suits your own, use it. Of course, these companies do not know your students, and so their systems should not be used without your input. Only teachers can determine the best practice books for their students because they know (1) the interests of their students, (2) the experiences their students have had with particular genres, (3) the word attack skills and reading strategies their students have been taught, and (4) the motivations and dispositions their students have toward reading. All of these factors matter in choosing texts.

STRATEGIES FOR TEACHING FLUENCY

It is widely accepted that fluency has been one of the most neglected parts of reading instruction, although it has gained increased attention since the publication of the NRP report and related reports. Since then, many educators have recommended the following strategies, which have their research base in the studies mentioned above.

Modeling Fluent Reading

Teachers must be good models of fluent reading. Some books may require a teacher to rehearse the reading before sharing it with children, to achieve the cadence and prosody intended. This is not a skill that comes naturally; it is a skill teachers acquire after multiple read-alouds. Take, for instance, this text by Pat Mora (1998): "Old Snake knows. Sometimes you feel you just can't breathe in your own tight skin. Old Vibora says, 'Leave those doubts and hurts buzzing like flies in your ears. When you feel your frowns, like me wriggle free from I can't, I can't. Leave those gray words to dry in the sand and dare to show your brave self, your bright true colors'" (p. 5).

Read as prose, the text is still beautiful. But read as a poem, as intended, the text is much more meaningful. Good readers of poetry know how to read the text aloud to make it meaningful, emphasizing essential words and slowing down the pace.

"Old Snake" (Mora, 1998)*

Old Snake knows.
Sometimes you feel
you just can't breathe
in your own tight skin.
Old Vibora says, "Leave
those doubts and hurts
buzzing like flies in your ears.
When you feel your frowns,
like me wriggle free
from *I can't, I can't.*
Leave those gray words
to dry in the sand
and dare to show
your brave self,
your bright, true colors."

Teachers can learn to read the poem (or any text) with expression that communicates just what it feels like to have doubts by slowing down the line "you just can't breathe" and expressing some pain in "I can't, I can't." Children will recall what it feels like to have doubts. When you boldly read, "Your brave self, your bright true colors" children will *feel* different, know they can be brave. You might see them lean in closer to listen and ask to hear it again. The picture book from which this poem comes, *This Big Sky* (Mora, 1998), features a giant, gorgeous red snake. The picture helps make this poem meaningful, too!

Running Starts

Sometimes students face a book and want to read it but think it is too hard. Or, they read the first page and put it away, not realizing just how good it is. Teachers can invite more children into more books if they give them a running start to the reading of these books. When teachers read the first page or chapter or just a little more (depending on the readers) and stop when the story is getting really good, chances are many children will pick it up. Because they have the context of the story in their heads, the readers can use prior knowledge to predict story events and even the words in each sentence. This helps them develop the necessary fluency to keep reading.

Choral Reading

Choral reading can be an excellent tool for older readers who are not confident but who want to read the good stuff. Children track print as they read, so it can also be a good tool for emergent and beginning readers. Thus, they can "read" material they cannot read on their own. Choral reading whets their appetite for more reading. It encourages

---

* Copyright 1998 by Pat Mora. Reprinted with permission from Scholastic, Inc.

risk taking and builds confidence. It helps build vocabulary as well as fluency. It also builds classroom community in the same way that singing does. It is excellent for older readers, too. Consider the first two stanzas of a Jack Prelutsky (1983) poem:

"The Bogeyman"*

In the desolate depths of a perilous place
The bogeyman lurks, with a snarl on his face.
Never dare, never dare to approach his dark lair
For he's waiting . . . just waiting . . . to get you.
He skulks in the shadows, relentless and wild
In search for a tender, delectable child.
With his steeling sharp claws and his slavering jaws
Oh he's waiting . . . just waiting . . . to get you. (p. 6)

Of course, this poem is not for young children. But the year Ellen taught sixth grade (with all students at seventh- or eighth-grade age because they had all been retained at least once), the students in her class loved it! In fact, Ellen believes today that her Jack Prelutsky and Roald Dahl books did more to improve students' reading than anything she did. The students read and reread those books. They are packed with high-level vocabulary the students craved. When they read chorally, all students were successful.

Repeated Reading

As the studies in the NRP report have shown, when students are repeatedly exposed to the same words in print, they develop word recognition and fluency. When teachers and researchers had children participate in repeated reading activities, they developed word recognition, speed, and comprehension, and this was true for average as well as struggling readers (Samuels, 2002). While there are several techniques for repeated reading, below are steps for a simplified method for beginning readers (Samuels, 2002).

1. The teacher selects a text.
2. The children work in pairs; one takes the role of student, the other as teacher.
3. The "student" reads and the "teacher" listens while looking at the words in the text. (Both students get practice this way.)
4. The students reverse roles, and each passage is read four times.
5. The children comment on their performances.

Buddy Reading

Teachers who encourage children to read in pairs often see more reading. It is fun to sit next to a friend and share a book. It can also help the readers as they assist one another

---

* Copyright 1983 by Jack Prelutsky. Reprinted with permission from HarperCollins.

with words and meaning. Some children love to read aloud to others and can be paired with ELLs who may not know enough English yet to be reading. Of course, we do not recommend that teachers always have proficient readers paired with struggling readers or ELLs. Good readers often want to read on their own silently and should be afforded many opportunities in the classroom to do this. But inviting and encouraging buddy reading can assist many students in different ways.

Guided Oral Reading

In guided oral reading the student reads aloud a text at his or her instructional reading level, and the teacher provides fluency, word identification, and vocabulary coaching during the reading. It is not round robin reading, the old practice in which children in a group all take a turn to read aloud a section of a text until the story is read. That practice does little to help children acquire reading skill of any sort. Guided oral reading is a one-on-one teaching time when the teacher works with the child on particular skills.

Readers' Theatre

Readers' Theatre is a staged reading of a play or dramatic piece of work designed to entertain, inform, or influence (Kerry-Moran, 2006). A script, play, or story is chosen that children want to read aloud. Children are assigned parts and practice their performances. The difference between Readers' Theatre and a play is that children do not have to memorize the script. They *read it* aloud with expression. This practice has wide acceptance as an excellent tool for developing fluency and comprehension.

There are many Readers' Theatre scripts available on the Internet, and several books have been written consisting of such scripts. Nancy observed a fourth-grade classroom in which students had been discussing perspectives and different points of view. The teacher had chosen to use a Readers' Theatre script based on *The True Story of the Three Little Pigs* (Sciezska, 1996), in which the wolf is depicted as the "good guy." Students were assigned roles, practiced at their seats and with partners, and then read the lines aloud together. In this case students did not actually act out the script, but they did focus on reading the lines aloud with expression. The reading and discussion of this book led students to examine the different viewpoints in the original and alternative versions of the story while developing their fluency.

Beginners or ELLs (if appropriate) can use texts with which they are familiar, due to prior reading. These should be short with several characters and simple story structures (Rieg & Paquette, 2009). Some children can write their own scripts (Peregoy & Boyle, 2008). Some tips for implementing Readers' Theatre include the following:

1. Choose developmentally appropriate texts.
2. Use visual and aural aids.
3. Determine the dramatic experience level of children.
4. Model expressive reading.

5. Make practice a priority.
6. Involve families.
7. Perform for an audience.
8. Do it often (Kerry-Moran, 2006, pp. 320–322).

Some teachers choose to make Readers' Theatre a regular part of the reading routine, whereas other teachers use Readers' Theatre from time to time. Young and Rasinski (2009) describe the integration of Readers' Theatre throughout the reading curriculum. The key to using this activity in your classroom successfully is to introduce the script and process thoroughly and to allow time for students to practice before performing.

More Drama

Students can also take part in poetry enactments. Teachers should choose poems that express strong emotions or attitudes (Tomlinson, 1986). Teachers use the cadence of poetry to promote more attention to rate and expression. Rieg and Paquette (2009) provide the following steps for helping children to enact poetry successfully:

1. The teacher first reads the poem aloud, paying special attention to the modeling of pronunciation and intonation.
2. The teacher discusses the challenging words with students.
3. The students read the poem chorally.
4. The students prepare plays or other sorts of dramatic interpretations to the class in pairs or in small groups.

Repetitive texts are especially good for ELLs because many children who are still learning English need to hear the same words repeated even more than native English speakers.

Name Game

Teachers can use the poem "Name Game," adapted from Jean Roberts (2009), a teacher who posted the poem on *thevirtualvine.com*, to celebrate children and develop fluency by writing the poem on a chart for all to see. At the beginning of each school year, Nancy has students read this poem together during the morning meeting. First, she introduces the poem to the students by reading it aloud to them. Then, she tells them that the poem consists of instructions for what to do with your name. She next reads the poem and says her name after each line. Each day of the first week of school the poem is read during morning meeting (or class meeting). First, the students have the support of their peers by reading the poem chorally and taking turns with different students' names. As the days go on, individual students ask to read the poem by themselves, until even the struggling readers have heard the poem enough that they feel confident reading it by themselves in front of their peers. Many students *love* to have an opportunity to read the poem themselves. It makes even the least proficient reader feel successful early in the year.

Growl your name. (JAVON!)

Howl your name. (JAVON!)

Stretch it 'til it's long. (JJJAAAVVVOOONNN!!!)

Chant your name. (Javon! Javon! Javon!)

Pant your name. (Ja Ja Ja Von Von Von!)

Sing it like a song. (Javon!)

Clap your name. (Clap the syllables of Javon.)

Snap your name. (Snap the syllables of Javon.)

Announce it loud and clear. (Say Javon loudly.)

Spell your name. (J-A-V-O-N!)

Yell your name. (JAVON!)

Tell the world you're here. (I'm here world!)

Practice, Practice, Practice: Mediated SSR

The studies summarized in the NRP report on fluency development show that (1) those who read a lot are better readers, and (2) good readers happen to read a lot. Yet, no studies show that the common practice of SSR *causes* improved reading skill. Instead, there is a correlation between reading a lot and being very good at it. So, why does this correlation exist? Stanovich (1986) has shown that the role of vocabulary might have something to do with it. The more a person reads, the more new vocabulary he or she learns. The more vocabulary learned, the easier reading becomes. If reading is easy, people read more. He also suggests, as do many other educators, that studies indicate that under specific conditions, practice at reading likely *does* cause reading improvement. But that practice must be *mediated* by appropriate texts and contexts.

Therefore, the practice of silent reading should not be stopped in schools! Teachers should create situations in which they know that their students are getting practice with accurate reading. The tips in Figure 6.3 may help you improve your students' practice of SSR.

Series Reading

A primary goal in reading instruction is to get children hooked on reading. One way to do that is to get them hooked on a favorite author or series. In our day, reading and rereading the Nancy Drew books, Encyclopedia Brown books, the Chronicles of Narnia, Babysitter's Club, and Archie Comic books got us addicted to reading. Today, the Captain Underpants series, Harry Potter books, the Twilight series, Bluford series, Cam Jansen, Magic School Bus series the American Girl series, and many more delight children and have them begging for more. Some children get hooked on topics and will read because of their fascination with a particular subject. If we can find the series or topics that our students crave, we will create readers.

- Have different kinds of SSR for different times of the day. For instance, during the morning SSR, designate a time and space for reading with teacher-selected books only. Some teachers put baskets of leveled or "matched" books on each child's desk and ask students to choose from those books only.

- During a shorter afternoon SSR, allow students to read anything they choose, even books too hard for them—to inspire motivation. Have favorites readily available. Children will return to favorites again and again, making repeated reading a strategy they can self-direct.

- Observe the readers carefully during SSR. If a child is not reading the print, intervene! Help the child find another book or avoid distractions. You may want to read with some children to get them started. Keep the tone and atmosphere fun and light, but also quiet. SSR time should be silent, except perhaps for the expected murmur of beginning readers voicing words.

- Keep the reading periods short for beginners. Some teachers have multiple short SSR periods rather than one longer one.

FIGURE 6.3. SSR revisited.

FLUENCY INSTRUCTION
AND CULTURALLY RESPONSIVE TEACHING

Fluency instruction lends itself easily to implementing culturally responsive instruction. First, there are many terrific books with themes related to culture, history, justice, ethnicity, and many other topics that are great choices for the fluency strategies described above. The choral repeated reading strategies will be familiar to some children who participate in religious or traditional celebrations that include readings. The lessons can be rigorous (think of the vocabulary in the Jack Prelutsky poem) while being developmentally appropriate and psychologically safe (mistakes go unnoticed). Children just learning to read and speak English can participate without feeling foolish for making mistakes. The strategies in this chapter also work well with the strategies that assist children with comprehension, which is the subject of the next chapter.

CHAPTER 7

Comprehension

"Clara, why don't you begin?" Ellen asks one of the four participants in her reciprocal teaching (Palinscar & Brown, 1984) lesson. Ellen has just finished modeling the comprehension strategies that make up the routine: summarizing, questioning, clarifying, and predicting. The children are reading a book on storms, and the chapter they are reading is about the famous New York City blizzard of 1888.

"OK," says Clara looking at her index card that designates her role. "I have *summarize*. This [the paragraph they just read] is about how the rain changed to snow and people had to make tunnels to get out of their house."

"What else?" asks Ellen.

"It was cold and people didn't have heat," responds Clara.

"How was this storm different from ordinary storms?" asks Ellen.

Clara looks back at her text. "Even telephone poles toppled."

"Do you know what that word *toppled* means?" asks Ellen.

"Fell down?" answers Clara.

"Yes, and that would make this storm quite severe, wouldn't it? Clara, you said that it snowed so much that the people had to make tunnels to get to the street, they did not have heat, and even telephone poles toppled. Can you think of one sentence that might say what this whole section is about?"

"This was a really bad storm, worse than any other storm, and people even died."

"It's true. Back then they didn't have the kind of help we have today with terrible snowstorms." Ellen turns to another child. "Bryan, you are the *questioner*. Do you have a question for the group? Be sure it is one that we can talk about, not just answer with one or two words."

"I have it," Bryan says confidently. "What do you think it was like to have snow all the way up to the second floor of your house?"

The group discusses Bryan's question for a bit, and then Shawn asks to participate. She has the index card that says *clarify*. Ellen knows there were some challenging parts to the text, and so she asks, "What part was confusing for you?"

"I don't know what *fierce gusts* means," she says. "I don't understand *towering drifts*."

"That's why the snow piled up!" Bryan interrupts.

Ellen nods and says to the group, "Asking about confusing parts of a text is what good readers do. They *clarify* or find out what they don't understand. Bryan, I am glad you understood that section, but I can see why some of you might have had some difficulty." Ellen rereads the section aloud and explains the references that gave Shawn difficulty.

Finally, it is Bonita's turn to *predict* what will be in the next section. She sees the subheading and predicts that there will be trouble on ships in the ocean due to the storm.

Before they begin to read the next section, the children trade index cards and roles. Each child will take a new role until they have practiced each strategy at least twice.

Reading *is* comprehending. If children can read the words of a text, but do not understand what they are reading, they are not really reading. How much and how easily readers comprehend depends on variables within and outside them. These key variables of reading comprehension include the *reader*, the *activity* of reading, and the *text* (RAND Reading Study Group, 2002), and these three intersect to affect how well comprehension occurs. For example, the reader's background knowledge and vocabulary (reader) interact with his or her purposes for reading (e.g., to scan for information, study for a test, or read for pleasure; activity) and the type of text (Internet website, textbook, novel)

to contribute to his or her comprehension. Because reading in today's world requires comprehension of a variety of types of texts for many different purposes, teachers must attend to these three variables now more than ever.

Good teaching is the most powerful means of promoting the development of proficient readers (RAND Reading Study Group, 2002). Good comprehension instruction includes demonstration, explanation, and guidance in *how* to read. Merely reading a lot does not make for better reading; reading more without guidance does not necessarily improve comprehension. Instruction in comprehension can help students understand what they read, remember what they read, and communicate with others about what they read.

Ellen's lesson in the beginning of this chapter includes multiple research-based comprehension strategies in a well-researched *routine* called reciprocal teaching (Palinscar & Brown, 1984). The routine includes high-level thinking, expectations that the students will perform the strategies, and the kind of scaffolding that encourages (rather than merely praises), making this lesson a research-based, culturally responsive lesson on comprehension. This chapter provides many examples and explanations for the teaching of comprehension to diverse populations of children in elementary classrooms. First, we summarize recent and classic research on comprehension instruction.

RESEARCH ON COMPREHENSION INSTRUCTION

In the last few decades, we have witnessed a surge of research on beginning reading, especially in the areas of phonological understanding. However, there has been less focus on reading comprehension. Nevertheless, there are enough important studies to guide us toward excellent comprehension instruction. One of the most important studies in the past few decades showed that there was very little teaching of comprehension in schools. Instead, what teachers called comprehension instruction was merely assessment of comprehension. Teachers asked children to read a text and then asked them what they recalled or interpreted from the text. They were not teaching children *how* to comprehend (Durkin, 1978–1979). The now famous *Becoming a Nation of Readers* (Anderson, Heibert, Scott, & Wilkinson, 1985) brought the problem to light, emphasizing the importance of reading comprehension *instruction*.

In one of the earliest reviews of research on comprehension instruction, Tierney and Cunningham (1984) categorized reading instructional strategies that occur before, during, and after reading. They showed that instruction in which teachers used tools such as *advance organizers*, which guide readers in anticipating and/or predicting what might be in the text, helped readers understand more. Other tools designed to improve comprehension include *graphic organizers* and *conceptual maps* (Pearson & Fielding, 1991; Pressley, 2000; Duke & Pearson, 2002). These aids not only assist learners with activating prior knowledge, but also help them to "work" the text, organizing their learning and remembering. Further, Tierney and Cunningham (1984) summarized studies that showed that providing students with objectives before they read also helps them comprehend texts better. Their review included studies of the routine directed reading–thinking activity (DR-TA), in which students declare their purposes for reading, predict answers to their own questions, and then read to test their purposes and predictions. Thus, what happens prior to actual reading is as important as what happens during reading.

This review also highlighted a key foundation of reading comprehension: *schema theory*. Schema theory (Anderson & Pearson, 1984) explains how knowledge is stored in the mind. Schema can be thought of as mental file folders that categorize the data the mind holds. Schemas organize the meanings of things and their characteristics (e.g., mammals, cities, apples), people and all they do and are (e.g., teachers, firefighters, Australians), processes (e.g., reading, skiing, surfing the Net), emotions (of all sorts), and more. Schemas are drawn from life's experiences. They are abstract representations organized in our minds through our associations, examples, and meanings. For example, a child's schema for insects might include small, crawling, six legs, roaches, ants, icky. This schema (accurate or not) includes descriptions, examples, attributions, and even emotions. The more schemas a reader has about the topic of a reading lesson or book, the more easily the child will comprehend the book.

In a later review of research on comprehension instruction, Pearson and Fielding (1991) illustrated how readers' prior knowledge of a story makes a significant difference in how well they comprehend. In one study, Hansen (1981) activated children's prior knowledge on the topic of the text through discussion and other activities. She taught them to predict what the text would be about and asked the children inferential questions. Her lessons led her students to better comprehend because she was *teaching* the children to comprehend rather than just assessing comprehension.

These studies also showed that if teachers explained how the text is structured or organized, the readers will comprehend the content of that text more easily. For example, if we teach children the structure of most narrative stories (plot sequence, character development, setting, and so on), they can then use this knowledge to comprehend future stories more easily. Of course, not all stories follow a "traditional" story sequence (Michaels, 1981), and teachers should remember this.

The studies of text structure included nonfiction texts as well. Researchers who explicitly taught children how historical texts (typically found in social studies) differ from categorical texts (often found in science), which differ from descriptive texts (found in multiple subject areas), helped the readers comprehend all genres better (Pearson & Fielding, 1991). All nonfiction texts differ in structure and language from stories. When children are taught these differences, they comprehend each type of text better.

Many studies have shown that when teachers directly explain how to do something, such as how to predict or how to summarize, the learners comprehend more (Duffy et al., 1987; Pressley, 2000). Teaching children how to summarize is *not* a matter of having them read a story and then asking the class, "Who can summarize the story?" That would be an example of assessing summarization for only the one child who responded. Teachers must explicitly teach children strategies for summarizing. Those who get this training do better (Pearson & Fielding, 1991; Pressley, 2000; RAND, 2002).

Studies show that instruction that focuses on self-questioning improves compre-hension (Pearson & Fielding, 1991). When readers question themselves while reading—about the content, about how well they understand—they comprehend better. In fact, this seems to be what good readers do. Thus, comprehension instruction should move away from having students answer questions toward having students *ask* questions as they read. When readers ask questions as they read, they make inferences, monitor their own understanding, and attend to the structure of the text. But they must be given explicit instruction in how to generate these questions (Pearson & Gallagher, 1983). This chapter shares examples of how to do this.

Some studies of reading comprehension focused on reading routines, processes, or general principles of good comprehension instruction. Teachers must provide explana-tions, modeling, guided practice, and application of any new skill or strategy and teach students to use these comprehension strategies flexibly and in combination with one another (Duke & Pearson, 2002). As suggested in earlier chapters, teachers must work alongside children, assisting their performance as they try the new strategies, providing feedback along the way as the readers participate in real reading events (Brown et al., 1989; Tharp & Gallimore, 1988). Thus, while explicit instruction is important as a first step, authentic and monitored practice in real comprehension situations is what actually helps readers transfer new reading skills.

Studies of "think-aloud protocols," or what readers say they are thinking while they read (Pressley, 2000), illustrate many characteristics of good readers. Here are some:

- They are aware of their own purpose (whether to enjoy a book or find informa-tion) for reading the text.
- They overview (skim) the text to see if it is relevant to their purpose.
- They read selectively for their purposes; that is, when they skim, they skip over text they do not need and slow down on material that suits their purposes.
- They evaluate and revise their predictions about the text as they read.
- They revise their schemas when they are inconsistent with ideas in the text.
- They figure out the meanings of words.
- They underline, reread, and make notes in efforts to remember points of the text.
- They interpret the text.
- They evaluate the text.
- They review the text.
- They think about how they will use the information from the text in the future.

Since we know what good readers do as they read, we can identify the best instruc-tional strategies for teaching students to comprehend. The NRP (National Institute of Child Health and Human Development, 2000) summarized the strategies that have been shown, through well-designed research studies, to increase students' comprehension. This report and other important studies and reviews of research studies (Anderson & Jetton, 2000; Block & Pressley, 2002; Palinscar & Brown, 1984; Pressley, 2000; RAND,

2002) recommend that teachers focus on several comprehension routines, such as those we just discussed, and some key research-based strategies. These include the following:

- Activating prior knowledge
- Predicting
- Drawing inferences
- Monitoring comprehension
- Questioning self, the author, and the text while reading
- Determining the most important ideas in a text
- Thinking aloud
- Summarizing
- Understanding text structures (fiction vs. nonfiction)
- Using text conventions

This chapter illustrates each of these strategies with examples that also highlight the features of the culturally responsive instruction emphasized in this book. We present reading strategies that, through instruction, (1) build on students' backgrounds, (2) build on students' home languages or dialects, (3) include group work and dialogic instruction, and (4) are rigorous and require high-level thinking.

PRINCIPLES FOR TEACHING COMPREHENSION

Figure 7.1 shares some general principles for teaching comprehension that teachers should keep in mind as they plan.

- Begin comprehension instruction in the earliest grades, even before children have moved into conventional reading.
- Consider the reader, the activity, and the text when planning instruction.
- Teach comprehension strategies through explanations, modeling (of thinking and actions), and guided practice. Repeat them often.
- Help learners understand when and why particular comprehension strategies are useful.
- Use a range of text genres.
- Use good books in which kids are interested.
- Conduct deep conversations about the meanings of texts.
- Whenever possible, employ paired or group learning.
- Plan for plenty of practice opportunities, especially in authentic contexts with real texts.
- Give lots of feedback.
- Design instruction that provides just enough scaffolding for students to be able to participate in tasks that are currently beyond their reach; that is, teaching within their ZPD.

FIGURE 7.1. Principles for teaching comprehension.

ASSESSING COMPREHENSION

Assessment of comprehension has been a challenge. We know that the reader's prior knowledge, the type of text read, and the purpose for reading are all important in measuring comprehension. So, how can we devise comprehension assessments that capture this information for teachers? Many standardized assessments cannot achieve this goal. They often assess only immediate recall or vocabulary. They merely compare children's abilities to read a particular text in a particular context.

There are, however, some principles for assessment that teachers can use as a guide. First, good assessments are tied to the curriculum (RAND, 2002). Teachers should assess (1) on what students have been taught; (2) a variety of reading tasks for the purposes of grouping children for lessons that address needs; and (3) students' attitudes and feelings about reading. There are many ways to link your curriculum to assessment. We suggest a few here.

Observation and Interview

Some teachers argue that the best way to assess students is by directly observing them in the targeted activity and asking them questions about it. For comprehension, this might provide teachers with the most useful information. If you take time to observe a student while reading, you can notice:

Does she read without stopping?
Does she skip parts?
Does she stay too long on some parts?
Does she quit easily?
Does she choose to read during free-choice time?

Further, many of the research-based strategies you will explicitly teach children to do can be excellent assessment strategies as well. As you observe children summarizing a story or synthesizing across multiple texts, their reading behaviors and products will reveal who needs extra support and who needs more challenging texts and tasks. That is the goal of assessment: to help teachers decide who needs what kind of assistance, when, how much, and on which strategies and skills.

Interviews can also reveal how well children comprehend. If you ask children how their reading is going, they may give you more information than you might get from a traditional test. Most importantly, if you ask them to tell you about what they just read, you will likely get a better notion of how well they comprehended that text. But, since comprehension is much more than recall of information, teachers must ask questions that go beyond the surface text. Even if children can retell a story completely or list facts from a text, they may not have deeply comprehended the text if they are not able to discuss it. Thus, interview prompts must be open-ended, such as:

"Tell me about what you read."

"How is this book like other books you've read?"

"Does the book teach you anything? If so, what?"

"What was the most important part of this book for you? Why?"

"Have you enjoyed reading this? Why [or why not]?"

"Would you recommend this book [article, story] to someone? To who? Why [or why not]?"

"What would you say about the book [article, story]?"

These sorts of informal assessments are usually directly tied to a teacher's curriculum, and supply the most critical information for what sort of support students need. At times, though, teachers want additional assessments that document many aspects of reading. One such assessment is the informal reading inventory.

Informal Reading Inventory

An informal reading inventory (IRI) is a set of tasks individually administered to determine a reader's needs and strengths. Usually the IRI is designed to assess several aspects of reading, such as word recognition, vocabulary, reading strategies, and comprehension. Commercially available IRIs have brief leveled texts, often in attractive packages, and separate booklets that guide teachers in how to administer the test.

One kind of IRI that Nancy and Vicky both use is the Developmental Reading Assessment or DRA (Pearson Learning; *www.pearsonlearning.com*). The DRA is designed to inform instruction within a guided reading model. It is intended to identify students' independent reading level (not their ZPD). It is also designed to identify students' reading strengths and weaknesses and to monitor reading growth. The DRA materials are appealing, with updated pictures and story situations that are free of stereotypical situations.

RESEARCH-BASED COMPREHENSION
READING STRATEGIES

The following strategies are taken from research studies that show improved reading achievement. They are described within lessons for elementary students and adapted for various groups of children without violating the integrity of their research-based characteristics. Some of the lessons are focused on a theme of diversity or justice. Others are simply lessons with great books we know all children enjoy. As suggested in Chapter 1 and supported by researchers, teachers should provide a balance of topics, genres, and purposes for reading.

Activating Prior Knowledge

This strategy is designed to elicit information from children about the topic on which they will soon read. At times it means bringing knowledge children already have to the surface, and at other times it means providing new knowledge they can apply to the reading act (Anderson & Pearson, 1984). The widely popular K-W-L (Ogle, 1986) in which the teacher asks children what they *know* about a topic, what they *want* to know, and then later what new information they *learned* is one example of how teachers activate prior knowledge. That strategy is used for nonfiction text. In the following lesson, Ellen activates first graders' knowledge so that they can use that knowledge to read increasingly difficult texts.

Ellen used three related books. The first book, *The Snowman*, by Raymond Briggs (1978), is a wordless picture book about a boy who wakes up to find it has snowed and rushes out to make a snowman. The snowman comes alive, and the two have wonderful adventures together. The second book is an "Early Step-Into-Reading" book, also by Briggs and also called *The Snowman* (1999a). This book has a sentence on each page, such as, "James wakes up." "James gets dressed." "He makes a pile of snow." In the third book in the series, *The Snowman Storybook* (Briggs, 1999b), the language is more sophisticated. On one page it says, "James and the snowman flew for miles through the cold, midnight air." Ellen knew that the children could read the second book somewhat independently, but probably not the third.

Ellen first shared the wordless book. The children were mesmerized by the beautiful pictures and delightful story. Ellen modeled how to pretend to read the pages using language found in books, emphasizing that they had to make up the words since there were no words in this book. She invited the children to give it a try, scaffolding them as needed. After they enjoyed and discussed the beautiful book, Ellen surprised the children with the easy reader version of the story. She led them through a prediction strategy and guided their reading, assisting them with the few words the children might not predict (e.g., *coal*). The children comfortably read the Early-Step-Into-Reading book, with a little assistance.

Then, when Ellen brought out the third book, the children gasped! They eagerly grabbed for the copies and scanned the pages, looking for the familiar. Ellen let them read the book on their own a bit before doing an oral reading. The children found that they could read this book! They had acquired the necessary background knowledge and vocabulary to predict many of the words. They used the knowledge of the story and the many words they encountered in the previous books and discussions to predict the words on the pages of the more difficult book. Ellen's assistance with decoding new words and the previously read books were the tools needed to scaffold the reading the children would not have been able to do on their own. This is an example of a lesson that activates prior knowledge, thus enabling readers to read more and better. This example also illustrates that children should be taught within their ZPDs, with texts that enable them to do what they cannot do alone. Many other activities can be used for the same purpose. Consider the following:

- See the movie version of the book before reading the book.
- Read related texts prior to the lesson text.
- Take a walk to study the trees before reading about trees.
- Do the science experiment before reading about the science concepts.
- Interview people from the country before you read the text about that country.

You get the idea. Teachers can find many ways to build students' background knowledge and vocabulary before a reading lesson to enable them to comprehend better. Activating background knowledge leads to better prediction capabilities. Teachers can also conduct direct lessons on how to predict.

Making Predictions

When teachers encourage children to make predictions about what they are going to read, they assist with comprehension. Teachers encourage students to use their existing knowledge of the topic to facilitate understandings of the ideas in the new text. What seems to help students most is when teachers explicitly demonstrate how to predict events in a story or content of a nonfiction text and then follow the lesson by comparing their predictions to the text content during and after reading. This verification or confirmation process is as important as making predictions (Duke & Pearson, 2002).

In Nancy's classroom, she invites children to "take a picture walk" before they read a book during shared reading. That is, she shows each page of the book, allowing time for the children to study each illustration, and then invites them to predict, based on the illustrations, what the story will entail. As she reads the book, the anticipation mounts: "Whose prediction will be closest to the text?" Nancy models the strategy often at the beginning of the year. Later, the students work in pairs to predict. One day she overheard Oscar, who was still learning English, say to his reading buddy, "First I'm gonna make a prediction." Through repeated exposure to the language of the strategy, Oscar was not only using the words correctly, he was demonstrating a strategy that aids his comprehension.

Another way to get students to practice making and checking predictions is by using *anticipation guides* (Herber, 1978). When creating an anticipation guide, teachers make a list of 6–12 true or false statements about the text the students will read. Students enjoy taking this true–false "quiz" before reading, making guesses about content, in some cases, and relying on background information, in other cases. Sometimes teachers have students complete the quizzes in pairs to encourage discussion and debate.

After reading the text, students check their work and change their responses to reflect the text. Some teachers also include a space in the anticipation guide for students to provide evidence to back up the statements they found to be true. Many examples of anticipation guides are available on the Internet.

An example from Nancy's second-grade classroom is shared here. Students read *Paper Crunch* (Rogers & Alexander, 2000) in guided reading groups. This book describes

		Anticipation Guide for Paper Crunch
True	(False)	Paper comes from insects. trees
(True)	False	Paper mills are places where paper is made.
True	(False)	Making paper takes energy, resources, time, and sugar. trees
True	(False)	You should throw paper away when you are done with it. recycle
True	False	One way to reuse paper is by turning it into balloons. a soft toy for my dog
(True)	False	You can wrap gifts with newspaper to reuse it.
(True)	False	You can reuse paper for arts and crafts.
(True)	False	When we recycle paper, we save trees.
True	(False)	Every ton of paper that is recycled saves 1 tree!
(True)	False	One thing I can do to save trees is recycle used paper.

Name Moneja

FIGURE 7.2. Anticipation guide for *Paper Crunch.*

where paper comes from, how it is made, and the need to recycle. Nancy had asked students to use both sides of paper when writing, so that they could save trees, and found that the students did not know there was a connection between trees and paper. So Nancy used this book to build from students' natural inquiry. In Figure 7.2, Moneja has corrected the sentences to reflect her new understandings about the origins of paper.

Drawing Inferences

Inferring is the act of using background knowledge and clues within a text to interpret the meaning of that text (Hansen, 1981). Inferring is sometimes called "reading between the lines." Students can be guided to make inferences while listening to a story read aloud in shared reading time. For instance, while reading *The Secret Olivia Told Me* (Joy, 2007) aloud, Nancy draws students' attention to the red balloon that grows and grows as a secret gets passed from one child to another. The students had just played the game Telephone (in which a story is passed from one person to another around a circle, until it reaches the last person and is retold, usually producing a completely new story) and talked about how the story changed in transition. Using what they gleaned from the game Telephone, the context of the story, and the clues within the pictures, students are able to *infer* that the secret is changing and growing each time it is told. Students can also infer, using their own background knowledge and the clues from the story, that Olivia might be upset with her friend for telling her secret.

Inferences can be made by paying attention to the way characters act or by the characters and the setting. For instance, in the book *My Name Is Yoon* (Recorvits, 2003), students can infer that Yoon is beginning to feel more comfortable in her new school because she imagines herself as a cupcake, which makes the other kids excited. Another story, *Taming the Taniwha* (Tipene, 2001), tells about Tama, who is bullied by James. (It can be viewed online at the International Children's Digital Library; it is displayed on-screen for students to follow along.) Tama tries many ways to get James to stop bullying him: fighting back, telling the teacher, and finally by getting to know him. One day Tama sits next to James at lunch and sees that he doesn't have food. James takes Tama's apple and runs off. At this point in the story, the teacher can lead students to draw inferences from the text about James's situation.

"Why do you think James took Tama's apple?"

"Why do you think James does not have a lunch?"

"Hmmm . . . James is always so mean to Tama. Why do you think James is so mean to Tama?"

The teacher can lead students toward inferences by linking background knowledge of bullies and hunger to the events in the book.

Monitoring Comprehension

Teachers can explicitly teach children to monitor their comprehension, constantly checking with themselves, "Is this making sense to me?" Good readers consistently monitor their comprehension; they know when they understand what they read, and they know when they don't. In order to teach students to monitor their own comprehension, they need to learn to recognize the difference between understanding and not understanding the text.

Nancy has students practice monitoring comprehension in a number of ways. A group of beginning readers might read a book chorally and then talk together about the meaning of each page, retelling what they read with small chunks of text. After it is clear that students can monitor their own understanding one page at a time, they might be asked to read several pages and then talk to a partner about the meaning of the text. After talking with a partner, it is still important that students share their interpretations with the group, so that the teacher and other students can help with any breakdowns in comprehension and so that children can learn that sometimes we interpret things in different ways that still make sense.

When Nancy's second graders were silently reading *The Giraffe and the Pelly and Me* (Dahl, 2001), a book with many unfamiliar words, students wrote questionable vocabulary words from the text on Post-it notes and stuck them to the pages where they found them. This helped students to monitor their comprehension without breaking up the reading. After they had finished reading a predetermined amount of text, the students discussed the words with which they'd had trouble, used various strategies to help one another with the words (with help from the teacher and a dictionary when necessary), and talked about what was happening in the book. When students disagreed about the meaning of some portion of text, the group looked back in the text to make clarifications.

Questioning

Comprehension instruction is about getting students to *ask* questions instead of answer them. When children ask questions before, during, and after reading, they become more engaged in the purpose for reading and in monitoring their own understandings. Readers can be taught to question themselves, the authors, and the texts they read (Raphael, 1984). There are many ways teachers can encourage productive questioning in their classrooms. Some of these are described here.

Question–Answer Relationships

One successful technique to helping students learn to ask questions of text is called Question–Answer Relationships (QAR; Raphael & Pearson, 1985). This technique was invented to help students differentiate the types of questions they asked of text. Students learned to identify "right there" questions, in which the answer to a question was explicitly stated in the text. They recognized "think and search" questions, which had answers in the text that required searching and some inferencing. "On my own" questions were those in which the question was generated by the reader's personal motivations and had to be answered by the reader's background knowledge. When children were gradually expected to take over the questioning role, they were able to ask more high-level questions of their text.

The book *Sélavi: A Haitian Story of Hope* (2004) by Youme, is a terrific story with which to illustrate the kinds of questions students might ask. This book, written long before the tragic and devastating 2010 earthquake, is a story of homeless children in Haiti who work together to protect one another and provide friendship. They begin to organize and with the help of community members, build a shelter for themselves and others like them. They eventually create Radyo Timoun, a children's radio station. QAR questions might include:

> *Right there:* "How did the children get food? How did some of the children become homeless? What did the children do after the home burned?"
> *Think and search:* "Why is Sélavi homeless? What made the children share? What sort of place did Sélavi go to in his efforts to get help from the adults?"
> *On my own:* "Why were there so many people with guns? What did they want? What does 'the might river' mean and what does it do? Do you have a might river in your life? Why do you think people were so cruel and burned Sélavi's new home?"

Thick and Thin Questions

Similar to QAR, Harvey and Goudvis (2007) encourage children to distinguish between types of questions as a way to help them focus on the most important aspects of a text. "Thick questions" are those that ask about the deep meaning of the text, whereas "thin questions" are less complex and typically ask for clarification, meanings of words, or require an answer of a number or yes or no. Students can be taught to identify thick and thin questions and begin to ask more thick questions. Harvey and Goudvis (2007) describe a classroom that uses 3" x 3" Post-it notes to mark thick questions and sticky flags to mark thin ones. Students write the questions on the Post-it notes and attempt to answer them on the back of the notes. They can later clarify them when and if they find the answers. QAR and thick and thin questions can be used to create more dialogic lessons, as we share in Chapter 8.

Questioning the Author

This strategy involves teachers in modeling how to ask the author questions (about what is in the text, the author's intentions, etc.) to help readers better understand the text and the author's purpose (Beck, McKeown, Hamilton, & Kucan, 1997). Good readers challenge the contents of a text when it doesn't make sense. This strategy helps students learn that sometimes a breakdown in comprehension is the fault of an unclear author, not that of a struggling reader. Some questions students might ask the author as they read include:

"What is the author trying to tell me?"
"Why is the author telling me that?"
"Is the author clear in his or her writing?"
"Is there a way the author could be clearer?" (Duke & Pearson, 2002)

Questioning Center

In Nancy's classroom, one of her learning centers for self-directed work is the questioning center. After lessons such as QAR and questioning the author, students are directed into the center with a self-selected book and a pencil. In a bucket placed in the center are "Questioning Center" forms (see Figure 7.3). Before and during reading, children think of questions they have about the characters, setting, conflict, author, or any other aspect of their book, and they write the questions on the left side of the form. When they finish reading the book (for beginning readers) or chapter (for more advanced readers), they write the answers to their questions on the right side. Sometimes the answers are found within the text and other times they are not (if they are "on my own" questions). These Questioning Center forms are not only tools for assisting comprehension but they can lead to such inquiry-based activities as Internet searches on topics.

Think-Aloud

An instructional strategy with a strong research base is the think-aloud. A think-aloud involves making your thoughts audible and public, saying what you are thinking while you are performing a task (Duke & Pearson, 2002). When teachers think aloud in front

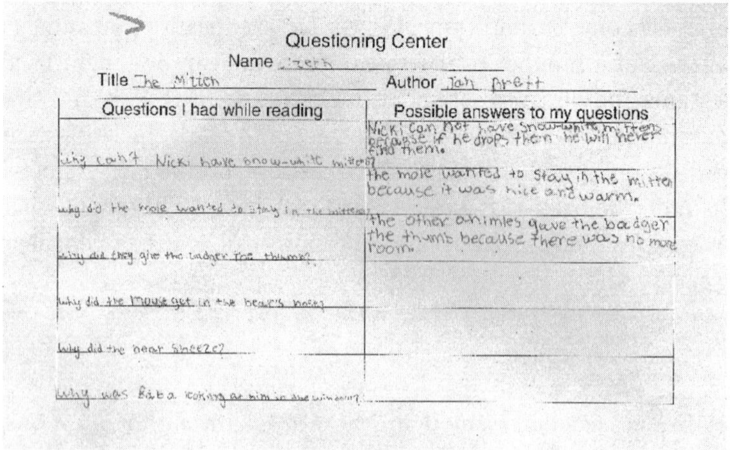

Questioning Center

Name Izeth

Title The Mitten Author Jan Brett

Questions I had while reading	Possible answers to my questions
why can't Nicki have snow-white mittens?	Nicki can not have snow-white mittens because if he drops them he will never find them.
why did the mole wanted to stay in the mitten?	the mole wanted to stay in the mitten because it was nice and warm.
why did they give the badger the thumb?	the other animles gave the badger the thumb because there was no more room.
why did the mouse get in the bear's nose?	
why did the bear sneeze?	
why was Baba looking at him in the window?	

FIGURE 7.3. Questioning center.

of their students, they demonstrate the effective comprehension strategies they want children to use independently. Thinking aloud makes teaching *metacognitive*. It helps learners "think about their thinking" and thus monitor their comprehension. When teachers think aloud, they provide students a glimpse into the mind of a good reader with examples of "inner conversations" (Harvey & Goudvis, 2007) readers have with text.

Vicky demonstrates the think-aloud technique during read-aloud time or shared reading. To model how to make inferences during reading, Vicky selected Amy Littlesugar's *Jonkonnu: A Story from the Sketchbook of Winslow Homer* (1996). Beginning with the colorful illustrations, Vicky modeled how to infer what the characters were feeling by the expressions on their faces.

> "When I first picked up this book, my eyes were drawn to the man on the front cover. I noticed that he is wearing a colorful outfit, while the little girls are dressed in ordinary clothes. I wonder what that means. I'll bet he is going to a party or a festival of some kind. His face looks peaceful and calm, so he is probably doing something he really wants to do. There are two little girls—one is on the back side of the fence. She's not smiling. I wonder what she might be thinking."

Vicky continued the read-aloud as she encouraged children to study the character faces and make inferences about the story. She turned to a page with a man and three women sitting down to lemonade and cookies in the afternoon.

> "When I try to make inferences, I also listen to the dialogue between the characters to figure out what's going on. 'He better be careful,' warned the gentleman on the ladder-back chair. 'Folks 'round here, they don't take kindly to strangers comin'

and pokin' their noses into things.' When I read this, I think there might be some trouble ahead for Mr. Homer."

Vicky continued through the story, stopping to allow the students to think aloud and make inferences, but also modeling attention to specific words. The Southern dialect demonstrated through the characters' dialogue was also a topic to be discussed.

"I noticed that when the characters are talking, the g's were left off the end of words like *lookin'* and *workin'*. Have you ever heard words like this? This is how an author shows that the speakers are from the South. It's called a Southern dialect."

Vicky's think-aloud led to an instructional conversation about dialect. The children explored how talk is different from written language and why it is important to understand the difference in ways to communicate. Through Vicky's think-aloud model, the students were able to "think through" the reading and dig more deeply into the meaning by using strategies that will eventually become automatic.

Determining Important Ideas in a Text

At the beginning of this chapter, you read how critical it is that children understand the text they are reading and the factors that can influence that understanding. Children are asked daily to read a variety of messages in a variety of formats, from textbooks to Internet advertising. Some of the facts and opinions they absorb are useful, some are not. They must learn to distinguish between the two in order to make appropriate decisions.

Determining important ideas (Palinscar & Brown, 1984) is one strategy readers use to wade through vast amounts of detail in order to infer big ideas and themes. Students underline parts of text, highlight key words and phrases, record notes on sticky pads, and use highlighting and comment applications on the computer. Teachers use many resources to draw students' attention to important facts and rich details.

Vicky explored the strategy with a group of fifth graders. The students had strong verbal skills, but often showed misconceptions in the comprehension of written text. She asked the students to create a double-entry journal in their response notebooks. To model the double-entry journal, Vicky drew one using the "Windows Journal" software on her laptop. One column was labeled "Topic" and the second column was labeled "Key Details." Using the nonfiction text *Different Places, Different Faces* (Davidson, 2003), she allowed the students some time to look through this book, which focuses on rain forest cultures across the globe. Vicky encouraged the students to select one section that they thought would be interesting. The group unanimously agreed to read about the Sing-Sing festivals of Papua, New Guinea.

Vicky read the text aloud the first time. Pictures of the elaborately dressed warriors and the colorful birds celebrated during the festival created enthusiasm in the students and provided a detailed visual to accompany the descriptive text. Students were allowed to make connections and comments and to ask questions about the reading. The students did not possess a great deal of background knowledge about the topic, so Vicky allowed them time to discuss the pictures and other text features with their elbow partner. After regaining the students' attention, Vicky used the text headings for the topic side of the double-entry journal and modeled how to return to the text to find the important ideas that would be recorded on the right.

Vicky modeled how to reread a section of text and ask oneself, "Is this detail important to know about the Sing-Sing festival? What other details do you think a reader would need to know?" Students created a bulleted list on the right side of the journal. Partners continued to read, stopping to ask each other if a point is important enough to record, while Vicky listened to the discussions. Vicky recalls Nadia and Damont debating the importance of information in the text box. Their discussion went like this:

NADIA: It says you need a plane or boat to get there.

DAMONT: Is that important to know about the Sing-Sing?

NADIA: Yes, transportation is important.

DAMONT: But I don't think that tells about the festival.

Both students made good arguments, asked the right questions, and carefully considered the importance of the details. The students moved on to other sections of the text to collect important ideas. The double-entry journal gave them a place to record and categorize information, which led to a deeper understanding of the text. Reading small sections and pausing to question their relationship and importance to the overall topic drew students' attention to details they may otherwise have missed, thereby heightening their comprehension.

Summarizing

One of the most important skills for readers to learn, and one of the most challenging to teach, is summarization. Summarizing is not merely a retelling of the text. Students have to be able to dispense with unnecessary information, interpret vocabulary, analyze events, and, at times, determine the author's purpose. Teaching readers to summarize requires explicit demonstration and thinking aloud and much practice by the children with feedback from the teacher. A few strategies for teaching summarization follow.

Rules for Summaries

Duke and Pearson (2002) describe the work of researchers who have taught children rules for creating summaries. The teacher explains the rules and models how to use them. The children participate in both group and individual practice. Teachers give feedback, helping children create excellent summaries. The strategy should be repeated often. The rules are as follows:

1. Delete unnecessary material.
2. Delete redundant material.
3. Compose a word to replace a list of items.
4. Compose a word to replace individual parts of an action.
5. Select a topic sentence.
6. Invent a topic sentence if one is not available (Duke & Pearson, 2002, p. 221).

GIST Procedure

The GIST procedure (Cunningham, 1982) stands for generating interactions between schemata and texts. This strategy assists readers and writers as they organize notes for class discussions, research, or summary writing. Teachers first model each stage of the process.

1. Read one sentence from a nonfiction text to the class and then help students summarize that sentence in 15 words or less.
2. Read a whole paragraph and have the class summarize the paragraph in 15 words or less.
3. Read a whole section and have students summarize it in 15 words or less. Write the summaries on the board and negotiate the best ways to include the important material.
4. Have students work in pairs to continue to summarize sections of the text.

Graphic Organizers for Summarizing

Graphic organizers, or visual representations of text, assist students with many comprehension strategies, including summarizing. Vicky taught summarizing to a small group of struggling fourth-grade readers who had revealed an inability to find and support the main idea of a passage. Students created an organizer in their response journals to write details from the text that would support the main idea (see Figure 7.4).

Students read a short two-paragraph passage from the biography *Matthew Henson, Arctic Explorer* (Podojil, 2000) to practice identifying main idea and supporting details. Vicky modeled how to read through a portion of text and predict the main idea. She recorded her predictions in the top box of the organizer. Then she modeled how to return to the text, select a key phrase, and record it below the main idea. To encourage the students to constantly monitor and focus their thinking, she asked them, "Does this detail support the main idea?" Heads nodded up and down in agreement. Vicky continued, "How do you know?"

Kandace replied, "It shows how much he wanted to learn and where he wanted to go when he grew up." Next, Vicky asked the students to find a second important detail that also supported the main idea and record it into the graphic organizer. Students took a few minutes to review the text and record another piece of information. Again, she asked students to share a detail they selected.

Main Idea:

Supporting Details:

- _____
- _____
- _____

FIGURE 7.4. Graphic organizer for determining importance in text.

Manuel chimed in, "He had dreams to see the world because he liked to read maps." Once the organizer was completed, they turned over the page. Vicky scribed a group summary on a chart based on the concepts recorded in the organizer. She asked the students to try to write their own summaries using the chart as a guide. She decided to try the same format with two more sections of text, each longer in length. Once students had completed the organizers, she instructed them to write their own short summaries. Students read their summaries to a partner, compared these to the organizers, and gave one another feedback on details that may have been missing. While more summary practice would follow, the organizers proved to be a key strategy to help kids analyze the reading. Teaching students to paraphrase a summary can help them distinguish between a laundry list of facts and a true summary of the author's message.

Understanding Text Structures

When teachers teach students to use the structure and organization of texts to organize their understanding and recall of important ideas, children comprehend better. The idea is that if we teach children how different types of texts are structured, they can transfer the knowledge and apply it to new texts with similar structures. Teachers can teach story structure to children through story maps to guide children's comprehension of stories. They can also teach the structure of the many kinds of nonfiction texts. Figure 7.5 lists several kinds of texts and their characteristics.

Vicky was working with a group of fourth graders who were struggling with comprehension. In the lesson, the students were analyzing two texts, discussing how the authors had chosen to present their ideas. The first article was about astronaut Ellen Ochoa. Vicky read the passage aloud to the students for the first reading and then posed the following question for a partner discussion: "What clue words can you find to help decide what kind of text the author used?" Students turned to their partners to decide and underlined words and phrases such as *first, finally, before long, a year later,* and *as a child.* Each pair shared one underlined word or phrase. The students referred to the

Sequence	Text information is presented in chronological order. Text clues include *first, next,* and *finally* or are historically ordered by dates.
Comparison	Text information is presented by comparing and contrasting two or more topics. Frequently includes the words *like, both, similar, contrast.*
How-to	Text is organized as a series of steps, often accompanied by flowchart diagrams or numbered directions.
Description	Texts that describe the topic using sensory imagery, strong adjectives, and vivid details to paint a picture for the reader.
Categorical texts	Texts that describe and distinguish, often found in science.
Problem–solution	Text information is presented as a problem with accompanying solutions.
Cause and effect	Text is organized as a set of events and the corresponding causes.

FIGURE 7.5. Nonfiction text structures and characteristics.

chart of structure types and decided that the author had used *chronological sequencing* to organize the passage.

The second article, about astronaut Mae Jemison, was read by students in partner groups. They were again instructed to search for clue words and phrases to help them identify which structure the author had used. Vicky listened to the group discussions. One pair of students had underlined several phrases, but they couldn't decide on the text structure.

HECTOR: This one is sequence too. It tells a list of all the things she did. And I found the word *first* in this sentence. (*Points* to "In 1992, she took her first trip into space aboard *Endeavor.*") Then, it says after in this sentence . . . (*Points to another sentence.*)

VICKY: Yes, *first* is a clue word for sequence. (*Turns to the other student.*) What type of structure do you think it is?

BILLY: Cause and effect.

VICKY: Tell me more. Why do you think it is cause and effect?

BILLY: It says, "*Because* of her experiences, she decided to help others by becoming a doctor." Then it says what she did because of that. She *went* to other countries and worked with people in Africa, Asia . . . (*Looks back at the book.*) and Latin America.

VICKY: You both have good arguments, and the author may be using more than one type of text. Reread and search for more phrases. See if you can decide which one the author used more than the other.

Labels	Help the reader identify what they are seeing.
Photographs	Help the reader see exactly what something looks like.
Captions	Help the reader better understand a picture of photograph.
Cutaways	Help the reader understand something by looking at it from the inside.
Maps	Help the reader understand where things are in the world.
Types of print	Help the reader by emphasizing certain words.
Close-ups	Help the reader see details in something small.
Table of contents	Help the reader identify key topics in the book in the order they are presented.
Index	An alphabetical list of almost everything covered in the text, with page numbers.
Glossary	Helps the reader define words contained in the text.

FIGURE 7.6. Text conventions to teach young readers. Based on Miller (2002).

The boys continued to search and compare their results to the anchor chart of key-words from the previous page. After finding "*As a result*," they decided that the author was using more cause-and-effect techniques because each paragraph showed actions Mae Jemison took only after the author had explained what had caused her to make those choices.

What careful reading the students had to do! They searched closely and realized that the author had left clues. When it came time to answer questions independently, the students referred to what they had underlined in the texts to complete the questions.

Using Text Conventions

Nonfiction texts are full of features and conventions that can aid readers in understanding. But many children ignore these features because they do not know their purposes or how they help with the meaning of the text. When teachers point out, explain, define, and invite discussion on text conventions, they assist students in reading all kinds of texts (see Figure 7.6).

COMPREHENSION WITHIN CULTURALLY RESPONSIVE READING INSTRUCTION

Comprehension instruction lends itself to culturally responsive instruction probably more than any other component of reading instruction. Teachers can find books that engage students and reflect their backgrounds, identities, and interests. They can choose books that focus on important messages they want their classes to learn. They can choose texts with particular language and dialect forms that match those of their students and expose students to new language forms. Comprehension strategy instruction is often best conducted in pairs and small groups for dialogic instruction. When teachers focus on the reader, the activity of reading, and the text, they can plan instruction that is appropriately rigorous for all learners while still keeping instruction within children's ZPDs. The weaving of research-based reading instruction and culturally responsive instruction can be achieved when teachers commit to both agendas.

CHAPTER 8

More Comprehension Tools
Vocabulary and the Instructional Conversation

In Jodi's combined first- and second-grade classroom, which serves mostly white and Hispanic rural students, one group of students is struggling with the meaning of the word *bully*. Simon believes that the word means a person who physically harms someone. Below, Jodi guides an instructional conversation with a group of seven first and second graders (all of whom happen to be white, except Alex, who is an ELL child born in the United States of Mexican parents). Jodi had just asked if they had ever witnessed a bully. (Question marks inside brackets indicate we could not understand exactly what the child said.)

> ASHLEY: I . . . I saw someone take Jason's [?? food item] and I told them.
>
> JODI: You told? Who did you tell?
>
> SIMON: (*interrupting*) That's not a bully . . . I mean, he's not a bully.
>
> JODI: Why do you say that?
>
> SIMON: He did something bad, I mean, he stole. But he didn't hurt someone.
>
> ASHLEY AND MARCUS: He did! Yea . . .
>
> SIMON: Well, I mean . . .
>
> JODI: What? What do you mean, Simon?
>
> SIMON: Well, no one got hurt (*sarcastically*). Did he break her arm or something? Was he starving to death? I mean . . . what he did was bad . . . [??] punished, but he didn't hurt anybody.
>
> MARCUS: I think . . .
>
> ASHLEY: No . . .
>
> ALEX: I think . . .

SIMON: What I am trying to say is . . .

JODI: *(to Alex)* Alex, you are trying to say something? What do you think?

ALEX: I think Jason was hurt. I think he was hurt because he wanted [??the food item] and it was his own . . .

JODI: What do you mean by *hurt?*

SIMON: I mean . . .

JODI: Let's let Alex explain. He has an idea and he wants to explain. Being hurt doesn't always mean your body is hurt. Alex?

MARCUS: Yea. He was hurt *inside.* My . . .

ASHLEY AND OTHERS: Yea! [Some unintelligible speech.]

JODI: So, hurt can happen inside, like when you get your feelings hurt or you are upset about something.

KIDS: Yea . . .

JODI: So, if someone hurts you on the inside, is that person a bully? (*A whole 3 seconds of silence follows.*)

KIDS: Yea . . .

MARCUS: Yes, he hurt him.

Word knowledge is complex. When children learn the meanings of new words, it is not an "all-or-nothing" experience. They do not go from a total lack of knowledge of a word to full and complete knowledge. Instead, word knowledge falls along a continuum; sometimes students' word knowledge is quite vague and filled with misconceptions. Or they might use a word well in one context but poorly in another. Because of its complexity, word knowledge is difficult to assess and teach. Jodi did some things well in this conversation about vocabulary, but she also could have limited Alex's oral language in some ways. We further analyze this brief conversation later in the chapter.

There is no one best way to teach word meanings. However, most educators interested in children's developing word knowledge agree that teachers should lead discussions with students in which they grapple with the meanings of words in the context the words are used. Thus, a primary tool for research-based, culturally responsive teaching of vocabulary (and deeper meanings of texts) is the *instructional conversation* (Goldenberg, 1993; Tharp & Gallimore, 1993; Saunders & Goldenberg, 1996). The instructional conversation (IC) is a structured form of dialogue that begins with teachers setting a goal about the content they want students to learn through the dialogic lesson. Saunders and Goldenberg (1996) define ICs as when:

> Teacher and students engage in discussion about something that matters to the participants, has a coherent and discernible focus, involves a high level of participation, allows teacher and student to explore ideas and thoughts in depth, and ultimately helps students arrive at higher levels of understanding about topics under discussion (e.g., content, themes, and personal experiences related to a story). (p. 142)

Not all academic talk is instructional conversation. Classroom talk can be merely "dialogue" or "discussion" if it is not rigorous and does not advance the thinking of students (McIntyre et al., 2006). This chapter links vocabulary instruction and the instructional conversation because they are two key tools for helping students comprehend. We include research-based word knowledge and vocabulary instruction such as word-learning strategies, modeling, using the context of passages, webbing, word play, and word derivation (Bear et al., 2004; Graves & Watts-Taffe, 2002). We begin with research on vocabulary instruction, followed by principles and strategies for teaching vocabulary. We then present examples of ICs that help children build word knowledge and a healthy "word consciousness" or "word awareness" (Graves & Watts-Taffe, 2002; Nagy & Scott, 2000), and which also helps readers develop deeper meanings of texts.

RESEARCH ON VOCABULARY LEARNING AND INSTRUCTION

The research on vocabulary is focused on two primary areas: how children learn vocabulary and how teachers teach vocabulary. The two are related, of course, but researchers are still attempting to understand the relationship. We know that children's home environments have much to do with their vocabulary development (Hart & Risley, 1995), but school instruction makes a difference, too.

Word Learning

Linguists are fascinated by how children learn words. They have studied why there is often an explosion of word knowledge in 4-year-olds and why some children develop elaborate vocabularies early, whereas others do not. All agree on the importance of word learning and have concern when children lag behind. Word learning is essential because vocabulary strongly influences listening and reading comprehension. Indeed, vocabulary knowledge is the best indicator of verbal ability, and the lack of a strong vocabulary can be a crucial factor in school failure (Graves & Watts-Taffe, 2002; Hart & Risley, 1995; Stahl & Fairbanks, 1986).

Word learning is highly complex because words are so complex. As we showed in the conversation that opened this chapter, "knowing" a word is a matter of degrees; one can "sort of" know what a word means. Sometimes, learners might be able to use the word accurately but not define it. Or, people can use a word correctly in one context but incorrectly elsewhere. And of course, words have different meanings, and many children and adults learn some meanings and not others.

We learn different sorts of words in different ways. People tend to learn function words (e.g., *the, and, whether*) in the context of speaking, listening, reading, and writing. They can learn content words (e.g., *spices, weather, gleeful*) in the same way, but often need more explicit instruction to learn them (Anderson & Nagy. 1991; Nagy & Scott,

2000). What makes the learning of both function and content words so difficult is that words do not have only one connotation. Anderson and Nagy (1991) show how the literal meaning of a word is not always tenable. Consider the following sentence.

Uncle Jim kicked the bucket.

Most adults automatically read this sentence as *Uncle Jim died*. But until children learn the multiple connotations of words, they will picture Uncle Jim putting his foot to a bucket and sending the bucket across the room. These sorts of connotations are learned mostly through discussion with others about words. In talking about words, phrases, and their meanings, children begin to develop a "word consciousness," which is an awareness of and interest in words and their meanings. It includes a cognitive and affective stance toward words (Anderson & Nagy, 1991; Graves & Watts-Taffe, 2002; Nagy & Scott, 2000). This concept is important because it would be impossible to directly teach all the words children need to learn. Nagy and Scott (2000) explain:

> Not only are there too many words to learn, but there is too much to learn about each one; thus learning words must occur through other means than explicit vocabulary instruction. Instruction must provide multiple encounters with the word. Knowing a word cannot be identified with knowing a definition. Knowing a word means begin able to do things with it. More like knowing how to use a tool than it is like being able to state a fact. (p. 273)

Hence, for teachers, vocabulary instruction must be about more than just the meanings of words. It must be about how words are used in the English language to create multiple meanings.

Vocabulary Instruction

Because word learning is so complex and still somewhat mysterious, vocabulary instruction is also challenging. While studies show there is no superior method for teaching vocabulary, research has shown that some practices clearly do *not* work. Children do not learn words and how to use them through memorizing definitions (Beck & McKeown, 1991; Blachowicz & Fisher, 2000; Graves & Watts-Taffe, 2002; Nagy & Scott, 2000; Shanahan & Beck, 2006). In one example, Miller and Gildea (1987) had students generate sentences after they were given definitions of unfamiliar words, and the sentences clearly showed that little learning had occurred. The researchers concluded that the instructional practice was "pedagogically useless" (Nagy & Scott, 2000, p. 277).

While much vocabulary is learned incidentally, teachers can create classroom opportunities that encourage vocabulary development. Most educators recommend that teachers stock their classrooms with rich literature and provide opportunities for wide reading, word play, and much conversation about words. Although it is almost impossible for researchers to conclude that any of these practices cause vocabulary learning, there is evidence that these opportunities are correlated with strong vocabularies (Beck

& McKeown, 1991; Blachowicz & Fisher, 2000; Graves & Watts-Taffe, 2002; Nagy & Scott, 2000).

Studies have shown that *explicit* instruction of words can also be useful. Studies of explicit practices included planned conversations around words, word play, teaching rules for using the context of sentences to figure out targeted words, semantic mapping of words, and instruction on roots and affixes. All these strategies have been shown in well-designed studies to increase students' word learning (Beck & McKeown, 1991; Blachowicz & Fisher, 2000; Graves & Watts-Taffe, 2002; Nagy & Scott, 2000). These researchers also found that when teachers use varied strategies and repeated exposure to the words, students retain more. Again, the strongest forms of direct instruction of vocabulary are those in which the teacher engages students in a discussion about a word's meaning (Nagy & Scott, 2000). Immersion in rich language environments combined with explicit instruction in vocabulary and repeated exposure seem to have the biggest effects.

Vocabulary learning is essential and even more complex for ELLs. It may be the most difficult task facing teachers of ELLs (Linan-Thompson & Vaugh, 2007). As we said in previous chapters, instruction that is effective for native speakers of English is also effective with ELLs, with some adaptations (Amendum & Fitzgerald, 2010; Linan-Thompson & Vaugn, 2007; Shanahan & Beck, 2006). The same components of teaching reading (phonemic awareness, phonics, fluency, vocabulary, and comprehension) still apply. Vocabulary is particularly critical for ELLs because they have not had the same opportunities as native speakers to learn words orally, prior to learning to read. In their reviews of the very few studies ever conducted comparing vocabulary instruction for native speakers and ELLs, Amendum and Fitzgerald (2010) and Shanahan and Beck (2006) found that the same principles lead to greater learning of vocabulary for all learners of vocabulary, such as repetition of words and meaningful or "deep processing" (p. 430).

PRINCIPLES FOR TEACHING VOCABULARY

Figure 8.1 lists general principles for teaching vocabulary.

ASSESSING VOCABULARY

Assessment of vocabulary has long been puzzling to educational researchers and psychologists. Because word knowledge is not an all-or-nothing phenomenon, it would be inaccurate to give students either a "yes she knows it" or "no, she does not know it" score. Beck and McKeown (1991) discuss the limitations of multiple-choice tests, noting that they do not test how well one knows a word; correct responses do not differentiate between words that are known well and words that are known vaguely. One famous example of excellent work in vocabulary assessment from decades past is that of Cronbach (1943, cited in Beck & McKeown, 1991). Cronbach conducted a study in which students were asked to distinguish between examples of a word and nonexamples that

- Offer students a choice in the words they want to learn, when possible.
- Expose students to rich literature.
- Find ways to repeat exposure to the same words in different contexts.
- Have students map concept words to illustrate relationships among words and ideas.
- Encourage wide reading.
- Encourage discussion of words.
- Use multimedia methods (especially for ELLs) as often as possible.
- Teach students about regional word usage and how dialects differ in vocabulary.
- Teach children how to use dictionaries and other reference aids, such as a thesaurus, to learn word meanings and to deepen knowledge of word meanings. Many reference tools on the Internet are easy and efficient to use.
- Teach children how to use information about word parts (affixes, base words, word roots) to figure out the meanings of words in text.
- Teach students how to use context clues to determine word meanings.
- Model your interest in word meanings.
- Practice "think-alouds" about word meanings in front of your students.
- Combine immersion in rich language environments with explicit instruction in vocabulary and repeated exposure to words for the biggest effects.

FIGURE 8.1. Principles for teaching vocabulary.

might be confused with the word. His assessment was a much more precise assessment of what students knew about those words. Yet, these sorts of assessments do not exist for teachers because the words teachers and children want to learn are contextual. They have to do with the content the class is studying and the goals of the teacher, school, and district.

Teachers should, however, attend to vocabulary assessment through observation, listening, talking with children, and examining students' written work for strong, average, or worrisome (weak) vocabulary use. It is often easy to diagnose a child who has a strong vocabulary. These children use words that surprise and humor us. But it is easy to neglect the child whose vocabulary should concern us. Teachers must make special efforts to attend to words children use and do not use. If some students seem to lack a rich vocabulary, these might be the children ripe for the explicit, research-based strategies we describe below.

STRATEGIES FOR TEACHING VOCABULARY

The following strategies are supported by research and fit with the principles for culturally responsive instruction we highlight in this book. Because all research on vocabulary instruction recommends use of a variety of strategies and repeated exposure, we invite teachers to use as many different strategies as they can across the school week, month, and year.

Modeling and Think-Aloud

Teachers should model their own interest in words and their word consciousness. They can do this with think-alouds, as described in Chapter 7, to wonder about a word's meaning. A think-aloud about word meanings from the book *Uncle Jed's Barbershop* (Mitchell, 1993) might sound something like this.

"In the sentence '*I know that three hundred dollars delayed him from opening the barber shop,*' I am wondering about the word *delayed*. Three hundred dollars did what to the barbershop? It didn't stop it from opening because Uncle Jed finally got his barbershop at the end of the book. But he had to wait many years because he had to pay for Sarah Jean's operation. Maybe *delayed* means *wait* or *slow down*. That three hundred dollars did slow Jed down from getting his barbershop."

This sort of modeling of thinking teaches word consciousness and interest in word learning.

Student Choice

When students experience some sense of ownership in what they learn, they tend to learn the material better and to sustain the learning longer. Learning vocabulary is no exception. Studies have shown that allowing students to select the words they want to learn improved comprehension (Blachowicz & Fisher, 2000). In addition to simple choice, training students on how to choose the words also helps. Students who received instruction in a process showing them how to recognize words to learn that were important to the selection learned more than those who did not receive that training (Blachowicz & Fisher, 2000).

Teachers can use children's reading practices as one way to help them choose words to learn. Teachers might ask children to choose a book they like that has several words of which they are unsure. Children enjoy this sort of activity more and learn more when they work in pairs or small groups. Teachers can then invite the children to write 5–10 words from the book that they *think* they know but are not totally sure. They can fill out a prediction chart (see Figure 8.2) or choose to fill out one of the webs (shown later in this chapter). Then, after doing a dictionary or thesaurus search, they complete the chart. The teacher then invites children to "teach" the class a new word or two. The words from the prediction chart in Figure 8.2 came from Pat Mora's *Dona Flor* (2005). Mora often writes in both English and Spanish.

Reading Aloud Rich Literature

Great children's literature is a key tool for teaching vocabulary. Think of the students in Ellen's sixth-grade classroom (mentioned in Chapter 6) who loved Jack Prelutsky's (1983) *Nightmares: Poems to Trouble Your Sleep*. The students read and reread the poems

Word	What do I think it means?	What do my resources say?
respect		
commotion		
exhausted		
mesa		
trickled		
pueblo		
luscious		
estrella		

FIGURE 8.2. Word prediction chart.

and memorized many of them. Had Ellen known better (she didn't; she was in her first year of teaching), she would have used her students' general interest in these poems to select words they wanted to learn. In only two lines of the poem "Bogeyman," there are several words she is sure the students would have chosen to learn:

In the *desolate depths* of a *perilous* place
The bogeyman *lurks* with a *snarl* on his face.

Some of Ellen's students probably did learn these definitions incidentally. But by combining exposure to rich literature with explicit teaching and student choice in which words to learn, Ellen could have created a much more powerful learning experience.

Often, a terrific piece of literature is valued for its story, its deeper meaning, or its illustrations, and word meanings are secondary. After all, children can understand stories well without knowing all the words. For example, the book *Brave Irene* (Steig, 1986) is a story of a young girl who braves a winter storm to take a handmade dress from her mother's sewing machine and deliver it to the duchess. The story is gripping, and children ages 5 through adult love it. Some of the words and phrases Steig uses to convey the intensity of the adventure include *coaxed, splendid, whirled, squinting, resented, cautioned, pressed on, squalled, wrestled, walloped, snatched, trudge, plodding, strode, delirious.* Even more impressive are the sentences that use ordinary words in unique ways, such as "*The ball gown flounced out and went waltzing through the powdered air with tissue-paper attendants.*" Teachers can take advantage of children's deep connections with stories to explicitly teach vocabulary. While most teachers teach target words before or during a reading lesson, some literature is best if dissected after the reading. This is one such book. Children will be much more interested in learning words like *delirious* and *squalled* after experiencing those words in the story. A few other books that have words with multiple meanings include:

The King Who Rained (Gwynne, 1970)

Pun and Games: Jokes, Riddles, Rhymes, Daffynitions, Tairy Fales, and More Word Play for Kids (Lederer, 1996)

How Much Can a Bare Bear Bear? (Cleary, 2005)

A Chocolate Moose for Dinner (Gwynne, 1976)

Dear Deer (Barretta, 2007)

In a Pickle: And Other Funny Idioms (Terban, 1983)

Teach Us Amelia Bedelia (Parrish, 1977)

Eight Ate: A Feast of Homonym Riddles (Terban, 1982)

Teaching about Dialects

We recommend that teachers learn as much as they can about the regional and cultural dialects of their students, as suggested in Chapter 4. One of the primary features of dialect differences is word meaning. Do you carry a *pocketbook, purse*, or *handbag*? Do you drink *cola, soft drinks, pop*, or *cokes*? What words from Latin America do we all know? What new words can we learn? Children become fascinated by word usage and are familiar with multiple uses of everyday words such as these. If we talk about them, it increases students' word consciousness and acceptance of linguistic differences.

Context Clues

Children can be taught to use the context of a sentence to figure out the meanings of unknown words (Kuhn & Stahl, 1998). Sometimes words are defined directly in sentences, but many times a synonym or embedded definition or description of the word will provide a clue to the meaning of the target word. In the following sentence, a definition is provided indirectly for the word *relentless*.

> She would not give up; in fact, she was relentless.

Teachers can use think-alouds to illustrate how readers can use the context of sentences to understand new words. However, to be cautionary, this strategy does not work well to predict or identify words in print that students already know from oral language, as researchers once thought (Stanovich, 2000). This strategy is reserved for learning the *meanings* of words through sentence context.

In Nancy's classroom, when a guided reading group was reading *The Giraffe and the Pelly and Me* (Dahl, 2001), they encountered many new words. Nancy taught the students how to use context clues to help them determine the meaning of the new words in the following excerpt.

> The Pelly is starving, the Monkey is famished and I am perishing with hunger. The Pelly needs fish. The Monkey needs nuts and I am even more difficult to feed. (p. 23)

Nancy began with the following statement: "Hmmm . . . I just read this [she reads the excerpt aloud] and I'm not sure about the word *famished*. One strategy I can use to help me is to look at the words and sentences surrounding the mystery word to help me figure out what it means. I've heard the word *starving* before. Jessica, what do you think *starving* means?"

"If you're starving, you're really hungry. You haven't eaten in a long time," Jessica offered.

"OK, so according to Jessica the Pelly is really hungry. Let's read the next sentence to see if we get some more clues. 'The Pelly needs fish.' Yep. We already know he's hungry. 'The Monkey needs nuts and I am even more difficult to feed.' José, what do you think Monkey's problem is, based on the last sentence?"

"I think the Monkey is hungry cuz he *needs* nuts, just like it said the Pelly *needs* fish. If you need nuts and fish, you're hungry probably."

"Great. So according to José, the Monkey and the Pelly are hungry. Let's look at the excerpt from the book again. 'The Pelly is starving, the Monkey is *famished*. . . . . . Anybody want to make a guess about what the word *famished* means now?"

Leonel speaks up. "It's another word for *hungry*."

"I think I agree with you, Leonel. *Famished* and *starving* both mean really hungry. It's cool how we used the word *starving*, which we knew, and the sentences after this one to figure out that the word *famished* means really hungry. This is a strategy for figuring out words you don't know. You use words and sentences around a word you don't know to help you figure out the meaning of the new word. Let's look back at the excerpt. It says 'and I am perishing with hunger.' Anybody want to guess what *perishing* means?"

Vocabulary Stair Steps

Based on the work of Beck, McKeown, and Kucan (2002), vocabulary stair steps are visual representations of synonyms that go from more basic to more specific or advanced. In the previous example, the words *hungry, starving,* and *famished* could have been written on vocabulary stair steps to help students visualize the progression of complexity in the words' meanings. It would look something like Figure 8.3. Figure 8.4 illustrates some vocabular stair steps from Nancy's class.

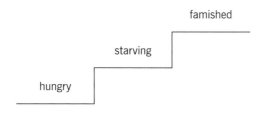

FIGURE 8.3. Stair-step vocabulary.

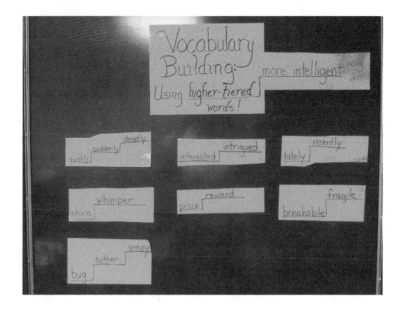

FIGURE 8.4. Nancy's stair steps.

Vocabulary Teams

One year, Nancy divided her class into two teams: the Vocabulary Vipers and the Word Wizards. When the students used new vocabulary words they had learned in science, social studies, mathematics, or reading *correctly* in the context of the instructional day, their vocabulary team got a point. For example, if a student made a comment about a character in a read-aloud that she seems to have "gone through a metamorphosis," that child would have earned a point if, in fact, that character had undergone a dramatic change and if the child used the word appropriately.

Semantic Webs

A semantic web is a way to organize information graphically according to categories. The target word is written in the middle of the web and associated words are written at the end of the spokes. Depending on whether the word is an adjective, adverb, or noun, the teacher can choose among these questions to ask the children to brainstorm responses to the word, such as: What is it? What is it like? What are some examples of it? What does it mean? What does it make you think of? What are similar words? What are some examples of its use? An example is shared in Figure 8.5.

Character Webs

The character web includes the name of the character from a book shared in class and associated features of the character at the end of the spokes. An example from *Brave Irene* might look like in Figure 8.6.

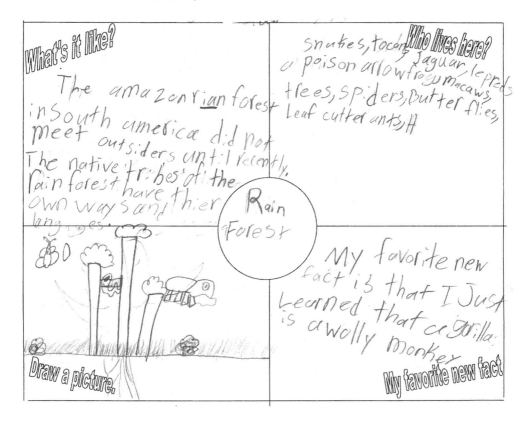

FIGURE 8.5. Semantic web.

Concept Webs

Some webs start with an idea or concept in their center, and children brainstorm related words (see Figure 8.7). Of course, webs such as these can be used to explore all sorts of words, such as synonyms, antonyms, analogies, and homonyms.

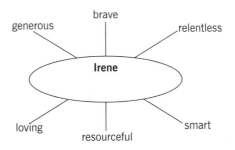

FIGURE 8.6. Character web.

FIGURE 8.7. Concept web.

Concept Ladders

The concept ladder is another graphic way to organize information that can help students learn words, concepts, ideas, and relationships among the ideas. These tools work well in science lessons (see Figure 8.8).

Semantic Feature Analysis

Semantic feature analysis (Anders, Bos, & Filip, 1984) is a tool that enables readers to compare several terms or concepts at once. The terms are placed in a grid, and students are asked to respond "yes" or "no" to questions relating to these concepts. The example in Figure 8.9 came from the book *Monster Bugs* (Penner, 1996).

Word Derivation

As children get older, vocabulary learning becomes more important, not less. They quickly must learn specialized vocabulary for science, social studies, mathematics,

What is a hurricane?	How are hurricanes formed?	Can people prevent hurricanes?
What are recent examples of hurricanes?	What happens to people and property in hurricanes?	How can people prepare for hurricanes?

FIGURE 8.8. Concept ladder for hurricanes.

	Sucks victims blood?	Lays eggs?	Is an insect?	Does it stink?
Bombardier beetle	no	yes	yes	yes
Giant waterbug	yes	yes	yes	no

FIGURE 8.9. Semantic feature analysis.

music, and anything else they want to learn about. Children who acquire some knowledge of word parts and how words are derived from other words will gain a huge advantage. Most words can be learned if the root or base of the word is learned, followed by prefixes and suffixes. Think of the word *biology.* If children learn that *bio* means *life* and that *ology* means *the study of,* they can quickly figure out the meanings of words such as *geology, topology, pharmacology, ecology, climatology,* and *astrology.* In Chapter 5 we described the word study program developed by Bear et al. (2004). Their program includes extensive word sorts and other activities for exploring word derivations.

Make Words Fun!

We all know that everyone learns more when they are having fun. Nancy's second graders loved Vocabulary Extravaganza. During one week they focused on the many new words they had learned throughout the year. Since *extravaganza* is one of Nancy's favorite words, she included it in the week's name. Much time was spent reading favorite books, playing vocabulary games such as Pictionary with white boards, synonym match, and charades in which kids acted out vocabulary words. The week culminated in a Vocabulary Parade, such as the one portrayed in the book *Miss Alaineus: A Vocabulary Disaster* (Frasier, 2007), in which kids dressed up as their favorite new vocabulary word and marched around school.

THE INSTRUCTIONAL CONVERSATION: TOOL FOR TACKLING TEXT

In Chapter 4 we described what typical classroom discourse looks like. The IRE sequence (Cazden, 1988)—in which a teacher initiates the discussion with a question, a student responds, and the teacher evaluates the response—is still the predominant way teachers lead classroom discussions, even though we know that these discussions are highly ineffective for learning. Surprisingly, in traditional classroom discussions, the teacher (one person) does twice or even three times as much talking as all students in the class *combined!*

In Chapter 4 we described what we call dialogic instruction, in which children participate in much discussion as they learn content. The instructional conversation (IC) is one type of dialogue that teaches content. Children are encouraged to talk with and learn from each other. The teacher facilitates this process by asking good questions and redirecting students as needed. In ICs the students talk more than the teacher. Researchers from the Center for Research on Education, Diversity, and Excellence (CREDE), at the University of California at Berkeley (mentioned in Chapter 1), have conducted multiple studies on ICs. From these studies, they have illustrated "indicators" of successful ICs (Figure 8.10).

Learning to conduct excellent ICs is not easy. In the study that grounds this research-based, culturally responsive reading model, the teachers found the IC the most challenging principle to practice. Jodi, the first/second-grade teacher in the opening vignette of this chapter, was a beginner at conducting ICs yet she conducted that particular IC well, for the most part. She had a definite goal for the content she wanted her students to learn, which included a thorough understanding of the concept of bully. This is important. ICs are not goal-less discussions on whatever students feel about a book or topic. They are intentional and designed to stimulate students' thinking.

Jodi also made sure that Simon did not dominate the conversation and so she jumped at the chance to involve Alex, the one ELL in the group. In typical class discussions, it is easy to permit the same children to contribute repeatedly. Jodi also asked high-level, open-ended questions that pushed students' thinking. "Why do you say that?" and "What do you mean?" are scaffolding questions that ask students to dig a bit deeper, to use vocabulary they might not be used to, and to form thoughts while forming sentences.

Jodi also made mistakes, common for all teachers attempting rigorous ICs. At one point, she saw where Alex was going, knew it was important, and said, "Let's let Alex explain. He has an idea, and he wants to explain." Yet, she went ahead and provided the answer for Alex! She said, "Being hurt doesn't always mean your body is hurt. Alex?" Alex had little else to say because his teacher had provided the words. That moment

---

The teacher:

1. Arranges the classroom to accommodate conversation between the teacher and a small group of students on a regular and frequent basis.
2. Has a clear academic goal that guides conversation with students.
3. Ensures that student talk occurs at higher rates than teacher talk.
4. Guides conversation to include students' views, judgments, and rationales using text evidence and other substantive support.
5. Ensures that all students are included in the conversation, according to their preferences.
6. Listens carefully to assess levels of students' understanding.
7. Assists students' learning throughout the conversation by questioning, restating, praising, encouraging, etc.
8. Guides the students to prepare a product that indicates the instructional conversation's goal was achieved.

FIGURE 8.10. Indicators of instructional conversations. From Center for Research on Education, Diversity, and Excellence (CREDE), University of California, Berkeley. *www.crede.berkeley.edu*. Reprinted by permission.

would have been a perfect opportunity for Alex to practice explaining a difficult concept, had Jodi allowed it.

In Mara's rural third-grade classroom, most of the children are white. She has seven nonwhite students, four of whom are ELLs (including Kevin and Lili in the lesson below). The conversations in her room were deeper than in Jodi's classroom, and students seemed to develop new understandings from their peers as well as from their teachers. Of course, the students in her classroom were older (by 1–3 years). But Mara was also more expert at scaffolding in-depth conversation. She seemed to be able to redirect misconceptions, pull more information out of the students, and encourage peer-to-peer talk and even argumentation—features of excellent ICs (Billings & Fitzgerald, 2002; Christoph & Nystrand, 2001). An excerpt from one of Mara's conversations illustrates these patterns. In this lesson, Mara leads a discussion of the book on Maya Lin, the woman who designed the Vietnam memorial. The children wrestle with concepts such as heritage, ancestors, and racism.

> MARA: I am going to move to having us read on our own today. But before I do, I want to reread one part . . . because I would like your reaction to this comment. (*Reads the section again, slowly and distinctly, about how some people were upset that someone of Chinese descent had won the competition to design the memorial. After she reads, there is a 2-second silence.*) Are there any questions or reactions to that statement in this text? (*2-second pause*) Rebecca?
>
> REBECCA: Even though Maya was Chinese heritage, she had the best design, and the people picked it because they liked it. And other people thought what *they* thought, and the people that picked it thought what *they* thought.
>
> MARA: What do *you* think?
>
> REBECCA: I think that it doesn't matter if she is Chinese, she should still win.
>
> MARA: Why do you think that?
>
> REBECCA: It doesn't matter where you come from, if you are black or white, you should be treated fairly.
>
> MARA: Do you think she was treated fairly?
>
> REBECCA: Well . . . no . . .
>
> BLAINE: (*interrupting*) Well, she *was* picked.
>
> CHARLIE: She was picked.
>
> HARPER: Yea, she was picked!
>
> [After more lively discussion and argument]:
>
> MARA: OK, listen to one another. . . . I like the way you interact with one another, and I want to keep talking without raising hands as long as we listen to each other. . . . Are there reactions to what has been said?
>
> LILI: I thought she was born in America, but her father was Chinese. And that makes her a little bit American. . . .

MARA: She was.

BLAINE: Oh. Well, she was . . . that makes her an *American.*

MARA: At one point, as you remember her reading, it says that her parents were from China. She was born in the United States.

BLAINE: So she is really American—she is just like us.

LILI: I agree that she . . .

ANN: Is she, um, is she honoring the Americans who died in the Vietnam War or is she honoring the Vietnamese?

MARA: What did it say in the text? Often we can find the answers in the text if we look back. (*Reads that only American soldiers' names were placed on the wall.*)

JENNIFER: There were Chinese people on there, too.

MARA: No, it says here American soldiers. The purpose of the memorial was to honor the Americans who lost their lives in the Vietnam War.

JENNIFER: Don't you think her idea was a little plain, though. I would also like to see the other people's ideas of [??].

MARA: The question that we're talking about is not if she *should* have won, do you remember? Let me look back at the text again. You guys are doing a really good job of thinking along these lines. (*Looks at Kara.*) I haven't heard from you. I'd love to hear your feelings.

KARI: I think it's kinda, like, um . . . like I was in a war, or something, and um . . . and I died and there was a Chinese person, like honoring me, and that would be kinda cool.

[More argument]

KEVIN: I know how they're feeling because their father or mother or somebody might have died in the Vietnam War. And they want to know if a Chinese or Vietnamese man killed their father or guy or [??] killed them. Well, they wouldn't want those people that their ancestors shot, the American ancestors, to bury their father or mother. So I can see why they would get mad. But Kari made a good point because a Chinese person is honoring the Americans, but I still don't think that would be right, though, because then that would show, I think, that would show a little mercy. I'm not being, like, racist or something like that, but it makes me mad because . . . a lot . . . the Chinese people. . . . Her ancestors might have killed 20 American soldiers, and those 20 American sons or daughters get mad because that Chinese lady [Maya Lin] is burying their American fathers. . . .

JENNIFER: She's just honoring them, she's not *burying* them.

[More conversation and some argument revealing some misconceptions about the Chinese]

HARPER: They're building this in America and she's. . . . I don't have anything against them, but she's Chinese, and she's building a pretty big thing in another country and she should be building it in like . . . in like . . . in a Chinese country.

MARA: Well, she was born here, in America, and. . . .

BOBBY: That's probably why she did it.

MARA: She's not . . . I think it's really interesting. I'm fascinated by all your responses. I'm fascinated by them. I disagree with some of what I heard. I feel like she designed this with her heart, and she did such a wonderful job. She's Chinese by heritage but that shouldn't have anything to do with her winning, and so I disagree with what some of you were saying, which is fine. That's a good thing for us to be able to disagree with each other and that you all feel comfortable doing that. I'm fascinated.

[Several more minutes of conversation]

MARA: And you know what we really brought up is that, in the book, they mention this controversy and we have it right here. So we brought it right into our room what happened when she was named the winner. Just as Rachel Carson was like that with the pesticides that we read about this morning. There was controversy about her life. So any time . . . you read about big things that happen in the world, there [might be] controversy. . . . Now, we're gonna buddy-up and let you all work in partnerships. Let's start with Rebecca and Ann. Girls, I have your materials here for you. . . .

In this instructional conversation, Mara feels free to disagree with her students, correct them when necessary, and allow her students to debate one another, all the while showing deep respect for their views. She and her class discuss the big ideas, the controversies of the book, not just the chronology. The students talk more than the teacher, and, despite some misconceptions about the role of the Chinese in the Vietnam War, they begin to understand a little bit about what Maya Lin went through when her sculpture proposal for the Vietnam Memorial in Washington, D.C. won the competition to honor the lives lost in that war.

Mara made some mistakes in this conversation, too, which is not uncommon when teachers first learn how to conduct ICs about controversial topics. First she privileges the United States over other countries by insisting that Maya Lin was an American (not a little bit American!). But more important, she allowed some misconceptions that border on racism to go unchallenged. While her students clearly heard more viewpoints than they would have had the IC not been conducted, some students still may not have been challenged enough. ICs are a powerful tool for constructing new understandings about the world, but they are not always easy to conduct.

Indeed, teachers often need help teaching their students how to participate in such conversations. First grade teacher and author Debbie Miller (2002) explicitly teaches her students how to participate in ICs around books. She tells them:

You know how readers make connections from the books they read to their lives, other books, and the world? When readers talk together about books, they make connections from the thinking of others to their own thinking, too. Whether it's to better understand a tricky part of text or talk about a favorite page, thoughtful readers engage in dialogue to better understand books and each other. (p. 96)

Miller (2002, p. 95) teaches her students to ask themselves the following questions before joining in an instructional conversation:

"Does what I have to say connect to the question or topic?"

"Can I connect what I have to say to what someone else has said?"

"Can I support what I have to say? What evidence or personal experience do I have to make my point?"

"Has someone else already said what I am about to say?"

"If I am speaking to disagree, can I state what I heard the other person say and explain how and why my thinking is different in a nice way?"

"Does what I want to say take the conversation deeper?"

VOCABULARY INSTRUCTION AND INSTRUCTIONAL CONVERSATIONS IN CULTURALLY RESPONSIVE CLASSROOMS

Vocabulary learning can be quite personal. The communities, homes, and cultural groups to which students belong are the sources for the development of word consciousness and understandings of words and word meanings. This knowledge should be valued and validated by the classroom teacher, and in this way, teachers build on students' home knowledge and linguistic patterns. Teachers can conduct all the vocabulary strategies in pairs or small groups to build on how students learn best.

As emphasized, vocabulary learning is critically important to reading comprehension for all learners, but even more so for ELLs. Many teachers have already witnessed the remarkable ability of their first- and second-generation immigrant students to pick up vocabulary from their friends, community, and teachers. But we should also not be satisfied that ELL students learn basic communication skills. We must have the same expectations for their vocabulary learning—especially academic vocabulary—as we do for all of our students, so that they are ensured the same educational opportunities.

Teachers can also build in much dialogic instruction by practicing the IC and by allowing small groups and pairs to discuss and argue about meanings of words. They can challenge students with books that include new words and concepts, rather than keeping to safe and predictable texts. In these ways, teachers can honor both research-based strategies and culturally responsive instruction.

CHAPTER 9

Writing

In Vicky's fifth-grade class, the students are conducting studies of their neighborhoods. The children live in different neighborhoods because many in the large urban district are bused long distances to school. To assist the students in writing their descriptive pieces, Vicky first modeled her own writing process, using an overhead projector to talk through her decisions on describing her neighborhood. Then she led the students in a lesson on word choice. After the chart of descriptive adjectives was completed by the class, the students selected three or more words they might use in their neighborhood descriptions and entered them in their writers' notebooks. Most students sat at round tables, while a few wrote directly on a computer. In the center of each table was a bin that included a children's dictionary, thesaurus, pencils, and crayons. The children on the computers had bookmarked dictionaries and a thesaurus for easy reference. The students had all the tools they needed and had begun to write.

Vicky stayed in the carpeted area a few minutes where she could observe the writers. She wrote two names of students she wanted to check in with, Marcus and Janine. They had offered little during the class lesson and had previously written only a few vague notes about their neighborhoods. Vicky was unsure whether they had walked through their neighborhood with their notebooks or interviewed an adult, as they were assigned. Indeed, when she spotted the two children, both were engaged in nonwriting activities. She invited them to bring their notebooks and come with her. She tapped a third child, Hector, and invited him to the group, too, as she knew he was struggling with basic word choice in all his writing.

She asked the students to repeat the directions for the assigned task and to share the notes they had generated about their neighborhoods. Then they each shared the words they had chosen from the morning lesson that would help them describe their neighborhoods with detail. When Vicky asked how they planned to use their words, Marcus and Janine claimed to be "stuck." Vicky asked them, "What are some things writers do when they are stuck?" The children responded by naming the resources they could go to for help, referring to the chart and the description the class had written together, other classroom tools, and each other. Vicky said to Janine, "Tell me about your neighborhood."

"We live in an apartment, and there are lots of cars, but we have trees in the back where I swing and my little sister slides sometimes."

After assistance from Vicky, it became clear that Janine was describing her neighborhood playground. She eventually added details such as a "yellow, twisty slide, wooden swings, and a large grassy field where kids play baseball."

Vicky turned to Hector, who had been listening intently to Janine's description. He held a digital Spanish–English dictionary and was eager to use the tool to enliven his description of the streets of his neighborhood. With guidance from Vicky, Hector was able to write that he lived in a neighborhood with "much green grass and hilly streets."

For some children, writing is easy. The words seem to flow naturally from their minds, through the pencil or keyboard and onto the page, with ideas fully developed, elegant grammar, and lively word choice. They tell funny stories, record dialogue, describe with detail, and develop a carefully laid-out plot. They make sound arguments backed with much evidence and convince their readers. This is not the majority of children.

For most children—like Marcus, Janine, and Hector—and even adults, writing is a challenge and is not easily learned. Like reading, writing skills do not develop naturally, but only through explicit teaching on *how* to write, much exposure to excellent writing, and ample opportunities to practice writing with corrective feedback. Like reading well, writing well requires background knowledge of the topic, vocabulary, knowledge of text structures or genre, and knowledge of the strategies that help writers focus their efforts and create products that bring to life the purpose for which they have written.

This chapter provides an overview of how writing instruction fits into the overall language arts instructional program in elementary classrooms. We describe the writing process and the writing workshop (its *promises* and *problems*) and the research-based writing strategies that can take place within a workshop environment. We also suggest principles for conducting the writing workshop that are especially important for diverse classrooms. First, we briefly review important research on writing and the teaching of writing.

RESEARCH ON WRITING AND WRITING INSTRUCTION

Elementary-age children develop from emergent writers who draw, scribble, and use random letters and letter-like forms to communicate a message to conventional writers, who use adult grammar, familiar organization, and lively word choice. As described in Chapter 2, even ELL writers follow the same general developmental patterns as native English speakers (Amendum & Fitzgerald, 2010; Samway, 2006). How does this development happen? In the past few decades, research on writing and the teaching of writing has provided some answers. The studies focused on what good writers do as they write and how teachers can create environments conducive for productive writers. As with reading, the field of writing research and instruction comes from multiple perspectives, which we address. While it is impossible to do an exhaustive research review here, we highlight key studies of writing processes and instruction and illuminate the promises and problems of some approaches.

Writers and Writing

We know from descriptions of young writers that some children learn to write even before they learn to read (Bissex, 1980; Clay, 1975), and we know that many children desire to write and to do so for many purposes, if encouraged. What goes on in the mind as people compose? Researchers have discovered that the way to understand how to help novice writers is to first understand what good writers do as they write (Emig, 1971; Florio & Clark, 1982; Flower & Hayes, 1980; Langer, 1986; Murray, 1980). Some researchers had high school students "think aloud" as they composed to explain their decisions while in the process of writing. These think-aloud protocols allowed researchers a window into the writing process of proficient writers. They discovered that writers participate in many of the same processes. For example, most writers do some *prewriting* activities such as brainstorming ideas, chatting with someone about their goals for writing, outlining the text they plan to write, or even viewing films, reading other texts, drawing, or just thinking before they actually compose.

Good writers also were observed creating messy *drafts* or early versions of their texts without attention to conventions. But the writers also regularly *revised* and *edited* their compositions as they composed, rather than waiting until they had completed an entire draft. They engaged in ongoing planning as they wrote (Langer, 1986), even young children. Finally, writers *published* their texts in some way by sharing it with someone else—their teacher, peers, or another audience. These typical actions of many (not all) came to be known as the *writing process*. It has dramatically affected the teaching of writing. However, because many of the researchers on writing have emphasized that this process is not linear (Emig, 1971; Hillocks, 1986; Langer, 1986), it is important that teachers not insist that children participate in the "stages" of the writing process with each text. We elaborate on this point later in this chapter. These studies set the stage for research on the teaching of writing.

The Teaching of Writing

Before research emerged on what writers do as they write, there was almost no research on the *teaching* of writing. When researchers turned their attention to writing instruction in the 1970s, they found that teachers did not *teach* writing; they merely assigned writing topics and then judged the writing for grades (Scardamalia & Bereiter, 1986). Even that was not often done in elementary classrooms. Young children were not thought of as writers.

Educators began to focus on teaching after the publication of seminal books on the relationship between writing and the teaching of writing, such as Donald Murray's (1980) book, *A Writer Teaches Writing*. A group of teachers in the Bay Area of California began a writing project that focused on their own writing and the teaching of writing. The project became popular and soon became a national movement called the National Writing Project (NWP). The NWP is widely viewed as one of the most effective professional development movements in education. For many teachers, the NWP is a life-changing experience.

The work of Donald Graves in *Writing: Teachers and Children at Work* (1983) dramatically advanced the field of elementary writing instruction. Graves showed through his classroom studies that many young children can write meaningful texts. One of his primary findings was that simply by allowing children to write on topics of their choice, some children will write much more. He showed that many children want to express themselves in writing and will do so, given the appropriate conditions for writing. He also illustrated the writing development of some children across a 2-year period, showing the promise of his suggested practices.

Sowers (1985), who worked with Graves and his colleagues, illustrated how the researchers affected the environment in which the young children wrote, thereby producing the outcomes of the study. She writes of the promise of the approach: the trust that grew between and among teachers and students as they learned to write in the collaborative setting and the teacher buy-in that resulted when they observed what their students *could* write that they had previously never expected. However, Sowers also noted that the writing students produced varied greatly in amount and quality. In 1 year, "The most prolific first grader produced 117 pieces of writing, yet a few third and fourth graders finished only about a dozen pieces in a year" (p. 304). This finding, along with many like it, begin to highlight the problems of this approach.

These early studies grounded the writing workshop approach to writing instruction but also brought out its critics. One common problem with education in general is that implications of studies are interpreted differently by many, and the implications of the research on writing was no exception. Some educators began to view the writing process as "orthodoxy" (Graves, 1985). Teachers began "teaching" the stages of the writing process as if all writers must proceed through these stages in a linear way. Even though Graves argued against it (1985), the writing process "approach" had become institutionalized in many classrooms.

Further, many became concerned that the writing workshop approach was good for some children and not others. In 1986, with the publication of Delpit's article, "Skills and Other Dilemmas of a Progressive Black Educator," the NWP came under some criticism. Delpit wrote about friends who viewed the writing workshop approach to teaching writing as appropriate for white kids but not for black kids. She worried that process writing instruction focused so much on process or fluency that skills instruction was neglected. She emphasized that many African American children are already fluent. What they needed were the writing skills that would get them into college. The belief was that a focus on process neglected product, and it is the product of writing on which we are judged. Her argument, in the midst of the reading wars, as mentioned in Chapter 1, impacted the field dramatically.

At the same time, Hillocks (1986) produced a critical review of research on writing instruction. He analyzed differing methods for teaching writing, including the writing process approach. Hillocks worried that the studies of the workshop approach (e.g., Graves's 1983 book) selected data examples to illustrate important points about the writing of particular children without consideration for the achievement of other children in the classroom. Hillocks claims that studies such as these imply that certain practices *cause* results. (Refer to Chapter 1 about the difference between causal studies and other types of studies.) This argument about writing process approaches was similar to that made about whole-language studies (described in Chapter 1) in which researchers focused only on a few children and not the effects of the instruction on the learning of whole classrooms of children. Further, Hillocks's concern with the lack of explicit teaching on how to write also corresponds to the criticism of whole-language instruction.

Other researchers raised additional concerns about the writing workshop that had become so popular through the NWP. Tim Lensmire, in *When Children Write* (1994), exposed that what elementary children do in the writing workshop is not always productive. In fact, even with the expert teaching by Lensmire himself, the third graders he taught were far from the productive little writers described in previous books on writing instruction. The students often cruelly inserted unpopular children into negative characters in their stories or purposely excluded students they did not like in group writing projects. Even with conferences to direct the children in more productive ways, the 8- and 9-year-olds remained focused on the social class dynamics and not on writing, continuing to reflect biases of gender and social class. The book shows that despite Lensmire's knowledge of writing and his care for the children, he was not entirely successful as a writing workshop teacher.

In another case study of six children learning to write in an urban primary school, Dyson (1993) illustrates how a talented teacher can help students bridge their social and academic worlds. She harnessed the oral performances of African American children to help them create conventional texts, illustrating the "hybrid" nature of the instructional context. Her study illustrates what can happen in culturally responsive classrooms in which teachers continue to expect the "official curriculum" to be addressed.

Despite the few studies of writing instruction and writing processes of children of color mentioned above, there is a serious dearth of research on the writing instruction that focuses on whole classrooms of children and specifically on the achievement of ELLs (Olson & Land, 2007; Samway, 2006). One study, however, illustrates much promise. Olsen and Land (2007) conducted a study of writing instruction in a California school district in which 95% of the students were ELLs. In the Pathway Project teachers learn cognitive strategies for reading and writing that were shown to work in previous research studies. The authors of the project had rejected both traditional forms of teaching and some aspects of the workshop model as well. Instead, they favored cognitive strategies but within an environment of explicit teaching of specific writing skills (e.g., using symbolism) and components (e.g., plot, commentary, supporting detail), rigorous curriculum, high expectations, and a trusting, collaborative environment for teachers and students. The students in the program were measured on both traditional and non-traditional measures and found to be significantly successful.

Our model of the writing instruction takes into consideration both the promises and the problems of the writing process or writing workshop approach. While we believe that the workshop approach as a framework for teaching elementary literacy allows for culturally responsive instruction, we also believe that explicit teaching of the cognitive writing processes must occur within the workshop environment. We believe strongly that careful monitoring of all students' progress, rigorous curriculum with high expectations, explicit feedback and correction, and much modeling and practice must prevail within the workshop framework. We also emphasize that teachers must adapt instruction for ELL and other children for whom writing might be especially challenging, and we stress the importance of teaching children explicitly how to improve their writing products and how to conduct themselves respectfully during the writing workshop. These elements are essential in classrooms serving diverse groups of students.

PRINCIPLES FOR WRITING INSTRUCTION

Figure 9.1 offers general principles for the teaching of writing.

- Read aloud from excellent models of writing; explicitly teach what good writers do.
- Model *how* to write through thinking aloud and showing your procedures, illustrating how other writers have accomplished goals, etc.
- Give younger children the most choice in topic and form. Older children need to be exposed to, and explicitly taught how to write on, many topics for various audiences and purposes.
- Use writing "stages" flexibly; allow children to move through them as their pieces need them, not necessarily in a linear way.
- Plan and deliver lessons on various genres: journals, persuasive writing (argument), letters, e-mails, "tweets," memoir, biographies, expository writing (description, sequence, comparison, cause and effect), stories, and poetry.
- Teach specific skills (e.g., sentence combining; show, not tell; punctuation; word usage) explicitly and often; link these lessons to the writing of whole texts. Provide this explicit instruction on whatever skills children need. Insist that they use the skills they know when they revise and edit.
- Be open-minded about new ways students create multimedia texts. (More on this in Chapter 10.)
- Never allow children to disrespect others during the writing workshop (or at any time).
- Provide many opportunities for students to share their writing.
- Celebrate all students' texts in some way.

FIGURE 9.1. Principles for writing instruction.

THE WRITING PROCESS: NONLINEAR AND MESSY

The writing process includes five phases through which many students move from the seed of an idea to a finished piece of writing ready for publication: prewriting, drafting, revising, editing, and publishing. Each phase of writing can build on the previous phase, but as suggested, many children overlap these phases and return to planning (i.e., prewriting) throughout the process. Writers move back and forth between and through the phase and even skip phases. Sometimes a writer will draft a piece and never return to it. Other times, a writer will revise a piece multiple times and publish it in various formats. Let's take a closer look at each stage of the writing experience.

Prewriting

Prewriting is what writers do before they write. Rarely does a writer have his or her intended text all worked out before writing. So, even *writing* can be a prewriting activity, as sometimes writers write to figure out what they know (Murray, 1980). The essential point of prewriting is to choose a topic and a purpose for writing. "Just get your thoughts down" is a popular phrase used by teachers to encourage students to begin to explore a topic or purpose.

If the writing is an elaborate investigation, such as when Vicky's class studied their own neighborhoods, prewriting can involve many activities for the students: taking a walk through the neighborhood and recording what they see, asking an adult to drive them through the neighborhood and taking notes, interviewing people who live and work in the neighborhood, drawing a map of the neighborhood, reading what others have written about the neighborhood, and more. Once a researcher has a pile of "data" such as this, he or she can begin to write her descriptions. Later lessons on word choice and sentence structure can enliven the work. Typical prewriting activities include:

- Talking with someone
- Writing to figure out what you know or want to write about
- Brainstorming ideas with a group or on paper
- Reading
- Viewing something (e.g., on the Internet)
- Drawing
- Mapping, webbing, or making some sort of outline

Drafting

Drafting can happen after prewriting, though it does not necessarily. Drafting is where poems begin to show white space and rhyme scheme. Short stories develop in sequence and dialogue. Humor and argument begin to take shape. When students draft, they should be encouraged to focus on the content of what they want to communicate and not worry about the mechanics of writing. Many writers simply begin to write to discover what they want to write about or to discover what they know. Often called a "free write," researchers suggest it helps build fluency and idea development. However, Hillocks (1986), who favors a cognitive approach to writing instruction, suggests that simply giving time to write does little to teach writing. The drafting stage is important, but not without explicit instruction in *how* to write. Letting ideas flow is key to producing a good draft. In drafting, students:

- Narrow topic choices
- Choose an audience
- Experiment with the appropriate voice, tone, and style for the given genre
- Decide an organizational form (e.g., separate ideas into paragraphs)
- Explore strategies to "hook" the reader and catch the attention of the audience

Teachers can scaffold the drafting stage by first modeling good writing of their own or of professional writers, dissecting what good writers do, and then providing time to write. During drafting, teachers can scaffold by simply asking "How can I help?", "Can you read what you've got so far?", "How is it going?", and "What are you trying to say?" The questions are open-ended and nonjudgmental. The idea is to help the writer keep writing.

Many students today want to draft on computers rather than by hand, so we recommend that teachers scramble to get as many laptop computers as possible in their classrooms. Also, children have learned to download a lot of material from the Internet and will want to create their pieces by compiling materials from multiple sites and media forms, creating original hybrid pieces (Burke & Hammett, 2009). They can produce some highly creative texts and should be encouraged. But teachers will need to conduct multiple lessons on how to give credit to the originators of material that students use in their own texts.

Revising

The main goal for revising is to make the ideas in the text clear. To clarify, writers rewrite sections, reorganize the piece, add text, remove material that just confuses or is irrelevant, and so on. Revision is one of the most difficult stages because many children are used to writing something only once. They do not see a need to revise. Yet, what we learned from research about what good writers do is that they constantly revise as they write. Revising is an ongoing process. It happens throughout the completion of a piece as the writer expands his or her thinking and adds to the existing set of ideas he or she has written. The primary tool for revising is to read and reread what was written. During revising, students:

- Add details appropriate to the genre
- Reorganize or resequence the text ("cut and paste" sections of the piece)
- Take out parts that no longer seem appropriate

- Alter sentence structure to match tone or correct problems in sentence writing
- Change words to reflect voice
- Change words to become more precise
- Reread to consider the readers' understanding of the piece
- Talk with a partner or the teacher to improve the written piece
- Include citations from all sources

Teachers can assist writers who are attempting to revise by asking such questions as "What else can you add?", "What is in here that might confuse your readers?", "Can you expand this section so it is clearer to your readers?", and "Can you write this section as if you are writing it for someone who knows nothing about this topic?" Each of the above revision strategies can and should be taught in explicit lessons.

Editing

Idea development governs the first three areas of the writing process. The next section requires that the reader attend to the conventions of writing. Sentence structure and grammar take a front seat, and students must read their own piece as if they were the audience. This requires a command of written language, rules of punctuation, and an understanding of what makes sense. During editing, students:

- Correct punctuation.
- Check sentence structure.
- Delete or add words and phrases.
- Check for accurate spelling.

Teachers tend to teach such skills in mini-lessons (described below) or in small groups of children who all need the same skills.

Publishing

To publish something means to make it public. Publishing can take many forms; it can be as simple as reading the text aloud to another person or as elaborate as uploading a polished work onto an Internet site for all to read. Many teachers provide multiple opportunities for children to publish stories or other texts into hardcover class-made books, which are then displayed in the classroom for all to read. Examples of publishing can include:

- Read the writing aloud to the class.
- Display the writing in the classroom or on a school wall.
- Add the piece to a class or school newspaper.
- Send the piece through the mail for others to read.
- Send it to a pen pal.

- Post it on the class or school website.
- Upload to one of the many Internet sites that publish children's works.

Some children's products can be published in online magazines such as *www.stonesoup.com* and *www.kidpub.com*.

ASSESSMENT OF WRITING

In the writing workshop teachers assess both *process* and *product* (Tompkins, 2000). They assess students' process by observing them as they write (and prewrite, revise, edit, and publish), and they attempt to understand students' writing goals, strategies, struggles, and successes. Teachers assess how children are spending their time (productively or not?) and intervene when students seem stuck, as Vicky did in the teaching vignette that opened this chapter. Teachers must be aware of what they are assessing, especially with respect to ELLs. Too often teachers assume that ELL students cannot write (Samway, 2006) as if the issue is writing rather than their English acquisition in general.

Many teachers use an *assessment notebook* to record students' behavior during the workshop period. Comments such as the following might be included in a notebook:

"James and Steve are writing together again. They seem productive, but should I invite them to choose new partners?"

"Maggie sat quietly alone today and produced only one sentence. Check on her."

"I took dictation from Gael today, and he seemed amazed as his words were put on paper. See if he can read it back tomorrow."

"More kids are refusing to write on paper and needing the computers. We need more laptops in here!"

"Met with those writing memoirs. They are ready to read aloud and get feedback."

You can see that the teacher is not always sure of what she might do with each of the children. Nonetheless, the act of writing in an assessment notebook often forces the teacher to attend to the concerns of the class. If teachers have a page marked in their notebooks for each child, they can thereby keep track of each student. If at the end of the week, the teacher notices that he or she has not written anything about a few of the children, he or she can (1) check their products (what they have written all week) to be sure they are on track, and (2) be sure to attend to them the following week.

Teachers must also assess *products*. An important study by Hillocks (2002) shows the problem that school districts have with standardized writing assessments. He says that most state assessments produce formulaic writing that is actually quite poor in many cases because the assessment drives what the teachers do. In one school district teachers were expected to teach the "five paragraph theme" from third grade on up, and the state assessment only examined whether the five paragraphs were present with their requisite topic sentences. They failed to assess the true quality of the writing.

The one exception in his study was in Kentucky, where Vicky and Nancy teach. The state assessment has a portfolio in which students produce multiple pieces of different genre, written without time constraints. The state provides teachers with rubrics and writing continuums that are guides for how the state will assess students' products. This rubric includes scales that evaluate idea development, organization, language use, spelling and grammar, and even visual characteristics of the published product. Figure 9.2 is a page from the rubric. The full rubric and guidelines can be found at *www.education.ky.gov/NR/rdonlyres/6B49A59F-81FF-417F-B63A-48192A382807/0/AnalyticalRubricFINAL.pdf.* Importantly, this rubric is for print products and not the multimedia products many children produce today. We address assessment of these "new literacies" in the next chapter.

Kentucky Writing Scoring Rubric

0	1	2	3	4
CONTENT				
Purpose and Audience; Idea Development and Support				
The writing: ☐ Lacks purpose	The writing: ☐ Attempts to establish a general purpose; lacks focus	The writing: ☐ Attempts to establish and maintain a narrowed purpose; some lapses in focus	The writing: ☐ Establishes and maintains an authentic focused purpose throughout	The writing: ☐ Establishes and maintains an authentic and insightful focused purpose throughout
☐ Lacks awareness of audience	☐ Indicates limited awareness of audience's needs	☐ Indicates some awareness of audience's needs; makes some attempt to communicate with an audience; may demonstrate some voice and/or tone	☐ Indicates an awareness of audience's needs; communicates adequately with audience; conveys voice and/or appropriate tone	☐ Indicates a strong awareness of audience's needs; communicates effectively with audience; sustains distinctive voice and/or appropriate tone
☐ Lacks idea development; may provide random details	☐ Demonstrates limited idea development with few details and/or support; may attempt to apply some characteristics of the genre	☐ Demonstrates some idea development with details/support; support may be unelaborated, irrelevant and/or repetitious; may apply some characteristics of the genre	☐ Demonstrates depth of idea development with specific, sufficient details/support; applies characteristics of the genre	☐ Demonstrates reflective, analytical and/or insightful idea development; provides specific, thorough support; skillfully applies characteristics of the genre
0	1	2	3	4
STRUCTURE				
Organization: unity and coherence; Sentences: structure and length				
The writing: ☐ Demonstrates random organization	The writing: ☐ Demonstrates ineffective or weak organization	The writing: ☐ Demonstrates logical organization with lapses in coherence	The writing: ☐ Demonstrates logical, coherent organization	The writing: ☐ Demonstrates careful and/or subtle organization that enhances the purpose
☐ Lacks transitional elements	☐ Demonstrates limited and/or ineffective transitional elements	☐ Demonstrates some effective transitional elements	☐ Demonstrates logical, effective transitional elements throughout	☐ Demonstrates varied and subtle transitional elements throughout
☐ Demonstrates incorrect sentence structure throughout	☐ Demonstrates some ineffective or incorrect sentence structure	☐ Demonstrates simple sentences; may attempt more complex sentences but lacks control of sentence structure	☐ Demonstrates control and variety in sentence structure	☐ Demonstrates control, variety and complexity in sentence structure to enhance meaning
0	1	2	3	4
CONVENTIONS				
Language: grammar and usage, word choice; Correctness: spelling, punctuation, capitalization, abbreviation and documentation				
	The writing: ☐ Demonstrates lack of control in grammar and usage	The writing: ☐ Demonstrates some control of grammar and usage with some errors that do not interfere with communication	The writing: ☐ Demonstrates control of grammar and usage relative to length and complexity	The writing: ☐ Demonstrates control of grammar and usage to enhance meaning
	☐ Demonstrates incorrect or ineffective word choice	☐ Demonstrates simplistic and/or imprecise word choice	☐ Demonstrates acceptable word choice appropriate for audience and purpose	☐ Demonstrates accurate, rich and/or precise word choice appropriate for audience and purpose
	☐ Demonstrates lack of control in correctness	☐ Demonstrates some control of correctness with some errors that do not interfere with communication	☐ Demonstrates control of correctness relative to length and complexity	☐ Demonstrates control of correctness to enhance communication

FIGURE 9.2. A state writing rubric.

THE WRITING WORKSHOP: PROMISES AND PROBLEMS

The writing workshop in many elementary teachers' classrooms is structured much like the reading workshop. In the writing workshop, the "work" of the morning is to *write*. Some —but not all—of the writing that is done is decided by the writer. At time, children decide what to write about, to whom to write, and for what purpose. The teacher acts as a guide, assisting the child's performance. The teacher must attend to whether the writing task a child has chosen for him- or herself is rigorous and challenging. The teacher must look for ways to assist the writer, whether through a mini-lesson on a skill, through pairing the child with another writer for a project, or through inviting collaborative writing projects.

Modeling How to Write

Children learn to write from other writers. Teachers can model the writing process in front of students, thinking aloud as they compose. In Figure 9.3, a kindergarten teacher demonstrated her thinking and writing as she explored what to write about. One of her students picked up on how to write from her demonstration (Figure 9.4). Children learn what they are taught! What you do as a teacher will have a direct effect on what children produce.

The most important way to model excellent writing is to share the writing of favorite children's authors. Children learn a great deal from the styles and language of chil-

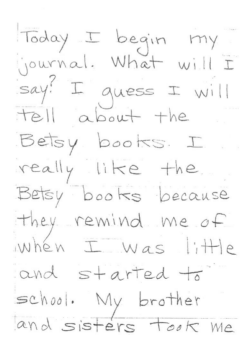

Today I begin my journal. What will I say? I guess I will tell about the Betsy books. I really like the Betsy books because they remind me of when I was little and started to school. My brother and sisters took me

FIGURE 9.3. A kindergarten teacher models writing.

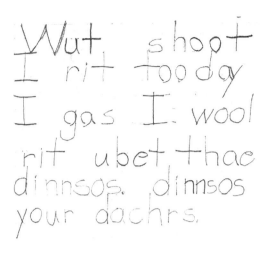

FIGURE 9.4. A child learns from his teacher.

dren's authors, especially if the teacher makes writing explicit. When teachers point out the literary language, the humor, the word choice of authors, children take notice. Simple, informal comments such as the following teach children what great writers do.

> "Listen to how William Steig makes us feel cold as he writes: '*Now the wind drove Irene along so rudely she had to hop, skip, and go helter-skeltering over the knobby ground. Cold snow sifted into her boots and chilled her feet.*'"

Good teachers remind children that good authors attend to language when they write. Teachers often like to read the first page or first line of many books to show children how important "leads" are. A brief discussion of the following leads can inspire children to think of their own creative ways to begin a piece of their own.

> "My name is India Opal Buloni, and last summer my daddy, the preacher, sent me to the store for a box of macaroni-and-cheese, some white rice, and two tomatoes and I came back with a dog." (*Because of Winn-Dixie*, by Kate DiCamillo)
> "With mournful moan and silken tone, itself alone comes one trombone. Gliding, sliding, high notes go low; one trombone is playing solo." (*Zin! Zin! Zin! A Violin* by Lloyd Moss)
> "Leo couldn't do anything right." (*Leo the Late Bloomer* by Robert Kraus)
> "All along the meadow where the cows grazed and the horses ran, there was an old stone wall." (*Frederick* by Leo Lionni)

The above lines from these great books are openings that teach. Teachers' best tool for teaching children to write is quality children's literature. In one third-grade classroom, the teacher loved Chris Van Allsburg's books and pointed out the beautiful and mysteri-

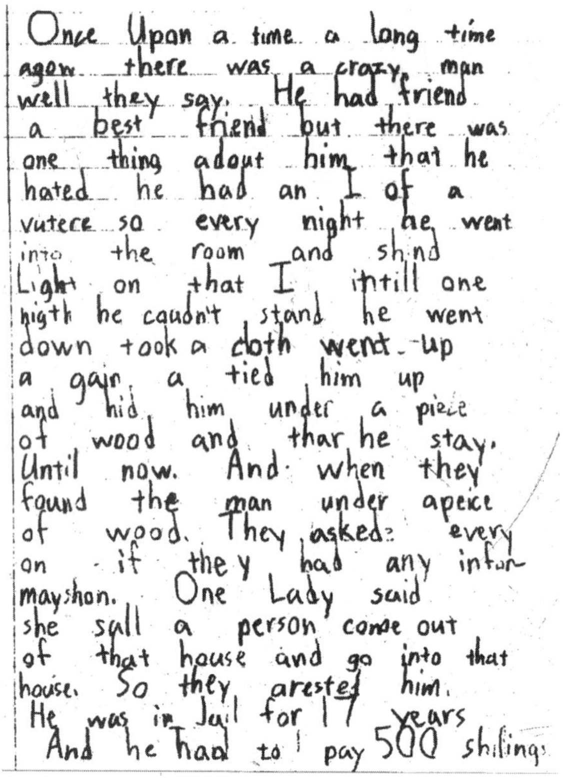
Once Upon a time a long time
agow there was a crazy man
well they say. He had friend
a best friend but there was
one thing adout him that he
hated he had an I of a
vutece so every night he went
into the room and shind
Light on that I intill one
nigth he caudn't stand he went
down took a cloth went up
a gain a tied him up
and hid him under a piece
of wood and thar he stay.
Until now. And when they
found the man under apeice
of wood. They asked: every
on if they had any infor-
mayshon. One Lady said
she sall a person come out
of that house and go into that
house. So they arested him.
He was in Jail for 17 years
And he had to pay 500 shilings.

FIGURE 9.5. Literary writing.

ous language he uses. One of her students produced the story in Figure 9.5. Notice the language the child uses. It is similar in style to Van Allsburg. This third grader's literary language and grammatical structures are reflective of the many children's books he has read and his teacher has shared with the class.

Explicit Teaching on How to Write: The Mini-Lesson

The mini-lesson (Tompkins, 2000) is an explanation or demonstration of writing concepts, strategies, or skills that some or all members of the class need. The lesson can also involve an explanation of procedures for operating in the writing workshop. A teacher might use the lesson to demonstrate (1) how to reorganize a piece of writing, (2) how to create a web of details for a personal narrative, (3) a strategy for combining sentences instead of using all short sentences, or (4) how to make a persuasive argument using claims, warrants, qualifiers. The teacher may read an excerpt from a book that instructs students in some aspect of the writing process, such as from Ralph Fletcher's *A Writer's Notebook* (Fletcher, 1996). The explicit lesson can also be a time of discussion wherein students ask questions or solve writing problems, such as where to search for certain ideas, how to cite sources, or where they can go for topic ideas. The lessons are usually brief to allow more time for writing practice, and they should naturally segue into the independent/conference part of the workshop.

A Mini-Lesson on "Show, Don't Tell"

Vicky's fifth graders had begun drafting personal narratives, essays that focused on one memorable event. Vicky had conducted teacher–student conferences with each to assess the children's progress. She noticed that many of the children were accurately recording the facts of their experiences; however, most of the pieces lacked the kind of description that would help the readers *visualize* the stories. This was the perfect opportunity to teach a mini-lesson on "Show, Don't Tell" to add creativity, emotion, and depth to the narratives. On the projector screen, Vicky displayed the following sentence that she had written on her tablet PC.

I cried because it hurt.

She said to the class, "If I were writing a personal narrative about going to the doctor to get a shot, this might be a sentence I would include. What do you visualize when you read it?" Antoine raised his hand and smiled. "I see you crying like you were a little girl." Small chuckles arose throughout the room.

"Yes, Antoine, I don't like getting shots any more than kids do. But do you think it's a good sentence for my piece? Thumbs up or thumbs down." The majority of students thrust thumbs down to the ground, as she had expected. They recognized that it wasn't a descriptive sentence. Vicky explained, "When I read my own writing, I sometimes notice that I just *tell* the reader what is going on; but good writers actually *show* the reader what is happening by using vivid descriptions. You might say that they 'paint a picture with words.' I'm going to try it again." Using the stylus pen, Vicky then wrote:

> Tears began to well in the corners of my eyes long before the doctor brandished the syringe full of medicine. I yelped in anticipated anguish, "Owwwwww!" Fat tears rolled down my cheeks as I held back cries. After a few seconds, the doctor asked, "Are you OK?" "Sure," I said, and she stuck the needle in my arm.

"What do you think is the difference between the first description and the second description?"

Lin raised his hand. "The second one had lots more details and wasn't so boring, like when you said 'fat tears rolled down my cheeks.' The first one just told that you cried."

Faustina waved her hands wildly and said, "I cried like that when my mom took me to the doctor even though nothing hurt!"

"Ha! You must have been expecting it to hurt, just like I was. How else did I *show* the reader I was crying?"

Yolanda, a very quiet and soft-spoken student, looked carefully at the screen, and Vicky invited her to come to the front to point out the answer. She took the stylus pen and underlined *Tears began to well up.*

"Thank you, Yolanda. That is another way to show crying. What else paints a picture?" Other students responded by coming to the tablet and circling words such as *yelped* and *Owww.* Vicky wrapped up the mini-lesson by saying, "We are going to practice 'Show, Don't Tell' in our own writing today." The students reviewed their drafts and found places where they could expand their descriptions.

Figure 9.6 presents other examples of explicit lessons.

Conferencing: Support and Feedback

The purpose of the writing conference is to provide additional support and feedback at any stage in the writing process. The structure of a conference can vary, but the most productive conferences occur when the student has reviewed his or her goals and progress before the conference session begins. Because we could not find research evidence that supports peer conferencing (in which children assist one another), we favor teacher–student conferences. These can take place one on one or with small groups of students who need the same feedback on developing pieces.

Sometimes students want a conference simply because they want feedback on their piece. How do students know when their work is adequate? What prompts them to

Building a writing community	Writing process
• Creating a writer's notebook • Writing workshop routines • How to conference • How to conference with peers • Share time expectations • Respecting others	• Generating ideas • Prewriting • Planning with a graphic organizer • How to do a "fast write" • Narrowing a topic • Word processing
Writing conventions and structure	**Content/ideas/genre studies**
• Does my sentence make sense? • Sentence combining for better writing • Using vivid verbs • Cutting out unnecessary words • Using a dictionary or thesaurus • How to use spell-check • Grammar and usage • Punctuating dialogue • How to cite Internet sources • Using an editing checklist	• Analyzing my own work • How to add clipart to a feature article • Characteristics of a personal narrative • Adding sensory imagery to a poem • Story map for short stories • Who is my audience? • Getting my reader's attention • Captivating conclusions

FIGURE 9.6. Other examples of explicit lessons.

end a day of writing with confidence that they have been successful writers? Giving feedback to students lets them know how close they are to reaching their goals and motivates them to continue improving their work. Feedback language should always be presented positively but helpfully. It can also be a time to correct students' attempts, if those corrections will not stifle their efforts. Knowing when to correct and when to back off takes knowing students well. The conference should help writers recognize what they did well and encourage them to continue. The prompts in Figure 9.7 are positive and helpful.

Vicky and a collaborating teacher had co-taught a series of lessons on how to narrate an event for a specific purpose to a fifth-grade class. After analyzing the students' progress, they created a chart of possible topics in which students may need support. Students listed their names beneath the topic that most closely defined an area of concern they had for their persuasive piece. As she reviewed the list, Vicky chose a girl who had moved quickly through the writing process and seemed to have a firm grasp on the characteristics of the genre. The student had chosen a topic, planned her work using a graphic organizer, and written a first draft. She requested a conference because she felt that her piece needed more details.

VICKY: What can I help you with today?

MICHELLE: I need some more details in my persuasive piece.

VICKY: Let's take a look. Read your work to me. (*Listens as the child reads.*) You told me that your grandmother was talking to your aunt. Do you remember our lesson on "Show, Don't Tell"? How can you show the reader instead of just telling about the conversation?

MICHELLE: I can use dialogue and write exactly what she said!

- "I like how you described the _____."
- "Can you add some more details _____?"
- "What did _____ sound like?"
- "How did _____ make you feel? Do you think that would give your reader more information?"
- "Tell me more about _____. Can you include that here?"
- "I noticed that you didn't include this point from your organizer. Do you think it is something your reader needs in order to understand your story?"
- "Why did you choose this _____?"
- "What else would you like to try in this piece?"
- "Here is something I want you to attend to: Remember when I did the lesson on what sentence fragments are? You have one here. How can you make that a full sentence?" (corrective feedback)
- "How can I help?"

FIGURE 9.7. Positive feedback prompts.

How was this conference helpful to the student? The conference allowed the student to take a fresh look at her own writing as if she were the reader. Vicky guided her to read the text aloud, recall previous lessons in which she had learned key strategies, and make writing decisions based on her own knowledge and abilities. The conference also allowed Vicky to tailor some individual time strictly to work within the student's ZPD, which moved her writing forward and gave her the confidence she needed to finish the work.

Writing in Different Genres

The older and more experienced children get with writing, the more they should be exposed to and expected to write in varied genres. In elementary school, children can make journal entries, write memoir pieces, and/or write expository pieces with description or persuasion. They can try their hand at poetry and story writing. All children should learn to write letters. Even in the age of e-mail and texting, letter writing is still important because attention to voice and audience are critical when writing to others, whether through traditional mail or electronic mail. Many excellent books on writing instruction give details on lessons for each specific genre (e.g., Atwell, 2002; Davis & Hill, 2003; Fletcher, 1996; Forney, 2001; Hillocks, 2007; Tompkins, 2000). Whereas many teachers allow the various genre, expert teachers provide explicit instruction in *how to produce* such texts.

Ellen worked with a group of fourth graders for 4 weeks, and one series of lessons focused on how to write biographies. She first spent time teaching the children how to synthesize text and write comparative essays. To teach the reading skill of synthesis, she took the children through several reading lessons in which they read several books on Martin Luther King and took notes from each book. The children concluded that the books included some of the same information but each provided specific information the others did not. From a diagram of notes from the books, Ellen composed in front of the children, thinking aloud how she made decisions on what to include in her biographical essay. After the demonstration, she worked with the children on choosing famous Americans about whom they wished to write. They were required to read at least three texts on the person and take notes in the same way Ellen had demonstrated. One child's biography appears in Figure 9.8.

After the biography writing, Ellen shared how to write comparative essays. She illustrated how to take two similar people, places, events, or ideas and, after much reading, create a Venn diagram of similarities and differences. She demonstrated when and how to separate paragraphs on both people. One product by two students appears in Figure 9.9.

Writing to Learn: Science, Social Studies, and Mathematics

We often think that children learn new material and then write about it. The examples above of biography writing and comparative essays might suggest this. But it is not

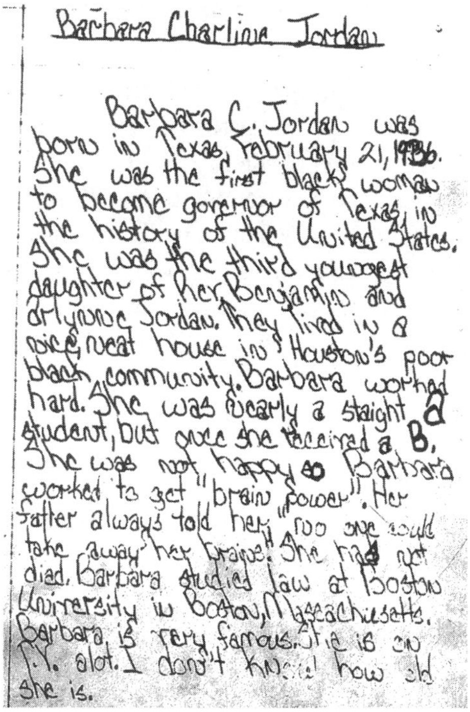

Barbara Charline Jordan

Barbara C. Jordan was born in Texas, February 21, 1936. She was the first black woman to become governor of Texas in the history of the United States. She was the third youngest daughter of her Benjamin and arlynne Jordan. They lived in a nice, neat house in Houston's poor black community. Barbara worked hard. She was nearly a staight A student, but once she received a B. She was not happy so Barbara worked to get "brain power". Her father always told her "no one could take away her brains." She has not died. Barbara studied law at Boston University in Boston, Massachusetts. Barbara is very famous. She is on T.V. alot. I don't know how old she is.

FIGURE 9.8. Biographical essay.

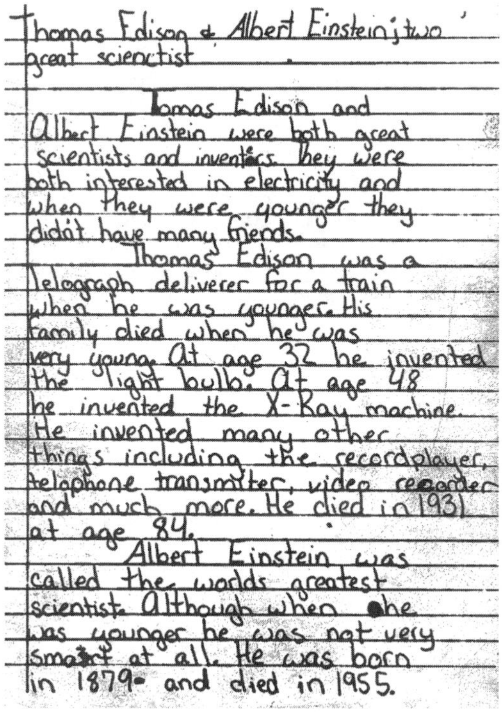

Thomas Edison & Albert Einstein; two great scienctist

Thomas Edison and Albert Einstein were both great scientists and inventors. They were both interested in electricity and when they were younger they didn't have many friends.

Thomas Edison was a Telegraph deliverer for a train when he was younger. His family died when he was very young. At age 32 he invented the light bulb. At age 48 he invented the X-Ray machine. He invented many other things including the recordplayer, telephone transmitter, video recorder and much more. He died in 1931 at age 84.

Albert Einstein was called the worlds greatest scientist. Although when he was younger he was not very smart at all. He was born in 1879 and died in 1955.

FIGURE 9.9. Comparison essay.

always the case. In fact, it is often *through* the writing that children come to understand what they know. Writing is a tool for thinking, and teachers use this tool to help children better understand concepts in science, mathematics, social studies, and more. In the examples above, the children were able to learn much through their decisions about what to include in the essays. What is *really* important about Barbara Jordan? What is *really* important about a great scientist? In the example in Figure 9.10, the third grader was asked to explain, conceptually, a multiplication problem that another child brought to the class and the teacher made into a class project. The child said that he had gone to a store and found a deal. For every folder he bought, he received three pens. The teacher asked, what if he needed *15* pens so that everyone in the group could

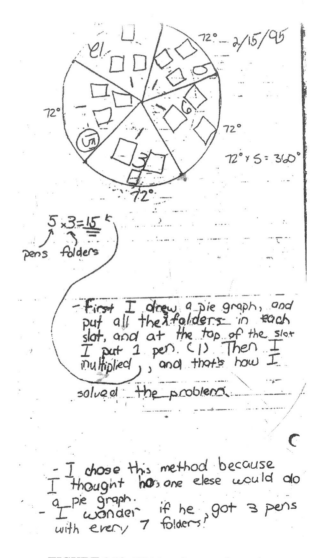

FIGURE 9.10. Writing about mathematics.

have one. How many folders would they need to buy? The teacher asked the children to write their explanations and use any other tools they needed. (The teacher's notations of angle degrees on the child's graph was a one-on-one lesson she had given this child.)

In the next example, in Figure 9.11, a child is writing what he had learned that week. This exercise is useful as a learning and assessment tool. Again, sometimes a learner does not internalize what was learned until he or she talks through or writes what he or she knows. As we described in detail in Chapter 2, language is a primary tool for learning.

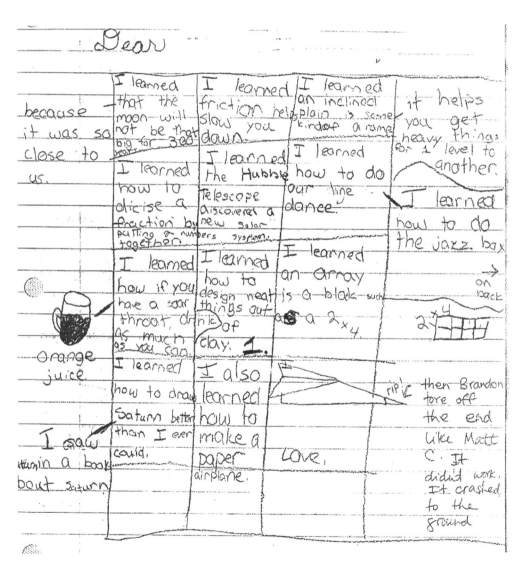

FIGURE 9.11. A child writes about what he learned one week.

MANAGING THE WRITING WORKSHOP: STRATEGIES IN A WORKSHOP FRAMEWORK

The writing workshop provides the perfect opportunity for a teacher to learn more about his or her students—their backgrounds, strengths, likes, dislikes, and needs. To teach young writers in their ZPD, the establishment of a safe, caring, rigorous environment is critical. Teachers and students create this environment together; however, it is a direct result of careful planning, organization, and a commitment to the consistent support structures we describe in Chapter 4, which lead students to feel free to express themselves and grow as writers. How do teachers structure this time to best meet the needs of students?

Establishing a Routine

The daily schedule for a writing workshop will vary based on the needs of the students, the preferences of the teacher, and the schedules and guidelines of the school and district. The basic framework may look something like this:

Mini-lesson	5–20 minutes
Independent writing/conference time	15–30 minutes
Sharing	5–10 minutes
Closure/self-reflection	5–10 minutes

The schedule may fluctuate depending upon the teachers' choice for the lesson introduction. He or she may decide to share a picture book with rich illustrations one day or instruct students to do a "quick write" on another day. Share time may vary in length and number of students selected to discuss their work. Self-reflection may be a simple "thumbs up, thumbs down" on Monday or a written reflection checklist another day. The important point to remember is that children feel comfortable with the expected flow of the workshop. Culturally responsive classrooms must maintain a consistent, yet flexible, schedule. The first consideration is what the students need in order to accomplish the goals they have created with their teacher.

Materials

Preparing the right materials helps to make the most of writing workshop time. When students have access to available resources, they can spend the majority of their time writing or sharing their writing. Materials should be introduced during mini-lessons, and the teacher should model how and when to use them. Students should also learn routines for returning them to their proper places at the close of the workshop, as well as routines for how to replenish consumable items. Great materials to have in a workshop include:

- High-quality literature, both fiction and nonfiction
- Writer's notebooks for each child to capture thoughts, illustrations, and writing ideas (paper or electronic)
- Writing folders to organize written pieces (paper or electronic)
- Pencils, pens, erasers in easily accessible, clearly labeled containers
- Paper, lined and unlined, for a variety of tasks
- Chart paper to create anchor charts, posters, and story boards
- Index cards
- Sticky notes
- Dictionaries and thesauruses (paper and electronic) in languages the students in the class speak
- Magazines representative of diverse populations to spark interest in writing topics
- Favorite online magazines, stories, and websites bookmarked for easy access
- Ideally, one laptop per child!
- Projectors and document cameras for analyzing and sharing writing in whole-group settings

Creating a Supportive Environment

A culturally diverse classroom has a distinct look and feel. The walls reflect authentic student work, the classroom library is full of multicultural, high-interest books, and students are actively engaged in reading and writing activities. Students are confident because all around them they see themselves and have clear expectations for what is required. Another important characteristic of a supportive learning environment is a place with a routine students can count on, with few or no surprises. Teachers should clearly define their expectations for the writing workshop and the roles of the students and the teacher (see Figure 9.12).

Student	Teacher
• Respects the workshop materials and space. • Respects others. • Brainstorms ideas. • Selects topics from experience. • Utilizes independent time for writing. • Prepares material for conferences. • Talks actively during conferences. • Collaborates with others. • Self-reflects on progress. • Develops goals.	• Organizes the workshop environment. • Respects each child. • Encourages students' ideas. • Explicitly teaches genres and their skills. • Consistently maintains writing time. • Facilitates student thinking. • Listens intently during conferences. • Teaches and models collaborative strategies. • Assesses progress and gives feedback. • Differentiates instructional goals.

FIGURE 9.12. Teachers and students' roles in the writing workshop.

Additional Lessons for Students Who Need More Support

Typically, children who need more support writing do not just need more time to write. Think of Vicky's students in the opening vignette of this chapter. She met with the three students who needed additional help, two of whom she could see were not using time wisely in the workshop and one student who was an English learner just beginning to get words into print. To her, the students' need for more help was not an indication of something wrong with them. Rather, it was an indication that she needed to provide something else for them. Vicky and Nancy have both used paired writing as one way to assist students. At times, they scribe the text for children who cannot yet get much on paper. Other times, they sit and take turns writing sentences for students to illustrate how one type of text might unfold. In any case, they do not merely provide more time for the students, they provide more *instruction*.

CULTURALLY RESPONSIVE WRITING INSTRUCTION

Writing instruction in a workshop environment is based on principles of culturally responsive instruction. When children are encouraged to write about what they know, they quite naturally connect school with their lives outside of school. They draft their pieces in the language and style most comfortable for them and only change that language at appropriate times for particular pieces with the guidance of the teacher. The teacher pushes the students to develop new skills and new ways of writing, which keeps the process rigorous. Also, children are encouraged to write collaboratively, and in doing so, learn much from one another. If teachers take care to be sure that all children are engaged, producing excellent work, and in the process taking care of their classroom community, a writing workshop can be highly reflective of culturally responsive instruction.

The writing workshop may be useless, however, if there is little excellent instruction on how to write. Because the goal of this book's instructional model is higher achievement for all students, teachers should plan explicit lessons on the writing strategies and skills that will push them toward better products. Teachers must carefully monitor the progress of their students, constantly asking themselves, "Whose needs are getting met? Who is writing most and why? Who is writing little and why? Whose products need more attention? How can I help them?" Research-based, culturally responsive writing instruction is about providing what individual students need to achieve.

CHAPTER 10

New Literacies

Audrey's class of fourth graders has had to face the challenge of school bullying. One member of the class was repeatedly called derogatory names on the playground by members of other classes. After addressing the situation with the principal and the students' teachers, Audrey spoke with her own class, emphatically insisting that this sort of behavior never, ever come from them. She emphasized the importance of protecting one another against bullies, and she read books to the group about bullying.

Today, Audrey leads her class in Internet searches on the topic of bullying. The search is conducted after extensive teaching on how to look for relevant information. Working in small groups (the class has only nine laptops), Audrey brainstorms with the class the most concise and precise search words and phrases. Then, in an effort to get the students to think critically, she says, "If you can click on only *one* link to get the information you want, what will it be?" She teaches them to examine and dissect the hyperlinks associated with the term under study, and to anticipate what they might be clicking on before they click. Will an advertisement pop up? The title of a book? An organization? Photographs? How will you know the information is useful or relevant? Audrey's lesson on searching for Internet information is repeated for all students in the class over multiple lessons. It seems there is always something new to learn about how to use the Internet to increase academic learning.

What is new about literacy? Well, a lot! The recent burst of Internet use and the many new corresponding tools in the last decade have changed our understandings of literacy dramatically and permanently. The challenge, and part of the excitement, is that we don't know where it will lead. We know that literacy has changed, but because of the rapid evolution and creation of new technologies, we are not sure exactly what it means for literacy development and teaching. Some educators are redefining literacy to

177

mean interpreting and communicating meaning through multiple media and modality forms, such as the Internet, an iPhone or iPad, or even YouTube. "Reading" means much more than reading print; it also means interpreting coded print, pictures, graphs, moving images, and constantly changing print. Reading is also synthesizing these multiple forms found within one text. It means problem solving, analyzing, and critically evaluating images and print on the screen. It is knowing how and when to make wise decisions when using technologies for meaning making (Coiro, Knobel, Lankshear, & Leu, 2008). It is learning how to adapt reading and writing skills for new media forms such as instant messaging, blogging, or posting photos on Facebook. New literacies are redefining what it means to be literate in the 21st century (Coiro et al., 2008; Williams, 2009).

The term *new literacies* has many meanings to educators from a variety of fields. We define it in this book as the new strategies and dispositions required for meaning making using the Internet and other *information communication tools*, or ICTs. ICTs include any form of technology used for communication, such as computers, phones, cameras, electronic readers, or instruments that combine several of these tools, such as the iPad. Technology has changed how we read, write, listen, compose, and communicate information and has thus brought about different or "new" literacies.

Where is all of this taking us? Do the Internet and ICTs help or hinder literacy? This debate will certainly be lively for many decades to come. The rise of the Internet and other ICTs has caused distress among some educators. Just as people worried that radio and television would create imbeciles, people worry that too much time on the Internet will do the same. A report published by the National Education Association (2004), called *Reading at Risk*, suggests that people simply are not reading anymore. Especially, the report emphasizes, people are not reading the sort of literature that develops intellectual engagement and social responsibility. The book points to the rise of the Web culture as one of the culprits. Jaron Lanier, one of the inventors of virtual reality in the 1980s, also expresses deep concern about our society's Web-focused culture. His book, *You Are Not a Gadget* (Lanier, 2010), questions whether what is created in the Web 2.0 era—an era of creation of knowledge on the Internet—is any better or even as good as what we have in traditional technologies such as the book. Lanier's book is actually about much more, including a critique of artificial intelligence and where it may take us. But the point is similar. Should those of us who care about literacy worry or jump on the bandwagon?

We believe, both. We certainly lament any decline in the reading of wonderful stories. We are all readers of literature ourselves. Yet, we are also wary of claims that online reading is replacing the reading of literature. We believe that there are highly intellectual texts (both print and multimedia) available on the Internet that, while they may not be considered classic literature, are worthy texts for many reasons. Further, it seems some young people may be reading more, not less, as they give up television viewing for multimedia devices that require reading. Of course, we also have concerns. While new technologies bring much promise for education, if they are overused or used without clear intention or planning, they can also take the place of experiences that are truly educational. Just as students can waste a lot of time watching mindless television, they can also waste a lot of time on computers and hand-held devices. Teachers can waste a lot of time with cute activities in which the technology tool is central rather than the learning of content. The goal is not to use technology; rather, it is to *enhance learning through technology*. There are many educational experiences, such as reading aloud a wonderful picture book or having a face-to-face discussion about a book, that cannot be replaced by technology.

RESEARCH ON NEW LITERACIES

As noted, new literacies are the new strategies and dispositions required for meaning making when using the Internet and other information communication tools (ICTs), which include computers, phones, cameras, electronic readers, or any other new technology. Because technology has changed how we read, write, listen, compose, and communicate information, researchers have begun to conduct studies on the effects of new literacies on the learning of young people. These include

- Investigations of what students do on the Web
- How websites affect learners' content knowledge and attitudes
- How visual texts are understood
- How ELLs use the Internet and its effects on their learning
- What people do with instant messaging
- The literacy embedded in electronic games
- Writing on blogs or wikis
- Issues of ethics and safety raised by new literacies
- How teachers encourage or discourage new literacies
- How gender, economic status, and race play into who uses ICTs, how they use them, and why

Many of these studies are summarized and compiled in the *Handbook of Research on New Literacies* (Coiro et al., 2008). We highlight the key findings of this research that seem most relevant for elementary teachers.

Comprehension on the Internet

We learned a lot about comprehension in Chapters 7 and 8. Yet, in comparison to print comprehension, there is scant information on comprehension of new literacies. There is also little research on how teachers teach comprehension of digital material. What is resoundingly clear is that comprehension of digital texts is different from comprehension of print text (Coiro, 2003; Dalton & Proctor, 2008). Better said, comprehension of digital text is everything we said it was in Chapters 7 and 8 and *more*.

Much of the important research has focused on what people do as they read on the Internet. Researchers asking this question have observed and interviewed students in and outside of school. These studies show that mostly what people do is "answer-grab" (Kuiper, Volman, & Terwel, 2005) in their quest to find information. Students who are not skilled at navigating the Internet may end up with inaccurate or irrelevant answers. Reading on the Internet includes many of the same skills as reading print (Coiro, 2003; Dalton & Proctor, 2008), such as decoding words, recognizing main ideas, making inferences, and making connections across texts. It also includes the skill of critically evaluating hyperlink information and the content found on the Web. The role of prior knowledge, critical thinking, and metacognitive skills becomes paramount when reading on the Web. So, the question becomes: How do we teach students to read and understand these texts so that they become both critical consumers and producers? (Dalton & Proctor, 2008).

We know the power of pictures and video for teaching. If a person does not understand a written description of the water cycle or phases of the moon, visual images can help. On the Internet or through software programs, a person can listen to a passage read aloud about the water cycle or phases of the moon, view a graphic illustration of the processes, and observe real photographs and videoclips. Researchers have documented the promise of what children can learn through well-designed multimedia packages (Mayer, 2008; Palinscar & Dalton, 2005). In one study, researchers compared learners' experiences from three different versions of multimedia text on the topic of "light and vision." The students reading with interactive diagrams and instructional scaffolding demonstrated significantly greater vocabulary and concept learning than did their peers reading the same texts without the enhancements, even though their text was read aloud to them through a text-to-speech (TTS) function and had an accessible glossary (Palinscar & Dalton, 2005). In another study, Mayer (2008) showed that people understand scientific explanations more deeply when they read both words and pictures together than words alone.

Much of what people do on the Web is engage in projects of inquiry, which involves generating search terms and browsing, critically reading search results and selecting sites, skimming sites for relevant and credible information, reading embedded hyperlinks, synthesizing information across links and sites, and more (Coiro, 2003; Coiro & Dobler, 2007; Dalton & Proctor, 2008; Karchmar, 2008). But students do not always perform these tasks successfully or efficiently. Coiro and Dobler's study of online reading comprehension of sixth graders illustrated the choices the students made as they used the Internet for finding information. They found that reading on the Internet was much more complex than reading print. Students had to use all their print reading skills and strategies and much more. The reading was shaped by the technology; the reading process demanded much inference, prediction, evaluation, and anticipation of the *relevance* of information.

Teachers' Varied Uses of Technology

Teachers are "all over the map" when it comes to the use of technology for teaching. Whereas some classrooms have gone paperless, other classrooms have almost no new technology use at all. Many teachers relegate usage to software programs as supplements to their general instruction or have found occasional ICTs useful for particular lessons. Other classrooms are equipped with laptops for every learner, and they are used every minute of every day.

There is a growing body of research on the use of software programs that claim to raise reading achievement. Not surprisingly, though, researchers (Kulik, 2003; Slavin, Lake, Chambers, Cheung, & Davis, 2009) have found that instructional technology is no magic bullet. Certainly when software is used in one-on-one tutoring sessions, few studies show the desired results. Kulik (2003) found that integrated learning systems (ILS)—software programs that provide an instructional sequence and tool for student self-monitoring—did not lead to increased reading achievement when compared with students who did not use ILS. Slavin and colleagues (2009) reviewed studies on instructional software in reading instruction and found small effects on reading tests at all grade levels. They emphasize that software must not be used in place of a teacher, and it must be used with clear intentions and in conjunction with expert and intentional reading instruction. Obviously, software programs should not be used for a total reading instructional program, but rather as a supplement to instruction (Kulik, 2003).

There is also a growing number of studies on the use of ICTs and their benefits in the classroom. One such tool is the multimedia book or e-book, which can be found online or on CD-ROMS, with sound effects incorporated in electronic texts. This tool has been shown to promote reading comprehension of struggling second-grade readers by indicating the mood and action of the story (Labbo, 2000; Lefever-Davis & Pearman, 2005; Pearman, 2008). Some electronic texts allow the reader to interact with the text, in essence reinventing the feeling of the "Choose Your Own Adventure" books (e.g., Montgomery, 1982). In some electronic texts, the reader can choose the level of scaffolding he or she receives (e.g., to be read aloud to, to see words highlighted). There are some concerns with the use of these materials in classrooms. For instance, readers may rely on the program to do the reading, rather than reading themselves. Children have been observed spending more time on automatic animations, sound effects, and hot spots that initiate actions in the programs than on actual reading. In fact, one study showed that 65% of the time children spent "reading" was actually spent in nonreading activities (Lewis & Ashton, 1999). While sound effects and graphic animations that further the storyline can provide support for the struggling reader, those that do not reflect story events or further the storyline can actually inhibit children's abilities to recall story information (Trushell, Maitland, & Burrell, 2003).

Recent studies have also shown how teachers use the Internet in their classrooms. Karchmar (2008) explored 13 teachers' (8 elementary teachers) reports on how the Internet influenced literacy instruction in their classrooms. The eight elementary teachers focused on the appropriateness of reading material found on the Internet (mostly with respect to the reading level of the material). The teachers looked for material with a lot of white space and visuals for beginning and developing readers. They found that the biggest problem with websites was too much print and two few graphics. Some teachers did not permit the struggling readers to use the Internet and considered this work supplemental, creating an equity issue (discussed in the next section). The teachers also taught students to evaluate information accuracy. While the teachers had always taught their students to question print text, they believed it was even more important to teach them to question digital texts. They discussed with their students that not all texts were accurate and taught them how to use multiple resources to check information. The teachers also published student work on the Internet. Elementary teachers noticed an increase in their students' motivation to write when their work was published on the Internet.

New Literacies in Diverse Classrooms

Like many technologies of the past (radio, television), educators saw possibilities for the equal access of information across all populations of people through the rise of the Internet. Poor children in underdeveloped countries as well as in the United States could now have access to information all people have, as long as they have a computer nearby. Still, a digital divide exists. More middle-class and wealthy youth have access to the advantages of the Internet and ICTs than do poor and working-class kids. The question, then, is: Can *schools* be the great equalizer by providing access to these tools and the scaffolding necessary for children to learn to use them successfully and efficiently?

Unfortunately, many educators have fallen into a traditional pattern of deficit thinking about poor students and Internet use. Studies are beginning to show that poor kids have less access to the Internet and ICTs *in school* than do middle-class and wealthy kids. It seems educators still view computer use as an "extra," rather than as a tool to engage and scaffold kids who may be disengaged from school or who need additional help. In some cases, economically challenged school districts seem to be denied online reading because school officials view online reading as something that will not raise school test scores (Anderson & Balajthy, 2009; Coiro & Dobler, 2007; Dalton & Proctor, 2008). When children in schools serving kids of poverty are invited to use ICTs and computers, it is usually with skill-oriented software programs rather than inquiry-based projects (Karchmar, 2001, 2008). This is sometimes the case, regardless of the students' reading skills. There is a digital divide in computer use *by school*, not always by individual.

Of course, some concerns rest with the skills students need in order to successfully navigate the Internet. Students who already struggle with print (who come from all socioeconomic backgrounds) may lack the reading speed and critical reading habits that are essential to effective reading on the Internet (Dalton & Proctor, 2008). Some tools can assist in this regard. We know that with print reading, word recognition and fluency act as gatekeepers, restricting access to the texts kids can read independently. With digital texts, readers have multiple cues to use for meaning making. Kids can learn to read digital texts before print text. Many of us have witnessed 3- and 4-year-olds who can spend 30 minutes of uninterrupted time at the computer with a game of some sort, clicking here and there for their purposes. They are "reading" digital texts, even though most of what they are reading are images with some print embedded in them. They quickly learn words such as "Go" before they can decode because reading that word serves their function in playing the game.

Further, with TTS technology, printed texts found on the Internet can be read aloud to students. TTS can serve as a scaffolding tool to help learners who cannot read the digital text independently (Dalton & Proctor, 2008). The use of TTS can allow students to focus on meaning, within a hybridized reading–listening task with the computer as scaffold. Teachers must be careful not to disenfranchise the kids who struggle with print literacy by keeping them away from inquiry-based projects and relegating them to print texts or merely skill-and-drill software programs on the computer. That would bring us back to the old basic skills argument of the print reading wars, discussed in Chapter 1. Certainly, the field of new literacies requires greater attention to issues of diversity and individual differences than ever before.

PRINCIPLES FOR TEACHING NEW LITERACIES

Figure 10.1 outlines general principles for teaching new literacies.

- Focus instruction on the key skills and strategies that kids need to learn to comprehend information on the Internet: how to locate information, ask important questions, critically evaluate the sites and information in them, synthesize information, use the information, and communicate it to others.
- Avoid using skill and drill software for struggling readers and writers. All kids need opportunities for exciting inquiry-based projects using the Internet.
- Broaden your views of what constitutes text to include images of all sorts.
- Use the tools that truly enhance learning, not just those that seem cool.
- Recognize that increased use of the Internet as a resource will increase instructional planning time initially.
- To use software programs purported to help readers, observe carefully what the children are doing while they use the program. If they are not productive, have them spend their time differently. Critically examine online material, just as you do for traditional print materials, regarding appropriateness.
- Allow sufficient time for each child to use the varied technology.
- Model ethical use and safe practices on the Internet. For example, if a child wants to use an image from a published webpage, show him or her how to e-mail the supervisor of that site and ask permission. Prevent students from writing personal information on blogs, wikis, or message boards.
- Never forget that reading a great picture book and having a meaningful conversation about important topics cannot be replaced by technology, no matter how cool or sophisticated the tool might seem. Some things cannot replace the most important elements of teaching.

FIGURE 10.1. Principles for new literacies teaching.

ASSESSMENT OF NEW LITERACIES

The field of new literacies is so new that assessments have not been developed for classroom use. Past attempts to evaluate the work young people do online has resulted mostly in teachers questioning the legitimacy of these activities (Burke & Hammett, 2009). New literacies products look so different that teachers often do not know where to begin to assess them. Further, as children learn to use social networking spaces, YouTube, and other video sites, music sites, and endless websites to incorporate into *their* texts, they often see these "hybrid" texts as original pieces, while to teachers they seem like plagiarism (Burke & Hammett, 2009). The notion of what makes a "good text," as represented by the writing rubric we shared in Chapter 9, is dramatically changing. Children (and adults) may quite legitimately reject a product that includes merely printed text. If we know how to engage through still pictures, moving pictures, music, and video, why limit ourselves to print? This plethora of possibilities makes assessment of products much more complex.

Further, new literacies scholars (Burke & Hammett, 2009; Coiro et al., 2008) emphasize the importance of assessing the process of communicating as well as the product. How well do students use new literacies? What sources do they take up and which do they reject and why? How effective and efficient are they in accomplishing their goals? In accomplishing the teachers' goals? They are both important.

Currently, teachers' most powerful tool for assessing their students' use of ICTs and the effects of their use is through careful observation. When teachers observe what their students do online, for example, they can see whether the students are engaged in efficient, purposeful, and productive activities. They can see whether children are wasting time or making use of the many tools. Teachers should also carefully observe students' products, whether they are traditional print products such as an essay that extended from an Internet inquiry project or a multimedia project shared with classmates. Teachers can begin to discern which tools help their students and which do not. Assessment of new literacies, like all aspects of literacy instruction, should include observation of both process and product.

Many online activities such as blogs, wikis, message boards, and videoclips can serve as indicators of students' understandings of content. These interactive venues can help children shape their ideas with others. The creation of digital stories can offer content for students to retell and manipulate. Again, it is important to use technology as a tool with which students can learn, practice, and then show their understandings of content.

COOL TOOLS: STRATEGIES, TOOLS, AND ACTIVITIES WITH THE INTERNET AND ICTS

In this section we explore literacy tools we have found useful or that we see as having educational potential. This is not an exhaustive discussion, as new literacies and technologies are evolving rapidly. The selections are meant to provide ideas for diversifying and augmenting your instruction. Remember, technology is not meant to be a replacement for good teaching. It is meant to support instruction.

Software Programs

There are many software programs designed to assist students with literacy learning, including programs focused on fluency, phonics, comprehension, and vocabulary. Software programs are best used for practice, although some can be used for initial instruction when scaffolding is provided by the teacher. For example, the exciting program Time to Know (TTK) (*timetoknow.com*) is for use in a one-to-one teaching environment in which every child has a laptop and can upload stories and graphics that teach specific reading strategies (including many of those covered in this book) with various types of texts, including some with multiple reading levels on the same topic. Like any software program, though, the skills and strategies must be monitored by the teacher in order for the practice to be meaningful.

Software programs can also help children formulate their understandings into finished products, as can happen with programs like Kidspiration (Inspiration Software, Inc., 2009). However, it is important to remember that a computer–student tutoring session is ineffective in increasing reading performance without teacher input, as discussed above. Be wary of promises within these programs and resources, and take time to sit with your students when they are engaged with such media to monitor their progress in person.

Google Earth

Google Earth (*earth.google.com*) is a favorite among teachers. It is used to show students locations on the Earth via satellite. While reading literature that depicts locations around the globe, teachers can pull up maps of those regions to enhance understandings of the literature, practice map skills, and explore the global community. In studying their own neighborhoods, as Vicky's fifth-grade students did, students can find their communities from Google Earth. This site provides opportunities to integrate social studies, mathematics, and literacy instruction, just like many of the excellent new Web locations.

YouTube and Google Videos

YouTube has become a sensation in the last few years, making important video accessible to nearly everyone. Teachers can find videos to support content in their classroom lessons or to support information learned within books. For instance, when reading *Sadako and the Thousand Paper Cranes* (Coerr, 1977), Audrey and her fourth graders viewed a video on YouTube that showed them, step by step, how to make the cranes. For teaching kids how to think through steps in a process such as in sequencing, this technology is useful and can inspire in-class "how-to" videos. You can even find retro *Reading Rainbow* videos and similar content on YouTube.

Twitter in Second Grade

One second-grade teacher in an urban school district, Mike, has his second graders actively using several cool tools. They regularly use Twitter to report to those outside of class (parents, guardians, and other interested followers) what they are doing. The "tweets" from the students below (printed as they are found on Mike's Twitter site) give you an idea of how Mike is weaving technology use into his instruction.

> "Outside me and Sarah Duncan chopped up onions and made homes for insects and worms."
> "We are getting to watch a webcast from New Jersey at 1pm about the Magic School Bus and Earth Day."
> "We did math we worked on different starategys in math."
> "I just published Dolpin Watch on 4-19-10 on Scrib."
> "We did a lot of reading today."
> "We went to music today to practice the play. We did scene three and four."
> "In math I learned a new strategy. I learned how to make tens."

Inquiry Searches on the Internet

Audrey's lesson that began this chapter was an extension of the research conducted by Julie Coiro (2003), who studied what students do when they read on the Internet. She observed that when conducting an Internet search, students click on whatever link they see first after entering a word or phrase into a search engine. This can take students down roads teachers would prefer they not go (e.g., to ads, to inappropriate sites with inaccurate information). Like Audrey, above, teachers must explicitly instruct students on *how* to search on the Internet. Leu and Coiro (2009) suggest that teachers engage their students in an exercise in which they are told to click only once after they enter their search phrase. They then compare their choices with others. They see where they ended up, what sort of information they gathered, and how useful it was compared to the information gleaned by their peers. They then ask themselves what strategies they used to select the particular site on which they clicked. Online assessment of URL knowledge is critical when looking for social justice information because there are many racist and antijustice sites on the Internet.

Nancy's class conducted a research project on heroes. After the class visited the library and read books on various heroes, they completed an organizer Nancy had found on *www.Readwritethink.org*, called a BioCube Planning Sheet (see Figure 10.2). The students visited the computer lab, and with assistance from Nancy and the computer teacher, each conducted Internet searches of their heroes. The teachers first conducted a lesson on choosing sites with accurate information. Using the projector, Nancy demonstrated how to read through the search results by modeling her thinking and selection of useful links. She pointed out ways to identify advertisements. "Does Amazon really want to teach you about Maya Angelou, or does it want to sell you a book about or writ-

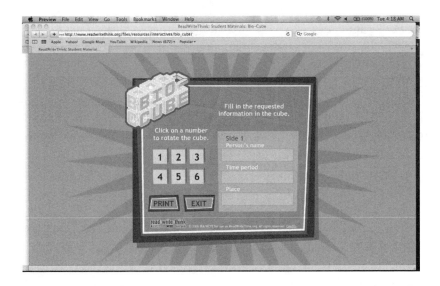

ReadWriteThink.org is a nonprofit website maintained by the International Reading Association and the National Council of Teachers and English, with support from the Verizon Foundation. The site publishes free classroom and professional development resources for teachers of reading and the English language arts. *www.readwritethink.org/files/resources/interactives/bio_cube*. Reprinted by permission.

FIGURE 10.2. BioCube.

ten by her?" Students then used the website's planning sheets to enter information into an interactive graphic organizer.

The BioCube prompts you to fill in information about a person you are studying: name, time period, place, personal background, personality traits, significance, biggest obstacle, important quotation. Each of these (except the first three) is entered in a different step of the program. Once you've entered information into all of the steps and hit print, it creates a cube with the information you entered on it. You can then print it, cut it out, glue the tabs and have a BioCube of the person you're studying. You could use it as a study tool for a group of students—they could swap cubes and quiz one another!

Cyberguides and WebQuests are predesigned inquiry activities that require students to use the resources on the Internet to answer questions and explore topics. Teachers can design cyberguides or WebQuests that lead students online from site to site (so the content is safe) in search of specific content and information. There are cyberguides and WebQuests already on the Internet for use. Examples of cyberguides by grade level can be found at *www.sdcoe.k12.ca.us/Score/cyberguide.html*.

Multimedia Literature/Electronic Texts/E-Books

Literature on the Internet is different from print literature because it is often multimedia; that is, it might include print, pictures, video, and interactive components that get the reader to respond to the text. Some variations of online literature simply illustrate pages from books and let children do the reading. Other variations have sound components in which the stories or text are read aloud. Still others are more interactive and require active participation from the reader.

The Kindle and other electronic readers could be paving the way for a revolution in reading. With her iPad, Ellen can read newspapers from around the world. Whenever she wants a word defined, it happens automatically with the press of a button. She can get the Spanish newspaper *El País* to learn what is going on in Spain and to practice her Spanish. She was even told she can download an "app" (application) that will translate Spanish words into English words simply by putting the cursor under any Spanish word. Think if children could have such a tool! Our ELLs could learn English so much more efficiently; our native speakers could learn a second or third language more easily; and all words could be defined immediately and efficiently, without ever resorting to paper dictionaries.

Digital Storytelling

Many teachers now have their students use digital tools (e.g., cameras, iPods, camcorders, computers for writing) to tell stories. Digital stories can incorporate print text, recorded audio for narration, videoclips, computer-based images, and/or music. Topics can be infinite and genre varied. We have seen personal stories from students' perspectives, descriptions of important people and events in history, and a funny (but accurate and informative) video of the effects of global warming. Completed digital stories can then serve as another resource for reading material for students while also providing an opportunity to express and produce ideas.

In creating digital stories, students must select a topic, write a plan or script, and collect and organize the data, images, and text for the story. Students can show their knowledge and comprehension of a story by creating their own versions of *Reading Rainbow*, using books that they select and endorse. They can exhibit good fluency by practicing a text or script several times, recording themselves reading the text, and then including that recording as the soundtrack for their digital story. Digital storytelling can be a useful tool in teaching vocabulary, in particular, to ELLs. An excellent inspiring online resource with which to launch the use of digital storytelling in the classroom comes from the University of Houston can be found at *digitalstorytelling.coe.uh.edu*.

Digital stories can also be found on the Internet and can serve as venues for recreational reading or practice for children. These include sites that do not read aloud the work, such as *www.childrenslibrary.org*, and those that do, such as *andersenfairytales.com/en/main*.

Podcasts

A podcast is an audio or video broadcast, such as a radio show, to which one can subscribe over the Internet. It can be played on the computer or transferred onto a portable media player such as an iPod. The information shared within a podcast is "inexpensive to produce, simple to use, portable, reusable, and beneficial to auditory learners" (Putman & Kingsley, 2009, p. 101). It can provide a convenient way for teachers to have their students listen to a radio program or view a downloaded video of news at any time of the day, not just during the original broadcast. Like many types of multimedia formats, podcasts can be used as a tool to teach novel concepts, reinforce content previously learned, remediate students who require extra practice or need to hear content reinforced, and to bring outside "experts" into the classroom. Students and classrooms can also create podcasts, demonstrating and sharing content they have learned, views that they hold, or skills they are practicing. You or your classroom can create podcasts through the use of online resources such as Audacity (*audacity.sourceforge.net*). Podcasts for classrooms can be posted to blogs and school, classroom, or district websites. Many examples can be found on iTunes, and you can learn a lot about the medium at sites such as *www.intelligenic.com/blog.*

Handheld Devices

Some handheld devices can be useful in helping students practice skills. The iPod Touch, for instance, can be used by students to practice vocabulary (e.g., Word Salad), phonics, and other types of drills. The iPod Touch "minilab" has a storage and charging cart with dozens of iPods and a laptop for downloading educational applications and transferring them to the players. In addition, there are handheld devices and applications that can serve as interpretive tools for ELLs.

Online Literature Discussions

Literature discussions on the Internet have the potential to build students' literacy skills, strengthen communication skills, and build a sense of community in the classroom (Larson, 2009). Online discussions include the use of message boards, wikis, blogs, and social networking sites. *Message boards* allow participants to add comments to a shared page. In a scholastic message board, for example, the participant responds to a prompt about Harry Potter that asks, "What do you think of the Dursleys?" He responds, "I think the Dursleys are mean. They're like a lot of people who just don't like people who are different. They're scared of Harry because he is different." Students can read other peoples' posts and add their own. Most message boards utilize written feedback, but some are introducing the use of voice recordings, as well. One such site is Voxopop (*www.voxopop.com*).

Wikis

Wikis are websites that allow for online collaboratively authored documents. Wikipedia is the ultimate example of a wiki. Wikis are often used in the workplace to create documents by multiple authors and are ideal for collaborative writing projects. They can be created by pairs, groups of students, or teachers. Students can work together to create a collaboratively authored document or they can help one another while creating individual documents. The teacher can contribute to the process as "collaborator, guide, editor, or site administrator" (Morgan & Smith, 2008, p. 80). A teacher can start a wiki by visiting several sites; two useful ones are PBWiki (*pbwiki.com*) and Wikispaces (*www.wikispaces.com*). These are easy to use and manage for most teachers, and are considered safe for use by most districts. Morgan and Smith (2008) offer the following advice to teachers interested in using wikis in the classroom:

1. Mistakes can be fixed easily, so don't fear the wiki.
2. Create a playground page first to practice; PBWiki and Wikispaces both offer this option.
3. Look at other wikis that you like, click on the page source code button, and borrow it by copy and pasting it to the pages of your wiki.
4. Plan the format of your wiki.

A variety of wiki types can be useful in the elementary classroom. These include *classroom wikis*, which allow teachers and students to relay assignments, work, and communications; *report wikis*, which show collaborative research projects; *school wiki* sites, which allow the school staff, students, and parents to engage in communication concerning the school; and *large-scale wikis for interschool projects*, which link multiple sites and encourage communication among them (Morgan & Smith, 2008).

Blogs

Blogs are online spaces that individuals, groups, or organizations can use for communication purposes. Blogs allow visitors to add comments to other peoples' entries or to add new strands of conversation. The difference between a blog and a wiki is that visitors can *add* comments concerning the content on a blog, whereas wikis allow visitors to *change* the content. Teachers can have their own pages with places for individual student work, areas for comments and information about homework, areas of study, and special events such as field trips or science fairs. You can set up a blog on *www.wordpress.com*, *www.edublogs.org*, and other places.

Different types of blogs are found in elementary classrooms (Zawalinski, 2009). There are classroom news blogs, which share news with parents and students; mirror blogs, which "allow bloggers to reflect on their thinking" (p. 652); showcase blogs, which highlight student work such as projects, podcasts, and writing; and literature response blogs, which are basically literature response journals in blog format. For a more thorough discussion of these types of blogs and "how-to" steps on setting up your own classroom blog, see Zawalinski (2009).

Although these are all exciting and potentially useful tools, teachers are the ones who must plan instruction *purposefully* while using these technologies. Think to yourself, does this technology actually enhance and further my students' understandings of the content I am trying to teach them? Is the technology inhibiting learning, or is it promoting learning? Am I using technology as a tool rather than as the focus?

NEW LITERACIES
AND CULTURALLY RESPONSIVE INSTRUCTION

The thoughtful integration of technology into the classroom lends itself to the inclusion of some aspects of culturally responsive instruction. With the use of digital storytelling, podcasts, publishing on the Internet, and other modes of communication discussed here, students can construct new knowledge by building on their backgrounds. Students can communicate globally to others who share their perspectives or with others who are quite different from them; they can learn about many people directly through those people. These global advantages should be harnessed as opportunities to make the classroom a welcoming space for children all over the world.

Teachers can encourage struggling and proficient readers to use their own voices in their writing, building on what they know and then expanding from the page to the podcast, movie, blog, etc. Wikis, blogs, and message boards can serve as places for students to voice their opinions, share ideas, and learn about others. Teachers can build curriculum from students' backgrounds using new literacies in many ways.

In addition, students can show their talents for home languages that are different than English by interpreting or helping to explain literature found on the Internet, such as on the International Children's Digital Library site. For instance, a child from Croatia can help to explain the finer points of life depicted in an online book about a Croatian family. Not only does this build on a student's home language patterns, but it makes the student the expert.

As previously stated, software programs should not be seen as one-on-one tutors because research shows that these programs are not effective in increasing reading ability. However, when students use technology in pairs or groups to read a text, create a product, or do research, they learn through the interaction. Group work and dialogic instruction are paramount in many forms of technology use. Many message boards allow visitors to practice writing, and some let them practice speaking new languages. The creation of podcasts, wikis, digital stories, and iMovies are just a few forms of collaborative work that are possible through the new literacies.

Finally, we must remember that technology must be used purposefully and must help to challenge students to reach new understandings and skill levels. A rigorous curriculum within a new literacy mindset includes content that furthers students' understandings while at times utilizing technology to enhance and push students' abilities within their ZPDs.

CHAPTER 11

Research-Based, Culturally Responsive Reading Instruction in Second Grade

Nancy teaches in a highly diverse school district, one of the largest in the country. Her school serves a student body in which 82% of students are on free or reduced lunch, 25.5% of the student body is European American, and 6% of students are identified as ELLs. Nancy's class is the second-grade "immersion" class, which includes all second-grade ELLs and many students with special needs who receive specialized instruction from additional teachers. Among the 24 students in her class, nine are African American, six Hispanic, six European American, two of self-described "mixed race," and one student from Myanmar. In this setting Nancy implements the research-based, culturally responsive reading model we describe in this book. She is a successful teacher of the model, but like all teachers, she finds some aspects of reading instruction more challenging than others. In this chapter she describes her schedule across a day and week, providing the details that illustrate how the components of the model fall into place across time, how instruction builds from previous lessons, how she finds time to reach every child, and how she makes on-the-spot decisions regarding instructional practices. The dialogue included is not an exact transcription; it is only remembered and recreated for this chapter. At the end of the chapter, Ellen reflects on Nancy's instruction, highlighting the research-based and culturally responsive aspects of her teaching.

MY DAY BEGINS

I was never a morning person until I became a teacher. Now I have my routine, with coffee in hand to start my day. On the drive to school I listen to National Public Radio and think through my goals for the day: I want to have patience, kindness, persistence, and understanding with my kids, their parents, and my colleagues. I like to get to school

30 minutes to an hour before the kids, just so I can get my head together and the room ready for the day. I also like to get there before others know I'm there, so that I can have quiet time to take in the morning, think through my plans, and talk to myself about why I am there every day.

I think about yesterday. I wonder if Nat will remember his glasses and if the bus driver protected him from the bully who tries to steal them; I wonder if Chantanay got any sleep last night, how Alex did in his basketball game, and whether Trae had trouble on his math homework. I call parents on my list and check my lesson plans to make sure I have everything ready for the day's activities.

I am absolutely not the most organized person in the world, but there is a method to the madness, and I lay things out the way it makes sense to me. I put the book we will read in shared reading on the easel with whatever materials we may need for response activities. Sometimes I use the big books provided in our district's adopted reading program, Rigby, and other times I use books from the school or public library or my own collection. I check the reading table to be sure I have the group sets of books ready, along with what I need for the individual lessons: letter tiles, response activities, dry erase boards, Elkonin boxes, etc. I make sure the materials are ready for our phonics activity, sometimes requiring partner sets of word sorts and other times individual materials. I also make certain that I have the supplies needed for our writing lessons: chart paper, books, sample writing, etc.

I glance over at our classroom library. This week's librarian (a job students take turns having) has organized the books by labeling them with sticky notes (e.g., animal books, picture dictionaries, chapter books). I am impressed by Maria's thoughtful categories and book placements. I sharpen pencils for the sharp box, from which students take pencils when they need them, and return dull or broken ones to the dull box. I do this because I can't stand to hear the sound of a pencil sharpener in the middle of instruction, so my kids were taught early on to use this system. A friend and fellow teacher once said to me, "I love teaching every day, not every moment of every day, but every day." I smile when I think about that statement.

JOURNAL WRITING: 9:10–9:25

When students enter my second-grade classroom in the mornings they hang their coats on the wall outside, place their take-home folders in our in-box, and get pencils. I am reminded of writing researchers such as Donald Graves who say that children learn to write by writing, and so the kids begin each day writing in journals on topics of their choice. Some kids are excited to get straight to business, while others are busy chatting in the hallway. I greet the three girls in the hallway and then gently nudge them into the classroom by putting my arms around their shoulders and walking them toward the door. I listen to their talk. "Hey, why not write about that in your journal today?" I suggest. The children find their journals in the boxes on each set of desks and begin writing about a topic of their choosing. The writing varies. Some write about their mornings or evenings before, their best friends, what they hope they will do over the weekend. Others try writing like some of their favorite authors. For instance, Orion loves the *Cam Jansen* books by David Adler, and so he writes mystery stories involving his friends and himself as the main characters. In any case, the choice is always up to the students. They arrive with much to say and when they eagerly get their words down, they build fluency in their writing.

After about 10 minutes, I pull a few names from my name cup (which is full of tongue depressors with the students' names on them) and invite those children whose names are drawn to read aloud. They can read what they wrote that day or read a piece they'd written previously. Their sharing helps us learn about one another and is an opportunity to hear different styles of writing and to practice sharing with peers. I encourage children to use some of the journal entries as drafts for fully developed writing pieces they produce in writing workshop.

The name cup helps me make sure that I don't choose the same kids to share over and over. It lets kids know they are accountable and might be called on to read to their friends on any given day. I must confess, though, that some days I cheat. When Lizeth wrote about her sister's quinciñera with great detail and voice, I asked her to read aloud. On the day I drew Julian's name and had seen he had written about how sad he was that he rarely saw his dad because of the divorce, I asked him if he wanted to read aloud and he chose not to. I didn't press, but asked if he would read for us another time.

GREETING: 9:25–9:35

I dismiss individual tables one at a time to sit in a circle on the rug for *morning meeting* (Kriete & Bechtel, 2002). We begin with a greeting in which I turn to the person beside me and say, "*Buenos dias*, Chardae" or another such greeting. She returns the greeting, "*Buenos dias*, Mrs. Hulan," and then turns to the person sitting to the other side of her to continue the greeting game. In the beginning of the year we always discuss how to shake hands and be attentive and friendly to our friends. There are many greeting ideas in *The Morning Meeting Book* (Kriete & Bechtel, 2002).

Depending on my schedule for the day (e.g., special area classes, lunch) and mandates of my school or district (when you must teach specific topics and for how long), I can tweak my literacy block to match my preference and the needs of my students. There have been years when I chose to combine the morning meeting with the shared reading and word work portion of our literacy block to make a seamless transition. Other years I followed morning meeting with guided reading groups and then shared reading and word work followed.

WORD WALL: 9:35–9:50

One weekly job in my class is Word Wizard. Most students in my classroom love this role. Ler, for instance, has recently been relocated from a refugee camp in Myanmar and has limited conversational English skills. When it was his turn to be the Word Wizard, he was ecstatic. He had observed how to do the job. He knew that the Word Wizard gets to lead our word wall activity each day for a week, that the Word Wizard uses a pointer selected from a variety of implements (stirrers, finger puppets, or wands) and randomly chooses an activity from a cup that tells how the class will read the word wall words that day. Ler selected his implement and activity and showed me. I read it aloud, "Imaginary Chalkboard," and demonstrated how to point to a word (e.g., the word *two*) and pretend to write the letters of the word on an imaginary chalkboard, forming the word in the air while saying each letter as I wrote it, "*T-w-o, two.*" Ler immediately remembered this from his participation in the activity and leapt into the Word Wizard role. His enthusiasm was contagious, and kids jumped in to spell the words. My students have learned so much about words from this activity. As we described in Chapter 5, there are lots of other ideas for making learning fun with word walls.

SHARED READING: 9:50–10:15

During shared reading, we discuss an important theme from a text, and I model skills and strategies I will later reemphasize during small-group guided reading. I use stories or poems from big books when possible (so all can see the print), standard-sized books, chart paper, or a projection screen. Sometimes I spend a week on one piece of literature, each day focusing on something different about the work or teaching and reteaching a needed research-based strategy. Other weeks, I may use two or more books that together illustrate a particular theme, skill, or strategy. One week, my class had been experiencing problems with name-calling and general intolerance toward one another on the school bus, in the cafeteria, and on the playground. One child, crying, had told me his friend had started calling him Big Head. I knew we needed to face this problem as a group. I decided to select literature for shared reading that would help us talk about intolerance and learn some new reading skills as well. The books I selected were *Titoy and the Magical Chair* (Molina, 2002) and *Why?* (Popov, 1996). I began the shared reading with the following statement.

> "This week we're going to read some really cool books together. I can't wait to share them with you. Before I introduce the first story, I want to remind you of something that all good readers do. It's called *inferring* or *making inferences*. Oh! I can tell from some of your faces that you have heard that word before. Can anyone help us remember what *inferring* means?"

Students share ideas such as "Making smart guesses" and "Thinking about what's happening in a story." I congratulate the children on good ideas and say something like the following: "When you make an inference, you use what you already have in your smart brains and what you see in the story to figure something out about the character, the setting, or the plot. We're going to read some books together and in our guided reading groups, and we'll work on making inferences together."

We then prepare for viewing the digital story *Titoy's Magical Chair*. This activity involves students clearing their desks and turning their chairs to face the white screen in the front of the room. Some kids move their chairs to different spots for a good view. Digital stories can be a real find. In my school district all teachers are given laptops and projectors for use in the classroom. I *love* having Internet access in the classroom and try to use it in ways that keep kids interested in the content. Consequently, I have seen some kids' interest leap when we use technological resources but then wane when we get into the content. So, I have had to be particularly careful that what I find on the Internet maintains students' interest. During the week described here, I chose to use a digital story I found on the International Children's Digital Library. The story is also in print, but since I didn't have access to the print version and could easily use the digital version, I chose to use it. *Titoy's Magical Chair* (Molina, 2002) is a book about a little boy and his friend Titoy who have exciting experiences every day in Titoy's chair. It is not until well into the book that readers realize that Titoy is in a wheelchair and has no legs. As I read this book for the first time, I thought it was a great text for teaching tolerance and for practicing making predictions and inferences, two skills that go hand in hand in comprehension.

We begin with a "picture walk" on Monday to assist students with the skill of prediction, and I do a think-aloud that includes making an inference based on the cover art.

> "I see two boys, and it looks like they're holding on to a big red chair, like they're holding on so they don't fall off. And I see birds around them. Now I know that birds fly in the sky and that you would only hold on to a chair like that if you were worried about falling. . . . I think that chair's flying in the sky! [pause] I used what I know about the sky, how we sit in chairs, and flying. Plus, I use what I see in this picture to make an inference about this book."

We continue taking a picture walk through the digital story, stopping to discuss what might be going on in the pictures and emphasizing using the pictures with what we already know to make inferences. Before the lesson I always read the books I will use and find good stopping places for teaching or practicing the strategy we're focusing on that day. After I model a few times for the students, I want them to try it. I ask the students to practice making inferences on the pages by talking with their neighbors about what they see in the pictures, what they hear in the text (if we are reading at that point and not just looking at the pictures), and what they already know that will help them figure out what's going on in the story. Students share what they come up with in their pairs. After reading part of the story and stopping on page 7, I ask the kids to turn to their neighbors to discuss what they can infer about Titoy's chair from the information in the text, the picture, and their brains. After conferring, Maria offers a suggestion.

> "The picture looks like it has lots of neat stuff that my chairs at my house don't have. And he says it doesn't use gas but goes places. Maybe they're playing make believe,

'cuz I do that with my friends, and we act like we're at the beach or at school or at Six Flags."

Another student, whose cousin uses a wheelchair, shares that he can tell by looking at the picture that Titoy's chair is a wheelchair because of the gadgets it has on it. It looks similar to his cousin's wheelchair. We continue to make inferences as we read the rest of the book. When we get to the end of the book, I ask students to talk with this prompt:

"We found out in this book that Titoy is a fun friend and that he is in a wheel-chair. The main character in this book—we don't know his name—but he isn't in a wheelchair and he plays with Titoy, and they both pretend that the chair is magi-cal. Do any of you have friends who are different than you in some way, like Titoy and the other boy? I want you to think about that and turn to a friend and talk to them about your friends who might be different than you and how that makes your friendship extra special."

Interesting discussions arise around the classroom, and I pop in and out of conversa-tions to listen to student's language use, encourage ELL students to use the language of their choice, to ask questions, give examples, or make remarks I hope will push kids' thinking on the subject. I listen to two children have this conversation:

"You're my friend and you speak a different language than me," Destiny tells Guadalupe.

"Yeah, I speak Spanish and English."

To push this to a higher level of thinking, I ask the girls, "How does that difference affect you as friends?" They look at me blankly. I press on. "Does the fact that Guadalupe speaks Spanish make it more fun or interesting to hang out with her? Can you learn something from her?"

Eyebrows raise, "Oh! Yeah. She's already taught me to count to 10 in Spanish, and when I go to her house to spend the night we have tortillas."

Nice, I think. They're onto the point. "OK, Guadalupe, what about you? Is there something that you can learn from Destiny or that makes Destiny very interesting?"

Guadalupe presses her lips together and looks down in thought. "Destiny takes karate and shows me how to do stuff like that. We have fun when we spend the night together."

I smile at the girls and do a hand clap to get everyone's attention and say, "I love what I'm hearing from you all. I heard some great ways that you all are different, and those things make each of you special. I heard ways that you can learn and *appreciate* the differences of others. That means that you understand that the way we are different is special."

During the second half of the week I chose to use the wordless picture book *Why?* (Popov, 1996) because it is perfect for making inferences. The illustrations are striking and gorgeous, and all kids can relate to the peaceful frog who is unfairly pushed off his rock by the bellicose mouse. It was particularly appropriate since our class had been dealing with name calling and bullying. The day after we finished with *Titoy* I intro-duced *Why?* by saying, "OK, you guys, we've been working on using a strategy that good readers use. What is it?" When I cup my hand behind my ears, they know they can let loose and yell it if they know it.

"Inferring!"

"OK, today I'm going to share with you one of my favorite books. It's called *Why?*, and it's by a Russian author whose name is Nikolai Popov. Mr. Popov grew up seeing lots of war and conflict. Will you please turn to a neighbor and talk about what you think the word *conflict* means?" There's a buzz in the room as kids share with one another.

Alexis shouts out, "A conflict is somebody who's in jail."

I respond, "I think you may have misunderstood the word I used. You are thinking of *convict*, and yes, convicts go to jail. The word I used is *conflict*, and in this book you will see what a conflict is. Mr. Popov grew up around lots of war and conflict or fighting. When we look at the pictures we're going to infer, using what we know about war and fighting and the pictures, to say what we think is going on in this book." I slowly show the pictures and the kids freely say what they think is going on in the story. The pictures are amazing and immediately capture the kids' attention and desire to participate. José always hangs back in the rear of the group, and although he is usually attending closely, he often must be prompted to speak. "José, what do you think is going on in this pic-ture?"

José begrudgingly smirks and replies, "Well, the mouse and the frog were fighting for the rock and now they've made everything uh. . . . " He looks up and asks, "What's the word?"

Other kids offer suggestions, "*Ugly*," "*Ruined*," "*Destroyed*," "*Polluted*."

José grins and says, "Yeah. All those." We continue to talk about how the two char-acters must feel at the end of the book, based on our experience with fighting and using the pictures for help. Students get out their reader response journals and reflect on the story in writing.

WORD WORK: 10:15–10:30

In my classroom we have a short whole-group word work period. I differentiate word work instruction for specific needs by incorporating word work into guided reading lessons using *Phonics Lessons* for second grade (Pinnell & Fountas, 2003), which is pro-vided in my district. This allows me to teach phonological skills in a systematic, explicit way that is closely based on kids' needs. Also, my assistant works with the groups alter-natively on specific skills I recommend.

As an example of the daily whole-class word work, we might focus on a skill such as spelling inflected endings, specifically /ed/ and /ing/. In the previous lesson, pairs of students sorted words that double the consonant (e.g., *hopped*) and those that don't (e.g., *hoped*) when adding an *-ed* ending. Today, students work in small groups to play sound dominoes (see Figure 11.1). In this game, each group gets a bag with dominoes in it. The

hopped	booted

borrowed	cracked

folded	bubbled

FIGURE 11.1. Sound dominoes.

dominoes have words with -ed endings that all sound different: /t/ ending as in hopped; /ed/ ending as in booted; and /d/ ending as in borrowed. I make these dominoes using cardstock, and when I'm especially ambitious (and the laminator works), I laminate them so that they will last longer. They can be made on the computer or with cardstock paper and marker.

Students each get five dominoes, and then each takes a turn adding a domino from his or her set to match the sound ending of a word that's already on the table. If they don't have a match, then students draw from the stack of remaining dominoes. We have played this game several times throughout the year, and the kids come to know exactly what is expected of them when we get out the bags. Since we only have 15 minutes to play, it is important that they know the routine, and therefore we go over the steps and expectations clearly whenever we play. I mill about the room, looking at the way kids place their dominoes on the board, paying attention to kids who seem to be having trouble and observing for any altercations that arise among groups.

GUIDED READING: 10:30–11:30

I transition from the whole-group shared reading/word work to guided reading groups by assigning children to work in learning centers. I try to plan activities for the centers that are research-based or build on the work we do as a whole class. I go to the center chart and explain to which centers each child is assigned. I often ask students to remind us of the routines and expectations for the centers. These centers are described in the next section.

Guided reading is the heart of my reading program. Sometimes, I group the children based on common reading levels and skills. Other times I form groups based on students' interests or even friendships. Other considerations for planning guided reading groups include the time frame, how many groups I have, and the help I have in my classroom (e.g., assistants, reading buddies, pull-out reading programs). I always try to give the students who struggle with reading the most time with me in guided reading groups. I see myself (as the classroom teacher should) as the most trained person in the room to help my students reach their reading and academic potential. Because of this, I spend as much time as I can with the students who struggle with reading in one-on-one and small-group settings to boost their skills, strategies, and interest in reading. Figure 11.2 shows how I scheduled our guided reading time when I had four reading groups and one assistant. The asterisk (*) indicates times when my assistant circulated and helped students at their desks and centers.

On the week shown above, my students are broken into four groups based on reading level. I meet with groups A and B daily because the children in those groups need my help the most. Groups C and D are reading on grade level, and although they certainly need my guidance, I meet with them less often. My goal for them is to find meaningful work in the centers so that their literacy skills are also pushed. Also, the children in these groups work with my assistant as needed. When I meet with children in these

	Time	10:30–10:50	10:50–11:10	11:10–11:30
Monday	What the other kids are doing	Centers (B, C)	Independent Reading/ Writers Notebook (C, D)	Centers (A, D)
	Teacher	A	B	C
	Assistant	D	A (making words)	B
Tuesday	What the other kids are doing	Independent reading/ writers notebook (C, D)	Centers (B, D)	Centers (A, C)
	Teacher	B	A	D
	Assistant	A	C	B
Wednesday	What the other kids are doing	Centers (B, C)	Independent reading/ writers notebook (B, D)	Centers (A, D)
	Teacher	A	C	B
	Assistant	D	A*	C
Thursday	What the other kids are doing	Independent reading/ writers notebook (C, D)	Centers (B, D)	Centers (A, C)
	Teacher	B	A	D
	Assistant	A	C	B
Friday	What the other kids are doing	Centers (B, C)	Independent reading/ writers notebook (C, D)	Centers (A, D)
	Teacher	A	B	C
	Assistant	D	A*	B

FIGURE 11.2. Nancy's schedule for guided reading group.

groups, I check in on their progress: I listen to them read, talk with them about their understandings of the books, words that confuse them, and whatever else needs attention.

Developing Readers: 10:30–10:50

This group is reading Eric Carle's *Slowly Slowly Slowly Said the Sloth* (2002). My goals for this lesson are to help student deepen their understanding of the hurtful consequences of verbal bullying. As well, I want them to develop reading skills such as summarization and inference and to continue to develop a stronger vocabulary. The book I have chosen is ideal for all three goals. The vocabulary in this book is rich and sophisticated and motivates children to learn new words. In the book, many animals of the rainforest question the sloth about his lifestyle with not-so-nice ways of describing him. They say he's slow, quiet, boring, and lazy. The sloth quietly listens to the other animals and ultimately responds by saying he is not lazy, he is "sluggish, lethargic, placid, calm, mellow, laid-back and, well, slothful" (Carle, 2002, p. 23). This one page is a great spot to practice our vocabulary strategies. I know that studies suggest much repetition of words we want the children to learn. I try to use the words as often as I can, and I invite the children to use them often, too.

The day before, I had led the group through prereading activities (a picture walk, making predictions, accessing prior knowledge). On this day I guided the students though reading the story. I invited them to read a few pages silently by prompting them with their own predictions from the previous day. "Read to find out . . . " was my usual prompt. We checked our comprehension every couple of pages, with students turning to their partners to retell what was going on in the text and how it made them feel. We also confirmed and rejected predictions we had made. When we got to the page quoted above, all the kids were stumped by the new and strange words, although they likely had some sense of their meanings from the context. I watched as kids started using the strategies they knew. Brian tried to find little words in big words by covering parts up with his fingers. Lizeth skipped the words she didn't automatically recognize (*sluggish, lethargic, placid*), reading only those she could pronounce. José came right out and asked, "What's *that* word?" These strategies might have helped them to decode the words, but not to understand what the words *meant*.

After kids do their best to decode the words on the page, I prompt them by saying, "OK, these are some really juicy words! I'm going to read the page aloud the way I think these words might sound, and I want you to think about what these words might mean by using the context, or other words around them, to help you." I read the page slowly but with expression. Then I show them a chart with all of the new words written down the left side. "Let's document our predictions about these words. I'm sure you have some guesses about what these words mean. Right now we're not worried about being perfectly correct. We just want to make smart guesses or predictions about what we think the words mean. So who wants to make a smart guess about the word *sluggish*?" As I say the word, I make sure to emphasize the *slug* part of it.

José was the first to respond. "I've heard the word slug before. They're *nasty*! They're slimy and they get on the sidewalk outside my dad's house. Grandpa says to pour beer on 'em."

"Thank you, José. So, maybe *sluggish* means slimy? Does that sloth look slimy?" (The children look at the picture closely.) "When Destiny and Shaun presented about sloths during our rainforest investigation, did they say that sloths were slimy?" The kids shake their heads no. "I really like how you're using that little word slug as a clue. What else do we know about slugs? Have any of you ever watched a slug move?"

"Well, I've seen a slug, but he didn't look like he was moving very much. He looked like a giant snail without a shell." Oscar had made a great connection.

"Wow, Oscar! I have to agree with you that they don't seem to move very much, so maybe they move slowly, *and* they look kinda like giant snails. If slugs move slowly, does that give us a clue about what the word *sluggish* means?"

"Maybe sluggish means slow or not moving much," Lizeth speaks up.

"Lizeth, will you please write that under the prediction part of the chart next to sluggish?"

The group continues like this with each word. Some have clues within them, as did *sluggish*, and others are complete mysteries to us, like *lethargic*. We make the best guesses we can using what we know about sloths, the mood and stance of the sloth, the pictures, and the surrounding words. Eventually, the chart (Figure 11.3) includes all the children's predictions.

Finally, we discuss the meaning of the book. I carefully plan the instructional conversation with the goals to help children construct meaning about this book, to learn what it takes (the kind of thinking) to gain meaning from future books they read, and help them develop oral language skills at the same time. Simultaneously, I have goals related to justice. I want the students to understand that the other animals were bullying the sloth, calling him names that could have hurt his feelings. I want students to

New word	Predictions	Dictionary check
sluggish	Not moving much Slow	
lethargic	Sleepy Skin like leather	
placid	Has dirty teeth	
calm	Peaceful	
mellow	Groovy	
laid-back	Chilled out	
slothful	Full of being a sloth	

FIGURE 11.3. Prediction vocabulary chart.

connect the theme of this book to the books we read during shared reading with the same theme. We talk about what happened to Frog and Mouse in *Why?*, and the fact that nothing good came from Mouse bullying Frog or the fight between the two creatures. I try to let the students do the talking, but nudge their thinking when I think it is needed. When students don't make the leap on their own, I ask them to think about Titoy and his friend. How are they different than Frog and Mouse? Students talk as a group, each trying to participate without talking during someone else's time, and decide that while Frog and Mouse argued over differences, Titoy and his friend, who also had differences, chose to have fun with what made them distinct, rather than fighting over it. The kids decide that having fun with differences is, well . . . more fun.

The following day, the group will look up the new words in dictionaries to see how accurate their predictions were. When we have learned the real meanings of the words, students will each get a sticker with "Ask me what *placid* [or another word] means." My students love this; they relish the experience when a lunchroom worker or the principal asks them what a word means and they can tell him or her the answer or use it in a sentence. I've even seen students trade word stickers in the middle of the day so that they can practice other words. As I said earlier, repetition of words is essential for learning them. The students will also write new pages for the book, choosing different choices for the animals, perhaps in which the animals say nice things to the sloth or acknowledge that he is different but OK. I love this book because there are so many wonderful life lessons and reading skill lessons that can spring from its pages. Our group time is almost up, but before the kids go to their centers I want them to reread the book once more, so I send them away in pairs with a copy of the book.

Developing Readers: 10:50–11:10

The goal for this lesson of developing readers is to help students develop a deeper understanding of the idea that racial and ethnic differences are only skin deep. We all dream, think, dance, feel, and love in much the same way. I am using the story *Am I a Color Too?* (Cole & Vogl, 2005) to address this issue. The main character of this story has a black dad and a white mom, and he begins by asking, "Am I a color, too?" This beautifully illustrated book includes images of children to whom the students in this group can relate, and ultimately makes the point that we are all human beings, "not a color, not a word." I also want these students to build skills in the spelling/phonics connection.

We have been working through many of the skill lessons in the "within-word pattern spelling" stage (Bear et al., 2004). This means that these students can read and write independently and can correctly spell short-vowel and single-syllable words. They are ready for a bit more advanced spelling/phonics connections. My goal is to help them both spell and decode words more easily. These skill areas build on one another.

Trae hurries over to get a seat next to me, while Donald is so engrossed in the book he's reading with his buddy that he needs to be asked several times to join the group. He comes over repeating the words "And Bear sleeps on" from the book he was just reading with a spring in his step. Finally everyone is at the table. "OK, guys, today we're going to do a Making Words (Cunningham & Hall, 2008) lesson with letter tiles. You will need one letter tile from each bag." We have practiced getting the letters out of the bags and passing them to our neighbors several times during the year. Kids learned to take just one tile, to hold the bag without letting any tiles fall out, and then to pass the bag to the person next to them. Each bag is passed around the group and then winds up back at my side. Like everything, passing the letters is practiced and I try to be clear about how to do each step. Students put all of the letters in a straight line in front of them.

"We have been reading *Am I a Color Too?* There are lots of great words and pictures in that book. Some of the words have the long *i* sound and are spelled with the letters *igh*. Today we're going to practice making long *-i* words with *igh*. Everybody, count your letters. You should have seven letters in front of you." I wait as everyone counts; if anyone is missing letters, we add the missing letters to his or her line.

"In front of you are the letters *s, f, h, i, g, t,* and *r*. I'd like you to use four of the letters to make the word *sigh*." Some of the students jump in and know from prior knowledge or from the prompt I gave them in this lesson that they should use *igh* to make the word. Others look around at their neighbors trying to get a little help. Eventually they all have the word spelled correctly in front of them. I ask one of the kids who created the word quickly to tell us which of the letters make the long *-i* sound. He answers, The letters *igh* make the long *-i* sound."

We continue. "Add one letter to turn *sigh* into *sight*." I ask a different child each time to explain what he or she did to make the new word and why it worked. For instance, Maria said the following: "I turned *sight* into *fight* because I took off the *s* and put an *f*." We make these words in order: *sigh, sight, fight, right, rights, frights*.

After the kids have made these words, I pass the letter bags around again and they put each individual letter tile in the appropriate bag and then pass the bag to their neighbor. After collecting the letter tiles, I pass out the individual copies of the book *Am I a Color Too?*

"You just made several words using *igh* to make the long *-i* sound. Now, we're going to reread this book chorally. As we read, I want you to pay attention to how the words are made and keep your eyes open for words spelled with the *igh* pattern." We begin to read chorally,

The group reads, "People call my dad Black, Like the dark night sky." Nicole raises her hand as she says, "Ooh, I found an *igh*." I ask her which word she found with the pattern, and she responds, "*Night* is *n-i-g-h-t*!"

"Great!" I respond. "Let's keep reading and see what other words we can find."

The group reads the next page of the book. "They say my mom is White, Like the clouds way up high."

Hands shoot up at lightning speed. I motion to Maria and she replies, "The word *high* has *igh*."

"Good! That's exactly right. You guys are on fire! I notice something else on this page, and I wonder if you guys do, too. There are other words on this page that have the long *-i* sound but that aren't spelled with *igh*. Can you find these words? Talk to your neighbor about it. See if you can work together to find the other words with the long

-i sound." Maria and Orion start to reread the page. Nicole, Donald, and Trae do the same.

As we discover more ways of making the long -i sound, we write the letter patterns on the left side of a paper and the words that have those patterns on the right side of the paper (Figure 11.4). This chart will be put up on the wall by the reading table for future reference and additions.

We finish reading the story and I ask them, "Yesterday when we discussed this book, some of you wondered about the end when Tyler says "I am a human being, not a color, not a word?" Let's talk about this again. Turn to your neighbor and share what you think he meant." After students talk for a few minutes, I send them back to their seats to write their reflections in their reader response journals. We will discuss their reflections tomorrow during our group time.

Beginning Readers: 11:10–11:30

This group is made up of beginning readers with many of the same skill needs. The goal of the lesson today is to help the students understand that differences among us are positive and healthy, and that we can all learn from our differences. Simultaneously, in this lesson I want to build students' fluency skills.

Yesterday, the group read *Bread, Bread, Bread* (1993) by Ann Morris. We talked about different kinds of bread we've had or seen and about how cool it is that people eat bread all over the world and why and how bread is different in different places. We followed this discussion with talk about differences within our class and how we like to celebrate those differences. Today we're going to focus on fluency.

"Today we're going to practice reading with fluency. Who can remember what the word *fluency* means?"

Kids chime in with their answers. "Where your voice goes up and down."

"When you read the words right."

"When you don't read too slow or too fast like /oooonce . . . upooooon . . . a . . . tiiii-ime/ or /onceuponatime/."

"You're right. When you read with your voice going up and down, it's called *expression*." I model reading with expression from the book. I write the word *expression* in big

Long *i*	
y	*sky, why*
i_e	*like, white, smiles, inside*
igh	*night, high, light, sight*
i	*find*
I	*I've, I'm, I*
Other	*eyes*

FIGURE 11.4. Word work with long i.

letters on a piece of construction paper with a wavy line that looks like hills and valleys next to it to show the up and down cadences of fluent reading.

"Kierra said that another part of fluency is when you read the words correctly—the word for that is *accuracy*." I also model reading with accuracy by stumbling a bit and rereading to fix mistakes. "Who would like to demonstrate reading this page accurately?" Jerman jumps in and reads the page the best he can with accuracy.

"Great work, Jerman! I noticed that Jerman read with expression, or up and down in his voice, and with accuracy. I did notice one little thing I'd like you to work on the next time you read this page, Jerman. I want you to listen to me read how Jerman did and see if you notice something missing. 'There are many kind, many shape, many size—' Jerman smiles at me and leans his head back. He grabs his book and automatically tries again. "There are many kinds, many shapes, many sizes." As he finishes, I write the word *accuracy* on the construction paper.

"Wonderful. The last part of fluency is speed. When we read, we don't want to go too fast and we don't want to go too slowly. I like to read about the same rate or speed that I talk. Let me show you how I read page 9 both too fast and too slowly before I read it just right." I read the words too quickly, too slowly, and finally just right. "Who would like to read this page with good speed or rate?"

Aaron volunteers and reads, "Skinny bread, fat bread, round flat bread, bread with a hole. . . . "

I smile and nod at Aaron. "Did you all notice how he took little pauses or breaks when he saw a comma? Commas and dashes help us to know that we need to take a little break when we're reading." I write the words *rate* = *speed* on the construction paper.

"Now each of you is going to practice reading the story with the three parts of fluency together. You are going to work in pairs, reading to one another, and scoring your partner's fluency. Remember to use kind words. After your partner reads, you will give him or her up to 3 points: 1 for expression, 1 for speed, and 1 for accuracy. I can tell you that even though I've been reading for a *long* time, I still need to work on my fluency when I read books that are tricky for me. We're doing this so that we pay attention to the parts of fluency—so if your partner tells you, after you read, that you need to work on your accuracy, don't let it upset you. It is supposed to help you become a better reader. Do you understand?"

I invite the children to choose a partner, take books to a cozy spot in the room, and practice reading with fluency for one another. I move from pair to pair listening, discussing the students' fluency and recording my findings in my assessment notebook.

Proficient Readers

This is the D group in the chart. The students in this group are not meeting with me today, but they did meet with my assistant. They have read *Boundless Grace* (Hoffman, 1995) twice and are now discussing Grace's family situation. In this book Grace lives with her grandma and mother in the United States. She receives an invitation from her dad to visit her other family in Africa. The visit helps her to realize that families are different, and that while her family doesn't look like families in the books she's read, her family is very special. The last line of the book is "Families are what you make them." Students respond to this line by writing about their own families. I will meet with them tomorrow to talk about and share their reflections on this statement and the book.

LEARNING CENTERS: MAKING INDEPENDENT WORK TIME MEANINGFUL

The following centers have been part of my classroom's literacy program. At the beginning of the year I begin centers by introducing the easiest one (i.e., easiest for kids to learn to do) first. It is called Read and Write the Room (shared below). When I introduce a center, I make sure I have everything labeled and that all supplies are ready. I put a laminated page with the steps kids can follow in each center. I model, explain, and actually *do* each step of the activity. I also show how to clean up after myself. I then have a child model the center activity and answer questions that arise.

After whole-class word work each morning, I go over to the center chart and list the centers each child will be visiting that day. I often ask kids to remind us of how to do the work at a particular center they are going to that day to make sure that they remember and to help other kids to do the same. The centers listed in Figure 11.5 are not my creations, but rather have been borrowed and tweaked from my fellow teachers throughout the years.

WRITING

Our writing time is based on the writing workshop model, and in this particular week we have been learning about memoirs. I know that excellent writing instruction must include explicit instruction in *how* to write, not just providing time to write. So, I plan lessons carefully. I like to begin teaching about new forms of writing by reading excellent children's books that exemplify the form we are studying. In the week described here, we have read *Smoky Night* (Bunting, 1994), a story about a child's experience during riots in Los Angeles. We also read Patricia Polacco's account of life with her brother, *My Rotten Redheaded Older Brother* (1998). Both of these memoirs describe events that led the main character to realize the value of someone or something they had not previously seen. After reading each of these stories aloud, we talk about how the authors told the stories, not simply listing events from the past but painting pictures with description and good word choice.

I asked the kids to talk to their neighbors about what they noticed about the writing that make these stories memoirs. While I eavesdropped, I discovered that some children had misconceptions about memoirs and were unable to talk about how the stories were constructed. But I also heard some developing ideas. My handclap got everyone's attention, and I asked for ideas. Kierra offers, "Both of those stories are about things that happened in the past." Elgin adds, "They're about an important thing that happens."

Center name	Description
Reader Response Journal	Students read a book or chapter at their seats and respond to that piece of writing in these journals. They begin their entries with a lead from a list that we staple inside their journals. Some of these include "I love the way . . . ," "If I were _____ I would . . . ," "I wonder . . . ," "I like how the author . . . ," etc.
Word Construction	Students build their spelling words or word wall words with magnetic letters.
Listening Center	Students listen to books on tape and complete a sheet that asks them to draw something from the story and to write about their favorite and least favorite parts. They can also write about how they would change the story.
Buddy Reading	Two students sit on beanbags (or wherever) next to each other, each with a copy of the same book, or read together. There is a basket of books supplied for them to read, and they inevitably read books more than once. They can either take turns reading pages or reading the whole book.
Read and Write the Room	Students walk around the room with a clipboard and a partner, reading words around the room and writing those they do not know on paper. I help them with those words later.
Poetry Center	Poems we have read in shared reading are written on sentence strips in this center. Students take the strips and put the poem in order in a pocket chart. They then practice reading the poem fluently together.
Writing Center	Students can choose to work on their own writing pieces, selected from their writing folders. Or, if children need a new idea, they might be asked to critique a book they have read, add a line to a story that previous students had been adding to, or write a letter to someone in the class or another teacher in the school.
Computer Center	Students can use the computer to compose new texts, work toward publication of one of their texts, or practice skills from a software program such as Earobics or Giggle Poetry.
Word Wall Center	Students write five words from the word wall, then put them in alphabetic order, then use them each in a sentence. Students who finish can try to write a story using as many of the word wall words as they can.
Vocabulary Box	This is a box that contains vocabulary words from the various content areas we study throughout the year. We start out with concepts that most students should know (e.g., *sister, friend*) and when new vocabulary is introduced (e.g., *prediction, pollution, legislative branch*), we talk about the words and explicitly add them to the box. In this center students select words (in my class we picked 12), write them, and draw pictures depicting what they mean.

FIGURE 11.5. One week's learning centers in Nancy's second grade (activities differ weekly).

Memoirs

Tell about something that happened in the past
Stories about memories
About important events
Made me feel happy, sad, scared
Described events, didn't just tell

FIGURE 11.6. Students' notes about memoirs.

Students continue to make observations about qualities they noticed in the memoirs we read (Figure 11.6). I write them on a chart and add my own to it. We will refer to these qualities when writing our own memoirs.

The day after this lesson, students will make a list of three important events in their lives (after I model this). Then they will select the one event about which they think they can write a good story. Students will complete a graphic organizer based on that one event, which will require them to add three details about the event, where it took place, how they felt, and who was there. Students will talk with their neighbors about their plans for writing and will offer suggestions to help one another.

After writing time, students line up for lunch. We are careful to store our writing in our writing folders so that no one loses his or her hard work. Returning to the classroom after lunch students listen as I read aloud to them. I often give introductions to several books and let students vote on which book we will read. Sometimes during read-alouds students listen quietly at their desks and soak in the stories. Other times we Sketch to Stretch, an activity in which children draw pictures of what they hear in the story being read aloud. This activity helps students to visualize what's going on in a story. At times these sketches are shared with classmates. This practice of sharing work encourages the understanding that we all interpret literature in our own personal ways.

RESEARCH PROJECTS

We sometimes conduct research in the library or computer lab during our reading time. During these times, students are broken into groups in one of three ways: randomly, based on interest, or based on skill level. Sometimes students choose their topics, and other times they are assigned. When we studied the rainforest, students chose three animals they wanted to learn about from a longer list I had created, and then I put them into groups accordingly. I try to tap into topics students might be naturally interested in and make connections between literacy, social studies, and science.

I collaborate with the librarian and the computer teacher so that kids can practice using a variety of texts in their research. When we do these projects, I conduct minilessons on beginning research skills such as how to Google a topic on the Internet (e.g., "animals in the rainforest") or how to use the index of traditional texts to find specific information. I teach them how to work effectively in a group, how to present findings to a group, and how to ask questions of presenters. I select books from the school library, the public library, my personal collection, and the Internet that focus on the topics that we've chosen and that are written in ways that are developmentally appropriate for my students. The computer teacher finds additional websites and programs that are age appropriate.

Many people I have worked with think I'm crazy to do research projects with second graders. They don't see how students so young could do such work. To make these lessons age appropriate and effective, it is important to keep high expectations and to scaffold students' budding research skills. To help them organize their inquiry searches, I provide a graphic organizer that guides the students in finding particular information. In the case illustrated in Figures 11.7 and 11.8, I asked students to find out something about where an animal lives, what food it eats, how it might camouflage itself, and another interesting fact. The figures show two pairs' products.

We always talk about the importance of being fair to group members, respecting the ideas of others, listening and respecting differences. When Kiya and Jerman investigated chimpanzees, they divided the information so that each presented two sections. Even this negotiation had to be modeled so that kids learn ways to work together.

I do a handclap to get students' attention. "I'm waiting for Julian's eyes." Finally Julian looks up and I have everyone's attention. "I want to tell you all about something cool I just saw. Kiya and Jerman finished filling out their graphic organizer about chimpanzees and needed to decide who would present which part. They didn't know it, but I was listening to them when they did it. Kiya asked Jerman which parts he wanted to present. He said that he liked the part about the habitat. Then Kiya said that she liked the part about the camouflage. Jerman said OK, that he would present about habitat and she could present about camouflage. Jerman and Kiya, how did you decide who would present the other parts?"

Kiya speaks up, "He had more written down about what they eat than me, so he took that part and I told him I really liked the interesting fact I wrote, so he said I could do that part." I knew my students were ready to present the organized information. The students transfer information from their graphic organizers to poster paper, thinking critically about the most important information. When their posters are finished, the students share them with the whole class (see Figure 11.9).

This research can easily be turned into a class-written book about animals in the rainforest. Each pair could compose an essay from their notes for a single-page or two-page-long chapter of the book. Children love to read class-written books. They take much pride in them and cherish them as any other book in the room.

END-OF-DAY THOUGHTS

After the kids have left for the day, I plop down at the reading table. I am tired and hungry, but I smile as I think about the funny and amazing things that have happened

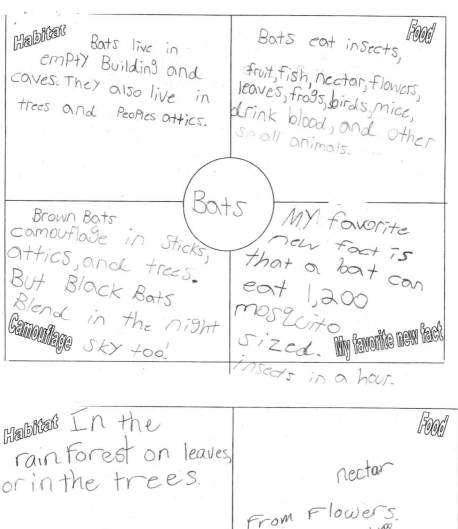

Habitat Bats live in empty Building and caves. They also live in trees and Peoples attics.

Food Bats eat insects, fruit, fish, nectar, flowers, leaves, frogs, birds, mice, drink blood, and other small animals.

Bats

Brown Bats camouflage in sticks, attics, and trees. But Black Bats Blend in the night sky too! **Camouflage**

MY favorite new fact is that a bat can eat 1,200 mosquito sized. **My favorite new fact** insects in a hour.

Habitat In the rain forest on leaves, or in the trees.

Food nectar From Flowers.

Butterflies

They camouflage in everything **Camouflage**

They live in fields, forests, wetlands, and deserts all over the world. They live on every continent except Antarctica. **My favorite new fact**

FIGURES 11.7 AND 11.8. Graphic organizers for research in second grade.

FIGURE 11.9. Kiya and Jerman share their graphic organizer with the class.

during the day. I laugh out loud when I remember what our new student said when a lunchroom worker asked him, "What's the magic word?" I replayed the image of his eyebrows raising as he exclaimed, "Y'all gotta magic word around here?" His reaction is a perfect example of the way we all too often expect kids to know the unwritten rules of school. I shake my head as I think about my fellow teacher who, during our faculty meeting groaned and said, "This sure is a lot of work for *literacy*." If we're not going to work for literacy, to excite kids about learning and reading and discovering, then we should not be teachers of reading. Such an important skill and life lesson should be molded carefully, proactively, and purposefully.

This peek into my classroom shows a week when I was able to find texts on social justice themes that were pertinent to my students' lives, namely bullying and acceptance of differences. These texts also leant themselves to several research-based reading strategies. They were appropriately situated within my students' ZPD and were excellent resources for the skills my students needed to practice. When we use books that reflect our students' experiences, cultures, and interests, they are naturally more engaged and motivated—which, in turn, leads them to learn the content and the skills more easily. Of course, it is not always possible to find books with social justice themes that are appropriately leveled and include places to practice needed skills. Often children need to read joke books (to develop fluency), adventure stories (to make predictions or practice summarizing), and books that are just plain fun to read. Many times I use books or other materials that either just interest the kids through a good story or are excellent sources for skills teaching. The important point is to consider what happens in my classrooms for each child across a week or month.

Our classroom culture is so important. I work very hard throughout the year, but especially at the beginning, to promote honesty, acceptance, and kind words in my classroom. I try to encourage this kind of thoughtful behavior by modeling and positively reinforcing positive behaviors and attitudes (e.g., "I love the way Elgin asked Jerman if he needed help"). I also conduct discussions about issues that arise in our classroom, school, and community; communicate with parents; and provide constant reminders that we are there to help and support one another. Students appreciate having a place where their bodies, minds, and emotions are safe.

There is no way to assess all center work. To make sure that kids do their best and to assess their progress, I choose certain centers to examine carefully each week. I also read through their reader response journals regularly, making comments in writing and in conferences with the children. I encourage them to use some pieces from these journals to create finished, polished writing products. I conduct running records in guided reading groups, using the text that we have been working on, to make sure that students are progressing. I carefully observe for students' comprehension of book contents and for their contributions to discussions concerning the books. I assess students using the Developmental Reading Assessment (DRA) at least three times a year—more often in special circumstances, such as when considering a referral for additional services or movement to and from reading interventions.

When I have students who are below grade level in reading, I often ask other children in the class to be their reading buddies during the center work or during whole-class lessons. I look for a child who likes to help others and who is patient and kind. It doesn't always have to be a super-proficient reader. Often a child who is a struggling reader can gain confidence and self-esteem when buddied with a child he or she can help with basic reading skills. At times I ask these kids to read books to and with the others, pointing to the words as they read. Other times I ask kids to practice a phonics chant with their buddy. Sometimes I have buddies play games using picture cards, encouraging kids to practice their oral vocabulary in a fun atmosphere.

Some of the students who read below grade level in my class receive special education services. This may be a result of a learning disability, mild mental disability, speech difficulties, emotional needs, or other such issues. At the beginning of the year, and regularly thereafter, I meet with our special education teachers to discuss students' progress, the modifications I've tried, and what I need to try next. I learned from a fellow teacher to keep "cheat sheets" of modifications that children need. I glean the information from their individualized education plans (IEPs) and make a sheet for each child. I keep these in my plan book for easy access. This makes my life much easier, as IEPs are complicated and the cheat sheet saves me time and keeps me focused on my students' needs throughout the year.

To effectively implement reading instruction that is both research-based and culturally responsive, I need to take time to prepare. I need resources on research-based strategies that are readily available, such as the "What Works" website of the U.S. Department of Education (*ies.ed.gov/ncee/wwc*). I need to get to know my kids and their families and caregivers. I need to get to know the books (and book sets) to which I have access in the school, library, and district. I talk with my fellow teachers about collaboration on inquiry projects, research, and field trips. I take time each day to reflect on what I love about my job and my students (especially on days when it's hard to think of anything). I use my students' real-world experiences, such as our problem with bullying and name calling, to create meaningful lessons. I try to use technology wisely. I get my students used to it so the glitz wears off and the content shines. Finally, I need to be sure of myself. I need to be equipped with knowledge of the research on effective reading instruction so that when a parent, administrator, or other teacher questions my practices, I can eloquently explain why I do what I do with the confidence that I am doing what is best for each learner in my classroom.

RESEARCH-BASED, CULTURALLY RESPONSIVE INSTRUCTION IN SECOND GRADE

Nancy's classroom is rigorous, motivating, and fun! But it is also much more than that. Upon careful analysis of her teaching, we can discern an *intentional* blending of research-based reading strategies and standards for culturally responsive instruction within a classroom culture of respect, dialogue, care for one another, and an expectation that the children will gradually become responsible for their own learning. This careful weaving of a blended model of instruction (McIntyre & Hulan, 2010) is the goal of our instructional model.

Nancy's natural enthusiasm and energy are quite effective with a diverse group of second graders who respond well to humor and active, hands-on work. But the enthusiasm is controlled, too, as we see by Nancy's use of tongue depressors to keep track of turn taking during discussions and the sharing of products to keep all students included. Nancy's use of the *Morning Meeting* book is her (and her school district's) response to the need for *class meetings*, described in Chapter 4. During these meetings, Nancy has the opportunity to create and sustain a warm, respectful classroom environment. She takes these meetings to conduct mini-lessons on classroom routines and the use of materials. Nancy is intentional with regard to the selection of the literature within her classroom library, ensuring that she has available a wide variety of multicultural literature and diverse genre. She supplements her own collection with titles from the library that support the topics that her class is studying. She also includes student work on the walls along with faces that reflect her students' racial and cultural identities.

Nancy's description of her shared reading period in this chapter highlights the blended nature of the culturally responsive, research-based character of this reading model. In that lesson, the children read a digital story about a boy named *Titoy*, who is in a wheelchair, and they discussed the importance of showing love and respect for people with physical disabilities. She follows the discussion with an explicit reading strategy lesson on how to make inferences, using think-aloud as her tool for modeling the strategy. She assists children as they gradually learn how to make inferences about the text. The students get a second opportunity to practice the inference strategy with another book, *Why?*, on a related theme. In this follow-up lesson, the children are encouraged to talk in pairs, connecting the lesson to their personal lives. There is much packed into these sequenced lessons, with both themes and skills from previous lessons.

Nancy weaves together the two strengths of this reading model through her whole-class word work lesson, in which she explicitly teaches a skill though choral and repeated reading, group work, and the active participation of all students. Nancy's strength is in modeling *how* to read and *how* to write, making the secrets of the processes transparent for children. For her writing lesson, she also enlists children's literature as models for how to write. Nancy does not just expect the children to do something, she teaches them *how* to do it first.

Nancy knows that her students are not too young to begin to learn to use the Internet in effective ways. Although lessons during research projects on evaluating Googled sites for accurate and reliable information may be challenging for many in her classroom, the children are ready to be introduced to such concepts. It will take many lessons across many years to teach kids to critically analyze the content found on the Internet. What a powerful lesson! This is not difficult for her, though, because she has taught her students all year how to critically and respectfully critique one another's work—a true life skill.

Nancy's guided reading lessons are the heart of her reading curriculum. In these small groups, she can be sure to teach skills based on students' needs, match texts to readers' skill levels and interests, and monitor progress carefully. In each of the four lessons described during this period, Nancy taught about the themes of name calling, racial differences, differences in people in general, and the variety of family structures in the world. Whereas in some lessons described here, the discussion of the theme was prominent, in other lessons the skill instruction was the focus. Across the lessons, Nancy modeled, explained, and had students practice decoding, predicting, inferring, retelling, repeated reading, and vocabulary learning. She also explicitly taught her students to monitor their comprehension, and she regularly and carefully assessed their performance to keep track of their development and needs. The whole atmosphere is rigorous and motivating. Nancy is clearly one who is focused on teaching her students to learn and love learning, a feature we found across all teachers implementing this model of instruction. Most importantly, this model enacted by Nancy is focused on student learning, the goal of the reading instruction described in this book.

CHAPTER 12

Research-Based, Culturally Responsive Reading Instruction in Fifth Grade

Vicky teaches in the same school district as Nancy, one of the largest in the country. Eighty-eight percent of the students are served by the free- or reduced-lunch program, 26% of the student body is European American, and 25% of students are ELLs. Vicky's class of 26 students is comprised of 11 African American students, five European American students, and 10 ELL students from the following countries: Bosnia, China, Korea, Mexico, Myanmar, Cuba, and Somalia. The research-based, culturally responsive reading model fits with Vicky's mission and her diverse set of students. Vicky is a successful teacher of the model. In some ways her classroom mirrors Nancy's because of district mandates to teach literacy in the morning

> 8:55–9:25 Morning Routines/Morning Meeting
>
> 9:25–9:50 Shared Reading (*Whole-Group Instruction*)
>
> 9:50–10:50 Guided Reading (*Small-Group Instruction and Literacy Stations*)
>
> 10:50–11:05 Word Work (*Whole-Group Instruction*)
>
> 11:05–11:45 Writing Workshop (*Whole-Group Instruction/Conferences*)

FIGURE 12.1. Vicky's schedule for literacy instruction.

and to include a community-oriented class or "morning meeting" daily, and the district's adopted resources. But Vicky's instruction differs from Nancy's, too, in part because of the grade level but also because she is different from Nancy, and teaching reflects background and personality to some extent. In this chapter, Vicky describes her schedule across a day (Figure 12.1) and week in her personal voice with her remembered dialogues, so that you can experience how the components of the model fall into place across several days. At the end of the chapter, Ellen reflects on Vicky's instruction, highlighting the research-based, culturally responsive aspects of her teaching.

It is a wonderful feeling to know where you belong. Every morning, as I step through the doors of my school, I am sure of one thing: I have chosen the right profession. Regardless of the papers waiting on my desk upstairs, the after-school committee meeting I cannot miss, or the daily uncertainty of issues that arise in a classroom of 26 distinctive personalities, I am in my zone.

Climbing the stairs to Room 303, I mentally break into my list of "need to's." I need to log on and check for e-mails from my principal; I need to change the class job list because it is Carole's turn to be the station manager, and she *loves* to be the station manager; I need to remember to take attendance so the clerk won't have to call me, yet again, with her gentle voice reminding me, "Baby, I need your attendance." The details of this job are many, to which anyone who has taught more than 5 minutes can attest. But by the time I reach my room, most everything miraculously comes together.

MORNING ROUTINES/MORNING MEETING: 8:55–9:25

It's 8:55 and away we go! Each morning, I stand waiting at the entrance of the room with my "Good morning" and firm handshake ready. They know to speak back clearly and make eye contact as I call them each by name. Students need to know that their teacher can *see* them and is genuinely glad they have come. Good communication governs every interaction we have, social and instructional, for the rest of our lives, so we make it a priority as we start our day. I teach best when I know my students' needs, wants, and habits. Although I'm not with them on the way in to school, I know that whatever has happened will affect much of what we do and it is often etched in their faces. Derrick looks distant;

did he eat breakfast this morning? What little-sister story was Mada bursting to share today? Did the translator explain the permission slip to Tha's parents so that he can go to the science museum next week? Who got into an argument on the school bus?

Print interactions start immediately and, by now, the projector displays the morning message or a provocative question we will read or discuss during our meeting. Also, an agenda has been posted in the meeting area to help us stay on task and maintain the structure of the meeting. After coats and book bags are put in their proper places, students make their way to the carpet for our morning meeting. I like them to read the message or question silently because it gives them time to think of connections or responses they may want to share later. Everyone needs a few minutes to get settled after the morning rush, so quiet chatter is the expectation.

I have my literacy materials ready on the table where I meet with reading groups, laid out in the order I will use them. Close by are pencils, index cards, white boards, and other resources that are staples of my instruction. Many of the resources I use are from our core reading program, *Rigby Literacy*, the series adopted by our district and used by the majority of schools. The transience of our students is a constant battle, so we try to maintain as much consistency as possible across the city. I like that students who enter my room from another school share the common strategy language and text experiences that the core texts provide. From these, I select the titles that simultaneously address the required state standards and move students through the levels that form the basis of the program.

I also choose materials from our school "Bookroom," a professional library of leveled book sets purchased over the years with grant funds. It is comprised of classic literature, multicultural texts, and many modern titles in every genre for teachers to check out. At times, I use our content-area textbooks and the accompanying leveled book sets to add more content to my strategy instruction. I've always felt fortunate to have so much at my fingertips, and I try to use it to expose my students to quality literacy materials at all times.

As in all diverse classrooms, there is a variety of literacy levels, and our classroom is no different. I hear my students wonder aloud about the question posed, pronounce words or make quiet comments, or laugh at a humorous line I may have included that day. As I observe them, I am reminded that different cultural groups have different communication styles and expectations, and I try to stay mindful of those differences as I teach my children how to share with one another and with the larger group. I remember my own shy nature as a child and how helpful it was to have time to develop my thoughts with peers to prepare myself for sharing with the whole class. There are other opportunities for spontaneity as we proceed through the day, but I believe that risk taking is born out of confidence. Part of my job is to encourage and strengthen children's confidence whenever and wherever possible. On cue, we stand, say the pledge, and in unison recite our school's self-esteem creed. I inhale deeply and exhale slowly, proud of the positive classroom community we are creating together.

I love morning meetings because it is a daily opportunity for our class to build community and develop literacy and oral language skills. This is not only important for

ELLs; fifth-grade expressive language abilities run the gamut from those who need to practice speaking in complete sentences of Standard English to students who are refining presentation skills. The meeting may be only 20 minutes in length, but it gives me an informative glimpse into my students' literacy needs. I listen to language patterns, vocabulary usage, grammar, and students' interests. *The Morning Meeting Book* (Kriete & Bechtel, 2002) is a source I use again and again to refine our meeting time. It is loaded with fresh ideas and models for how to conduct a meeting that is relevant to students' lives while simultaneously integrating language arts and content instruction.

Every meeting begins with a special greeting. One day we may say hello in one of the seven languages spoken by students in our room. One day the greeting might be a peace sign hand gesture or one hip handshake chosen by the students. I enjoy seeing the creative choices they make, like the pinky shake greeting or today's "two-sided" hand slide. Jackson slides hands and says, "Good morning, Charles." Charles replies, "Good morning, Jackson," and turns to the next student to do the same. Everyone in the group watches and listens respectfully as we go through the circle. I constantly look for what catches their attention and makes them smile so that I can later choose books and activities that match their needs and interests.

The daily greeting is followed by the morning question or morning message. The question is always an open-ended inquiry about something we are studying, something about our classroom, or just something I want the children to wonder about. For example, I might post:

> How do some mammals survive without food throughout the winter?
> How can we share the use of the computers more fairly in our classroom?
> How should our country help the victims of the Haiti earthquake?

The morning message is a letter written by me to the students. Some days I write it on chart paper, and some days I display it on the laptop projectors our school district has provided to each classroom. My fifth graders often consider themselves technology gurus, so today I used the laptop to write the message. This way, after their initial reading of the message, the students and I can collaborate to decide whether to delete text, highlight words, or add new material if necessary. Through this demonstration, children can experience the word-processing skills they need for present and future writing.

To begin, we might read the message aloud chorally. Even in the fifth grade, this is a good practice, especially if the message is more challenging. Sometimes I simply read it aloud, like today. Because of the variety of language abilities, we might stop to employ strategies such as *Think–Pair–Share* (Lyman, 1981) about the meaning of the message. Although I do not know whether this strategy is actually research-based, I do know that it gets students talking and thinking, and that much research has shown that students must practice academic talk, just like they practice anything else. The strategy Think–Pair–Share gets them talking about the topics I am teaching. As I read the morning message, the students follow the text so that we can discuss the interactive activity that is embedded in the message (see Figure 12.2).

Dear Fabulous Fifth Graders,

    Good Morning! Are you as excited as I am about our Science Museum field trip next week? I hope you remembered to ask your parents to sign the permission slip. I need them all by Friday. The exhibits are going to be exciting as well as informative. You may even find inspiration for your next science project.

    Do you like to read about history? Today we are going to step back in time and read about a very important event in our country's history.

    Also, I hope you are *pre*pared to *re*member our word sorts from word work. We will *re*view what we learned the *pre*vious week and add some new *pre*fixes to our chart. (Can you explain why some of the words have italic print? Sh-h-h, save your response for the morning meeting).

                                                  Respectfully yours,
                                                    Ms. Layne

FIGURE 12.2. Morning message.

When we respond to messages, I often use the text as word study (e.g., "Do you think this word ending makes sense?") or vocabulary support (e.g., "What might be synonyms for the word *exciting*? Who would like to record them on our synonym poster?").

We round out morning meeting with sharing time. Students sign up to share in advance so they are prepared to speak; but we also have time for last-minute news in case something happened the previous night or that morning. This morning, Colett, who signs up to share as often as possible, gave her time to Rondionna, whose mother came home last night from the hospital. These meetings are student centered, so I stay open to the unpredictable, delighted in Colett's show of empathy. I am reminded that flexibility is one of the most valuable qualities a teacher can possess. It is here, I think, that we practice building trust. We listen carefully to each other, and students are allowed to comment or question in a positive way. At the beginning of the year, there was sometimes a giggle or snide remark when some shared. And as uncomfortable as it might have been for the offenders, I used those moments as "teachable moments" to disallow such behavior. It has worked in my classroom this year (some years it takes longer than other years). I am proud of how my students have learned to respect one another and respond with helpful suggestions, insightful questions, or a simple "Good job." The goal is to extend these qualities throughout our classroom discourse across the day. I announce that we are moving back to our table groups for shared reading today. I decided that table groups were the best setup for our next activity. We have started on our path to a productive day!

SHARED READING
(WHOLE-GROUP INSTRUCTION): 9:25–9:50

Our official literacy instruction time begins with my personal favorite: shared reading. It is comprised of the teacher, students, and the excitement of sharing a book and learning from each other. My goal for this period is to explicitly teach my students to *be aware of* literacy skills and strategies in their reading experiences. I model fluent reading, word-learning skills, and comprehension strategies through "think-alouds." The key to shared reading is that all students can see and interact with the same text at the same time, whether it is a picture book, a poem, or a class set of chapter books.

Fifth graders have a great deal of content to cover: science, social studies, and mathematics. I've always been bothered by the philosophies that treat these as separate entities. I consider them all before deciding which books to choose for our lessons. Naturally, there will be a need to schedule time for each content area, according to a school's curriculum requirements. However, shared reading is a great opportunity to blend subjects together, allowing children to see how reading connects all subjects like the cog in a wheel.

This week I have planned a genre study of historical fiction, a perfect way to complement our upcoming social studies unit about the California gold rush and westward expansion. My first thought is *How can I place 21st-century kids into a 19th-century world that was very different from their own?* I'm not so concerned about my history buffs, Charles and Michelle. They are mesmerized by historical information and seek out biographies of famous historical figures such as Harriet Tubman and places such as Ellis Island. They read them voraciously and make a point to share new facts and questions that come up in the reading. As I consider the rest of my class, I ask other questions, too. How much background do the students have about this period of history? How deep is their understanding of the concept of change over time? What books or materials might support our study?

I stop there and focus my planning on developing lesson goals and objectives. I want to make sure that my choices are research-based and rigorous, with clear expectations and attainable outcomes. I use action verbs to target specific areas and post them for students to see. In this lesson, the students should be able to activate prior knowledge about a topic and identify the characteristics of historical fiction. I want them to be able to see how characters' behaviors are affected by the historical context of the time. These goals affect my assessments, too. I want to assess students' content and literacy learning.

For the unit, I have chosen two texts from our core programs to use this week. I read the teacher lesson guides for their strategy suggestions and then determine the lesson needs of my students. I also have to plan for the amount of time that I have to deliver the lesson. I've learned to be very intentional in developing these lessons. "The California Gold Rush" (Rigby, 2000) is a short article that I use to access prior knowledge about the time period. It describes how a modern-day boy, Henry, categorizes his own research about the topic. There are pictures and captions that can add to students' prior knowledge of the era so that later in the week, everyone enters the story with something upon which to build. *Rose's Gold* (Goldenstern, 2002), is a historical fiction story set in 1849. There is more text than pictures at this stage, so students have to get the majority of their information from the print. The book has strong characters that I think my students will enjoy. Even in my own reading for pleasure, I love a story with a strong character whose experiences shape his or her future. Through this shared reading experience, students learn how attractive reading can be for them as they identify with characters like themselves.

"When I say the words *California gold rush*, what thoughts come to your mind?" I ask my students. I watch their faces. Immediately, two or three hands fly into the air. I motion them to lower their hands for some think time. I am still learning how to effectively conduct instructional conversations, which is much more difficult to do with the whole class (rather than with a small group), but I have learned that a key is to insist that the children *think* before responding. After a bit of think time, I ask the children to share their thoughts with the person next to them. A low hum overtakes the room as they rehearse responses. As they talk, I display an artist's rendition of a miner panning for gold from the Internet (*www.history-for-kids.com/california-gold-rush.html*). Drawing their attention to the painting, Rondionna says excitedly, "Oh, yeah, I remember that! Everybody went to look for gold in California." The low hum turned into a loud chatter as students make remarks about the picture.

"Good readers use or *activate* their knowledge when they begin to read something new. That means you think about what you already know or think about the topic while you are reading the book. Today, we are going to use what we know or think about the California gold rush as we read this book." I model what I hope the students will do as they read. "This is an artist's illustration of some miners during the gold rush. I know from stories I have read in the past that the miners would sift those pans in the water and look for glittering rocks. There are several men in the picture, and their clothes look different than the clothes we wear today."

Elijah commented, "They all have on hats and boots. We only do that in the winter, but it doesn't look like winter there."

"Good observation. I like how you used what you know about the clothing we wear today to compare it with the men in the photo." This was a simple comparison, but Elijah is on the right track. I want students to start where they are and add to their existing knowledge.

"Let's take a look at some real photos of the California gold rush. Open to the table of contents and find 'The California Gold Rush.'" Pages turn and the students get quiet as they look at the photos. "A boy named Henry is doing some research about the gold rush. He already knows a little information, and he adds to it from the photos he finds." I continue to model how to connect prior knowledge to new knowledge from the text. "I notice that the pictures are in black and white. I know the first cameras didn't take color pictures, so these were taken a long time ago. I read that the gold rush was in 1849." I do a quick subtraction on the board: 2009 − 1849 = 160 years ago. "Things were very different then." Now I want them to try accessing what they know. "Stacee, tell me what you think about the picture."

"The men look dirty, like they've been working all day. They must really need to find gold."

"OK, Stacee, what else are you thinking?"

"Some of them were poor people. Sometimes they didn't have money to eat."

I comment, "I know that many of the men who went to California were very poor, and they sold what little they had for the dream of finding gold. How do you think their families felt when they left?"

This question sparks comments, as I knew it would. I am pleased with how the students took time to think through the text features and article details. I hope they understand that they come to reading with a wealth of experience and can draw on those experiences to lead them to new places. I will look for evidence of their understanding as we proceed throughout the week.

Now that students are better prepared through drawing on their prior knowledge of the gold rush, I introduce the story *Rose's Gold* (Goldenstern, 2002) the second day. One reason I chose this book as our follow-up story is that many of my students can connect to a story of a father who has to leave for a while to work in another town or set up the family in another country. I have students who can relate to a girl who is raised by her extended family and whose life is shaped by events she knows little about and cannot control. I want them to be able to see how the characters' behavior is affected by the historical context of the time. "We're going to take what we learned from yesterday's lesson and use it to help us understand our reading for today. Scan the text and make an inference about the genre of this piece with your partner." I model how to look at the pictures, activate my prior knowledge, and draw a conclusion about the genre. "Some of you mentioned that this is historical fiction. Why do you think that is the genre of this particular story?" As students raise their hands, we create a class chart with characteristics of historical fiction. I will post it in the room for easy references at other times, helping the students to distinguish it from other types of text structures, as described in Chapter 7.

"The first character is Rose," I say, "Let's see what she is all about!" I read: " 'Rose wished that her father would return home. As she closed her eyes to sleep, she thought again of a story she had heard from him. . . . . .'." The beautiful opening of the story begins our journey. During shared reading, I sometimes read aloud to the students, but most often I have the students read short sections silently, and we stop periodically to discuss the meaning of the book. We also reflect on our strategy use (whatever the focus might be that day), but most often, we discuss the deep meaning of the book. The goal is to inspire readers and create classroom community around a common book. The students' responses allow me to gauge thinking and comprehension, which I use to determine needed lessons for small-group guided reading or individual conferences. Shared reading is also an excellent opportunity for vocabulary teaching.

I ask the students, "The story describes Rose's father as being 'infected with Gold Fever.' What do you think this phrase means?" Some children may first assume that he is sick, so they talk in groups to make sure everyone knows the meaning. Later, when the term *infected* shows up in the social studies text, the children already have a beginning understanding of its meaning. Stopping to think about meanings and responding orally in a large group gives learners a scaffold to begin to do this during their independent reading.

We further explore historical fiction and compare the information about Rose's father to our first day's lesson on the California gold rush. These activities later become part of our literacy stations and social studies units. Our class charts and organizers remain in view of students, and we continuously make connections and inferences. Students open their response notebooks and select a character to write about, careful to paraphrase details from the text.

GUIDED READING (SMALL-GROUP INSTRUCTION AND LITERACY STATIONS): 9:50–10:50

Students complete their responses and I make my way to the literacy station management chart. On the way, I move among the desks to get a glimpse of the students' work. A responsive teacher is always aware—observing, assessing, revising. This is the day I take notebooks home and I get the chance to write feedback, so I don't linger over their work. After the shared reading, the class moves into small-group guided reading. In order to maximize literacy learning at this time, the students work independently in literacy stations while I meet in small groups for guided reading.

My first experiences with literacy stations often left me feeling exhausted. Were the activities research-based and rigorous enough to engage the students? Why are some students consistently on or off task? How do I know they are really learning when my attention is with this small group in front of me? Independent work can look many different ways, and I chose literacy stations to give my fifth graders choice and multiple literacy activities (see Figure 12.3).

If I could name two words of advice to any educator who wants to develop literacy stations, I would say *meaning* and *practice*. Students who understand *why* they are given a task do the task with better results. They need to know the purposes for which they are learning and view those activities as those that will get them there. Pretty stations students do not understand are exercises in futility. Each station should have child-friendly purposes posted (related to what students will learn from the activity), along with clear expectations for assigned tasks. This leads me to my second piece of advice. Regardless of the age and ability of the student, station work is always *practice*. New materials should be modeled, taught, and used a number of times before students are expected to be adept at the skill. They can think at higher levels when the focus is not on the basic understanding of the activity. During guided reading, students are not allowed to ask me questions; the station manager is the go-to person, or the students are taught to ask others in the same station. Literacy stations are the "gradual release theory" in action. To be successful, students need to know how to utilize everything they have at their disposal, including transition time and behavior expectations. At least once a week, I skip one group lesson and spend my time observing the work in the stations and making notes of activities that are working in the best interests of the students. From there we change, we adapt.

I have many students, so I have to be intentional when scheduling guided reading groups. Each day I meet with Group 1, comprised of children who seem to struggle most with reading. They are not always the same children each week, but they often are. Usually, these children have difficulty with decoding, which affects their comprehension and causes difficulty with grade-level text. Many of them receive extra services with an

Station	Purpose	Sample contents of literacy stations
Word Work	Students explore words, word patterns, and word meanings.	Word sorts Word games *Mad Libs* *Scrabble* Dictionaries/thesauruses
Reading Response	Students read independently and write for authentic responses.	Books Response journals Response stems Question cubes Pencils Index cards
Writing	Students practice writing skills that improve idea development and fluency with grammar and conventions.	Writer's notebooks Creative writing ideas Pencils/pens/paper Sticky notes Scissors, markers Editing/revising checklists
Computer	Students explore technology literacy or conduct research.	Chart of approved Internet sites (bookmarked, if possible) Ethics reminders Selected software Headphones
Buddy Reading	Students share and discuss books with a partner.	Fiction/nonfiction books Graphic organizers Pencil paper Question stems/questions for discussion
Content	Students use literacy skills with content-area reading materials.	Nonfiction trade books Map/globe question cards Math word problems Science investigations
Fluency	Students practice speed, accuracy, and prosody.	Poems, songs Readers' Theatre scripts Short passages Timers Pointers
Newspaper	Students explore real-world materials for a variety of purposes.	Newspapers/news magazines for kids Highlighters/highlighter tape Graphic organizers Scissors

FIGURE 12.3. Literacy stations in fifth grade.

adult later in the day, so I often choose to work with them first to free them for special services and work in the literacy stations. My school favors a collaborative model for interventions (see Chapter 13 for many types of interventions). In my room this year, the reading specialist pulls a group for reading interventions on one side of the room. Her lessons run simultaneously with my groups and the literacy stations. Having another adult who knows your students' behaviors, skills, and personalities is a blessing to me as I search for the best materials, texts, and strategies to develop my students' reading skills. Scheduling is tight and the activity level in the room is high, but the more exposure students have to a qualified reading professional, the more strides they make in reading. Also this year, a specialist works with ELLs during their daily classroom activities to help them navigate through new expectations and language barriers. I am pleased and happy about all the help.

Groups 2, 3, and 4 meet on an alternating schedule, two to three times per week. Group 2 students decode well, but they struggle to comprehend dense text and answer questions with precise detail and sequence. (They sometimes rush through the reading.) Groups 3 and 4 are grade-level or above-average readers, and I meet with them in flexible groups depending on the comprehension skill or strategy they need. A typical weekly schedule looks something like Figure 12.4.

Once students are settled into their literacy stations, I turn my attention to the students who are waiting for me at the reading table. Even though I need to get started, today I pause momentarily to watch them. Rereading the familiar texts I placed on the tables keeps them engaged during the few minutes the others are listening to tips and instructions, checking the station chart, and moving into position. Watching their reading behaviors, I can see who is still struggling with a text we have read, who is interested in the book selections I have made, and who is ready for new materials. I smile, make a couple of notes and set the timer, the signal for us to begin.

Group 1: Struggling Readers

As mentioned, some of the children who struggle as readers have the same primary problem: decoding complex word patterns. Using the DRA (Beaver, 2006), I found that

	9:50–10:10	10:10–10:30	10:30–10:50
Monday	1	2	4
Tuesday	1	2	3
Wednesday	1	3	4
Thursday	1	2	4
Friday	1	2	3

FIGURE 12.4. Guided reading schedule.

seven students started the year at the mid-third-grade level or below, and for many weeks I have grouped them together for lessons focused on decoding and fluency. At this time in the year they still "use but confuse" vowel pairs, r-controlled vowels, and words with three or more syllables. I begin the lesson teaching the skills explicitly through word sorts and other activities. If appropriate, I connect the word work skills with the skill lesson from shared reading that morning. I follow the word work with reading connected text. The students' comprehension levels vary; some members are ELLs and use comprehension strategies well in their own language, but are still adjusting to the complexities of English. One week I scaffold their reading with a lower level of text that allows us to practice fluency and comprehension skills, and the next week I choose instructional level text that exposes us to more complicated language patterns that we can work through in the smaller setting.

This week I choose the book *Dancing in the Wings* (Allen, 2000), for a number of reasons. It is not a part of our district series, but it has many features of high-quality literature that will engage this group. This book still has much picture support, and since three of the students in the group are incredibly artistic, I think it is a wise choice. Kadir Nelson, the illustrator, created lush paintings that capture the individual facial expressions—varieties of tone, texture, and actions—to match the author's brilliant descriptions. I try to connect these ideas to heighten the students' interest in the specific details that will enable us to eventually synthesize the characters' experiences to understand the intended theme. The text is written with a dialectical pattern familiar to some of my students. The author uses `cause and *lookin'*, which gives me the opportunity to compare these to Standard English spellings. As you probably inferred from Chapter 4, issues of dialect are often a question on reading assessments, as a student's home language can override what is printed on the page, and it may be taken for a miscue.

The final reason I choose this book is that the main character, Sassy, struggles with issues of self-esteem. Many fifth graders, like Sassy, are beginning to deal with the emergence of social cliques, and they can also relate to the sibling rivalry many of us have experienced at some point or another. I have my own copy of this book and was lucky to find a copy in our school library and three at the public library, so we are sharing copies with partners.

"Have you ever wanted to do something so badly that you tried everything to make it happen?" Hands fly into the air! Almost everyone has a connection. I make them wait to think and remind them to listen to their classmates and *respond to them*, not to me. After Anthony shares his story of trying out for a football league at church, I go deeper. "What are some of the things you have to do if you want to excel at something?" I model my own interest in vocabulary, or as mentioned in Chapter 8, "word consciousness." "*Excel* means to be very good or try your best. "I had to work hard in school to excel at playing the clarinet. Talk to your partner about something in which you have excelled at home or at school."

This is a group of six students, so we can evenly divide into partners. During our group conversations, there is rarely time for all students to share. Partner sharing gives everyone a voice. I listen briefly to each pair and intervene if partners are having trouble communicating. Monica and Anthony are just sitting there so I attempt to get them started. "So, who is going to share first?" No response, following a moment of awkward silence.

Monica says, "I haven't tried out for anything."

"What about at school? You wrote a beautiful personal narrative. What did you have to do to write such an awesome piece?"

"Oh, yeah," she smiles, "I had to conference about it and type it in on the computer."

"So Anthony, did she do it perfectly the first time?"

"No, she had to spend a lot of time on it."

"So she had to . . . " They chime in together, "Work hard!" By now, the other four kids are getting fidgety, but I really needed to take the opportunity to develop the students' partnering skills.

"Adrian, tell me what your partner said." She is a very attentive listener but doesn't always volunteer to talk, unlike her partner, so I ask her to comment first.

"Dzemila said you have to practice hard and that her sister practices every day even when she doesn't want to; but she is good at the piano."

"OK, good listening and nice connection, Dzemila!" I proceed. "The main character of this book wants to, as you can infer from the cover, become a dancer."

Anthony sighs, "This book is for girls."

"Yes, but as you scan the book, I think you'll see it is a book for boys, too. You may find characters doing things you can connect to as well. As I was saying, our main character, Sassy, wants to be a dancer, but she has a problem—or at least something she *thinks* is a problem. She says and does some things we can use to infer the theme of the story and . . . "

"What's *theme*?" Anthony blurts. I pause to look at him. "Oh, sorry!" he replies. In this less formal setting, I like the children to speak openly; however, I failed to set the rules before I started. I should have stated whether to "popcorn" (call out our responses) or to raise quiet hands. In this case, I wasn't quite finished with my statement, so it was confusing for us both. Students need to know expectations for our instructional conversations. "Popcorn is OK today, just be sure the other person is finished speaking."

We have used the term *theme* before, but some students need to hear strategy words multiple times before they can actually own them. I point to the chart behind me, where the word is defined. Adrian, who feels more comfortable speaking out because of her earlier success, says, "It's the message in the story—what the author wants you to learn."

"Good. Scan the pictures and see if you can predict the author's message."

Anthony nods once and grins, taking it all in. Once he reached the picture of Sassy's football-toting brother, he seemed to relax, tapping his partner's arm and giggling. Fifth-grade boys are notoriously concerned about gender images.

"So, let's go back to the beginning. We are going to read Sassy's story to see what Sassy has to do to excel at being a dancer." We read the first few pages chorally as I lead them, modeling fluency and observing closely for signs of struggle. Since we have read it once together, I invite one volunteer to read aloud a portion of the text for discussion.

" 'My mom calls me Sassy, 'cause I like to put my hands on my hips and 'cause I always have something to say. Well, if you had feet as big as mine, you'd understand why' " (Allen, p. 2). On the dry erase board, I write 'cause and ask, "Why is there an apostrophe at the beginning of the word?"

Manuel answers, "That is supposed to be *because*." I write *because* beneath it, lining up similar letters. "Let me show you another way we do this sometimes." Below that, I write 'cuz. "When we write, we often want to use the whole word, *because*, so our readers know what we mean. But at times, like when you write stories with dialogue, you might use the other forms. Authors write like this to make language sound more like the way we talk at home sometimes. Be on the lookout for other examples of this in the story."

I then ask, "How do you think Sassy feels about her feet?"

Ming responds, "She don't like them."

"How do you know?"

" 'Cause . . . "

I tap the board and smile at her.

"*Because* they are big," Ming says. Ming rereads the sentence and looks up at me for approval. She then finishes her thought, "Because . . . she says 'if you had feet as big as mine you'd understand,' and her brother makes fun of her feet, too. She doesn't like it that she has big feet."

We continue to read the text chorally as we identify Sassy's struggle with being taller than all of the other kids and how that feels.

"What can you infer about Sassy from this page?"

"She doesn't let her big feet stop her from dancing!" Giggles abound. "Do you think her feet are really bigger than anybody else's, or is she just picking on herself?" Silence. "Keep that in mind as we read the rest of the story. Can you predict the theme from what we have read so far?"

Anthony raises a hand as he simultaneously speaks out, "Don't let other people tell you that you are not good enough. You can still try hard and be good . . . excel.

I turn to Adrian who looks like she will explode any minute, "Do you want to add something?"

"I'm guessing that she is a hard worker and will practice very hard to dance her best when she gets the chance." I think, *I love this job.*

Struggling readers in fifth grade are often kids who can gain a deep understanding of the meaning of text, but they struggle with phonological problems and have a difficult time processing print. Chorally reading the text eliminates the decoding issues and allows us to focus on the instructional conversation that propels their comprehension forward. As the week progresses, we will select words and phrases from the text and devote considerable time to decoding. Using a strategy from Words Their Way (Bear et al., 2004), we will sort for inflected endings. Chorally we read: "Mr. Debato walked around prodding and poking, making corrections. He stopped once and looked right at me but didn't say a thing. I held my breath as he dismissed almost half the kids after the first round. But not me" (Allen, 2000, p. 18).

I prepared a word sort to help the children review how words change with the addition of an inflectional ending (Figure 12.5). We will sort into three categories: words that double, words that drop the e, and words with no change. I modeled how to sort the selected words as we discussed what change had to be made and how, if applicable, the meaning was changed or altered.

As we continue throughout the week, I add other examples and let the students sort with partners or individually. We also reread other portions of the text and search for words that fit the categories. When I feel comfortable with the students' ability to recognize the patterns, I add the activity to the word work station. It is easy to differentiate with different levels of words, and students can continue to practice the very effective strategy of sorting.

To wrap up today's lesson, I close with "As you are reading in your stations today, see if you can predict the author's theme before you read and find some evidence to support your prediction." My timer rings almost on cue. Students begin to clean up stations and move. I lay out some familiar books for the next group, do a quick running record on a student, and move to Group 2.

Doubled	e-drop	No change
prodding	*poking*	*dismissed*
stopped	*making*	*looked*
		walked

FIGURE 12.5. Word sort for struggling readers in fifth grade.

Group 2: Proficient but Careless

This group of readers, brought together for the first time this week, is comprised of children who struggle with some aspects of reading, but not all. They characteristically speed through text, with fairly accurate decoding, but their comprehension suffers. They often fail to support their thoughts with text details and often cannot detect the main idea. Their decoding skills are more accurate than members of Group 1, but they still guess at some of the more difficult words, while ignoring context clues and other support the text may offer. They are not careful readers, and they need some skills that will make them more attentive to the text. My goal is to also challenge them to look past basic surface-level ideas and to push themselves to critically comprehend the text. I select one section from the *Rigby Literacy* book, *Between the Lines*, a biography of the writer Roald Dahl, by Tim Arnold for our lesson today.

We have been exploring the life of Roald Dahl and how it shaped his writing using the "questioning the author" strategy from Chapter 7. Roald Dahl books have become popular in our class, and so we activated prior knowledge in a previous lesson using an article I downloaded from the Internet. We tied together what we knew of him from books we have read, and today we are prepared to read a brief biography of his life.

"This author has written a biography about Roald Dahl's life. When I'm reading a biography, I know that the author has researched someone's life very carefully. The author would be able to answer many of the questions I have about the focus of the biography or about the author's style of writing. One question I might ask the author is, 'How did Roald Dahl's childhood help him to create stories?'" I record the question on a whiteboard, then read the first section aloud, modeling prosody, as this section has many complex sentences. "The author writes that Roald Dahl was bullied a lot by the older boys in his private school and came to be known as a bully himself. I can draw a conclusion that this is why he included bullies in many of his stories, such as the family in *The Magic Finger* (Dahl, 1964) and the parents in *Matilda* (Dahl, 1988). Does the author use any other examples from his childhood?"

"Yes . . . the author talks about how lots of his characters have only one parent or are on their own because their parents died or were bad." Colett answers knowingly, as she has lived with a single father for most of her life. I nod in recognition as I think about how this book has empowered her to reflect on her life. "I agree. The author uses clear examples and a description of Dahl's background to get his message across to us."

I read aloud more in this group today than usual; some of the text is difficult and I want to model how to carefully read and use questioning to monitor my own comprehension. So, I purposely stumble a bit, and then reread the sentence. I follow with a think-aloud about what I just read to be sure it makes sense. The goal is to explicitly teach students that they cannot carelessly stumble over the words and still gain meaning. Reading requires both print processing and comprehension. Students need this explained, modeled, and practiced. The closure for this group—and there should *always* be some learning-focused closure to any lesson—is to have students write in their notebooks two questions they may want to ask the author when we meet next time. Later in the week, students will read about other favorite authors and continue to try the question-the-author strategy. Two groups down, one to go.

Group 3: Skilled Readers

Themes of social justice are prevalent in my classroom, as in all classrooms characterized by culturally responsive instruction. Students in U.S. schools have such a rich, historical well from which to draw. There is so much literature on topics like the development of freedom in our country, the civil rights movement, immigration, fair workplace practices, and racism. *All* of the students in my classroom are the descendents of people who were directly affected by one or more of these topics, regardless of the "side" they were on. Many are still in the midst of those same struggles.

I selected *Making the World a Better Place: The Stories of Social Reformers* by Jyotsna Sreenivasan (2002), also from our core program. I think of how perfect the text is for this particular group of students. Two of them participate in our school's "Conflict Mediator" program. When students have arguments, they complete a form explaining the incident, and the mediators are assigned as the go-between that helps them solve the problem with words. Two students help collect the recycling bins each week, and the other one serves as a member of the safety patrol. The text is written with rich vocabulary, complex sentences, and references to historical people, places, and events. As I said before, content integration is critical in fifth grade. Advanced readers can handle more content because there is less need for decoding help. I want my students to learn to summarize text. I know this is a life skill and also quite challenging to teach. I work at teaching this skill all year with my students.

So, on our first meeting, I take time to conduct an explicit lesson on how to summarize. I use another chapter from the book on social reformers because it is close to what I want them to read on their own. I choose to use the GIST strategy mentioned in Chapter 7. The GIST procedure (Cunningham, 1982), as noted, stands for generating interactions between schemata and texts. This strategy helps my students gradually increase the task of summarizing increasingly longer texts. I model each stage of the process. First, I choose Susan Sygall, an advocate for individuals with disabilities, and read one sentence from the text aloud to the class. I then say, "I have to summarize this sentence in 15 words or less." I summarize that sentence through a think-aloud, saying "Susan's training programs made people with disabilities aware that they had rights."

Then I read a whole paragraph from the story, and again I model how to summarize, thinking through what I believe are the key ideas, but keeping the summary to 15 words or less. I like to model on the overhead projector or laptop so my students can see me cross out words and ideas as I decide what is *most* important. Finally, I read a whole section aloud and model the summary process (15 words or less) for this longer text. I write the summaries in front of them as a model for how to do this. I allow the children to help me decide what might be the most important material.

After the demonstration, the children are given time to skim the text they were assigned to read on their own and prepare notes for their literature discussions. Literature circles (Daniels, 2002) are an activity I do with *all* students (not just this advanced group), but some texts are better suited for this type of discussion. Literature circles, as a process, may not have been researched in studies, but what students do while in these groups (ask and answer high-level questions, summarize, predict, attend to and discuss vocabulary) are highly valuable research-based strategies important for reading development. And so, I implement this process whenever I can.

In a typical literature circle period, students meet with their literature circle group and read an agreed-upon portion of text. Each reader is assigned a different role in the group, and they all prepare ahead of time. One role is the "Summarizer," and so my explicit lesson on how to summarize will help this particular a lot.

On this day, I function as "Discussion Director," as I often do the first time the group meets over a new book. I enjoy watching the students challenge one another. I give them some discussion starters to help guide the conversation; if I don't hear what I think I need to hear, I ask questions to check for understanding. I listen as they begin to discuss the social reformers. The following is a summary of what I recall from this group as we discussed the work of Marian Wright Edelman:

DISCUSSION DIRECTOR: We read pages 32–37 about Marian Wright Edelman. (*I point to and read our focus question for the book.*) How can one person's contributions change the world? First we need the summary.

SUMMARIZER: Marian finished law school and moved to Mississippi to help poor black people. She helped to get the Head Start program started there. Parents got to decide on the teachers and be a part of the program. Some men didn't want black people to get help, so she had to work hard to keep it. Then she left to live in Washington. That was when Martin Luther King and Robert Kennedy got killed. She got married and helped pass bills that became laws. (*I think*, "She did a bang-up job! I must mention this to the group after the others finish reporting.")

DISCUSSION DIRECTOR: Are there any new or interesting words on those pages?

VOCABULARY RESEARCHER: I found three words to look up: *victims, activists*, and *vetoed*. I kinda' knew what they meant, but I looked in the dictionary for the definitions. *Victims* are people who get hurt by somebody. An *activist* works to help people, and a *veto* is when the president doesn't pass a new law. Marian was an activist who helped poor people get food and schools and health care.

[Other literature discussion jobs include the "Literary Luminary" and "Illustrator." These students also report what is in their notes. Then they turn to the Questioner, who shares questions he has written about the text.]

QUESTIONER: One question I had was, why didn't President Nixon want to help the children?

LITERARY LUMINARY: Yeah, it said she couldn't believe it. Some people just don't think it's important. Sometimes the whole family needs help, like when you need to live in a shelter. [The Literary Luminary is supposed to share text that is particularly literary, although that is not the case in this transcript.]

VOCABULARY RESEARCHER: Like when all of those people were in Hurricane Katrina.

ILLUSTRATOR: She said, (*turning to the page*) "I was shattered" [p. 35]. That means she was very angry and unhappy that he wouldn't give money.

QUESTIONER: Um, Ms. Layne also asked us to talk about how did Marian's work help us today? Well, I know how. Kids get a good education now, and they have enough food to eat. Maybe she could have made a bunch of money and kept it all for herself, but she made sure that other people could be safe and healthy too. She was generous. (*I think*, "Good use of vocabulary!")

LITERARY LUMINARY: She started the Children's Defense Fund, too. Look on page . . . 37. (*Turning to the page, he reads the paragraph aloud.*)

DISCUSSION DIRECTOR: OK, yes. Now we have to tell something new that we learned.

The students share something new they learned and return their notes to the folders I will review this evening. They will meet tomorrow for the final section of the book, and they will meet without me in their literature discussion groups. I will change the roles so that others will work on summarizing. I will also have all students practice the strategy using the graphic organizers mentioned in Chapter 7.

Literature circles are effective when students are taught how to conduct them. Our morning meeting routines guide the discussion. Only one person can talk at a time. Students take turns with the different roles, including the leadership position. There are occasional issues with behavior, disagreements, or absences, but if routines are consistent, students can fill in and carry on when issues arise.

I give the schoolwide signal "Gimme five." Students stop where they are, and we share what went well and what we can improve next time. We reflect on work stations each day to build accountability for time spent in independent or paired work. I make mental notes to check reading notebooks, replace books in the Buddy Reading station, and finish the organizer from Group 2. As we clean up stations, turn in work, and have a couple of minutes of talk time, I feel good about the work that has been completed so far this morning. Later in the week, we complete and extend the texts and strategies we learned. We take a few minutes from the rigor of the morning to sharpen pencils, lightly chatter, and transition back to whole-group instruction.

WORD WORK (WHOLE-GROUP
INSTRUCTION/CONFERENCES): 10:50–11:05

The word work lessons I choose come from cues I take from my students. My fifth grad-ers have been ushered into more sophisticated word patterns. We have moved from com-pound words to studying multisyllablic terms. Simple base words have grown to include prefixes and suffixes. Words with multiple meanings become increasingly important to know in order to comprehend their choices of books, which often contain dense plots, humor, and multiple themes. Reading response journals, science notebooks, and open-ended responses provides very telling information about students' vocabulary. So, I read and I plan.

I know I must differentiate instruction for word work, as some of my students need very little and others need a lot of a very specific kind. In guided reading groups, I address needs characteristic of the group of students, and the instruction is systematic and sequenced for those with the greatest needs (e.g., the children in this week's Group 1). In whole-class word study, I scaffold where necessary for individual student needs by incorporating buddy sorts, table discussions, and carefully selecting words tailored to the concept we are studying. In my reading conferences, I listen to individuals read books they have self-selected. They often choose the popular titles that contain unfa-miliar words or words they may have heard. They can understand the gist of these texts, but often guess at words and keep right on reading, muddling the medial syllable or leaving off the ending altogether. (This was typical of my Group 2!) Inside, I cringe, my inner "word nerd" wanting to stop them in their tracks. I check to see how these mis-cues affect the meaning, and my reflections become the basis for a conversation after the reading. But more than this, listening to students read gives me evidence for the types of word activities they need, how they approach unknown words, and how they make meaning based on words they already know.

Word sorts are effective for comparing and contrasting the similarities and differ-ences in words. We start this week with an open word sort. I want to see what similari-ties the students naturally gravitate toward. In partners, students sort 10 words with the prefixes *mis-*, *un-*, and *dis-* (Figure 12.6). When we first begin to explore a concept, I keep the number of words low so as not to overwhelm students who struggle with the concept and to allow advanced students to delve deeper into the meanings of the few words I have selected.

mistake	untie	discover	unlike
distaste	misuse	misread	unopened
disturb	unseen		

FIGURE 12.6. Prefixes word sort.

A couple of different patterns emerge as some groups sort by the prefixes, some groups sort by word endings, and one group sorts by the vowel sounds in the base words. Again I think, *I love this job*. It is interesting how my students notice things I have never considered. I begin to question their choices and allow them to explain their thinking. "Why did you choose to sort this way? What connections do you see between the words?" When I notice misconceptions, I may point out a pair of words for the groups to rethink. "Is there another group where this word may fit *better*?" They record their open sorts in their notebooks and write a quick explanation for how they decided to sort the words. Later, they can compare.

The following day, I add or alter the choice of words for the sort. We have conversations about the meanings of the base words and how they change with the addition of the prefixes. I like to include exceptions to the patterns, such as *disturb* from the above list, which is already a base word but will later appear in our study of word roots. I let students finish the sort, again recording them in their notebooks. Then I encourage them to extend their list by adding words they know.

A lesson from *Words Their Way* (Bear et al., 2004) finishes the week. I had created a homemade spinner and a set of cards with base words, divided into *mis-*, *dis-*, *un-*, as well as *re-* and *pre-* from a previous lesson. Students select a base word and spin the prefix spinner. If the two make a word, the players can record; if not, the other player proceeds. Students with a limited vocabulary may find the latter part of this lesson more difficult because they may not be familiar with whether or not the words they make are actually legitimate. I create a chart of all the possible combinations that could be made from the spinners for cross-checking. This lessens the anxiety and gives students additional exposure to new words in a safe environment. All of these resources will go into the word work station for students to practice in the coming weeks.

WRITING WORKSHOP (WHOLE-GROUP INSTRUCTION/WRITING CONFERENCES): 11:05–11:45

We transition into the daily writing workshop with a quick switch from reading notebooks to writing notebooks. We've prepared during the first 6 weeks of the year by building the writing community. We've discussed how to use a writer's notebook as a "garden for planting the seeds of writing ideas." Throughout the year, these ideas and new ones germinate, grow strong, and eventually blossom into authentic writing pieces. Writers' notebooks lie at the center of our writing workshops. Developing writers use them daily to record their thoughts and practice writing skills and strategies. Writers' notebooks are different from reading response journals or science notebooks. The writing notebooks eventually become a resource for the students' writing as they return to them frequently to inform their writing choices.

My vision for the students as writers is that they will find the tools to express what is in their hearts. The experiences that have shaped them also shape their learning outcomes. In culturally responsive classrooms, these experiences are the foundations that teachers can build upon and extend to pull out students' very best. I introduce resources that I believe will help draw out their thoughts; but our daily experiences with writing skills and strategies is only a small part of the puzzle. The published writing should, in some way, reflect the capabilities of a fifth grader no matter what literacy level a student happens to be in at the time the piece is written.

Writing workshop always begins with a strategy mini-lesson. My lessons are based on series of writing lessons in a genre unit, exploration of the author's style of writing in shared reading or the read-aloud, and/or examples from student writing in the classroom. We take each writing piece through the writing process (as described in Chapter 9), and students learn to take ideas from a thought to a visible product. I begin by modeling strategies and allow students to make comments orally to prepare them for writing practice. Some students do not yet possess the vocabulary to express all they want to say. Their vocabulary develops, over time, as they orally explain their thinking and gradually proceed through the stages of writing toward complete autonomy and writing fluency.

The reading–writing connection is always a focus in my workshop. For a few weeks, we have studied writers' attention to the specific details of their own lives. We read Cynthia Rylant's *When I was Young in the Mountains* and excerpts from *Through My Eyes: The Autobiography of Ruby Bridges* (1999). Today we are composing our shared class poem (Figure 12.7), patterned after *Where I'm From* by George Ella Lyon (2010). It is a beautiful poem that drives home the power of the small things in our lives as she chronicles her childhood through remembrances. We explore the poem's mood, dissect its structure, and then connect its meaning to the members of our class by creating a group list of details about our class. At the prewriting stage, each group brainstorms events and characteristics we have shared as a class: our first day, our reading and content-area experiences, school groups, and our classroom routines. For drafting, we type these details into the computer, cut and paste them to provide some organization, and today we extend the events to mimic the reflections Ms. Lyon infused to intensify the poem's mood and emotion. I enjoy listening to their comments and reflect on how our classroom community has created a fun and memorable experience.

Shared writing experiences are a great tool of culturally responsive classrooms. Working together to collaborate on a project develops a sense of camaraderie, and for students who are new to the country or just new to the classroom, this can make the difference in how quickly they begin to communicate with the teacher and other students.

As students write, I formatively assess their progress, offer suggestions about topics, share resources, and question them about their writing choices. When necessary, I conference with individuals or small groups to clarify, reteach skills and strategies, or encourage them to stretch their writing pieces by going deeper into the strategy when they are ready to revise. Editing and word processing are built in to complete the writing process, and students are then given opportunities to write and publish pieces on their own. *It's lunchtime! Where did the time go?*

Where We're From (based on *Where I'm From* by George Ella Lyon, 2010)

We are from E_____,
From good grades and respectful behavior
We are from the grass on the kickball field
Green and soft
Easy to run around during PE.
We are from Morning Meetings
Share time
Where we listen to each other like
Brothers and sisters

We're from academic team and basketball
From cheerleading and safety patrol
We're from fighting sometimes
But learning our lessons
From Gimme Five and Ms. Layne's voice

We're from Myanmar, Mexico, and Bosnia
Somalia, Korea, and China
From the United States of America,
The pledge we say that stands for liberty

In our library is a compliment box,
Full of written notes
Kind words when we see our friends do good things
We are these pieces
Fitting all together
Leaves fall from our classroom tree.

FIGURE 12.7. Vicky's class poem.

REFLECTIONS

It's a wonderful feeling to know where you come from. As an African American girl growing up in Eastern Kentucky, a region of Appalachia, I recognize my rich cultural history. I read books voraciously. The people I met and places I traveled through books opened my eyes to possibilities that have brought me to where I am today. As a teacher in an urban school district, I think of the similarities and differences between these two environments: one rural and one urban, yet we needed the same things. My students *need* to read, not just for the curricular purposes we devise, but for their own personal purposes. I carefully select activities to interest and motivate, consider the outcome from different perspectives, and implement instruction with the best resources I can find. This takes planning and knowing what drives my students.

Culturally responsive instruction is empowering! Using the great body of reading research to guide my thinking, I implement this model when I collaborate with colleagues to introduce the most effective strategies, involve parents, and build upon the wealth of knowledge that each student brings with him or her into my classroom every day. To successfully implement CRI, instructional conversation and higher-level questioning take the forefront to stretch students' thinking and encourage them to create and develop ownership of the events that occur in the classroom.

As I descend the stairs at the end of the day, my need-to list grows, but other thoughts capture my attention. I reflect on the respectful conversations and ideas expressed during our morning meeting and how long we worked to achieve this caring environment. I muse over how the students built relationships with each other and engaged with the stories we shared. I think of the uncertainty of tomorrow and of the diversity it holds. I think of how to reach my students—how to connect with them through the barriers of language and culture that no longer have the power to keep us apart.

RESEARCH-BASED, CULTURALLY RESPONSIVE INSTRUCTION IN FIFTH GRADE

Vicky's deep respect and love for her students and work come through in nearly every line of this description. She has set high expectations for her students both in terms of behavior and academics. For instance, she is respectful of children's dialects and includes literature written in a dialect familiar to many of her students, but she insists, with great warmth and high expectations, that they learn and use standard forms of English ("*Because*," she repeats with a smile when a child says "'cause"). Vicky is aware of how the age of her students impacts learning. Fifth graders have identity issues, and teachers must attend to them if they are to sustain engagement with their students. I wondered if Vicky missed an opportunity when she allowed the boy to consider dancing to be a girl thing. Maybe. Or, Vicky decided this was not the lesson she wanted to focus on at that moment. These moments often come and go in classrooms, and teachers do their best to make the on-the-spot decision whether or not to address particular issues that arise.

Vicky's guided reading lessons were appropriate for each of her groups. The children who struggled with reading did not miss out on the high-level discussion on the meaningfulness of the text they were reading. Too often, the learners who struggle the most get to participate only in lessons on skills. Yet, Vicky is also aware that this group must have more explicit phonological work; she seems aware that students at this age, who are still struggling with reading, are often those who still cannot decode with ease (Torgeson, 2002a). Vicky provides instruction on these skills as well. She also shows students how to read through her explicit demonstrations and explanations, such as when she modeled how to summarize using the GIST procedure.

Other aspects of Vicky's culturally responsive classroom come through with her constant attention to the individual child, the choice she affords the students for their work, the topics she chooses to have students read about, the careful wait time she provides for them during discussions, the opportunities for paired and group work, and the numerous chances for classroom academic talk, with and without her present.

Vicky weaves these standards for culturally responsive instruction into her research-based reading strategies. She has planned her instruction carefully to include the components of reading necessary in elementary classrooms, but she differentiates that instruction to be appropriate for the different groups of learners. She provides systematic phonics instruction for one group and focuses on word consciousness and vocabulary learning for the whole class. Vicky is well aware of the power of words, and she intends to arm her students with the tools they need to enter into any discourse group of their choice. Vicky's content lessons are also packed with research-based reading strategies, such as inferencing, scanning, and summarizing. She knows the importance of first explicitly explaining and demonstrating a strategy before she gradually releases the responsibility to the children to practice the strategy independently.

The use of the literature circle roles is one way to move toward instructional conversations. Assigning the students roles (and teaching them explicitly how to carry out their roles) can be a useful step toward the true instructional conversation we witnessed in Chapter 8. The roles give the students a chance to practice critical skills for contributing, and they ensure that all participate. Finally, Vicky (like Nancy) is lucky to work in a school district that has been able to provide for the extra reading interventions (the topic of Chapter 14) for students who still struggle, even given the excellent research-based, culturally responsive instruction described here.

CHAPTER 13

Family Involvement

Recently, Ellen had lunch with several community members interested in the local district's controversial school assignment plan. The conversation moved from the school assignment plan to the role parents play in children's education. Much of what Ellen was hearing was the deficit-oriented, blame-the-family talk we wrote about in Chapter 3. One man in his early 70s lamented that children today were not disciplined enough to learn. He just shook his head and said, "Well, I just don't understand schools today. Classrooms are just chaos. You go in there and kids are talking and moving around. When I was in school, we sat in rows, we faced the teacher, we listened, and we behaved. And we learned!"

Of course, this man probably went to a demographically homogeneous school. He may have had no problem learning, but did *all* his classmates learn equally? And *what* did they learn? Did they learn to work with others? To respect differences? To see others' points of view? To respectfully challenge one another? To dig for accurate evidence for a collaborative project on an authentic problem? To ponder big questions and seek solutions to issues? Ellen didn't get the sense the answer would be yes to any of these questions.

Schooling in the 21st century *must* be different from that in recent decades because kids, families, and society are different. For the most part, this is a good thing! Society in the 1950s served white men well, but not many others. Today, girls and students of color have vastly different experiences and more opportunities. Teachers want all students to be prepared for all sorts of opportunities and challenges. To enable success for all, teachers must reach out to the students' families *to learn from them* how to best meet the needs of their children. Our model of instruction, which is focused in part on culturally responsive instruction, also connects the school curriculum to students' out-of-school lives. Doing so requires that teachers know something about families and reach out to them in nontraditional ways (Kyle et al., 2002). Knowing the students' outside-of-school interests and passions, their families, families' jobs, and home routines, and then using this information to connect in meaningful ways can have huge rewards in fostering happier, healthier, and smarter youth (Edwards & Turner, 2010; Long & Volk, 2010; McCarthey, 2009; Schultz, 2010).

Traditional parent involvement is not the goal. We do not expect parents to volunteer in the classroom (but are thrilled if they do!), and we understand when parents or guardians cannot come to traditional evening school events. Family involvement is not intended to get parents to do at home what we wish they would do, but instead it is for teachers and parents to share information that can improve instruction at school through the building of lasting, trusting relationships between homes and school. Parents are experts on their children; they are teachers' primary resources for understanding students and knowing what and how to teach them. Our perspective is one of mutual respect. Yet, we know that at times developing respect is not always easy. We have found that many families have lives different from our own, and we have learned to see these differences as just that, and in no way as deficiencies or faults on the part of the families.

Family involvement takes time and reflection, two resources scarce in the lives of teachers. We propose ways to do this work that are time, energy, and cost efficient. We also offer general principles for family involvement that can fit the working styles of most teachers and the circumstances of most schools. First, though, we review some of the key research findings on family involvement in culturally and linguistically diverse settings.

RESEARCH ON FAMILY INVOLVEMENT

Much of the recent work on building positive home–school connections is grounded in research that has shown the discontinuities between traditional schooling and the home cultures of many students. With her groundbreaking work *Ways with Words*, Shirley Heath (1983) illustrated how literacy discourse patterns in rural African American and Appalachian communities differed from those found in schools operating from European American middle-class standards. As we described in Chapters 1 and 3, the differences between the school and community cultures disenfranchises students of poverty and students of color and complements the achievement of the mainstream community. We have also shown, in Chapter 4, how differences in some dialects (usually Southern and African American), are viewed by some teachers and school administrators as deficient languages in need of eradication. Studies indicate that Hawaiian ways of sharing (Jordan, 1985) and Native Americans' (Philips, 1972) and African Americans' (Michaels, 1981) storytelling patterns and interaction styles (Foster & Peele, 2001) are also often viewed as problem behaviors.

In another important study, Valdés (1996) studied the lives of 10 Mexican immigrant families. She found that the caregivers of the families had a deep respect for schools, but they saw the role of schools differently than their roles as parent educators. The families believed that their role was to teach their children to be respectful, obedient, and moral people. They viewed what schools did as separate, and while valuable, not the sort of work the families were supposed to do. Lareau (2000), who studied several working-class families, found many families with the same views. The roles of home and school were perceived differently; academic achievement was the responsibility of the schools and families; intervention in the teacher's work was viewed as inappropriate. Rios (2010) found that some teachers have more favorable opinions about some groups than others. They might celebrate the community practices of one group but show disdain for other groups, particularly those they suspect do not have proper documents for being in the country.

Families' literacy levels can also be misunderstood. Although a strong correlation exists between education levels and poverty (Grissmer, Flanagan, & Williamson, 1998), there are also studies that have shown that not all poor families are low in literacy (Purcell-Gates, 1996; Taylor & Dorsey-Gaines, 1988; Teale, 1986). What seems to be problematic is the distinction made about what constitutes literacy. Bloome and his colleagues (2000) distinguish between school literacy and community literacy. *School literacy* is characterized by the practices we see in school: reading as an assignment, completing homework, drilling and practicing with print to "get better" at it. This is in contrast to *community literacy*, which includes practices that serve a community function: to find something out (e.g., what happened to the fired police chief), for entertainment (e.g., to find out when the game is on), to run the family more efficiently (e.g., writing grocery lists), and so on. Historically, most educators have worked toward changing home literacy practices to more closely reflect school literacy with the goal of changing families (Gorman & Balter, 1997). In our view, teachers can and should do the opposite by building school experiences from students' backgrounds and interests.

When differences exist between families and schools teachers can find themselves confused and distrustful of parents and other caregivers. Teachers might interpret the families as unwilling to help or purposefully ignoring their wishes, in consequence which teachers might develop deficit views of families and begin to believe that families do not care. Many children's cultural ways of interacting have been viewed in schools as *deficits*. Without being aware, teachers who hold these views unwittingly undermine the academic progress of their students. Differences in parental attendance at school functions and parent–teacher conferences has also led to widely held myths. Many teachers interpret parents' absence at school functions or unfinished homework as indicating a lack of concern for education on the part of parents. As we shared in Chapter 3, we have heard teachers complaining about parents with phrases such as "They don't care," "They can't read," "They don't know how to help," or about parents of an ELL student, "All their other mail comes in English!" [so why can't they read our mail?], without evidence that any of this is so.

Instead, reviews of research on parental involvement suggest that a large majority of parents want to be involved in their child's education (Dantas & Manyek, 2010; Hoover-Dempsey & Sandler, 1997). *All* the parents we have worked with care about their children and want them to learn, and they want better life conditions and opportunities for their children than they have for themselves; indeed, many see schools as the "ticket" for their children's entry into middle-class life. However, since many parents had negative experiences in schools themselves, they may be uncertain about how to ask for help and often feel unwelcome when they do.

Much of the current work in this area operates from a *difference*, rather than *deficit*, model (Dantas & Manyek, 2010; Edwards & Turner, 2010; McCarthey, 2009; McIntyre, 2010; McIntyre, Rosebery, & González, 2001; Moll & González, 1997). These educators have been working toward understanding families in ways that respect their knowledge base and discourse patterns and building school communities around those ideas. These studies have shown that when teachers get to know families in deep and personal ways, they begin to understand and break down the barriers to school literacy success. They begin to see how to build on the successes of students' community literacy, which in turn may affect school achievement. Many of these studies have also reported increased parental involvement (McIntyre, Kyle, Hovda, & Stone, 1999) when teachers make these kinds of efforts.

Our instructional model is built in part on the work of Moll and González (1997), who use families' "funds of knowledge" upon which to build school curricula. "Funds of knowledge," first used by Vélez-Ibáñez and Greenberg (1992), refers to the various social and linguistic practices and knowledge that are essential to students' homes and communities. In some households, funds of knowledge might consist of craft making and car mechanics. In others, it might be knowledge of the Bible and canning. Teachers use a variety of ways to assess families' knowledge and build activities and curricular units around those topics. This interweaving of school and family not only serves to motivate children and families, but it contextualizes (Tharp et al., 2000) instruction in what the children already know, increasing the likelihood that the children will learn. However, we caution that teachers could further disenfranchise students if they implement a "funds of knowledge approach to teaching" without a simultaneous focus on research-based instruction (McIntyre, 2009).

For 5 years in the late 1990s, Ellen and her colleagues studied the academic development of more than 50 young children. They knew that to truly understand children's development, they needed to know children in a deeper, richer way than just their academic experiences. Their work took them into the homes and communities of the students, and they began to investigate families' funds of knowledge. In doing so, they also built stronger relationships with parents and guardians. They not only learned about families' goals, backgrounds, and knowledge, but they learned much about what families were doing to assist children with learning and the ways they wanted to be involved with their schools (Kyle et al., 2002; Kyle et al., 2005). Many of the principles in Figure 13.1 are based on this work.

PRINCIPLES FOR FAMILY INVOLVEMENT

Figure 13.1 outlines general principles for family involvement.

- Recognize that families' ways of being and caregiving are different across cultural groups; these differences are no better or worse than any other sort of parenting.
- Work hard to uncover their own biases and assumptions about families.
- Meet caregivers "where they are and wherever they are" (Rios, 2010, p. 267).
- Begin the year with a positive note or phone call home to initiate a climate of support.
- Share yourself, particularly those things about you that you have in common with the family member with whom you are connecting.
- Show interest and concern in the lives of your families. Let them know you see them as more than your students' caretakers.
- View the child as more than just a student; he or she has interests and needs outside of school as well.
- Show up in the community, in places your families are likely to be, even if just a short walk in the neighborhood, a visit to the local drugstore, and so on.
- Ask parents, "How is everything with you these days?" and "Is your child getting what she needs?"
- Invite parents to share what they know about their children in a survey or interview.
- Invite parents to share their opinions about the school year through a survey or interview.
- Ask families to share their knowledge with your class through class visits when possible.
- Use interpreters as often as possible. Show, don't tell during Family Nights.
- Smile a lot—it means the same thing across languages.
- Learn greetings and critical phrases in the families' first language.

FIGURE 13.1. Principles for family involvement.

STRATEGIES FOR INVOLVING FAMILIES

Involving families begins with an examination of our own biased beliefs toward some children, families, and communities and learning to deal with the discomfort that comes from working closely with people who are not like you. Many teachers will face personal challenges while trying to connect with families. As long as the families "look like" their own, family involvement is easy. But teachers must think deeply about this question: "How comfortable am I with people who are not like me?" The families of children in our nation's classrooms reflect differences in many ways: ethnicity, race, class, language, sexual orientation, religion, and cultural practices. While no one can know everything about these differences prior to getting involved in connecting with families, beginning the process requires that one have an attitude of respect for and appreciation of differences and a willingness to learn more. Reaching out to families, then, will be meaningful only if teachers overcome this barrier and decide that they have much to learn and families have much to teach.

While teachers must think about their biases, they must also be prepared for what they might find when entering the homes. When Ellen and her colleagues visited families, they found drug use, seemingly ceaseless television viewing, racism, and homophobia. They had to meet to "unpack" their strong emotions after the visits and try to process what they were seeing without resorting to deficit thinking. When Nancy visited families of her students who were refugees, she was always met with warmth and food. In several instances families spoke to her in their native language, of which she knew very little. Sometimes mothers and grandmothers began crying, obviously telling stories about what had happened in their native countries in their native tongues. A nod, smile, hug, or an attentive ear are often understood regardless of linguistic and cultural differences.

But school doors and attitudes swing both ways. Edwards and Turner (2010) warn that teachers must also be prepared for caregivers who visit the school and begin to identify the weaknesses of the school, class, and the teacher. Rios (2010) asks, "Are we ready for that?" (p. 267). Below we share some of the primary principles and activities we have found to be successful with all sorts of families. We encourage teachers to work collaboratively with their colleagues to create an inviting school, not just an inviting classroom, where families know they are welcome, cared about, and valued.

Building Trust

No amount of effort toward improving home–school relationships will be effective without trust. Our students' families must trust that we truly want for their children what we want for our own children. We must communicate that we want to become partners with families in improving education for the children. Building trust takes sharing of ourselves, seeing parents' lives as complexly as we view our own, getting and valuing the knowledge and opinions of the parents, and sincerely working together toward common goals.

Sharing with Families

For many families, teachers are a mysterious group who sometimes must be avoided, tolerated, confronted, or even manipulated. The gulf between school and home is often wide, with little contact outside of the classroom and rarely, if ever, on topics unrelated to student progress or behavior (Kyle et al., 2002). When parents and children see teachers as adults with lives outside school consisting of families, interests, concerns, and struggles, the gap between school and home can be narrowed. When they see teachers as humans, they can begin to trust, which is critical for building the kind of respectful relationships necessary for student success.

One way teachers can begin to be seen as human is for teachers to share their lives with families, particularly when there are similarities among them. Sometimes this might mean sharing similar struggles. For instance, when one mother discussed her great difficulty with being a single parent on welfare and without a job, Ellen told her about her sister who had been recently left by her husband of 14 years. She had three school-age kids and no job and suffered great trauma and struggles for years. With another parent, Ellen shared that a young child she was helping to raise has difficulty going to sleep at night, and she described her frustration in being controlled by a 3-year-old. Those parents both said how much they appreciated hearing these stories. They helped the mothers feel less alone with their struggles and provided hope that their lives might get easier, too. One teacher we know shared with a parent that her own son struggled with reading, a surprising fact from a reading specialist! How enlightening it is for parents to realize that a child's learning problem is not the fault of the parent.

Being visible in the community outside school is another way teachers can get to know families. When teachers can occasionally attend a student's ball game, performance, or celebrations, the respect between home and school groups escalates. The thrill for the students in seeing their teachers outside of school and there *for them* is evident (even when the children pretend not to notice). Nancy often shopped at stores surrounding her school, hoping to run into the families from her school. Students' eyes grew wide as she waved with a friendly "Hey!" while toting groceries. The next day at school those kids, whether they were her own students or not, would seek her out and say, "I saw you at Walmart!" and turn to a friend say, "She was buying groceries!" A church in the neighborhood near Vicky's school sponsored a Saturday reading program for all students in the school. Vicky and some other teachers showed up to lend an air of familiarity with the hope of making the children and their parents feel comfortable in the different setting as well as to help make the in- and out-of-school connection. Another teacher we know, who didn't live in or near the community in which she taught, took her laundry to school once a week and visited a laundry in the late afternoon in an effort to be available for her students' parents in an informal place for a legitimate reason.

Another fun and interesting adventure that teachers can experience is to visit the school's community with the eyes of an anthropologist. Go into the community, make drawings and maps of what you see, eat at a local establishment, talk to people who work in the community (e.g., the postmaster or mistress, a gas station attendant), and "walk the walk" of the students in the school. JoAnn, another teacher with whom we have worked, uses this term when describing how she walks around on the streets that take children from school to home so she can see the neighborhood through their eyes. JoAnn has written about her experiences (McIntyre & Archie, 2001) visiting her school's community prior to beginning to teach there. As an African American woman teaching in a working-class European American neighborhood, she did not know what she did not know about her students' families. Her principal took the teachers on a field trip through the neighborhood before school began, and she realized that she had harbored the same assumptions about her European American students that she knows some European American teachers hold about their African American students. Sometimes it is not until we experience a culture other than our own do we realize the prejudices we hold. The goal in these activities is to try to experience the community as the children who live there do. Then, come back into the classroom and talk with the students about it. Tell them where you've been and with whom you've spoken. Show them your maps and have them help you make better ones!

Of course, parents are people too. They are not simply the caretakers of our students, but people with complex lives beyond their children. Sometimes we neglect to truly see what many of our parents are dealing with outside of their children's (our students') lives. We need to consciously realize that parents have their parents and siblings to worry about, work issues, economic issues, scheduling difficulties—essentially the same problems *we* have in our lives. When we remember this, and try to see situations and issues through the eyes of our students' parents, we can make adjustments in our attitudes, expectations, and interactions with families as necessary.

Making Families Visible in the Classroom

When families do visit the school, it is sometimes difficult for them. They may not speak English well and will be nervous about that. They may feel uncomfortable in schools because they had unhappy experiences in schools in their youth. Or, they may just be nervous because they want the teachers to like their child and to know that their child is learning.

To create a warm, welcoming atmosphere for families, many teachers intentionally have art and photographs in the room that reflect the population of the class. Even better, many invite children to take photos of themselves at home and in their communities, with their family members, and to hang these pictures on the walls in the room. Teachers can make connections to content when children use photos to create a timeline of their lives and post them in the classroom, or students can decorate their writing notebooks with pictures of family and friends to use for inspiration for writing topics. It provides a sense of security for children to see their loved ones represented in the classroom. Families love it too and become partners with their children's teachers when they see themselves in the classroom.

Parents as Experts

Parents are the experts on their children, and teachers can and should let parents know this. This acknowledgment helps build trust. As teachers, the goal is to gain as much information about each child outside of school to better meet his or her needs inside of school. Thus, we can view the parents as experts and seek to learn from them—about their child's routines, literacy habits, interests, social relationships, and family knowledge and skills. Vicky begins every initial parent–teacher conference in the fall with "Tell me about [your child]." If possible, teachers should meet face to face with each parent, but this information can be accessed through a survey as well. Some questions we have used include:

"How would you describe [child's name]?"
"What are some things she is interested in? What does she like to play?"
"Who are her friends?"
"How does he get along with others? Siblings? Friends? Adults?"
"Does he have responsibilities around the home?"
"What is he good at?"
"How does she react when she is upset?"

"Does he like books? What kind?"

"Does he like to draw, color, or write? What kinds of things? How often?"

"Does he like to sort things, organize, measure, count?"

"What does he like and dislike about school?"

"What are your goals for him this year at school? What would you like him most to learn?"

"Is there anything we should know that would help us during the school year?"

Respecting Families' Wishes and Perspectives

We have emphasized that the role of family involvement is not necessarily to get students to do at home what we wish they would do at school. However, this maxim changes if the parents want and ask for help with school-related tasks. When Ellen and a teacher visited with one grandparent, the teacher asked the grandmother what we could do to help the child. The grandmother was ready for the question and had a list! She wanted flash cards for both reading and math and paper for drawing. Our own ideas for literacy practices at home were quite different from using flash cards, but we decided on the spot to get her what she wanted. We had invited the grandmother to say what she wanted, and so we needed to honor her answer. The child was thrilled with the cards and loved using them.

When Vicky served as a reading coach for her school, a second-grade teacher had come to her frustrated after meeting with a parent who did not grasp her son's reading difficulties. The parent had described her son as reading just fine at home, but the teacher had assessed him as generally below grade level in reading. She said that the boy attempted to read grade-level texts but got distracted easily. He did not apply taught strategies and often appealed for help. When she read instructional-level texts with him in guided reading, he participated and responded well.

The school had purchased a site license for Reading A–Z (*www.readinga-z.com*). This site is loaded with printable reading resources at a variety of levels that address all components of reading from the NRP report. There are leveled books, fluency passages (e.g., Readers' Theatre, poetry), phonics and phonemic awareness lessons, vocabulary lessons, and questions to target comprehension. Vicky had used these successfully in reading groups and knew it was a great way to get books into the homes of her students.

Vicky then called the boy's mother and asked her to describe the student's reading. The mother described her son as a good reader, but she agreed that he read only easy books, and she said she wished for more difficult books. Vicky explained that she and the teacher hoped that the child would become an advanced reader and they believed he could if he practiced with both easy texts and some more challenging texts as well. Vicky compiled two levels of text. She downloaded books at the child's instructional level and also his grade-level text. She wrote instructions for the mother so that she could see the difference between what he could read comfortably and what he needed to be able to read to be considered a grade-level reader. Each week she asked the boy to choose a book from several she had selected at that level. Then she sent the books home so that his mother could read with him. Reading A–Z lessons also come with activities and questions that she sent home as well to guide his mother and demonstrate appropriate activities. Each one offered an opportunity for him to respond in writing so that he could bring it to his teacher for feedback.

After about 4 weeks, with weekly monitoring and ongoing teacher assessment, both mother and teacher were pleased with the child's performance. They began to notice that he needed higher levels of books until eventually with he was choosing and reading grade-level texts independently. Vicky continued to check in periodically with the mother, who through the changes in her son, seemed to begin to appreciate the extra support. Through the combination of consistent home practice and his teacher's persistence, this child demonstrated great improvement in reading.

Parents in the Classroom

Letting parents take part in the school day is a great way to connect with them, to learn about them, and to let them see what happens in a child's day. Teachers can invite parents to visit during the literacy block or any other time parents are able. Parents sit with their children and live through the experience of being in school, helping kids with activities, learning about routines and expectations, and sharing insights with teachers. Before beginning this type of visit, teachers must be very clear about their expectations of students and parents. Parents must *not* treat this as a reason to bring cupcakes or distract children. It is meant to be an opportunity for parents to learn about the day and for the teacher to learn about the parent. Parents sit in chairs next to their kids or in centers with their kids for a designated time. Teachers can create an exit ticket on which parents can leave feedback. In Nancy's experience, these exit tickets help teachers to learn interesting information about their students. For example, one parent wrote, "My child is good at helping other kids. She really likes reading with her little sister." This information helped the teacher learn that this student might be a great buddy for struggling readers.

Some teachers have taken this concept and invited parents to come to their classrooms every Friday to read with a student. This time is always met with excitement and makes an event within the school day based on reading. Parents can read with their own children, but are also encouraged or are assigned to read with other children. This predetermined time can also be used as times for students to present their work from various subjects in front of an authentic audience.

Family Nights

Some of the teachers we have worked with claim family nights (Kyle et al., 2005) as the most successful activity for connecting with families. These events can be formal (in which the teacher teachers the caregivers how to assist with reading) or informal (pot luck, get-to-know-you suppers). Teachers should decide the purpose of the workshop and proceed from there. We recommend that some food and transportation be provided so all can attend. We also recommend that the teacher go beyond the traditional stand-and-deliver workshop in which the teacher explains his or her curriculum while families sit in children's desks and listen. Ellen and her colleagues (Kyle et al., 2005) designed and implemented 13 different family nights that cover all curricular areas. The events include collaborative activities families can do together and cross many interests. Examples include scrapbook night; game-making night; math morning; hobbies, talents, and interests night; and biographies night. Kyle et al. also provide tips for making the events run smoothly and include reproducible documents such as invitation letters.

Beyond the School: Community-Based Organizations

Community-based organizations (CBOs) are groups that assist families in obtaining health and education information and services. Many schools are partnering with CBOs to help students achieve academic success while first meeting basic needs (Adger & Locke, 2000). As one way to extend the family involvement in schools, we recommend that teachers and administrators seek out the CBOs in their school's community to build on the work that is being done in that arena.

What do CBOs do? There are hundreds of different kinds of CBOs that assist students and families in ways that can ultimately affect academic success. Some organizations provide programs that assist families with child care, health care, prenatal care, and alcohol and drug prevention. Some offer English language classes, general equivalency diploma (GED) classes, after-school programs, and tutoring. Many of these organizations have the same or similar goals as ours. Thus, it is not surprising that research has shown that some school and CBO partnerships have raised achievement of students thought to be at risk for school failure (Adger & Locke, 2000).

The primary way in which schools have been able to assist CBOs is by referring families to programs they might need or want. Some schools create parent centers, which are simply a place for parents to convene, get acquainted, and share information. Brochures from the CBOs are available, and teachers and principals stop by to welcome families. Each year, Vicky's school hosts a "back-to-school" bash the weekend before school starts. CBOs set up booths where parents can get health, education, and community information while the teachers lead games and activities to welcome families, new and old.

Other partnerships can be more elaborate. In Seattle, Washington, "Project Look" operates three "schools" in apartment buildings where many of the students live to provide a safe place for children in grades 1–6 to come after school for help with homework and tutoring. It began with a focus on academics, but expanded to include prevention of alcohol, tobacco, dropout, and violence. During school hours there are programs for parents such as GED preparation and language classes. Project Look grew out of a conversation between teachers, a principal, and a university professor and now includes 35 different community organizations (Adger & Locke, 2000).

Working together always results in more than what is accomplished working alone. Just being seen in the community can also be beneficial. Some families who see familiar faces in one setting (e.g., school) might well be interested in becoming part of another setting (e.g., a CBO). This is all part of the trust building that we discussed earlier—an essential ingredient for successful family–school relationships and the first step toward higher student achievement.

Family Involvement and Research-Based, Culturally Responsive Instruction

We know that there are no guarantees to students' academic success and that we might not always elicit the assistance of families. Yet, the kind of education we propose in this book is one way we can combat the alienation we know so many children experience today. We found, as have many other educators (Edwards & Turner, 2010; Li & Edwards, 2009; McCarthey, 2009; Schultz, 2010), we have a moral obligation to apply our most creative and sophisticated thinking to ensure that all students in our classroom learn, and the ideas contained in this chapter (and book) offer several possibilities. We believe that family connections provide teachers with a knowledge base from which to build meaningful, authentic instruction. Children engaged in learning that matters to them are likely to be more successful and to achieve at high standards. We believe they will be happier, more emotionally healthy, and more productive. Our hope is that they will also be more compassionate and committed to making the world a better place for everyone.

CHAPTER 14

"What If My Students *Still* Need Help?"
Effective Reading Interventions

The reading instructional model we present in this book is designed so that children do not slip through the cracks. Regular classroom instruction should provide the intensive (research-based) strategies through engaging (culturally responsive) pedagogy that will meet all students' needs. That is the goal: the prevention of reading difficulties. But in reality, even with expert teaching, some children need additional help (Allington & McGill-Franzen, 2010; Snow et al., 1998; Torgeson, 1998, 2002a, 2002b). This chapter addresses the need for planned interventions, summarizes key studies of supplemental instruction, and describes several research-based interventions. We end the chapter with a conclusion for the entire book.

WHY CHILDREN STILL STRUGGLE

In Chapter 3 we explored the many conditions of children's lives that might contribute to lower academic achievement. For example, we said that although poverty itself certainly does not cause reading disabilities, the common conditions of poverty may contribute to school failure. These conditions include fewer resources, less time in adult interactions, more health issues, and lack of connection between print and the children's personal and cultural identities. We also emphasized the many school conditions that might contribute to reading failure. Some of these have to do with low expectations of teachers, few school resources, and difficult working conditions for teachers. Certainly, one part of the problem is the inadequate teaching of the essential skills of reading.

As emphasized in Chapter 5, most children who struggle with reading need additional help in the area of phonological skill or *word-level reading* (Mathes, Denton, Fletcher, Antony, Francis, et al., 2005; Snow et al., 1998; Torgeson, 2002b). For some children, a neurological disorder prevents them from hearing sounds in words the way normally developing children do. But for many, the reasons for their struggle with reading is the lack of appropriate instruction on the essential phonological skills research has shown to be critical for reading acquisition and development. For this reason, many of the interventions we summarize in this chapter emphasize this particular group of skills.

SUPPLEMENTAL INSTRUCTION: THE NEW NORM?

Supplemental instruction in the form of interventions became popular with Reading First, a salient component of the No Child Left Behind (NCLB) law. One required component of Reading First was for states and districts to provide supplemental instruction to students who fail to progress within the regular classroom instructional model. Importantly, the regulations emphasize that the additional instruction *supplement*, not supplant, the students' regular reading instruction program, and that these programs target students who are still behind their peers. The regulations encourage intensive individual or small-group instruction.

The idea of supplemental instruction is that students are part of heterogeneous classes participating in the general "core" program with all the other children, and then during another part of the day, sometimes before or after school but often during academic time (literacy or otherwise), the children participate in small-group or one-on-one focused work on specific literacy needs with students of similar ability and often with a specially trained teacher. They participate in the additional instruction until their reading performance is demonstrably improved and on par with their classmates.

Despite complaints about some aspects of Reading First, the inclusion of provisions for struggling readers has been met with approval and even relief by many. Indeed, the International Reading Association (IRA) has issued a position statement on "children's rights" in regard to reading instruction (*www.reading.org*). One of these rights states that "children who are struggling as learners have a right to receive supplemental instruction from professionals specifically prepared to teach reading" (*www.reading.org/general/ positionstatements/childrensrightsposition*). Since the year 2000, many different types of reading interventions have been developed.

RESPONSE TO INTERVENTION

The response-to-intervention (RTI) approach fits philosophically with our research-based, culturally responsive instructional reading model. RTI emerged from the field of special education because too many students were referred for special education services but were not learning disabled. In RTI, teachers are encouraged to rethink the practice of automatically referring students for special services when a child has a reading problem and instead first to diagnose the learning environment or *sociocultural context* of the child's learning situation. Teachers ask the same sorts of questions we outlined in Chapter 3 about why some students struggle with reading. When teachers have a sense of the causes of children's struggles, they are more likely to address them effectively.

RTI is a multi-tiered intervention. Tier 1 consists of the core instruction (which might be the model we describe in this book) and initial interventions. Tier 2 is used with students who do not respond academically to Tier 1 interventions and consists of targeted interventions and progress monitoring (instruction that might look like the Targeted Reading Intervention described above). Tier 3 is used with students who do not respond to either Tier 1 or Tier 2 interventions and includes a more intensive intervention than used in the other tiers (e.g., Fast ForWord, described later). There is no single RTI method, but the concept is based on the same principles as our model: It seeks to be inclusive, adapts instruction for ELLs and anyone else with linguistic differences, and has the academic achievement of all learners as its goal.

Tiers 2 and 3: The Need for Intensive Interventions

Even when classroom instruction is of high quality, approximately 5–7% of students do not develop in reading as expected by the end of the primary grades (Mathes et al., 2005; Torgeson, 2002a). If these children are not attended to immediately, they may never catch up (Juel, 1988, 1991). However, much research, especially from the field of special education (e.g., Klenk & Kibby, 2000), has illustrated that it is quality teaching (not just amount) that is key to improved achievement. If children simply get more of the same bad teaching, it is reasonable to think that they will become more disengaged and continue to struggle. The quality of instruction matters. Researchers agree that interventions in Tiers 2 and 3 must be *systematic, explicit*, and *intense* until the child's reading performance is on par with others his or her age. As stated, children's difficulties with word identification skills, especially resulting from lack of phonological skill, are firmly established as the primary reason most children struggle with reading.

RESEARCH ON
SUPPLEMENTAL READING INTERVENTIONS

Studies of reading interventions for struggling readers clearly show that children who receive intervention services outperform children who receive only the "status quo" (Heibert & Taylor, 2000, p. 467) instruction, regardless of the focus of instruction. Some comparison studies, however, suggest that some instructional interventions are more helpful than others. Pinnell, Lyons, DeFord, Bryk, and Seltzer (1994) compared the effectiveness of Reading Recovery, a popular one-on-one reading intervention for first graders (described below), to three other instructional models and a control group. Two of the interventions were also one-on-one tutoring models, and the other groups were whole-class instructional models. The students who received Reading Recovery training in addition to their regular classroom instruction performed best on all measures, followed by the other tutoring models, illustrating that individual tutoring may be "necessary but not sufficient" for struggling readers to make adequate progress (p. 31). However, in an independent evaluation of Reading Recovery (Shanahan & Barr, 1995), effects of the program were mixed, raising questions about the program's cost effectiveness because of the intensive, year-long training required of Reading Recovery teachers who can work with only a few children daily.

Another comparison of tutoring programs (Wasik & Slavin, 1993) found that students who received tutoring that was integrated with their regular classroom instruction performed better than students whose intervention took place outside their regular classroom instruction. That is, in the Success for All model, children in grades 1–3 received tutoring every day for 20 minutes in addition to their regular instruction, which included the same content and pedagogical focus as the tutoring. Their performance was compared with other children who received a different one-to-one tutoring, small-group, or whole-group intervention. The Success for All children achieved significantly more (Wasik & Slavin, 1993).

In a review of five supplemental programs, Pikulski (1994) found similar results. A common feature among the five interventions she reviewed was that the interventions were all in addition to, not a substitute for, the instruction the students received as part of the regular programs. While some of the programs, such as Reading Recovery, were pull-out programs with little coordination with the instruction in the regular classroom, others were conducted in collaboration with the regular classroom teachers. All five programs were successful at preventing reading problems; however, the supplemental program that were coordinated with the regular classroom program resulted in highest gains on student achievement measures.

In a study of the effects of various reading interventions on first- and second-grade reading achievement, we found that children achieve on the skills they are directly taught in the intervention (McIntyre, Petrosko, et al., 2005). Across the various interventions, 39 first-grade children and 20 second-grade children served by daily, intensive reading instruction as a *supplement* to their regular classroom reading instruction achieved significantly higher on a reading inventory passage measuring fluency and comprehension than 84 first-grade and 43 second-grade children who did not receive supplemental instruction. However, there were no significant achievement differences in phonics instruction across the groups because in all five supplemental models, the instruction was focused on reading fluency and comprehension of connected text.

Other researchers have also shown that children learn what they are taught (Allington, 1983; Gunn, Smolkowski, & Biglan, 2002; Mathes et al., 2005). Gunn et al. (2002) found that primary-grade children who received intervention services that focused on word attack skills, word identification, fluency, vocabulary, and reading comprehension performed significantly better on measures of those aspects of literacy than those who had not received the intervention. The same was true for students whose first language was not English (Goldenberg, 1994; Gunn, Biglan, Smolkowski, & Ary, 2000). Certainly there is evidence that interventions of all kinds can and do make a difference, but there is also evidence that the focus of instruction (what it is emphasized and with what materials) also matters (Knapp, 1995; Wharton-McDonald, Pressley, & Hampton, 1998).

One question researchers posed aligns with our own interest in combining effective instructional practices from multiple perspectives. Mathes, Howard, Allen, and Fuchs (1998) asked how to balance or weave together the positive aspects of different instructional approaches in ways that are both practical for teachers and responsive to the specific learning needs of individual children. Their intervention, called PALS (peer assisted learning strategies), is a peer-mediated instructional program for first graders focused on phonological skills and repeated exposure to a variety of children's literature. The content of the lessons includes a balance of instructional practices from a behaviorist tradition (i.e., principles of the direct instruction) (Carnine, Silbert, Kame'enui, & Tarrer, 2004) with practices from a holistic (constructivist) tradition as implemented through partner read-alouds. In other words, the lessons include "sounds and words" activities that are scripted for the teachers to follow and paired reading of literature trade books, individualized to meet students' interests.

PALS was effective in improving reading performance of low-, average-, and high-achieving English-proficient students, including students with disabilities (Simmons, Fuchs, Fuchs, Mathes, & Hodge, 1995; McMaster, Fuchs, & Fuchs, 2006); ELLs (McMaster, Kung, Han, & Cao, 2008), including those with learning disabilities (Saenz, Fuchs, & Fuchs, 2005); and children in high poverty schools (Fuchs et al., 2001). Researchers have even found that students who participate in PALS enjoy more social acceptance than similar children in non-PALS classrooms (Fuchs, Fuchs, Mathes, & Martinez, 2002). In this study, however, the researchers were not able to determine whether it was the word study or the paired reading or the combination that helped children achieve.

In a later study that built on the PALS study, Mathes et al. (2005) compared two interventions from two different theoretical orientations. The first intervention, called Proactive Reading, entailed short, research-based activities that covered phonemic awareness, letter knowledge, word recognition, fluency, and comprehension. The texts read were "decodable," which meant that the language of the text was severely limited to match the word-level skill of the lesson. The skills were explicitly taught within a scope and sequence: The children practiced phonetic elements in isolation, then practiced decoding words in isolation, then read connected text. Over time, the types of words increased and story lines got more complex. Children were rewarded with praise and stickers, and all errors were corrected.

The second intervention was derived from cognitive strategy instruction grounded in Vygotskian theory. In this intervention, called Responsive Reading, the children were taught to problem-solve during reading, and mistakes were viewed as a natural part of the learning process. The teachers modeled what they wanted students to do and guided them through a lesson or activity with coaching and scaffolding. The "gradual release of responsibility" concept described in Chapter 4 is paramount in this intervention; the idea was for children to become independent problem solvers in the reading process. Responsive Reading also followed a scope and sequence. Teachers taught essential preskills, modeled strategies, and followed with reading connected text with scaffolding. The children's needs dictate the goals of the teacher (making it *responsive*), and the teacher planned instruction according to those needs.

As with previous studies, these researchers found that those who received the additional instruction performed better on reading measures than those who received only the core instruction. They also found, like so many other researchers (e.g., Allington, 1983; McIntyre, Petrosko, et al., 2005) that children learn what they are taught. In particular, because Proactive Reading focused on word attack skills, children who received that intervention performed better on that measure.

There have been a few studies of reading interventions with children who struggle with reading and who also happen to be ELLs. Vaughn, Mathes, Linan-Thompson, and Francis (2005) developed two interventions, one in English and one in Spanish. The struggling ELL students were assigned to one of the two interventions, matching the language of their core program. The English intervention was the Proactive Reading of the previous study. The lessons were augmented with teacher adaptations for ELLs, referred to in Chapter 4 as "comprehensible input" (Echevarria et al., 2004), including the use of visuals, gestures, facial expressions, clarifying, and opportunities for more student talk. Much vocabulary was discussed, especially the vocabulary associated with the activities, to ensure that the students understood the tasks. The second intervention, developed in Spanish, was also a version of Proactive Reading. But these lessons were careful to attend to the syllabic nature of the Spanish language and thus focused much on syllable reading. There was also an oral component for both interventions, which included daily read-alouds with discussions and retellings. The researchers found that the children participating in either intervention outperformed those who did not participate. Implications for instructional practices for ELLs from this and other studies (see Amendum & Fitzgerald, 2010) favor practices that maintain the general instructional procedures for the research-based model with additional opportunities for oral language development for ELLs.

More recently, a study of a promising new intervention, called Targeted Reading Intervention (TRI), designed for kindergarten and first-grade children in rural poor and working-class communities (Amendum, Vernon-Feagans, & Ginsberg, in press), has shown significant achievement on a battery of both phonological and comprehension measures. In a well-designed controlled experimental study of over 300 children in seven schools, the researchers found that after 1 year of TRI delivered by the regular classroom teacher, the children who received the services outperformed those who did not on all measures. Classroom teachers delivered the intervention in one-on-one, 15-minute teaching sessions, facilitated by in-classroom literacy coaching via an innovative webconferencing system using laptop computers and webcam technology. That is, researchers/coaches could watch lessons via webcam from another location in the state and give the teachers immediate face-to-face feedback through the webcam technology. This intervention (described below) is currently being conducted in urban schools, with much of the same success.

Train the Mind, Change the Brain

In 2007, Sharon Begley, former science writer for *Newsweek* magazine, published *Train the Mind, Change Your Brain*, a book that brings together many recent studies in the field of neuroplasticity to illustrate that the actual physical matter of the brain can change with intense effort and attention. Previously the field of neuroscience held that the brain was fixed and unchangeable after early childhood. Yet, the studies summarized in the book—of animals and people—show that the brain can be rewired through cognitive strategy training or mindfulness meditation to do many things not previously thought possible, such as eliminating compulsive disorders, decreasing depression, and compensating for the loss of sight or hearing. Important for us, the studies also illustrated that mind training can help increase compassion toward others and even unlearn racism and other prejudices.

One exciting series of studies was conducted with children with dyslexia, those with serious brain-based reading difficulties. Researchers developed a computer game-based reading intervention called Fast ForWord, in which children were taught to learn to hear phonological sounds they could not otherwise hear, among other skills. The training was intense; it took place for 100 minutes a day for 30 school days. The training significantly improved children's performance on essential reading skills for over 70% of the participants, some of whom were ELLs. The intensity and time required for these sorts of interventions may be best suited for children with the most serious learning disabilities. However, the field of neuroplasticity shows much promise for what might be achieved in school settings in the future.

PRINCIPLES FOR READING INTERVENTIONS

Figure 14.1 presents general principles for reading interventions.

- Ensure that regular "core" instruction is high-quality research-based, culturally responsive instruction that is differentiated for different learners.
- Assess students' reading skills and strategies regularly as they work in authentic contexts.
- Intervene immediately when students seem to fall behind; provide additional help for these learners in the form of instruction on targeted needs.
- If in-class extra help does not seem to move students toward improvement, elicit outside help or extra intervention services.
- Be sure interventions are well-designed research-based programs that engage the students.
- The interventions should be intense, regular, and focused on the skills the children need.
- If a technology-based program is used, teachers should monitor it closely to be sure that students remain engaged, as intended.
- Integrate the intervention content with regular classroom content as often as possible.
- Keep the intervention instruction of high quality so as not to waste the teacher's or the students' time.

FIGURE 14.1. Principles for reading interventions.

EFFECTIVE READING INTERVENTIONS

There are many types of reading interventions that fit the principles we outline above, and some are described above in our research review. We have chosen to elaborate on a few of our favorites that represent very different types of interventions (one-on-one, small-group, in-class, or computer-based interventions). The first four are popular and grounded in well-designed studies. The fifth is a research-based tutoring program that utilizes volunteers for the additional instruction. The final one is the computer-based program designed to "change the brain" for children with dyslexia.

Reading Recovery

Reading Recovery is a supplemental reading intervention created in the 1970s by Marie Clay. This program aims to reduce the number of first graders who have problems learning to read and write. Reading Recovery serves the lowest-achieving first graders. In Reading Recovery, the identified students meet one on one with specially trained teachers for 30-minute sessions every school day. Lessons are designed specially for the individual student, based on assessments conducted by the Reading Recovery teacher. Students are initially assessed using an Observation Survey of Early Literacy Achievement (Clay, 1995), which measures letter identification, word knowledge, concepts of print, writing vocabulary, hearing and recording, sounds in words, and text reading. Subsequently, Reading Recovery teachers assess students' reading and writing behaviors during lessons, take running records daily, and use observational data to inform instruction. During each lesson children read familiar or previously read books, and the teacher takes a running record as each child reads. In addition, children use magnetic letters to work with letters and/or words, write stories, assemble cut-up versions of the stories, and read new books. Each lesson also includes opportunities for students to problem-solve and use reading strategies in the presence of the trained teacher. Teachers work with children on rereading, reading strategies, decoding, and sentence writing. Children are also expected to practice at home.

Targeted Reading Intervention

TRI is a one-to-one instructional intervention designed for the most struggling readers in kindergarten and first grade (Amendum et al., in press). The regular classroom teacher delivers the instruction for 15 minutes each day for a period of several weeks, assessing students' achievement periodically. Instruction focuses both on phonological aspects and comprehension of reading. Each lesson has the following three component lessons: rereading for fluency (2–5 minutes), in which the teacher leads the child in reading and rereading appropriately leveled books, much like we describe in Chapter 6; word work (6–10 minutes), in which the child actively manipulates materials to help him- or herself hear and use more sound–symbol relations, similar to some activities we describe in Chapter 5; and guided oral reading (7–10 minutes), which emphasizes monitoring of reading connected text and comprehension, reflected in strategies we describe in Chapters 6 and 7. After the student has made sufficient progress to be able to learn better from the general classroom instruction, the teacher selects another student to receive the one-to-one teaching. Eventually, some teachers work with the children in groups of two or three.

What is exciting about TRI is that the teachers who receive training in the intervention find it doable. They seem to be able to fit the time into their busy schedules. They also begin to use the strategies learned for all kids in the classroom. It is not expensive, like Reading Recovery or some of the other models. Most importantly, it is highly effective. In its infancy, it has already shown results of increased student achievement for hundreds of children.

Early Intervention

This model is based on a study by Taylor, Strait, and Medo in Heibert and Taylor's (1994) *Getting Reading Right from the Start*. Students who are perceived as lagging behind the rest of the class are targeted early in the school year for an extra reading lesson each day. The teacher begins the day with this group, when he or she is freshest and while the other students are engaged in meaningful, independent work (reading, researching, problem solving, or completing tasks at literacy centers or stations). The teacher has students read and reread, discuss, read more, work on decoding skills, and read more during an intensive 30-minute period. Then the teacher's regular day begins with her usual grouping practices with all her students, again including those students in the intervention group. The intervention group students may graduate from the group after a few weeks or months, depending on what is needed. Other children may be drawn into the group, as needed. The key is that the teacher works with the bottom 20% of the class in the morning when he or she is freshest and when the other students are also freshest and therefore more likely to remain engaged in quality independent work. Planning for this kind of intervention is essential, as the teacher must ensure that the rest of the students are getting the academic support they need. The following sample lesson was observed by Ellen and her colleagues in a study of reading interventions.

The teacher works with a small group of six children outside the regular classroom and introduces a new book. It is called *Going to the Fair* and the teacher elicits from the children their experiences going to a state fair. The children mention animals, rides, games, and food they experienced at a fair. The teacher guides them through a "picture walk" and continues to elicit the students' knowledge about fairs and their expectations for this book. Then the teacher introduces the title page, incorporating some phonics attention in the context of reading the title. The teacher asks, "What's the title again, Billy?"

Billy says, "Going to the fair."

"Can you sound out the author's name for me?"

The child makes an attempt.

"Break it down into small parts that you know"

The child says, "Vack er all."

The teacher goes over it, "/vack ack/, we know that, /er/, we know that. . . . Then we sound out the name of the illustrator."

A child says something.

"Good. *Leach*, rhymes with *beach*."

Then the teacher guides the children through the rest of the book, asking several comprehension questions such as, "What about this picture makes you think it is a grandmother?", "How many of you have grandmothers who make jellies and jams?", and "What is this girl getting ready to do here?"

In addition to posing questions, the teacher elaborately explains and demonstrates what a "raffle" is (this concept is dealt with in the story). Then there is more phonics work with a sign in the book that says "refreshments" and the teacher has children write the word on their "lap boards"—individual wipe-off boards. This sequence of book introduction, skill lessons, and meaning construction discussion takes 22 minutes.

Then the teacher has the children read the book individually and silently, while he circulates and helps as needed. After a few minutes, he asks a child to come to his desk and read aloud while he listens and scaffolds the child's reading. This goes on for about ten minutes, during which all the children finish their readings. Before the children leave the room the teacher introduces a book they will read the next time they come—a Dr. Seuss book that happened to be one of his favorites. The lesson has lasted about 35 minutes. The teacher takes the group back to the classroom.

In the lesson above, the teacher includes the rereading, word work, vocabulary, and comprehension instruction within one cohesive, 30-minute lesson.

Peer Assisted Learning Strategies (PALS)

PALS is a peer tutoring strategy implemented in whole-class settings and directed by the classroom teacher. Students work in pairs, with readers of varied skill. To form these pairs the teacher makes a list of students in the classroom in rank order from strongest reader to weakest reader (on some area of reading with some sort of text; we are aware designations such as these can be arbitrary and temporary). He or she then divides the list in half and pairs the strongest reader of that type of reading task from the top half of the list with the strongest reader from the bottom half, until all students are paired (McMaster, Fuchs, & Fuchs, 2007). The partners take turns being the reader and the coach; the coach offers corrective feedback when necessary. Students are trained to give this feedback in helpful, positive ways and receive points for good reading and coaching. Partners change every couple of weeks, based on new tasks and new assessments. There are materials that must be purchased, but texts utilized along with these materials can come from the classroom.

In Kindergarten PALS, or K-PALS, students practice letter–sound correspondence, decoding, phonological awareness, and sight words. It takes 30 minutes per session and is conducted three or four times per week. In first grade, PALS students practice decoding and reading fluently three or four times per week for 35 minutes. In grades 2–6 the goal of PALS is to improve the use of reading strategies and thereby improve reading fluency and comprehension. Three main components are used: partner reading with retelling, paragraph shrinking, and prediction relay. In these higher grades students and teachers participate in PALS three times per week for 35 minutes each time. PALS is popular among participating teachers and students. Training and implementation materials are relatively inexpensive. More information, including sample lessons and materials, can be found at *kc.vanderbilt.edu/pals*.

Book Buddies

Book Buddies is a reading intervention designed for tutors. It is an instructional model written by some of the same authors (Johnston, Invernizzi, & Juel, 2009) as the word study program described in Chapter 5, Words Their Way. The manual is a comprehensive guide for volunteer tutors of emergent and beginning readers. While many volunteer programs exist across the country, only a few have been researched for their effectiveness (Morris, Shaw, & Perney, 1990; Invernizzi, Juel, Rosemary, & Richards, 1997; Juel, 1997). One of these is Book Buddies. In this program, each volunteer receives approximately 6 hours of training across a year, including videotaped analyses of lessons. A school coordinator arranges for materials, space, and the sessions, which take place twice weekly for 45 minutes each. The students are assessed three times a year for their achievement and needs. The program is primarily for first-grade children.

The lessons consist of reading, writing, and phonics. The instruction is based on several assumptions that are similar to those we share in our instructional model.

1. Children learn to read by reading in meaningful contexts.
2. Reading instruction should be differentiated based on diagnosed learner needs.
3. Phonics instruction should be taught explicitly and paced according to a child's developing hypotheses about how words work.

4. Reading, writing, and spelling develop in synchrony.
5. Learning to read occurs in a social context and through interactions with a more knowledgeable other. (Johnston et al., 2009, p. 8)

These principles sound much like the principles we have established in the early chapters of this book on children's development.

Fast ForWord

Fast ForWord (*www.scilearn.com*) is a computer training program designed for children with severe dyslexia. The child wears headphones to hear the instructions or stimuli and uses the computer mouse to respond. The training program consists of seven exercises presented in the form of computer games, which are organized such that the child first trains on basic acoustic reception abilities and progresses to exercises that are designed to improve the child's syntactic and semantic skills. Each exercise (game) begins with training at a level at which most children can perform. The difficulty level is continuously adapted so that the child gets the majority (about 80%) of answers correct. Initially, the acoustic elements of speech (e.g., phonic match, phoneme identification) are stretched in time or amplified. For example, the sound /ba/ might be pronounced /bbb-baaaaa/. The program reduces the elongated sounds to normal sounds as the child progresses. The ending level for all of the training exercises is normal, unmodified speech. During the exercises the child receives immediate and constant feedback.

Described in *Train the Mind, Change Your Brain* (Begley, 2007), researchers found the program to be highly effective for children with severe reading problems.

INTERVENTIONS AND RESEARCH-BASED, CULTURALLY RESPONSIVE TEACHING

Our goal is for all students to make progress in reading, and so we welcome all interventions that have been shown in studies to work well and in which students remain engaged. We caution that selecting an intervention must be made with cultural considerations. Teachers should examine texts carefully for their connection with students. Teachers must ask whether the instructional practices will frustrate, bore, or engage students. However, as we have mentioned often throughout the book, teachers must also consider the practices of the intervention that make it research-based. Often interventions work because of the text that is used or because of its somewhat rigid schedule. Teachers must use their judgment and assessments to determine which interventions are received well by students and increase student performance.

The goal of our instructional model is student achievement for all, and the reading interventions described here are the type that provides the most targeted help that struggling readers need. We believe that providing interventions is an equity issue. If some children are not succeeding in school, it is the responsibility of the school to find what will help them to succeed. We believe that teachers, principals, and school officials want their students to succeed. These interventions, combined with excellent overall core instruction, offer that opportunity.

CONCLUSION

We live and teach in an interesting, dynamic era of constant technological and demographic change. The diversity in U.S. classrooms has increased dramatically over the past few decades and will continue to do so for years. Teachers in all parts of the country have racial and ethnic minorities, large populations of ELLs, refugees from war-torn countries, and children with diverse religious and cultural values. It is difficult to keep up with it all, but change is what makes our lives rich and exciting.

Teaching in the 21st century demands a new way of thinking and being, but without disregard for the important educational research that has shaped our field in significant ways. The powerful research that affects reading achievement comes primarily from two areas: (1) research on the reading instruction that effectively improves learning and (2) research on educational practices that shows effectiveness for diverse populations of students. Because education is one of our society's greatest equity issues, we must attend to these multiple perspectives on what works for all learners.

The purpose of this book is to provide elementary teachers with a guide for implementing research-based reading instruction through an approach that attends to the cultural and linguistic backgrounds of the students in their classrooms. The reading instruction described is based on decades of research on what works in reading, focusing primarily on the five topic areas of an effective reading program: phonemic awareness, phonics, fluency, vocabulary, and comprehension. We address critical supporting areas of literacy as well, including classroom climate, academic talk and listening, writing, and new literacies. The instructional strategies included in the book for each of these literacy curricular components were only those that had a strong research base.

Our goal for the book is a lofty one. In addition to emphasizing the importance of using strategies we know from research help children improve their reading, we also explicate how to employ pedagogical standards that closely match students' cultural and linguistic backgrounds. This is not always easy, especially in the areas of phonemic awareness and phonics, because the instruction on those topics must at times be decontextualized from stories (which are a primary tool for engaging learners). Thus, these individual lessons or learning activities may not appear to be both research-based and culturally responsive. Instead, it is the *classroom* and the *perspective of the teacher* that can always be culturally responsive. The teacher's beliefs about children, their families, the goals of education, and how to treat people all become part of his or her cultural responsiveness. If teachers create environments like those described in Chapter 4, research-based lessons can occur *within* those culturally responsive contexts. If an activity, lesson, program, or model is studied under rigorous research conditions, as described in Chapter 1, then nothing can be changed in the lesson if the teacher is to maintain the integrity of the research-based (or proven) characteristic of the lesson. Thus, if a child says or does something that makes the teacher want to rearrange the sequence of the lesson, choose a different type of text, avoid particular skills in the sequence of the researched lesson, or make some other move because the teacher believes it does not reflect his or her learners, then the lesson or activity is no longer research-based.

What is a teacher to do? As we described in Chapter 1, the decision regarding what to do in such cases lies with the teacher. We recommend that teachers find lessons, programs, and interventions that they know are research-based and that they believe the children in their classroom will respond to with high engagement. However, teachers should also observe students closely to see if they are bored or disengaged or simply not learning. Teachers should always keep their students' needs, interests, backgrounds, desires, and ways of learning in their minds as they select lesson activities and texts. In this way, teachers can teach research-based lessons *within* culturally responsive classrooms. The model we present in this book is meant to be pragmatic in this way.

The reading components of fluency, vocabulary, comprehension, and writing lend themselves more easily to culturally responsive instruction. Research-based strategies such as repeated reading for fluency practice can be conducted with terrific multicultural texts, and comprehension strategies can be adapted pedagogically to connect more deeply to students' words, creating the sort of hybrid classrooms that allow for the voices of children often left out of traditional instruction (Dantas & Manyek, 2010; Gutiérrez et al., 2001). Dantas and Manyek emphasize that these classrooms are not just all "warm and fuzzy," however. Instead, they are challenging and engaging, with "careful, strategic, and rigorous use of such experiences to extend children's repertoire of skills, build meaningful connections to new knowledge and enhance students' engagement in school learning" (p. 13). Importantly, the model of instruction shared in this book illustrates how the components of research-based reading instruction and culturally responsive instruction can exist within the same classroom. The model includes these different instructional paradigms in a pragmatic, hopeful, yet realistic model that has the potential to meet the needs of all students in elementary classrooms.

Resources

SOME FAVORITE CHILDREN'S LITERATURE
FOR READING INSTRUCTION

Adler, D. (1986). *Martin Luther King, Jr.: Free at last.* New York: Holiday House.

Allen, D. (2000). *Dancing in the wings.* New York: Puffin.

Allen, D. (2000). *Dancing in the wings.* New York: Puffin.

Barretta, G. (2007). *Dear deer.* New York: Henry Holt.

Bogart, J. E., & Daigneault, S. (1991). *Sarah saw a blue macaw.* New York: Scholastic Press.

Bradby, M. (1995). *More than anything else.* New York: Orchard.

Bridges, R. (1999) *Through my eyes.* New York: Scholastic Press.

Briggs, R. (1978). *The snowman storybook.* New York: Random House.

Briggs, R. (1999). *The snowman.* New York: Random House.

Brown, P. (2009). *The curious garden.* New York: Little, Brown.

Browne, A. (1998). *Voices in the park.* New York: DK Publishing.

Bruchac, J. (2000). *Pushing up the sky: Seven Native American plays for children.* New York: Penguin Group.

Bunting, E. (1994). *Flower garden.* New York: Harcourt Books.

Bunting, E. (1994). *Smoky night.* Orlando, FL: Harcourt Brace.

Bunting, E. (2006). *One green apple.* New York: Clarion Books.

Carle, E. (2002). *Slowly, slowly, slowly said the sloth.* New York: Scholastic Press.

Castle, C. (2000). *For every child.* New York: Putnam Books.

Cherry, L. (1990). *The great kapok tree: A tale of the rain forest.* Orlando, FL: Harcourt Books.

Cherry, L. (1992). *A river ran wild.* San Diego, CA: Harcourt, Brace.

Cine-Ransome, L. (2003). *Satchel Paige.* New York: Simon & Schuster.

Cleary, B. (2005). *How much can a bare bear bear?* Minneapolis: Millbrook Press.

Coerr, E. (1977). *Sadako and the thousand paper cranes.* New York: Puffin Books.

Cole, H., & Vogl, N. (2005). *Am I a color too?* Bellevue, WA: Illumination Arts.

Cole, J. (1998). *The magic school bus in the rain forest.* New York: Scholastic Press.

267

Coleman, E. (1996). *White socks only*. Morton Grove, IL: Albert Whitman.

Collier, B. (2000). *Uptown*. New York: Henry Holt.

Cooper, F. (1994). *Coming home*. New York: Philomel Books.

Cunningham, P., & Hall, D. (1994). *Making words*. Torrance, CA: Good Apple.

Curtis, J. (1996). *Tell me again about the night I was born*. New York: HarperCollins.

Dahl, R. (1964). *The magic finger*. New York: Scholastic Press.

Dahl, R. (1985). *The giraffe and the pelly and me*. New York: Puffin Books.

Dahl, R. (1988). *Matilda*. New York: Scholastic Press.

Dahl, R. (2001). *The giraffe the pelly and me*. London: Puffin Books.

DiCamillo, K. (2000). *Because of Winn-Dixie*. Cambridge, MA: Candlewick Press.

Disalvo-Ryan, D. (1994). *City green*. New York: HarperCollins.

Dorros, A. (1991). *Animal tracks*. New York: Scholastic Press.

Edwards, P. (1997). *Barefoot escape on the underground railroad*. New York: HarperCollins.

Feelings, T. (1993). *Soul looks back in wonder*. New York: Puffin Books.

Fife, D.H. (1996). *The empty lot*. San Francisco: Sagebrush Education Resources.

Fleischman, P. (1999). *Weslandia*. Cambridge, MA: Candlewick Press.

Fleming, D. (1995). *In the tall, tall grass*. New York: Henry Holt.

Forney, M. (2001). *Razzle dazzle writing*. Gainesville, FL: Maupin.

Frasier, D. (2007). *Miss Alaineus: A vocabulary disaster*. Orlando, FL: First Voyager Books.

Garland, S. (1993). *The lotus seed*. Orlando, FL: Harcourt.

Goble, P. (2005). *All our relatives: Traditional Native American thoughts about nature*. Bloomington, IN: World Wisdom Books.

Goldenstern, J. (2002). *Rose's gold*. Barrington, IL: Rigby.

Grifalconi, A. (1986). *The village of round and square houses*. Boston: Little, Brown.

Grimes, N. (1984). *Meet Danitra Brown*. New York: Scholastic Press.

Grimes, N. (1999). *My man blue*. New York: Scholastic Press.

Grimes, N. (2008). *Barak Obama: Son of promise, son of hope*. New York: Simon & Schuster Books for Young Readers.

Gwynne, F. (1970). *The king who rained*. New York: Simon & Shuster.

Gwynne, F. (1976). *A chocolate moose for dinner*. New York: Aladdin Paperbacks.

Hall, B. E. (2004). *Henry and the kite dragon*. New York: Philomel Books.

Hawes, J. (1996). *Why frogs are wet*. New York: HarperCollins.

Hoffman, M. (1991). *Amazing grace*. New York: Dial.

Hoffman, M. (1995). *Boundless grace*. New York: Dial Books for Young Readers.

Hopkinson, D. (1993). *Sweet Clara and the freedom quilt*. New York: Dragonfly Books, Knopf.

Hopkinson, D. (1999). *Maria's comet*. New York: Atheneum Books for Young Readers, Simon & Schuster.

Hosking, C. (2000). *Encyclopedia of a rain forest*. Barrington, IL: Rigby Literacy.

Howard, E. F. (1991). *Aunt flossie's hats and crab cakes later*. New York: Clarion.

Howard, E. F., & Lewis, E. B. (2000). *Virgie goes to school with us boys*. New York: Simon & Schuster Books for Young Readers.

Johnson, A. (2007). *Lily Brown's paintings*. New York: Orchard Books.

Johnson, A., & Peck, B. (2007). *Just like Josh Gibson*. New York: Simon & Shuster.

Johnson, D. (2000). *Henry hikes to Fitchburg*. Boston: Houghton Mifflin.

Joy, N. (2007). *The secret Olivia told me*. Scholastic: New York.

Kalman, B. (1989). *China: The culture*. New York: Crabtree.

Kennedy, J. (1998). *Lucy goes to the country*. Los Angeles: Alyson Wonderland.

King, M. L., Jr. (1963). *I have a dream*. New York: Scholastic Press.

Kraus, R. (1971). *Leo the late bloomer*. New York: Windmill Books.

Krull, K. (1996). *Wilma unlimited: How Wilma Rudolph became the world's fastest woman*. New York: Voyager Books, Harcourt.

Kuklin, S. (1992). *How my family lives in America*. New York: Simon & Schuster.

Lawrence, J. (1993). *The great migration: An American story*. New York: HarperTrophy.

Lawrence, J. (1997). *Harriet and the promised land*. New York: Aladdin Paperbacks.

Lederer, R. (1996). *Pun and games: Jokes, riddles, rhymes, daffynitions, tairy fales, and more word play for kids*. Chicago: Chicago Review Press.

Lester, H. (1999). *Hooway for Wodney Wat*. New York: Houghton Mifflin.

Lester, J. (1994). *John Henry*. New York: Dial Books.

Levine, E., & Nelson, K. (2007). *Henry's freedom box*. New York: Scholastic Press.

Lindbergh, R. (1996). *Nobody owns the sky*. Cambridge, MA: Candlewick Press.

Lioni, L. (1967). *Frederick*. New York: Knopf.

Littlesugar, A. (1997). *Jonkonnu: A story from the sketchbook of Winslow Homer*. New York: Philomel Books.

Lorbiecki, M. (1998). *Sister Anne's hands*. New York: Puffin Books.

Louis, A.-L. (1996). *Yeh Shen*. New York: Putnam.

Lovell, P. (2001). *Stand tall Molly Lou Melon*. New York: Putnam.

Lyon, G. E. (2010). *George Ella Lyon: Where I'm from*. Retrieved February 14, 2010, from *www.georgeellalyon.com/where.html*.

Lysecki, M., & Murray, J. (2005). *They changed the world*. Parsippany, NJ: Celebration Press, Pearson Learning Group.

Margolies, B. (1990). *Rehema's journey: A visit in Tanzania*. New York: Scholastic Press.

Martin, R. (1976). *Brown bear, brown bear: What do you see?*. New York: Henry Holt.

Martin, R., & Shannon, D. (1992). *The rough-face girl*. New York: Scholastic Press.

McCain, B. R., & Leonardo, T. (2001). *Nobody knew what to do*. Park Ridge, IL: Albert Whitman.

McKissack, P. (2001). *Goin' someplace special*. New York: Scholastic Press.

Mitchell, M. K. (1993). *Uncle Jed's barbershop*. New York: Simon & Schuster, Aladdin Paperbacks.

Mochizuki, K. (1997). *Passage to freedom: The Sugihara story*. New York: Lee & Low Books.

Molina, R. (2002). *Titoy's magical chair*. Philippines: Adarna House.

Monk, I. (1999). *Hope*. Minneapolis: Carolrhoda Books.

Montgomery, R. A. (1982). *House of danger*. Waitsfield, VT: Chooseco.

Montgomery, R. A. (1982). *The abominable snowman/journey under sea/space and beyond/the lost jewels of Nabooti* (Choose Your Own Adventure 1–4). Waitsfield, VT: Chooseco.

Mora, P. (1997). *Tomas and the library lady*. New York: Knopf.

Mora, P. (1998). *This big sky*. New York: Scholastic Press.

Mora, P. (2005) *Dona Flor*. New York: Knopf.

Mora, P. (2006). *Marimba! Animals from A to Z*. New York: Clarion Books.

Mora, P. (2007). *Yum! Mmmm! Que Rico!* New York: Lee & Low Books.

Mora, P. (2009). *Book Fiesta!* New York: HarperCollins.

Morris, A. (1989). *Hats hats hats*. New York: Mulberry Book.

Morris, A. (1993). *Bread bread bread*. New York: HarperCollins.

Moss, L. (1995). *Zin! Zin! Zin! A violin*. New York: Simon & Schuster.

Nelson, V. (1987). *Almost to freedom*. New York: Scholastic Press.

Newman, L., & Thompson, C. (2009). *Daddy, papa, and me*. Berkley, CA: Tricycle Press.

Pack, L. (2002). *A is for Appalachia!: The alphabet book of Appalachian heritage*. Prospect, KY: Harmony House.

Parnell, P., & Richardson, J. (2005). *And tango makes three*. New York: Simon & Schuster.

Parrish, P. (1977). *Teach us Amelia Bedelia*. New York: HarperCollins.

Pellegrini, N. (1991). *Families are different*. New York: Holiday House.

Penner, L.R. (1996). *Monster bugs*. New York: Random House.

Perez, A.I. (2002). *My diary from here to there*. San Francisco: Children's Book Press.

Pinkney, A. (1998). *Dear Benjamin Banneker*. New York: Voyager Books.

Podogil, C. (2000). *Matthew Henson, arctic explorer*. New York: McGraw Hill Macmillan.

Polacco, P. (1998). *My rotten redheaded older brother*. New York: First Aladdin Paperbacks.

Popov, N. (1996). *Why?* Zurich, Switzerland: North-South Books.

Prelutsky, J. (1983). *Nightmares: Poems to trouble your sleep*. New York: Mulberry Books.

Raschka, C. (1992). *Charlie Parker played be bop*. New York: Orchard Books.

Recorvits, H. (2003). *My name is Yoon*. New York: Francis Foster Books.

Ringgold, F. (2003). *If a bus could talk*. New York: Aladdin Paperbacks.

Roberts, J. (2009). *Back to school and autumn poems*. Retrieved August 19, 2009, from *www.primarysuccess.ca/main_ca.htm*.

Rochelle, B. (1996). *When Joe Louis won the title*. New York: Sandpiper.

Rogers, K., & Alexander, J. (2000). *Paper crunch*. Barrington, IL: Rigby Literacy.

Romanova, N. (1983). *Once there was a tree*. New York: Dial Books.

Rosenberg, L. (1999). *The silence in the mountains*. New York: Orchard Books.

Rowe, L. (2001). *The hickory chair*. New York: Scholastic Press.

Ruchac, J. (1993). *The first strawberries: A Cherokee story*. New York: Dial Books for Young Readers.

Ryan, P. (2003). *When Marian sang*. New York: Scholastic Press.

Rylant, C. (1982). *When I was young in the mountains*. New York: Dutton.

Rylant, C. (1993). *When I was young in the mountains*. New York: Penguin Putnam.

Say, A. (1993). *Grandfather's journey*. Boston: Houghton Mifflin.

Scieszka, J. (1996). *The true story of the three little pigs*. New York: Puffin Books.

Scraper, K. (2005). *Maya Lin linking people and places*. Parsippany, NJ: Celebration Press, Pearson Learning Group.

Seeger, L. (2007). *First the egg*. New York: Roaring Brook Press.

Seeger, P. (1986). *Abiyoyo*. New York: Aladdin Paperbacks.

Seuss, D. (1971). *The lorax*. New York: Random House Children's Books.

Silverstein, S. (2004). *The giving tree*. New York: HarperCollins.

Simon, N. (1976). *All kinds of families*. Morton Grove, IL: Albert Whitman.

Sisulu, E. (1996). *The day Gogo went to vote*. New York: Little, Brown.

Skutch, R. (1995). *Who's in a family?* Berkeley, CA: Tricycle Press.

Soto, G., & Martinez, E. (1993). *Too many tamales*. New York: Putnam.

Spier, P. (1980). *People*. New York: Doubleday.

Sreenivasan, J. (2002). *Making the world a better place: The stories of social reformers*. Barrington, IL: Rigby.

Steig, W. (1986). *Brave Irene*. New York: Farrar, Straus, & Giroux.

Stein, R. (1986). *The story of the Montgomery bus boycott*. Chicago: Children's Press.

Steptoe, J. (1987). *Mufaro's beautiful daughters: An African tale*. New York: Scholastic Inc.

Stock, C. (2001). *Gugu's house*. New York: Houghton Mifflin.

Surat, M. M. (1983). *Angel child, dragon child*. New York: Scholastic Press.

Terban, M. (1982). *Eight ate: A feast of homonym riddles*. New York: Clarion Books.

Terban, M. (1983). *In a pickle: And other funny idioms*. New York: Clarion Books.

The Old Man's Daughter. Available online at *www.dragonrest.net/romanian/daughter.html*.

Thomas, J. (1993). *Brown honey in broomwheat tea*. New York: HarperCollins.

Tipene, T. (2001). *Taming the Taniwha*. Wellington, New Zealand: Huia Publishers.

Trivizas, E., & Oxenbury, H. (1993). *The three little wolves and the big bad pig*. New York: Aladdin Paperbacks.

Uchida, Y. (1993). *The bracelet*. New York: Philomel.

Udry, J. M. (1956). *A tree is nice*. New York: Harper & Rowe.

Venezia, M. (1993). *Getting to know the world's greatest artists: Monet*. Chicago: Children's Press.

Walker, P. (2001). *Ellen Ochoa*. New York: Children's Press.

Ward, H. (2001). *The tin forest*. New York: Dutton Juvenile.

Webster-Doyle, T. (1999). *Why is everyone always picking on me?: Guide to handling bullies*. New York: Wetherhill.

Weiss, G., & Thiele, B. (1994). *What a wonderful world*. New York: Atheneum Books.

White, E. B. (1952). *Charlotte's web*. New York: HarperCollins.

Wiles, D. (2001) *Freedom summer*. New York: Aladdin Paperbacks.

Williams, K. L. (1990). *Galimoto*. New York: Mulberry Books.

Winter, J. (1988). *Follow the drinking gourd*. New York: Trumpet Club.

Wood, J. (1991). *Jungles: Facts, stories, activities*. New York: Scholastic.

Woodson, J. (2001). *The other side*. New York: Penguin Putnam Books for Young Readers.

Woodson, J. (2004). *Coming on home soon*. New York: Putnam.

Yarbrough, C. (1996). *Cornrows*. New York: Putnam & Grossett Group.

Youme. (2004). *Sélavi: A Haitian story of hope*. Hong Kong: Morris Printing.

Young, E. (1996). *Lon Po Po: A red riding hood story from China*. New York: Putnam Juvenile Books.

MORE BOOKS ORGANIZED BY THEME

Fairytale Alternatives

These can be used to explore differences in cultures and how stories vary based upon cultural differences and similarities. There are also alternatives based on a character's point of view, which allow students to think about different perspectives.

Louis, A.-L. (1996). *Yeh Shen*. New York: Putnam. (Chinese version)

Martin, R. & Shannon, D. (1992). *The rough-face girl*. New York: Scholastic. (Native American version)

Scieszka, J. (1996). *The true story of the three little pigs*. New York: Puffin Books.

Steptoe, J. (1987). *Mufaro's beautiful daughters: An African tale*. New York: Scholastic. (African version)

The Old Man's Daughter (Romanian version). Available at *www.dragonrest.net/romanian/daughter.html*.

Trivizas, E., & Oxenbury, H. (1993). *The three little wolves and the big bad pig*. New York: Aladdin Paperbacks.

Young, E. (1996). *Lon Po Po: A red riding hood story from China*. New York: Putnam Juvenile Books. (Chinese version)

Rainforest Unit

Bogart, J. E., & Daigneault, S. (1991). *Sarah saw a blue macaw*. New York: Scholastic Press.

Cherry, L. (1990). *The great kapok tree: A tale of the rain forest*. Orlando, FL: Harcourt Books.

Cole, J. (1998). *The magic school bus in the rain forest*. New York: Scholastic Press.

Hawes, J. (1996). *Why frogs are wet*. New York: HarperCollins.

Hosking, C. (2000). *Encyclopedia of a rain forest*. Barrington, IL: Rigby Literacy.

Mitchell, S. K. (2007). *The rainforest grew all around*. Mt. Pleasant, SC: Sylvan Dell.

Wood, J. (1991). *Jungles: Facts, stories, activities*. New York: Scholastic.

Environmental Education

Brown, P. (2009). *The curious garden*. New York: Little, Brown.

Bruchac, J. (2000). *Pushing up the sky: Seven Native American plays for children*. New York: Penguin Group.

Cherry, L. (1992). *A river ran wild*. New York: Harcourt, Brace.

Dorros, A. (1991). *Animal tracks*. New York: Scholastic Press.

Fife, D. H. (1996). *The empty lot*. San Francisco: Sagebrush Education Resources.

Glaser, L. *Compost! Growing gardens from your garbage*. Minneapolis: Millbrook Press.

Goble, P. (2005). *All our relatives: Traditional Native American thoughts about nature*. Bloomington, IN: World Wisdom Books.

Romanova, N. (1996). *Once there was a tree*. New York: Henry Holt.

Seuss, D. (1971). *The lorax*. New York: Random House Children's Books.

Silverstein, S. (2004). *The giving tree*. New York: HarperCollins.

Stock, C. (2001). *Gugu's house*. New York: Houghton Mifflin.

Udry, J. M. (1956). *A tree is nice*. New York: Harper & Rowe.

Ward, H. (2001). *The tin forest*. New York: Dutton Juvenile.

Civil Rights and Freedom

Bradby, M. (1995). *More than anything else*. New York: Orchard.

Coleman, E. (1996). *White socks only*. Morton Grove, IL: Albert Whitman.

Edwards, P. (1997). *Barefoot escape on the underground railroad*. New York: HarperCollins.

Hopkinson, D. (1993). *Sweet Clara and the freedom quilt*. New York: Knopf.

Howard, E. F. (1991). *Aunt Flossie's hats and crab cakes later*. New York: Clarion.

King, M. L., Jr. (1963). *I have a dream*. New York: Scholastic Press.

Levine, E. (2007). *Henry's freedom box*. New York: Scholastic Press.

Lorbiecki, M. (1998). *Sister Anne's hands*. New York: Puffin Books.

Nelson, V. (1987). *Almost to freedom*. New York: Scholastic Press.

Ringgold, F. (2003). *If a bus could talk*. New York: Aladdin Paperbacks.

Uchida, Y. (1993). *The bracelet*. New York: Philomel.

Winter, J. (1988). *Follow the drinking gourd*. New York: Trumpet Club.

Woodson, J. (2001). *The other side*. New York: Penguin Putnam Books for Young Readers.

Families Are Different

Brown, A. (1998). *Voices in the park*. New York: DK Publishing.

Bunting, E. (1994). *Flower garden*. New York: Harcourt Books.

Collier, B. (2000). *Uptown*. New York: Henry Holt.

Hoffman, M. (1995). *Boundless grace*. New York: Dial.

Johnson, A. (2007). *Lily Brown's paintings*. New York: Orchard Books.

Kuklin, S. (1992). *How my family lives in America*. New York: Simon & Schuster.

Newman, L., & Thompson, C. (2009). *Daddy, papa, and me*. Berkley, CA: Tricycle Press.

Parnell, P., & Richardson, J. (2005). *And tango makes three*. New York: Simon & Schuster.

Pellegrini, N. (1991). *Families are different*. New York: Holiday House.

Say, A. (1993). *Grandfather's journey*. Boston: Houghton Mifflin.

Skutch, R. (1995). *Who's in a family?* Berkeley, CA: Tricycle Press.

Soto, G., & Martinez, E. (1993). *Too many tamales*. New York: Putnam.

Surat, M.M. (1983). *Angel child, dragon child*. New York: Scholastic Press.

Woodson, J. (2004). *Coming on home soon*. New York: Putnam.

Issues of Identity and Acceptance (Self-Esteem, Gender, Race, Physical Differences, etc.)

Allen, D. (2000). *Dancing in the wings*. New York: Red Bird Productions.

Cole, H., & Vogl, N. (2005). *Am I a color too?* Bellevue, WA: Illumination Arts.

Hoffman, M. (1991). *Amazing grace*. New York: Dial.

Howard, E. (2000). *Virgie goes to school with us boys*. New York: Simon & Schuster Books for Young Readers.

Lester, H. (1999). *Hooway for Wodney Wat*. New York: Houghton Mifflin.

Littlesugar, A. (1997). *Jonkonnu: A story from the sketchbook of Winslow Homer*. New York: Philomel Books.

Perez, A.I. (2002). *My diary from here to there*. San Francisco: Children's Book Press.

Recorvits, H. (2003). *My name is Yoon*. New York: Francis Foster Books.

Rochelle, B. (1996). *When Joe Louis won the title*. New York: Sandpiper.

Rylant, C. (1982). *When I was young in the mountains*. New York: Dutton.

Woodson, J. (2004). *Coming on home soon*. New York: Putnam.

Conflict Resolution and Bullying

Carle, E. (2002). *Slowly, slowly, slowly said the sloth*. New York: Scholastic Press.

Grimes, N. (1984). *Meet Danitra Brown*. New York: Scholastic Press.

Hall, B. E. (2004). *Henry and the kite dragon*. New York: Philomel Books.

Lovell, P. (2001). *Stand tall Molly Lou Melon*. New York: Putnam.

Popov, N. (1996). *Why?* Zurich, Switzerland: North-South Books.

Electronic Resources

www.teachingtolerance.org (book lists, curricular resources, etc.)

www.childrenslibrary.org (International Children's Digital Library)

www.pbskids.org (games, printouts, shows, etc., from PBS)

www.brainpop.com (videos on various content-area topics)

www.brainpopjr.com (videos and interactive games on beginning skills)

kids.nationalgeographic.com (videos, games, stories, activities)

www.readwritethink.org (lesson plans, online games, student materials from the International Reading Association)

www.mightybook.com (stories, songs, and other educational resources for students, teachers, and parents)

www.ncsu.edu/project/IT_programs/webquests/spires/webquest8/Webquest%20project.html (Web-Quest about *The True Story of the Three Little Pigs* by Jon Sieszka)

interactives.mped.org/view_interactive.aspx?id=775&title= (WebQuest about Patricia Polacco and her books)

www.colorincolorado.org (a bilingual site for parents and educators of ELLs)

References

Adams, M. J. (1990). *Beginning to read: Thinking and learning about print*. Cambridge, MA: Harvard University Press.

Adger, C. T., & Locke, J. (2000). Broadening the base: School/community partnerships serving language minority students at risk. Available at *escholarship.org/uc/item/8s47008n#*.

Adger, C. T., Wolfram, W., & Christian, D. (2007). *Dialects in schools and communities* (2nd ed.) Mahwah, NJ: Erlbaum.

Adger, C. T., Wolfram, W., & Christian, D. (2009). *Dialects in schools and communities*. New York: Erlbaum.

Allington, R. L. (1977). If they don't read much, how they are ever gonna get good? *Journal of Reading, 21*, 57–61.

Allington, E. L. (1984). Content coverage and contextual reading in reading groups. *Journal of Reading Behavior, 16*, 85–96.

Allington, R. L. (1983). The reading instruction provided readers of differing reading abilities. *Elementary School Journal, 83*, 548–559.

Allington, R. L. (2002). *Big brother and the national reading curriculum: How ideology trumped evidence*. Portsmouth, NH: Heinemann.

Allington, R. L. (2006). *What really matters for struggling readers: Designing research-based programs*. Boston: Pearson.

Allington, R. L. (2009). *What really matters in fluency: Research-based practices across the curriculum*. Boston: Allyn & Bacon.

Allington, R. L., & McGill-Franzen, A. (2003). The impact of summer reading setback on the reading achievement gap. *Phi Delta Kappan, 85*, 68–75.

Allington, R. L., & McGill-Franzen, A. (Eds.). (2010). *Handbook of research on reading disabilities*. New York: Routledge.

Almasi, J. F., O'Flahavan, J. F., & Arya, P. (2001). A comparative analysis of student and teacher development in more and less proficient discussions of literature. *Reading Research Quarterly, 36*, 96–120.

Amendum, S. J., & Fitzgerald, J. (2010). Research on reading instruction for English language learners in kindergarten through sixth grade: The last twenty years. In R. Allington & A. McGill-Franzen (Eds.), *Handbook of research on reading disabilities*. New York: Routledge.

Amendum, S. J., Vernon-Feagans, L., & Ginsberg, M. C. (in press). The effectiveness of a technologically-facilitated classroom-based early reading intervention: The Targeted Reading Intervention. *The Elementary School Journal*.

Anders, P., Bos, C., & Filip, D. (1984). The effect of semantic feature analysis on the reading comprehension of learning disabled students. In J. A. Niles & L. A. Harris (Eds.), *Changing perspectives on research in teaching: Research reviews* (pp. 77–117). Rochester, NY: National Reading Conference.

Anderson, R. C., & Balajthy, E. (2009). Stories about struggling readers and technology. *The Reading Teacher, 62*(6), 540–542.

Anderson, R. C., Heibert, E. H., Scott, J. A., & Wilkinson, I. (1985). *Becoming a nation of readers.* Washington, DC: National Institute of Education.

Anderson, R. C., & Jetton, T. (2000). Learning from text: A multidimensional and developmental perspective. In M. L. Kamil, P. B. Mosenthal, P. D. Pearson, & R. Barr (Eds.), *Handbook of reading research* (Vol. II, pp. 285–310). Mahwah, NJ: Erlbaum.

Anderson, R. C., & Nagy, W. E. (1991). Word meanings. In R. Barr, M. L. Kamil, P. Mosenthal, & P. D. Pearson (Eds.), *Handbook of reading research* (Vol. II, pp. 690–724). Mahwah, NJ: Erlbaum.

Anderson, R. C., & Pearson, P. D. (1984). A schema-theoretic view of basic processes in reading. In R. C. Anderson, E. H. Heibert, J. A. Scott, & I. Wilkinson (Eds.), *Becoming a nation of readers.* Washington DC: National Institute of Education.

Anyon, J. (1997). *Ghetto schooling: A political economy of urban education reform.* New York: Teachers College Press.

Aram, D., & Levin, I. (2001). Mother–child joint writing in low SES: Sociocultural factors, maternal mediation, and emergent literacy. *Cognitive Development, 16*, 831–852.

Arzubiaga, A., Rueda, R., & Monzo, L. (2002). Family matters related to the reading engagement of Latino children. *Journal of Latinos and Education, 1*(4), 231–243.

Atwell, N. (2002). *Lessons that change writers.* Portsmouth, NH: Heinemann.

August, D., & Shanahan, T. (2006a). (Eds.). *Developing literacy in second-language learners: Report of the National Literacy Panel on language minority children and youth.* Mahwah, NJ: Erlbaum.

August, D., & Shanahan, T. (2006b). Introduction and methodology. In D. August & T. Shanahan (Eds.), *Developing literacy in second-language learners: Report of the National Literacy Panel on Language Minority Children and Youth* (pp. 1–42). Mahwah, NJ: Erlbaum.

Bailey, G., & Tillery, J. (2006a). Sounds of the South. In W. Wolfram & B. Ward (Eds.), *American voices: How dialects differ from coast to coast* (pp. 11–16). Oxford, UK: Blackwell.

Bailey, G., & Tillery, J. (2006b). The lone star stage of speech (Texas). In W. Wolfram & B. Ward (Eds.), *American voices: How dialects differ from coast to coast* (pp. 36–41). Oxford, UK: Blackwell.

Banks, J. A. (2003). Teaching literacy for social justice and global citizenship. *Language Arts, 81*(1), 18–19.

Banks, J. A. (2006). *Race, culture, and education.* London: Routledge.

Barr, R. (1984). Beginning reading instruction: From debate to reformation. In P. D. Pearson, R. Barr, M. L. Kamil, & P. Mosenthal (Eds.), *Handbook of reading research* (pp. 545–582). White Plains, NY: Longman.

Barr, R., Kamil, M. L., Mosenthal, P., & Pearson, P. D. (Eds.). (1991). *Handbook of reading research* (Vol. II). Mahwah, NJ: Erlbaum.

Baugh, J. (2006). Bridging the great divide (African American English). In W. Wolfram & B. Ward (Eds.), *American voices: How dialects differ from coast to coast* (pp. 217–224). Oxford, UK: Blackwell.

Bear, D. R., Invernizzi, M., Templeton, S., & Johnston, F. (2004). *Words Their Way: Word study for phonics, vocabulary, and spelling instruction.* Upper Saddle River, NJ: Pearson.

Beaver, J. M. (2006). *Teacher guide: Developmental Reading Assessment, Grades K–3, Second Edition.* Parsippany, NJ: Pearson.

Beck, I. L. (2006). *Making sense of phonics: The hows and whys.* New York: Guilford Press.

Beck, I. L., & McKeown, M. (1991). Conditions of vocabulary acquisition. In R. Barr, M. L. Kamil, P. Mosenthal, & P. D. Pearson (Eds.), *Handbook of reading research* (Vol. II, pp. 789–814). Mahwah, NJ: Erlbaum.

Beck, I. L., McKeown, M., Hamilton, & Kucan, L. (1997). *Questioning the author: An approach to enhancing student engagement with text.* Newark, DE: International Reading Association.

Beck, I. L., McKeown, M. G., & Kucan, L. (2002). *Bringing words to life: Robust vocabulary instruction.* New York: Guilford Press.

Begley, S. (2007). *Train your mind, change your brain: How a new science reveals our extraordinary potential to transform ourselves.* New York: Ballantine Books.

Between the lines: Leveled reader grade 5. (2001). Boston: Houghton Mifflin.

Biemiller, A. (1970). The development of the use of graphic and contextual information as children learn to read. *Reading Research Quarterly, 6,* 75–96.

Billings, L., & Fitzgerald, J. (2002). Dialogic discussion and the Paideia seminar. *American Educational Research Journal, 39,* 907–941.

Bissex, G. L. (1980). *GYNS AT WRK: A child learns to write and read.* Cambridge, MA: Harvard Educational Books.

Blachman, B. (2000). Phonological awareness. In M. L. Kamil, P. B. Mosenthal, P. D. Pearson, & R. Barr (Eds.), *Handbook of reading research* (Vol. III, pp. 483–502). Mahwah, NJ: Erlbaum.

Blachowicz, C. L. Z., & Fisher, P. (1996). *Teaching vocabulary in all classrooms.* Columbus, OH: Merrill.

Blachowicz, C. L. Z., & Fisher, P. (2000). Vocabulary instruction. In M. L. Kamil, P. B. Mosenthal, P. D. Pearson, & R. Barr (Eds.), *Handbook of reading research* (Vol. III, pp. 503–523). Mahwah, NJ: Erlbaum.

Block, C. C., & Pressley, M. (2001). *Comprehension instruction: Research-based best practices.* New York: Guilford Press.

Bloome, D. D., & Green, J. (1984). Directions in the sociolinguistic study of reading. In P. D. Pearson, R. Barr, M. L. Kamil, & P. Mosenthal (Eds.), *Handbook of reading research* (pp. 395–421). White Plains, NY: Longman.

Bloome, D. D., Katz, L., Solsken, J., Willett, J., & Wilson-Keenean, J. (2000). Interpellations of family/community and classroom literacy practices. *Journal of Educational Research, 93,* 155–164.

Brandt, D. (2001). *Literacy in American lives.* New York: Cambridge University Press.

Brown, J. S., & Collins, A., & Duguid, P. (1989). Situated cognition and the culture of learning. *Educational Research, 18,* 32–42.

Brown, K. (1999). What kind of text—For whom and when?: Textual scaffolding for beginning readers. *The Reading Teacher, 53,* 292–307.

Burke, A., & Hammett, R. A. (2009). *Assessing new literacies: Perspectives from the classroom.* New York: Peter Lang.

Calderon, M. E., & Minaya-Rowe, L. (2003). *Designing and implementing two-way bilingual programs: A step-by-step guide for administration, teachers, and parents.* Thousand Oaks, CA: Corwin Press.

Cambourne, B. (1988). *The whole story: Natural learning and the acquisition of literacy in the classroom.* Jefferson City, MO: Scholastic.

Cambourne, B. (2000). Conditions for literacy learning. *The Reading Teacher, 53,* 512–515.

Christoph, J. N., & Nystrand, M. (2001). Taking risks, negotiating relationships: One teacher's transition toward a dialogic classroom. *Research in the Teaching of English, 36,* 249–286.

Carnine, D. W., Silbeert, J., Kame'enui, E. J., & Tarrer, S. G. (2004). *Direct instruction reading* (4th ed.). Upper Saddle River, NJ: Merrill/Prentice Hall.

Cazden, C. (1988). *Classroom discourse: The language of teaching and learning.* Portsmouth, NH: Hienemann.

Chall, J. S. (1967). *Learning to read: The great debate.* New York: McGraw-Hill.

Chall, J. S. (1983). *Stages of reading development.* New York: McGraw-Hill.

Chomsky, C. (1971). Write first, read later. *Childhood Education, 47,* 296–299.

Christoph, J. N., & Nystrand, M. (2001). Taking risks, negotiating relationships: One teacher's transition toward a dialogic classroom. *Research in the Teaching of English, 36,* 249–286.

Clay, M. M. (1968). A syntactic analysis of reading errors. *Journal of Verbal Learning and Verbal Behavior, 7,* 434–438.

Clay, M. M. (1975). *What did I write? Beginning writing behavior.* Auckland, NZ: Heinemann.

Clay, M. M. (1985). *The early detection of complex reading behavior.* Portsmouth, NH: Heinemann.

Clay, M. M. (1991). *Becoming literate: The construction of inner control.* Portsmouth, NH: Heinemann.

Clay, M. M. (1995). *Observation survey.* Portsmouth, NH: Heinemann.

Cline, R. K. J., & Kretke, G. L. (1980). An evaluation of long-term SSR in the junior high school. *Journal of Reading, 23,* 503–506.

Coiro, J. (2003). Reading comprehension on the Internet: Expanding our understanding of reading comprehension to encompass new literacies. *The Reading Teacher, 56*(5), 458–464.

Coiro, J., & Dobler, E. (2007). Exploring the online reading comprehension strategies used by sixth-grade skilled readers to search for and locate information on the Internet. *Reading Research Quarterly 42,* 214–257.

Coiro, J., Knobel, M., Lankshear, C., & Leu, D. L. (2008). Central issues in new literacies and new literacies research. In J. Coiro, M. Knobel, C. Lankshear, & D. L Leu (Eds.), *Handbook of research on new literacies* (pp. 1–24). New York: Erlbaum.

Conn, J. (2006). Dialects in the mist. In W. Wolfram & B. Ward (Eds.), *American voices: How dialects differ from coast to coast* (pp. 149–155). Malden, MA: Blackwell.

Cowen, J. E. (2003). *Toward a definition of a balanced approach to reading: Six major U.S. research studies.* Newark, DE: International Reading Association.

Cronbach, L. J. (1943). Measuring knowledge of precise word meaning. *Journal of Educational Research, 36,* 528–534.

Cunningham, J. W. (1982). Generating interactions between schemata and text. In J. Niles & L. Harris (Eds.), *Thirty-first yearbook of the National Reading Conference* (pp. 42–47). Washington, DC: National Reading Conference.

Cunningham, P. M. (2000). *Phonics they use: Words for reading and writing.* New York: Longman.

Cunningham, P. M., & Alligton, R. C. (1995). *Classrooms that work: They can all read and write.* New York: Longman.

Cunningham, P. M., & Cunningham, J. W. (1992). Making words: Enhancing the invented spelling–decoding connection. *The Reading Teacher, 46,* 106–107.

Cunningham, P. M., & Cunningham, J. W. (2002). What we know about how to teach phonics. In A. E. Farstrup & S. J. Samuels (Eds.), *What research has to say about reading instruction* (pp. 87–109). Newark, DE: International Reading Association.

Cunningham, P. M., & Hall, D. P. (2008). *Making words second grade: 100 hands on lessons for phonemic awareness, phonics, and spelling.* New York: Allyn & Bacon.

Daniels, H. (2002). *Literature circles.* Portland, ME: Stenhouse.

Dalton, B. (2007). *Five standards for effective teaching: How to succeed with all learners.* San Fransisco: Jossey-Bass.

Dalton, B., & Proctor, P. (2008). The changing landscape of text comprehension in the age of new literacies. In J. Coiro, M. Knobel, C. Lankshear, & D. L Leu (Eds.), *Handbook of research on new literacies* (pp. 297–324). Mahwah, NJ: Erlbaum.

Dantas, M. L., & Manyak, P. C. (2010). *Home–school connection in a multicultural society: Learning from and with culturally and linguistically diverse families.* New York: Routledge.

Davis, J., & Hill, S. (2003). *The no-nonsense guide to teaching writing: Strategies, structures, solutions.* Portsmouth, NH: Heinemann.

Delpit, L. D. (1986). Skills and other dilemmas of a progressive black educator. *Harvard Educational review, 56,* 379–385.

Delpit, L. D. (1988). The silenced dialogue: Power and pedagogy in educating other people's children. *Harvard Educational Review, 58,* 280–298.

Delpit, L. D. (1995). *Other people's children: Cultural conflict in the classroom.* New York: New Press.

Developmental Studies Center. (1996). *Ways we want our class to be: Class meetings that build commitment to kindness and learning.* Oakland, CA: Developmental Studies Center. Available online at *www.devstu.org/page/welcome-to-dsc-public-web-site.*

Dowhower, S. (1987). Effects of repeated reading on second grade transitional reader's fluency and comprehension. *Reading Research Quarterly, 22,* 389–406.

Duffy, G. G., & Roehler, L. R., Sivan, E., Rackliffe, G., Book, C., Meloth, M., et al. (1987). Effects of explaining the reasoning associated with using reading strategies. *Reading Research Quarterly, 22,* 347–368.

Duke, N. K., & & Pearson, P. D. (2002). Effective practices for developing reading comprehension. In A. E. Farstrup & S. J. Samuels (Eds.), *What research has to say about reading instruction* (pp. 205–242). Newark, DE: International Reading Association.

Durkin, D. (1978–1979). What classroom observations reveal about reading comprehension instruction. *Reading Research Quarterly, 15*, 481–533.

Dyson, A. H. (1993). *Social worlds of children learning to write in an urban primary school.* New York: Teachers College.

Dyson, A. H. (1984). Learning to write/learning to do school: Emergent writers' interpretations of school literacy tasks. *Research in the Teaching of English, 18*, 233–264.

Dyson, A. H. (1986). Transitions and tensions: Interrelationships between the drawing, talking, and dictation of young children. *Research in the Teaching of English, 20*, 370–409.

Echevarria, J., Vogt, M. E., & Short, D. (2004). *Making content comprehensible for English language learners: The SIOP model* (2nd ed.). Boston: Pearson.

Edwards, P. A., & Turner, J. D. (2010). Do you hear what I hear? Using the parent story approach to listen and learn from African American parents. In M. L. Dantas & P. C. Manyak (Eds.), *Home–school connection in a multicultural society: Learning from and with culturally and linguistically diverse families* (pp. 137–155). New York: Routledge.

Ehri, L. C, (1991). Development of the ability to read words. In R. Barr, M. Kamil, P. Mosenthal, & P. D. Pearson (Eds.), *Handbook of reading research* (Vol. II, pp. 353–417). Mahwah, NJ: Earlbaum.

Ehri, L. C., Nunes, S. R., & Willows, D. M. (2001). Phonemic awareness instruction helps children learn how to read: Evidence from the National Reading Panel's meta-analysis. *Reading Research Quarterly, 36*, 250–287.

Ehri, L. C., & Wilce, L. C. (1985). Movement into reading: Is the first stage of printed word learning visual or phonetic? *Reading Research Quarterly, 20*, 163–179.

Elkonin, D. B. (1973). U.S.S.R. In J. Downing (Ed.), *Comparative reading* (pp. 551–579). New York: MacMillan.

Emig, J. (1971). *The composing processes of twelfth graders.* Urbana, IL: National Council of Teachers of English.

Farstrup, A. E., & Samuels, S. J. (2002). *What research has to say about reading instruction.* Newark, DE: International Reading Association.

Ferguson, R. F. (1998). Teachers' perceptions and expectations and the black–white test score gap. In C. Jencks & M. Phillips (Eds.), *The black–white test score gap* (pp. 273–317). Washington, DC: Brookings Institution Press.

Ferreiro, E., & Teberosky, A. (1982). *Literacy before schooling.* Portsmouth, NH: Heinemann.

Ferreiro, E., & Teberosky, A. (1983). *Literacy before schooling.* Portsmouth, NH: Heinemann.

Finn, P. J. (1999). *Literacy with an attitude: Educating working class children in their own self-interest.* Albany, NY: SUNY Press.

Fisher, R. (2009). *Creative dialogue: Talk for thinking in the classroom.* New York: Routledge.

Fitzgerald, J. (1999). What is this thing called "balance"? *Reading Teacher, 53*, 100–107.

Fitzgerald, J., Noblit, G. (2000). Balance in the making: Learning to read in an ethnically diverse first grade classroom. *Journal of Educational Psychology, 92*, 3–22.

Fitzgerald, J., & Spiegel, D. L. (1983). Enhancing children's reading comprehension through instruction in narrative structure. *Journal of Reading Behavior, 15*, 1–17.

Flanigan, B. O. (2006). Different ways of talking in the Buckeye State (Ohio). In W. Wolfram & B. Ward (Eds.), *American voices: How dialects differ from coast to coast* (pp. 118–123). Oxford, UK: Blackwell.

Flesch, R. (1956). *Why Johnny can't read.* New York: Popular Library.

Fletcher, R. (1996). *A writer's notebook.* New York: HarperCollins.

Fletcher, R., & Portalupi, J. (2007). *Craft lessons* (2nd ed.). Portland, ME: Stenhouse.

Florio, S., & Clark, C. M. (1982). The functions of writing in an elementary classroom. *Research in the Teaching of English, 16*, 115–130.

Flower, L., & Hayes, J. R. (1980). The pregnant pause: An inquiry into the nature of planning. *Research in the Teaching of English, 15*, 229–244.

Foster, M., & Peele, T. (2001). Ring my bell: Contextualizing home and school in an African American community. In E. McIntyre, A. Rosebery, & N. González (Eds.), *Classroom diversity: Connecting curriculum to students' lives* (pp. 27–36). Portsmouth, NH: Heinemann.

Fuchs, D., Fuchs, L. S., Mathes, P. G., & Martinez, E. (2002). Preliminary evidence on the social standing of students with learning disabilities in PALS and No-PALS classrooms. *Learning Disabilities Research and Practice, 17,* 205–215.

Fuchs, D., Fuchs, L., Thompson, A., Al Otaiba, S., Yen, L., Yang, N., et al. (2001). Is reading important in reading-readiness programs?: A randomized field trial with teachers as program implementers. *Journal of Educational Psychology, 93,* 251–267.

Gay, G. (2000). *Culturally responsive instruction: Theory, research, and practice.* New York: Teachers College Press.

Gay, G. (2002). Preparing for culturally responsive teaching. *Journal of Teacher Education, 53,* 106–116.

Gersten, R., & Jiménez, R. T. (1994). A delicate balance: Enhancing literature instruction for students of English as a second language. *The Reading Teacher, 47,* 438–449.

Goldenberg, C. (1993). Instructional conversations: Promoting comprehension through discussion. *The Reading Teacher, 46,* 316–326.

Goldenberg, C. (1994). Promoting early literacy development among Spanish speaking children: Lessons from two studies. In E. Heibert & B. M. Taylor (Eds.), *Getting reading right from the start* (pp. 171–200). Boston: Allyn & Bacon.

Goldenberg, C., Rueda, R., & August, D. (2006). Synthesis: Sociocultural contexts and literacy development. In D. August & T. Shanahan (Eds.), *Developing literacy in second language learners* (pp. 249–268). Mahwah, NJ: Erlbaum.

Goodman, K. S. (1967). Reading: A psycholinguistic guessing game. *Journal of the Reading Specialist, 6,* 126–135.

Goodman, K. S., Watson, D., & Burke, C. (1987). *Reading miscue analysis.* New York: R. C. Owen.

Gorman, J. C., & Balter, L. (1997). Culturally sensitive parent education: A critical review of quantitative research. *Review of Educational Research, 67,* 339–369.

Grant, C. A., & Sleeter, C. E. (2001). *Doing multicultural education for achievement and equity.* New York: Routledge.

Graves, D. H. (1983). *Writing: Teachers and children at work.* Exeter, NH: Heinemann.

Graves, D. H. (1985). The enemy is orthodoxy. *Highway One, 8,* 153–163.

Graves, M. F., & Watts-Taffe, S. M. (2002). The place of word consciousness in a research-based vocabulary program. In A. E. Farstrup & S. J. Samuels (Eds.), *What research has to say about reading instruction* (pp. 140–165). Newark, DE: International Reading Association.

Grissmer, D., Flanagan, A., & Williamson, S. (1998). Why did the black–white score gap narrow in the 1970s and 1980s? In C. Jencks & M. Phillips (Eds.), *The black–white test score gap* (pp. 182–228). Washington, DC: Brookings Institute.

Gunn, B., Biglan, A., Smolkowsi, K., & Avy, D. (2000). The efficacy of supplemental instruction in decoding skills for Hispanic and non-Hispanic students in early elementary school. *Journal of Special Education, 34,* 90–103.

Gunn, B., Smolkowski, K., & Biglan, A. (2002). Supplemental instruction in decoding skills for Hispanic and non-Hispanic students in early elementary school. *Journal of Special Education, 36,* 69–79.

Gutiérrez, K. D., Baquedano-Lopez, P., & Alvarez, H. H. (2001). Literacy as hybridity: Moving beyond bilingualism in urban classrooms. In M. D. L. L. Reyes & J. J. Halcon (Eds.), *The best for our children: Critical perspectives on literacy for Latino students* (pp. 122–141). New York: Teachers College Press.

Hale, J. E. (2003). *Learning while black: Creating educational excellence for African American children.* Baltimore, MD: Johns Hopkins University Press.

Hansen, J. (1981). The effects of inference training and practice on young children's reading comprehension. *Reading Research Quarterly, 16,* 391–417.

Harste, J., Woodward, M., & Burke, C. (1984). *Language stories and literacy lessons.* Portsmouth, NH: Heinemann.

Hart, B., & Risley, T. R. (1995). *Meaningful differences in the everyday experiences of young children*. New York: Paul H. Brooks.

Harvey, S., & Goudvis, A. (2007). *Strategies that work: Teaching comprehension for understanding and engagement* (2nd. ed.). Portland, ME: Stenhouse.

Hazen, K., & Fluharty, E. (2006). Defining Appalachian English. In W. Wolfram & B. Ward (Eds.), *American voices: How dialects differ from coast to coast* (pp. 17–21). Oxford, UK: Blackwell.

Heath, S. B. (1983). *Ways with words: Language, life, and work in communities and classrooms*. New York: Cambridge University Press.

Heath, S. B. (1991). The sense of being literate: Historical and cross-cultural features. In R. Barr, M. L. Kamil, P. Mosenthal, & P. D. Pearson (Eds.), *Handbook of reading research* (Vol. II, pp. 3–25). Mahwah, NJ: Erlbaum.

Heath, S. B. (1994). The children of Trackton's children: Spoken and written language in social change. In R. B. Rudell, M. R. Rudell, & H. Singer (Eds.), *Theoretical models and processes of reading* (pp. 208–230). Newark, DE: International Reading Association.

Heibert, E. (1999). Text matters in learning to read. *The Reading Teacher, 52*, 552–566.

Heibert, E., & Taylor, B. (1994). *Getting reading right from the start: Studies of early reading interventions*. Mahwah, NJ: Erlbaum.

Heibert, E., & Taylor, B. (2000). Beginning reading instruction: Research on early interventions. In M. L. Kamil, P. B. Mosenthal, P. D. Pearson, & R. Barr (Eds.), *Handbook of reading research* (Vol. III, pp. 455–482). Mahwah, NJ: Erlbaum.

Henderson, E. (1990). *Teaching spelling*. Boston: Houghton Mifflin.

Herber, H. L. (1978). *Teaching reading in content areas* (2nd ed.). Englewood Cliffs, NJ: Prentice Hall.

Herrnstein, R. J., & Murray, C. (1994). *The bell curve: Intelligence and class structure in American life*. New York: Free Press.

Hillocks, G. (1986). *Research on written composition: New directions for teaching*. Urbana, IL: National Council of Teachers of English.

Hillocks, G. (2002). *The testing rap: How state writing assessments control learning*. New York: Teachers College Press.

Hillocks, G. (2007). *Narrative writing: Learning a new model for teaching*. Portsmouth, NH: Heinemann.

Homan, S. P., Klesius, J. P., & Hite, C. (1993). Effects of repeated readings and nonrepetitive strategies on students' fluency and comprehension. *Journal of Educational Research, 87*, 94–99.

Hoover-Dempsey, K. V., & Sandler, H. M. (1997). Why do parents become involved in their children's education? *Review of Educational Research, 67*, 3–42.

Horowitz, R. (1985). Text patterns. *Journal of Reading, 28*, 448–454.

Huey, E. B. (1908). *The psychology and pedagogy of teaching reading*. Cambridge, MA: MIT Press.

Inspiration Software. (2009). *Kidspiration*. Beaverton, OR: Inspiration Software, Inc.

Invernizzi, M., Juel, C., Rosemary, C., & Richards, H. (1997). At-risk readers and community volunteers: A three-year perspective. *Scientific Studies of Reading, 1*, 277–300.

Irvine, J. J. (2006). *Educating teachers for diversity: Seeing with a cultural eye*. New York: Teachers College Press.

Johnston, F. R. Invernizzi, M., & Juel, C. (2009). *Book buddies (2nd ed.): A tutoring framework for struggling readers*. New York: Guilford Press.

Jordan, C. (1985). Translating culture: From ethnographic information to educational program. *Anthropology and Education Quarterly, 16*, 105–123.

Juel, C. (1988). Learning to read and write: A longitudinal study of children in first and second grade. *Journal of Educational Psychology, 80*, 437–447.

Juel, C. (1991). Beginning reading. In R. Barr, M. Kamil, P. Mosenthal, & P. D. Pearson (Eds.), *Handbook of reading research* (Vol. II, pp. 759–788). Mahwah, NJ: Earlbaum.

Juel, C. (1997). What makes a literacy tutoring effective? *Reading Research Quarterly, 31*, 268–289.

Kagan, S. (1994). *Cooperative learning*. San Clemente, CA: Resources for Teachers.

Kamil, P., Mosenthal, P. D. & Pearson, P. D. (Eds.). (1991). *Handbook of reading research* (Vol. II, pp. 789–814). White Plains, NY: Longman.

Karchmar, R. A. (2001). The journey ahead: Thirteen teachers report how the Internet influences literacy and literacy instruction in the K–12 classrooms. *Reading Research Quarterly, 36*, 442–467.

Karchmar, R. A. (2008). The journey ahead: Thirteen teachers report how the Internet influences literacy and literacy instruction in their K–12 classrooms. In J. Coiro, M. Knobel, C. Lankshear, & D. L Leu (Eds.), *Handbook of research on new literacies* (pp. 1241–1280). Mahwah, NJ: Erlbaum.

Kerry-Moran, K. J. (2006). Nurturing emergent readers through readers theater. *Early Childhood Education Journal, 33*(5), 317–323.

Klenk, L., & Kibby, M. W. (2000). Literacy and children with learning disabilities. In M. L. Kamil, P. B. Mosenthal, P. D. Pearson, & R. Barr (Eds.), *Handbook of reading research* (Vol. III, pp. 667–690). Mahwah, NJ: Erlbaum.

Knapp, M. (1995). *Teaching for meaning in high poverty classrooms.* New York: Teachers College Press.

Kovarik, M. (2004). Selecting children's books for a multiracial audience. *Florida Libraries, 47*, 10–11.

Krietel, R., & Bechtel, L. (2002). *The morning meeting book.* Turner Falls, MA: Northeast Foundation for Children.

Kucan, L., & Beck, I. (1997). Thinking aloud and reading comprehension research: Inquiry, instruction, and social interaction. *Review of Educational Research, 67*, 271–299.

Kuhn, M., & Stahl, S. A. (1998). Teaching students to learn word meanings from context: A synthesis and some questions. *Journal of Literacy Research, 30*, 119–138.

Kuiper, E., Volman, M., Terwel, J. (2005). The Web as an information resource in K–12 education: Strategies for supporting students in searching and processing information. *Review of Educational Research, 75*, 285–328.

Kulik, J. A. (2003). *Effects of using instructional technology in elementary and secondary schools: What controlled evaluation studies say* [Final report]. Arlington, VA: SRI International.

Kyle, D. W., McIntyre, E., Miller, K. B., & Moore, G. H. (2002). *Reaching out: A K–8 resource for connecting families and schools.* Thousand Oaks, CA: Corwin Press.

Kyle, D. W., McIntyre, E., Miller, K. B., & Moore, G. H. (2005). *Bridging school and home through family nights: Ready-to-use plans for grades K–8.* Thousand Oaks, CA: Corwin Press.

Labbo, L. D. (2000). 12 things young children can do with a talking book in a classroom computer center. *The Reading Teacher, 53*(7), 542–546.

LaBerge, D., & Samuels, S. J. (1974). Toward a theory of automatic information processing in reading. *Cognitive Psychology, 6*, 293–323.

Ladson-Billings, G. (1994). *The dreamkeepers: Successful teachers of African American children.* San Francisco: Jossey-Bass.

Langer, J. A. (1986). Reading, writing, and understanding: An analysis of the construction of meaning. *Written Communication, 3*, 219–267.

Lanier, J. (2010). *You are not a gadget.* New York: Alfred A. Knopf.

Lareau, A. (2000). *Home advantage: Social class and parental intervention in education.* New York: Rowman & Littlefield.

Larson, L. (2009). Reader response meets new literacies: Empowering readers in online learning communities. *The Reading Teacher, 62*(8), 638–648.

Lee, C. D. (1998). Signifying in the zone of proximal development. In C. D. Lee & P. Smagorinsky (Eds.), *Vygotskian perspectives on literacy research: Constructing meaning through collaborative inquiry* (pp. 191–225). Cambridge, UK: Cambridge University Press.

Lee, C. D. (2008). The centrality of culture to the scientific study of learning and development: How an ecological framework in education research facilitates civic responsibility. *Educational Research, 37*, 267–279.

Lee, J. S., & Bowen, N. K. (2006). Parent involvement, cultural capital, and the achievement gap among elementary school children. *American Educational Research Journal, 43*(2), 193–215.

Lefever-Davis, S., & Pearman, C. J. (2005). Early readers and electronic texts: CD-ROM storybook features that influence reading behaviors. *The Reading Teacher, 58*(5), 446–454.

Lemke, J. L. (1990). *Talking science: Language, learning, and values.* West Park, CT: Ablex.

Lensmire, T. J. (1994). *When children write: Critical re-visions of the writing workshop.* New York: Teachers College Press.

Leseman, P. P. M. & de Jong, P. F. (1998). Home literacy: Opportunity, instruction, cooperation and social–emotional quality predicting early reading achievement. *Reading Research Quarterly, 33*(3), 294–318.

Leu, D., & Coiro, J. (2009, July). *Comprehension on the Internet.* Keynote address at the New Literacies Teacher Leader Institute. Raleigh, NC: North Carolina State University. Available at *www.fi.ncsu. edu/newliteraciesinstitute.*

Lewis, R. B., & Ashton, T. M. (1999). *Interactive books on CD-ROM and reading instruction for students with learning disabilities: What are your views?* In conference proceedings online: 1999 "Technology and Persons with Disabilities" Conference. Retrieved March 20, 2000, from *www.dinf.org/ csun_99/session0027.html.*

Li, G. (Ed.). (2009). *Multicultural families, home literacies, and mainstream schooling.* Charlotte, NC: IAR.

Li, G., & Edwards, P. A. (2010). *Best practices in ELL instruction.* New York: Guilford Press.

Linan-Thompson, S., & Vaughn, S. (2004). *Research-based methods of reading instruction for English language learners grades K–4.* Alexandria, VA: Association for Supervision and Curriculum Development.

Linan-Thompson, S., Vaughn, S. (2007). *Research-based methods of reading instruction for English language learners.* Alexandria, VA: Association for Supervision and Curriculum Development.

Long, S., & Volk, D. (2010). Networks of support: Learning from the other teachers in children's lives. In P. C. Manyak & M. L. Dantas (Eds.), *Home–school connection in a multicultural society* (pp. 177–200). New York: Routledge.

Luke, A., Cook, J., & Luke, C. (1986). The selective tradition in action: Gender bias in student teachers' selections of children's literature. *English Education, 18,* 209–216.

Luxford, H., & Smart, L. (2009). *Learning through talk: Developing learning dialogues in the primary classroom.* New York: Routledge.

Lyman. F. (1981). Think pair share: The responsive classroom discussion. In A. S. Anderson (Ed.), *Mainstreaming digest.* College Park: University of Maryland College of Education.

Mallinson, C., Childs, B., Anderson, B., & Hutcheson, N. (2006). If these hills could talk (Smoky Mountains). In W. Wolfram & B. Ward (Eds.), *American voices: How dialects differ from coast to coast* (pp. 22–28). Oxford, UK: Blackwell.

Marks, G., J. Cresswell, J., & Ainley, J. (2006). Explaining socioeconomic inequalities in student achievement: The role of home and school factors. *Educational Research and Evaluation, 12*(2), 105–128.

Marshall, J. C. (2002). *Are they really reading?: Expanding SSR in the middle grades.* Portland, ME: Stenhouse.

Marx, S. (2006). *Revealing the invisible: Confronting passive racism in teacher education.* New York: Routlege.

Mason, J. M. (1980). When do children begin to read? An explanation of four-year-old children's letter and word reading competencies. *Reading Research Quarterly, 15,* 203–227.

Mason, J. M. (1984). Early reading from a developmental perspective. In P. D. Pearson, R. Barr, M. L. Kamil, & P. Mosenthal (Eds.), *Handbook of reading research.* White Plains, NY: Longman.

Mathes, P. G., Denton, C. A., Fletcher, J. M., Anthony, J. L., Francis, D. J., & Schatschneider, C. (2005). The effects of theoretically different instruction and student characteristics on the skills of struggling readers. *Reading Research Quarterly, 40,* 148–182.

Mathes, P. G., Howard, J. K., Allen, S., & Fuchs, D. (1998). Peer-assisted learning strategies for first grade readers: Making early reading instruction more responsive to the needs of diverse learners. *Reading Research Quarterly, 33,* 62–95.

Mayer, R. (2008). Multimedia literacy. In J. Coiro, M. Knobel, C. Lankshear, & D. L. Leu (Eds.), *Handbook of research on new literacies* (pp. 359–366). Mahwah, NJ: Erlbaum.

McCarthey, S. (2009). Understanding English language learners' identities from three perspectives. In G. Li (Ed.), *Multicultural families, home literacies, and mainstream schooling* (pp. 223–244). Charlotte, NC: Information Age.

McDermott, R. (1977). Social relations as contexts for learning in school. *Harvard Educational Review, 47*, 198–213.

McGill-Franzen, A. (1987). Failure to learn to read: Formulating a policy problem. *Reading Research Quarterly, 22*, 475–490.

McGill-Franzen, A., & Allington, R. L. (1991). The gridlock of low reading achievement: Perspectives on practice and policy. *Remedial and Special Education, 12*, 20–30.

McIntyre, E. (1990). Young children's reading strategies as they read self-selected texts in school. *Early Childhood Research Quarterly, 5*, 265–277.

McIntyre, E. (1995). Teaching and learning writing skills in a low-SES, urban, whole language primary classroom. *Journal of Reading Behavior, 27*, 213–242.

McIntyre, E. (2007). Story discussion in the primary grades: Balancing authenticity and explicit teaching. *The Reading Teacher, 60*(7), 610–620.

McIntyre, E. (2009). Issues in funds of knowledge teaching and research: Key concepts from a study of Appalachians families and schooling. In M. L. Dantas & P. C. Manyak (Eds.), *Home–school connections in a multicultural society: Learning from and with culturally and linguistically diverse families* (pp. 201–217). New York: Routledge.

McIntyre, E. (2010). Sociocultural perspectives on children with reading difficulties. In R. Allington & A. McGill-Franzen (Eds.), *Handbook of research on reading disabilities*. New York: Routledge.

McIntyre, E., & Archie, J. (2001). Teaching history: A cultural approach for primary grade children. In E. McIntyre, A. Rosebery, & N. González (Eds.), *Classroom diversity: Connecting curriculum to students' lives* (pp. 85–91). Portsmouth, NH: Heinemann.

McIntyre, E., & Freppon, P. A. (1994). A comparison of children's development of alphabetic knowledge in a skills-based and a whole language classroom. *Research in the Teaching of English, 28*, 391–417.

McIntyre, E., Hulan, N., & Maher, M. (2010). The relationship between literacy learning and cultural differences: A study of teachers' dispositions. *Journal of Reading Education, 35*, 19–25.

McIntyre, E., Kyle, D. W., Hovda, R. A., & Stone, N. (1999). Nongraded primary programs: Reform for Kentucky's children. *Journal for Education for Students Placed at Risk, 4*(1), 47–64.

McIntyre, E., Kyle, D. W., & Moore, G. (2006). A teacher's guidance toward small group dialogue in a low-SES primary grade classroom. *Reading Research Quarterly, 4*(1), 36–63.

McIntyre, E., Kyle, D. W., Moore G., Sweazy, R. A., & Greer, S. (2001). Linking home and school through family visits. *Language Arts, 78*, 264–272.

McIntyre, E., Kyle, D. W., & Rightmyer, E. C. (2005). Families' funds of knowledge to mediate teaching in rural schools. *Cultura y Educacion, 17*(2), 175–195.

McIntyre, E., Petrosko, J. P., Powers, S., Jones, D., Bright, K., Powell, R., et al. (2005). Supplemental instruction in early reading: Does it matter for struggling readers? *Journal of Educational Research, 99*(2), 99–107.

McIntyre, E., & Pressley, M. (1996). *Balanced instruction: Strategies and skills in whole language.* Norwood, NJ: Christopher-Gordon Press.

McIntyre, E., Rosebery, A., & González, N. (2001). *Classroom diversity: Connecting curriculum to students' lives.* Portsmouth, NH: Heinemann.

McMaster, K., Fuchs, D., & Fuchs, L. (2006). Research on peer assisted learning strategies: The promise and limitations of peer-mediated instruction. *Reading and Writing Quarterly, 22*, 5–25.

McMaster, K., Fuchs, D., & Fuchs, L. (2007). Promises and limitations of peer-assisted learning strategies in reading. *Learning Disabilities: A Contemporary Journal, 5*(2), 97–112.

McMaster, K., Kung, S., Han, I., Cao, M. (2008). Peer-assisted learning strategies: A "Tier 1" approach to promoting English learners' response to intervention. *Exceptional Children, 74*(2), 194–214.

McNair, J. C. (2003). "But the five Chinese brothers is one of my favorite books!": Conducting sociopolitical critiques of children's literature with preservice teachers. *Journal of Children's Literature, 29*, 46–54.

Mesmer, H. A. (2008). *Tools for matching readers to texts: Research-based practices.* New York: Guilford Press.

Michaels, S. (1981). "Sharing time": Children's narrative styles and differential access to literacy. *Language in Society, 10*, 423–442.

Miller, D. (2002). *Reading with meaning.* Portland, ME: Stenhouse.

Miller, G., & Gildea, P. (1987). How children learn words. *Scientific American, 257*, 94–99.

Miller, L. S. (1995). *An American imperative: Accelerating minority educational advancement.* Cambridge, UK: Cambridge University Press.

Moats, L. C. (2000). *Whole language lives on: The illusion of "balanced" reading instruction.* Washington, DC: Thomas Ford Foundation.

Moll, L. C. (1994). Literacy research in community and classrooms: A sociocultural approach. In R. B. Rudell, M. R. Rudell, & H. Singer (Eds.), *Theoretical models and processes of reading* (pp. 22–43). Newark, DE: International Reading Association.

Moll, L. C., & González, N. (1997). Teachers as social scientists: Learning about culture from household research. In P. Hall (Ed.), *Race, ethnicity and multiculturalism* (pp. 89–114). New York: Garland.

Moll, L. C., & González, N. (2003). Engaging life: A funds of knowledge approach to multicultural education. In J. Banks & C. A. Banks (Eds.), *Handbook of multicultural education* (pp. 299–614). San Francisco: Jossey-Bass.

Morgan, B., & Smith, R. D. (2008). A wiki for classroom writing. *The Reading Teacher, 62*(1), 80–82.

Morris, D. (2008). *Diagnosis and correction of reading problems.* New York: Guilford Press.

Morris, D., Shaw, B., & Perney, J. (1990). Helping low readers in grades 2 and 3: An after-school volunteer tutoring program. *Elementary School Journal, 19*, 133–150.

Murray, D. (1985). *A writer teaches writing.* Boston: Houghton Mifflin.

Nagy, W. E., & Scott, J. A. (2000). Vocabulary processes. In M. L. Kamil, P. B. Mosenthal, P. D. Pearson, & R. Barr (Eds.), *Handbook of reading research* (Vol. III, pp. 269–284). Mahwah, NJ: Erlbaum.

National Center on Response to Intervention. (2009). *What is RTI?* Retrieved January 10, 2009, from *www.rti4success.org.*

National Institute of Child Health and Human Development. (2000). *Report of the National Reading Panel. Teaching children to read: An evidence-based assessment of the scientific research literature on reading and its implications for reading instruction* (NIH Publication No. 00-4769). Washington, DC: U.S. Government Printing Office.

Nieto, S. (1999). *The light in their eyes: Creating multicultural learning communities.* New York: Teachers College Press.

Ogbu, J. U. (1988). Diversity and equity in public education: Community forces and minority school adjustment and performance. In R. Haskins & D. McRae (Eds.), *Policies for America's schools: Teachers, equity, and indicators* (pp. 141–160). Norwood, NJ: Ablex.

Ogbu, J. U. (2003). *Black American students in an affluent suburb: A study of academic disengagement.* Mahwah, NJ: Erlbaum.

Ogle, D. (1986). K-W-L: A teaching model that develops active reading of expository text. *The Reading Teacher, 39*, 563–570.

Olson, C. B., & Land, R. (2007). A cognitive strategies approach tp reading and writing instruction for English language learners in secondary school. *Research in the Teaching of English, 41*, 269–303.

Palinscar, A. S., & Brown, A. L. (1984). Reciprocal teaching of comprehension-fostering and comprehension-monitoring activities. *Cognition and Instruction, 1*, 117–175.

Palinscar, A. S., & Dalton, B. (2005). Speaking literacy and learning to technology; speaking technology to literacy and learning. In B. Maloch, J. Hoffman, D. Schallert, C. Fairbanks, & J. Worthy (Eds.), *54th yearbook of the National Reading Conference* (pp. 83–102). Oak Creek, WI: National Reading Conference.

Pearman, C. (2008). Independent reading of CD-ROM storybooks: Measuring comprehension with oral retellings. *The Reading Teacher, 61*(8), 594–602.

Pearson, P. D., Barr, R., Kamil, M. L., & Mosenthal. P. (Eds.). (1984). *Handbook of reading research.* White Plains, NY: Longman.

Pearson, P. D., & Fielding, L. (1991). Comprehension instruction. In R. Barr, M. L. Kamil, P. Mosenthal, & P. D. Pearson (Eds.), *Handbook of reading research* (Vol. II, pp. 815–860). Mahwah, NJ: Erlbaum.

Pearson, P. D., & Gallagher, M. C. (1983). The instruction of reading comprehension. *Contemporary Educational Psychology, 8*, 317–344.

Pearson, P. D., & Johnson, D. (1978). *Teaching reading comprehension.* New York: Holt, Rinehart & Winston.

Pearson, P. D., & Stevens, D. (1994). Learning about literacy: A 30-year journey. In R. B. Rudell, M. R. Rudell, & H. Singer (Eds.), *Theoretical models and processes of reading* (pp. 22–43). Newark, DE: International Reading Association.

Peregoy, S. F., & Boyle, O. (2008). *Reading, writing and learning in ESL.* Boston: Pearson.

Peters, S. G. (2006). *Do you know enough about me to teach me?* Orangeburg, SC: Peters Group Foundation.

Philips, S. (1972). Participant structures and communicative competence: Warm Springs children in community and classroom. In C. Cazden, D. Hymes, & V. John (Eds.), *Functions of language in the classroom* (pp. 370–394). New York: Teachers College Press.

Pikulski, J. J. (1994). Preventing reading failure: A review of five programs. *The Reading Teacher, 48*, 30–39.

Pinnell, G. S., & Fountas, I. C. (2003). *Phonics lessons: Letters, words, and how they work.* Portsmouth, NH: Heinemann.

Pinnell, G. S., Lyons, C. A., DeFord, D., Bryk, A. S., & Seltzer, M. (1994). Comparing instructional models for the literacy education of high-risk first graders. *Reading Research Quarterly, 29*, 39.

Portes, P. R. (1999). Social and psychological factors in the academic achievement of children of immigrants: A cultural history puzzle. *American Educational Research Journal, 36*, 489–507.

Powell, R., McIntyre E., & Rightmyer, E. C. (2006). Johnny won't read, and Susie won't either: Reading instruction and student resistance. *Journal of Early Childhood Literacy, 6*, 5–31.

Pressley, M. (1998). *Reading instruction that works: The case for balanced teaching.* New York: Guilford Press.

Pressley, M. (2000). What should comprehension instruction be the instruction of? In M. L. Kamil, P. B. Mosenthal, P. D. Pearson, & R. Barr (Eds.), *Handbook of reading research* (Vol. II, pp. 545–562). Mahwah, NJ: Earlbaum.

Pressley, M., Woloshyn, V., & Associates. (1995). *Cognitive strategy instruction that really improves children's academic performance* (2nd ed.). Cambridge, MA: Brookline Books.

Purcell-Gates, V. (1988). Lexical and syntactic knowledge of written narrative held by well-read-to kindergartners and second graders. *Research in the Teaching of English, 22*, 128–160.

Purcell-Gates, V. (1995). *Other people's words: The cycle of low literacy.* Cambridge, MA: Harvard University Press.

Purcell-Gates, V. (1996). Stories, coupons, and the "TV Guide": Relationships between home literacy experiences and emergent literacy knowledge. *Reading Research Quarterly, 31*, 406–428.

Purcell-Gates, V., Jacobson, E., & Degener, S. (2004.) *Print literacy development: Uniting cognitive and social practice theories.* Cambridge, MA: Harvard University Press.

Putnam, S. M., & Kingsley, T. (2009). The atoms family: Using podcasts to enhance the development of science vocabulary. *The Reading Teacher, 63*(2), 100–108.

RAND Reading Study Group. (2002). *Reading for understanding: Toward a R&D program in reading comprehension.* Arlington, VA: RAND.

Raphael, T. E. (1984). Teaching learners about sources of information for answering comprehension questions. *Journal of Reading, 27*, 303–311.

Raphael, T. E., & Pearson, P. D. (1985). Increasing students' awareness of sources of information for answering questions. *American Educational Research Journal, 22*, 217–236.

Rasinski, T. V. (1990). Effects of repeated reading and listening-while-reading on reading fluency. *Journal of Educational Research, 83*, 147–150.

Rasinski, T. V., & Padak, N. (2000). *Effective reading strategies: Teaching children who find reading difficult.* Cols, OH: Merrill.

Read, C. (1971). Preschool children's knowledge of English orthography. *Harvard Educational Review, 41*, 1–34.

Reitsma, P. (2002). Reading practice for beginners: Effects of guided reading, reading-while-listening, and independent reading with computer-based speech feedback. *Reading Research Quarterly, 22*, 219–235.

Reutzel, R. D. (1999). On balanced reading. *The Reading Teacher, 52*, 322–324.

Rios, F. (2010). Home–school–community collaborations in uncertain times. In M. L. Dantas & P. C. Manyak (Eds.), *Home–school connections in a multicultural society: Learning from and with culturally and linguistically diverse families* (pp 265–279). New York: Routledge.

Rist, R. C. (1970). Student social class and teacher expectations: The self-fulfilling prophecy in ghetto education. *Harvard Educational Review, 40*, 411–451.

Roberts, J., Nagy, N., & Boberg, C. (2006). Yakking with the Yankees (New England). In W. Wolfram & B. Ward (Eds.), *American voices: How dialects differ from coast to coast* (pp. 57–62). Oxford, UK: Blackwell.

Rogoff, B. (2003). *The cultural nature of human development.* New York: Oxford University Press.

Rothstein, R. (2002). *Class and schools using social, economic, and educational reform to close the black–white achievement gap.* New York: Teachers College Press.

Rowe, M. B. (1972). Wait time: Slowing down may be a way of speeding up. *American Educator, 11*, 38–43, 47.

Rueda, R., & McIntyre, E. (2002). Toward universal literacy. In S. Stringfield & D. Land (Eds.), *Educating at-risk students* (pp. 189–209). Chicago: University of Chicago Press.

Saenz, L., Fuchs, L., & Fuchs, D. (2005). Peer-assisted learning strategies for English language learners with learning disabilities. *Exceptional Children, 71*(3), 231–247, 408.

Salvucci, C. (2006). Expressions of brotherly love (Philadelphia, PA). In W. Wolfram & B. Ward (Eds.), *American voices: How dialects differ from coast to coast* (pp. 88–92). Oxford, UK: Blackwell.

Samuels, S. J. (2002). Reading fluency: Its development and assessment. In A. E. Farstrup & S. J. Samuels (Eds.), *What research has to say about reading instruction* (pp. 166–183). Newark, DE: International Reading Association.

Samuels, S. J., LaBerge, D., & Bremer, C. (1978). Units of word recognition: Evidence for developmental changes. *Journal of Verbal Learning and Verbal Behavior, 17*, 715–720.

Samuels, S. J., Miller, N., & Eisenberg, P. (1979). Practice effects on the unit of word recognition. *Journal of Educational Psychology, 71*, 514–520.

Samway, K. D. (2006). *When English language learners write: Connecting research to practice, K–8.* Portsmouth, NH: Heinemann.

Samway, K. D., & Pease-Alverez, L. (2005). Teachers' perspectives on Open Court. In B. Altwerger (Ed.), *Reading for profit: How the bottom line leaves kids behind* (pp. 142–154). Portsmouth, NH: Heinemann.

Saunders, W. M., & Goldenberg, C. (1999). Effects of instructional conversations and literature logs on limited- and fluent-English-proficient students' story comprehension amd thematic understanding. *Elememtary School Journal, 99*, 277–306.

Scardamalia, M., & Bereiter, C. (1986). Research on written composition. In M. C. Wittrock (Ed.), *Handbook of research on teaching* (pp. 778–803). New York: Macmillan.

Schreiber, P. A. (1980). On the acquisition of reading fluency. *Journal of Reading Behavior, 22*, 177–186.

Schultz, M. M. (2010). Building connections between homes and schools. In P. C. Manyak & M. L. Dantas (Eds.), *Home-school connections in a multicultural society* (pp. 94–111). New York: Routledge.

Shanahan, T. (2002). What reading research says: The promises and limitations of applying research to reading education. In A. E. Farstrup & S. J. Samuels (Eds.), *What research has to say about reading instruction* (pp. 8–24). Newark, DE: International Reading Association.

Shanahan, T., & Barr, R. (1995). Reading Recovery: An independent evaluation of the effects of an early instructional intervention for at-risk learners. *Reading Research Quarterly, 21*, 360–406.

Shanahan, T., & Beck, I. (2006). Effective literacy instruction for English language learners. In D. August & T. Shanahan (Eds.), *Developing literacy in second-language learners* (pp. 415–488). Mahwah, NJ: Erlbaum.

Shaywitz, B., Pugh, K. R., Jenner, A. R., Fulbright, R. F., Fletcher, J. M., Gore, J. C., et al. (2000). The neurobiology of reading and reading disability (dyslexia). In M. L. Kamil, P. B. Mosenthal, P. D. Pearson, & R. Barr (Eds.), *Handbook of reading research* (Vol. III, pp. 229–250). Mahwah, NJ: Erlbaum.

Shelton, N. R. (2005). First do no harm: Teachers' reactions to mandated reading mastery. In B. Altwerger (Ed.), *Reading for profit: How the bottom line leaves kids behind* (pp. 184–198). Portsmouth, NH: Heinemann

Simmons, D. C., Fuchs, L., Fuchs, D. Mathes, P., & Hodge, J. (1995). Effects of explicit teaching and peer tutoring on the reading achievement of learning disabled and low-performing students in regular classrooms. *The Elementary School Journal, 95*(5), 387–408.

Sindelar, P. T., Monda, L. E., & O'Shea, L. J. (1990). Effects of repeated readings on instructional- and master-level readers. *Journal of Educational Research, 83*, 220–226.

Slavin, R. E., Lake, C., Chambers, B., Cheung, A., & Davis, S. (2009). Effective reading programs for the elementary grades: A best-evidence synthesis. *Review of Educational Research, 79*(4), 1391–1466.

Smith, F., & Goodman, K. S. (2008). On the psycholinguistic method of teaching reading revisited. *Language Arts, 66*, 61–65.

Snow, C. E., Burns, M. S., & Griffith, P. (Eds.). (1998). *Preventing reading difficulties in young children.* Washington, DC: National Academy Press.

Sowers, S. (1985). Learning to write in a workshop: A study in grade one through four. In M. Farr (Ed.), *Advances in writing research: Children's early writing development* (pp. 297–342). Norwood, NJ: Ablex.

Spiegel, D. L. (1992). Blending whole language and systematic direct instruction. *The Reading Teacher, 46*, 38–44.

Spiegel, D. L. (1998). Silver bullets, babies, and bath water: Literature response groups in a balanced literacy program. *The Reading Teacher, 52*, 114–124.

SRA Reading Mastery. (2003). New York: McGraw-Hill.

Stahl, S. A., & Fairbanks, M. M. (1986). The effects of vocabulary instruction: A model-based meta analysis. *Review of Educational Research, 65*, 72–110.

Stanovich, K. E. (2000). *Progress in understanding reading: Scientific foundations and new frontiers.* New York: Guilford Press.

Stanovich, K. E. (1986). Matthew effects in reading: Some consequences of individual differences in the acquisition of literacy. *Reading Research Quarterly, 21*, 360–406.

Stanovich, K. E., & Cunningham, A. E. (1998). What reading does for the mind. *American Educator, 22*, 8–15.

Stauffer, R. (1969). *Directing reading maturity as a cognitive process.* New York: Harper & Row.

Street, B. (1985). *Literacy in theory and practice.* New York: Cambridge University Press.

Sulzby, E. (1985). Children's emergent abilities to read favorite storybooks: A developmental study. *Reading Research Quarterly, 20*, 458–481.

Sulzby, E., & Teale, W. H. (1991). *Emergent literacy. Writing and reading.* New York: Ablex.

Taylor, B. M., Frye, B. J., & Maruyama, G. M. (1990). Time spent reading and reading growth. *American Educational Research Journal, 27*, 351–362.

Taylor, B. M., Strait, J., & Medo, M. A. (1994). Early intervention in reading: Supplemental instruction for groups of low achieving students provided by first-grade teachers. In E. H. Heibert & B. M. Taylor (Eds.), *Getting reading right from the start: Effective early literacy interventions.* Needham Heights, MA: Allyn & Bacon.

Taylor, D., & Dorsey-Gaines, C. (1988). *Growing up literate: Learning from inner-city families.* Portsmouth, NH: Heinemann.

Taylor, N. E., Wade, M. R., & Yekovich, F. R. (1985). The effects of text manipulation and multiple reading strategies on the reading performance of good and poor readers. *Reading Research Quarterly, 20,* 566–574.

Teale, W. H. (1986). Home background and young children's literacy development. In W. H. Teale & E. Sulzby (Eds). *Emergent literacy: Writing and reading* (pp. 173–206). Norwood, NJ: Ablex.

Teale, W. H., & Sulzby, E. (1986). *Emergent literacy: Writing and reading.* Norwood, NJ: Ablex.

Tharp, R. G. (1989). Psychocultural variables and constants: Effects on teaching and learning in schools. *American Psychologist 44,* 349–359.

Tharp, R. G., Estrada, P., Dalton, S. S., & Yamauchi, L (2000). *Teaching transformed: Achieving excellence, fairness, inclusion, and harmony.* Boulder, CO: Westview Press.

Tharp, R. G., & Gallimore, R. (1993). *Rousing minds to life: Teaching, learning, and schooling in social context.* Cambridge, UK: Cambridge University Press.

Tierney, R. J., & Cunningham, J. W. (1984). Research on teaching comprehension. In P. D. Pearson, R. Barr, M. L. Kamil, & P. Mosenthal (Eds.), *Handbook of reading research* (Vol. I, pp. 609–655). White Plains, NY: Longman.

Tobin, K. (1987). The role of wait time in higher cognitive level learning. *Review of Educational Research, 57,* 69–95.

Tomlinson, B. (1986). Using poetry with mixed ability language classes. *English Language Teaching Journal, 40,* 31–45.

Tompkins, G. (2000). *Teaching writing: Balancing process and product.* New York: Prentice Hall.

Torgeson, J. K. (1998). Catch them before they fall. *American Educator, 22,* 32–38.

Torgeson, J. K. (2002a). Lessons learned from intervention research in reading: A way to go before we rest. In *Learning and teaching reading* (pp. 89–103). The British Psychological Society.

Torgeson, J. K. (2002b). The prevention of reading difficulties. *Journal of School Psychology, 40,* 22–42.

Tracey, D., & Morrow, L. M. (2006). *Lenses on reading: An introduction to theories and models.* New York: Guilford Press.

Trushell, J., Maitland, A., & Burrell, C. (2003). Pupils' recall of an interactive storybook on CD-ROM. *Journal of Computer Assisted Learning, 19*(1), 80–89.

Turner, J. D., & Edwards, P. A. (2009). *Implications of home literacies for teacher education K–12 schools and family literacy programs.* Charlotte, NC: Information Age.

Valdés, G. (1996). *Con respeto: Bridging the distance between culturally diverse families and schools.* New York: Teachers College Press.

van Steensel, R. (2006). Relations between socio-cultural factors, the home literacy environment and children's literacy development in the first years of primary education. *Journal of Research in Reading, 29*(4), 367–382.

Vaughn, S., Mathes, P. G., Linan-Thompson, S., & Francis, D. J. (2005). Teaching English language learners at risk for reading disabilities to read: Putting research into practice. *Learning Disabilities and Practice, 20,* 58–67.

Vélez-Ibáñez, C., & Greenberg, J. (1992). Formation and transformation of funds of knowledge among U.S. Mexican households. *Anthropology and Education Quarterly, 23,* 313–335.

Vygotsky, L. S. (1978). *Mind in society: The development of higher psychological processes.* Cambridge, MA: Harvard University Press.

Vygotsky, L. S. (1987). *Thought and language* (A. Kozulin, Ed.). Cambridge, MA: MIT Press.

Wasik, B. A., & Slavin, R. E. (1993). Preventing reading failure with one-to-one tutoring: A review of five programs. *Reading Research Quarterly, 28,* 178–200.

Weaver, C. (1998). *Teaching grammar in context.* New York: Boyton-Cook.

Weinberger, J. (1996). A longitudinal study of children's early literacy experiences at home and later literacy development at home and school. *Journal of Research in Reading, 19,* 14–24.

Weinstein, R. (2004). *Reaching higher: The power of expectations in schooling.* Cambridge, MA: Harvard University Press.

Wells, G. (1986). *The meaning makers: Children learning language and using language to learn.* Portsmouth, NH: Heinemann.

Wells, G., & Wells, J. (1989). Learning to talk and talking to learn. *Theory into Practice, 23*, 190–196.

Westby, C. (2004). A language perspective on executive functioning, metacognition, and self-regulation in reading. In C. A. Stone, E. A. Silliman, B. J. Ehren, & K. Appel (Eds.), *Handbook of language and literacy: Development and disorders* (pp. 398–428). New York. Guilford Press.

Wharton-McDonald, R., Pressley, M., & Hampton, J. M. (1998). Literacy instruction in nine first grade classrooms: Teacher characteristics and student achievement. *The Elementary School Journal, 99*, 101–128.

Williams, B. T. (2009). *Shimmering literacies: Popular culture and reading and writing online.* New York: Peter Lang.

Wilson, G. P., Wiltz, N. W., & Lang, D. (2005). The impact of reading mastery on children's reading strategies. In B. Altwerger (Ed.), *Reading for profit: How the bottom line leaves kids behind* (pp. 172–183). Portsmouth, NH: Heinemann.

Wolfram, W., & Ward, B. (Eds.). (2006). *American voices: How dialects differ from coast to coast.* Oxford, UK: Blackwell.

Yaden, D. B., Rowe, D. W., & MacGillivray, L. (2000). Emergent literacy: A matter (polyphony) of perspectives. In M. L. Kamil, P. B. Mosenthal, P. D. Pearson, & R. Barr (Eds.), *Handbook of reading research* (Vol. III, pp. 425–454). Mahwah, NJ: Erlbaum.

Yaden, D. B., Smolkin, L. B., & Conlin, A. (1989). Preschoolers' questions about pictures, print conventions, and story text during read aloud at home. *Reading Research Quarterly, 24*, 188–214.

Yokota, J. (1993). Issues in selecting multicultural children's literature. In M. F. Optiz (Ed.), *Literacy instruction for culturally and linguistically diverse students* (pp. 184–197). Newark, DE: IRA.

Yopp, H. K. (1995). A test for assessing phonemic awareness in young children. *Reading Teacher, 49*, 20–29.

Young, C., & Rasinski, T. (2009). Implementing Readers' Theatre as an approach to classroom fluency instruction. *Reading Teacher, 63*(1), 4–13.

Young, T. A., Campbell, L. C., & Oda, L. K. (1995). Multicultural literature for children and young adults: A rationale and resources. *Reading Horizons, 35*, 374–393.

Zawalinski, L. (2009). HOT blogging: A framework for blogging to promote higher-order thinking. *The Reading Teacher, 62*(8), 650–661.

Children's Literature Cited

Allen, D. (2000). *Dancing in the wings*. New York, New York: Dial.

Barretta, G. (2007). *Dear deer*. New York: Henry Holt.

Bridges, R. (1999) *Through my eyes*. New York: Scholastic Press.

Briggs, R. (1978). *The snowman storybook*. New York: Random House.

Briggs, R. (1999a). *The snowman*. New York: Random House.

Briggs, R. (1999b). *The snowman storybook*. New York: Random House.

Bunting, E. (1994). *Smoky night*. Orlando, FL: Harcourt Brace.

Carle, E. (2002). *Slowly slowly slowly said the sloth*. New York: Philomel Books.

Cleary, B. (2005). *How much can a bare bear bear?* Minneapolis: Millbrook Press.

Coerr, E. (1977). *Sadako and the thousand paper cranes*. New York: Puffin Books.

Cole, H., & Vogl, N. (2005). *Am I a color too?* Bellevue, WA: Illumination Arts.

Dahl, R. (1964). *The magic finger*. New York: Scholastic Press.

Dahl, R. (1988). *Matilda*. New York: Scholastic Press.

Dahl, R. (2001). *The giraffe and the pelly and me*. London: Puffin Books.

DiCamillo, K. (2000). *Because of Winn-Dixie*. Cambridge, MA: Candlewick Press.

Fleming, D. (1995). *In the tall, tall grass*. New York: Henry Holt.

Frasier, D. (2007). *Miss Alaineus: A vocabulary disaster*. Orlando, FL: First Voyager Books.

Goldenstern, J. (2002). *Rose's gold*. Rigby Literacy: Comprehension Quarterly, Grade 5 Volume 1. Barrington, IL: Rigby.

Gwynne, F. (1970). *The king who rained*. New York: Simon & Shuster.

Gwynne, F. (1976). *A chocolate moose for dinner*. New York: Aladdin Paperbacks.

Hoffman, M. (1995). *Boundless grace*. New York: Dial Books for Young Readers

Joy, N. (2007). *The secret Olivia told me*. New York: Scholastic.

Kraus, R. (1971). *Leo the late bloomer*. New York: Windmill Books.

Lederer, R. (1996). *Pun and games: Jokes, riddles, rhymes, daffynitions, tairy fales, and more word play for kids*. Chicago: Chicago Review Press.

Littlesugar, A. (1996). *Jonkonnu: A story from the sketchbook of Winslow Homer*. New York: Philomel.

Lionni, L. (1967). *Frederick*. New York: Knopf.

Lyon, G. E. (2010). *George Ella Lyon: Where I'm from*. Retrieved February 14, 2010, from *www.georgeellalyon.com/where.html*.

Martin, B. (1967). *Brown bear, brown bear, what do you see?* New York: Henry Holt.

McCain, B. R., & Leonardo, T. (2001). *Nobody knew what to do*. Park Ridge, IL: Albert Whiteman.

Mitchell, M. K. (1993). *Uncle Jed's barbershop*. New York: Aladdin Paperbacks.

Molina, R. (2002). *Titoy and the magical chair*. Philippines: Adarna House.

Montgomery, R. A. (1982). *House of danger*. Waitsfield, VT: Chooseco.

Mora, P. (1998). *This big sky*. New York: Scholastic Press.

Mora, P. (2005). *Dona Flor*. New York: Knopf.

Morris, A. (1989). *Bread, bread, bread*. New York: HarperCollins.

Moss, L. (1995). *Zin! Zin! Zin! A violin*. New York: Simon & Schuster.

Parrish, P. (1977). *Teach us, Amelia Bedelia*. New York: HarperCollins.

Penner, L. R. (1996). *Monster bugs*. New York: Random House.

Podogil, C. (2000). *Matthew Henson, arctic explorer*. New York: McGraw Hill Macmillan.

Polacco, P. (1998). *My rotten redheaded older brother*. New York: First Aladdin Paperbacks.

Popov, N. (1996). *Why?* New York: North-South Books.

Prelutsky, J. (1983). *Nightmares: Poems to trouble your sleep*. New York: Mulberry Books.

Raschka, C. (1992). *Charlie Parker played be bop*. New York: Orchard Books.

Recorvits, H. (2003). *My name is Yoon*. New York: Frances Foster Books.

Rigby. (2000). *The California gold rush*. Literacy: Comprehension Quarterly, Grade 5, Volume 1. Barrington, IL: Author.

Roberts, J. (2009). *Back to school and Autumn poems*. Retrieved August 19, 2009, from *www.primarysuccess.ca/main_ca.htm*.

Rogers, K., & Alexander, J. (2000). *Paper crunch*. Barrington, IL: Rigby Literacy.

Rylant, C. (1993). *When I was young in the mountains*. New York: Penguin Putnam.

Sciezska, J. (1996). *The true story of the three little pigs*. New York: Puffin Books.

Scraper, K. (2005). *Maya Lin: Linking people and places*. Parsippany, NJ: Celebration Press.

Sreenivasan, J. (2002). *Making the world a better place: The stories of social reformers*. Barrington, Il: Rigby.

Steig, W. (1986). *Brave Irene*. New York: Farrar, Straus & Giroux.

Terban, M. (1982). *Eight ate: A feast of homonym riddles*. New York: Clarion Books.

Terban, M. (1983). *In a pickle: And other funny idioms*. New York: Clarion Books.

Tipene, T. (2001). *Taming the Taniwha*. Wellington, NZ: Huia.

Weldon-Owe. (2003). *Different places, different faces*. Boston: Houghton-Mifflin Harcourt.

White, E. B. (1952). *Charlotte's web*. New York: HarperCollins.

Youme. (2004). *Sélavi: A Haitian story of hope*. Hong Kong: Morris Printing.

Index

AAVE. *See* African American Vernacular English
Achievement gap
  deficit views and, 44–45
  definition of, 41
  educational factors in, 48–53
  historical and cultural factors in, 46–47
Activating prior knowledge strategy, 120–121
Adult–child interactions, 43
Advance organizers, 114
African American Vernacular English (AAVE), 71, 72
Analytic phonics, 80
"Answer-grabbing" in Internet, 180
Anticipation guides, 121–122
Assessment
  of comprehension, 118–119
  of fluency, 101–103
  of new literacies, 184
  of phonological knowledge, 82–86
  of vocabulary learning, 138–139
  of writing, 162–163
Assisted performance, 37–38
Audacity site for podcasts, 189

B

Backgrounds of students, connecting curriculum to, 12–13, 212, 241–242
Balanced literacy approaches, 5–6

Basal reading programs, 2, 49–50
Beginning reading, 20, 27
Beginning writing, 35–37
BioCube Planning Sheet, 186–187
Biography writing, 170, 171
Blogs, 190–191
Book Buddies, 263–264
Books. *See* Literature; Texts
Brain, plasticity of, 259
Buddy reading, 107–108, 213

C

Call and response, 13
CBOs. *See* Community-based organizations
Center for Research on Education, Diversity, and Excellence (CREDE), 9, 74
Character webs, 144, 145
Child Development Project, 55, 56
Children's literature. *See* Literature
Choice in student work, 59, 140
Choral reading, 106–107, 230
Civil rights and freedom, books about, 272–273
Clapping syllables strategy, 87
Class meetings
  description of, 55–57
  in fifth grade, 218–219
  in second grade, 214
Classroom discourse, 9, 16

Classrooms
    diversity in, 18–19, 63, 182–183
    listening in, 64–65
    parents in, 250
    turn taking in, 66–67
    See also Class meetings
Closed sorts, 89
Code-emphasis approach, 2
Cognitive perspective on literacy development,
    21
Community-based organizations (CBOs),
    251–252
Community literacy, 243
Comparison essays, 170, 171
Comprehensible input, 86
Comprehension
    assessment of, 118–119
    fluent reading and, 98
    key variables of, 113–114
    of new literacies, 179–180
Comprehension instruction
    activating prior knowledge, 120–121
    culturally responsive instruction and, 132–133
    determining important ideas, 127–128
    drawing inferences, 122–123, 195–198
    making predictions, 121–122, 201–203
    monitoring comprehension, 123
    overview of, 112–114
    principles for, 117
    questioning, 124–125
    research on, 114–117
    strategies for, 117, 119–132
    summarizing, 128–130
    think-alouds, 125–127
    understanding text structures, 130–132
    using text conventions, 132
Concept ladders, 146
Conceptual maps, 114
Concept webs, 145–146
Conferencing in writing workshops, 168–170
Conflict resolution and bullying, books
    about, 273
Content area literacy instruction, 59–60
Context
    of reading, 21
    of sentence, 142–143
Controlled scribbling, 29–31
Core reading program, 10, 11
CREDE. *See* Center for Research on Education,
    Diversity, and Excellence

Culturally responsive instruction
    blending with research-based instruction, 10,
        12–16
    comprehension instruction and, 132–133
    family involvement and, 252
    in fifth grade, 237–240
    fluency instruction and, 111
    goal of, 17
    home language patterns and, 13–14
    new literacies and, 191
    phonics and, 18
    phonological instruction and, 96
    preparation for, 213–214
    principles for, 54
    purpose of book and, 265–266
    in second grade, 214–215
    standards for, 13
    supplemental interventions and, 264–265
    techniques for, 14–15
    themes of, 9
    vocabulary instruction, instructional
        conversation, and, 152
    writing instruction and, 176
Cultural practices and achievement gap, 47
Curriculum
    achievement gap and, 48–51
    for comprehension development, 16
    connecting to students' lives, 12–13, 212,
        241–242
Cyberguides, 187

D

Debate about reading instruction, 2–3
Decodable text, 94
Deficit views
    of struggling readers, 41–42, 45
    of students and families, 241, 243
Determining important ideas in texts strategy,
    127–128
Developmental issues in reading instruction,
    39
Developmental Reading Assessment (DRA),
    119, 213, 226–227
Developmental Studies Center, 55
Dialects, American
    overview of, 71–73
    phonological skills and, 80–81
    teaching about, 142

Dialogic instruction
    building skills in, 68–70
    for comprehension development, 14–15
    as culturally responsive, 10
    listening and, 64–65
    overview of, 64
    teacher questioning and, 65–66
    teacher responses and, 67–68
    wait time and turn taking, 66–67
    See also Instructional Conversation
Difference model compared to deficit model,
    244
Difficulty of texts, 104–105
Digital storytelling, 188
Directed reading–thinking activity, 115
Disengagement during phonics instruction, 78
Diversity in classrooms
    increase in, 18–19
    new literacies and, 182–183
    workshop approach and, 63
DRA. *See* Developmental Reading Assessment
Drafting phase of writing process, 159–160
Drawing inferences strategy, 122–123, 195–198

E

Early intervention model, 261–262
Editing phase of writing process, 161
Electronic resources, 274
Electronic texts, 181, 187–188
Elkonin boxes, 88
Emergent literacy, 20
English language learners (ELLs)
    CREDE, 9
    literacy instruction for, 73–75
    phonemic awareness instruction for, 86
    repeated readings and, 101
    SIOP, 74
    supplemental instruction for, 258
    vocabulary learning and, 138
    workshop approach and, 63
    writing instruction for, 157–158
Environmental education, books for, 272
Environment for writing workshops, 175
Expectations of teacher, 51–53
Experts, parents as, 248
Explicit teaching
    description of, 9–10
    phonemic awareness and, 79

whole-language movement and, 4–5
    of words, 138
    of writing process, 166–168

F

Families
    books about, 273
    literacy levels of, 43–44
Family involvement
    importance of, 241–242
    principles for, 244–245
    research on, 242–244
    strategies for, 245–252
Family nights, 250–251
Fast ForWord intervention, 259, 264
Feedback language, 169
Fifth-grade instruction
    culturally responsive instruction and,
        237–240
    greeting time, 219
    morning message, 219–220
    morning routine, 217–220
    schedule for literacy instruction, 217
    school district information, 216
    shared reading, 220–224
    sharing time, 220
    word work, 235–236
    writing workshop, 236–238
Fluency, 97–98
Fluency assessment, 101–103
Fluency instruction
    culturally responsive instruction and, 111
    principles for, 102
    research on, 98–101
    in second grade, 205–206
    strategies for, 105–111
Four Corners learning strategy, 69–70
Fun, making words, 147
"Funds of knowledge," 244

G

Genres
    studying in fifth grade, 221–224
    writing in different, 170, 171, 207, 209
GIST (generating interactions between
    schemata and texts) strategy, 129

Good readers, characteristics of, 116
Google Earth, 185
Gradual release of responsibility, 62–63, 258
Graphic organizers
    comprehension instruction and, 114
    for research in second grade, 211, 212
    for summarizing, 129–130
Graphophonic information, 23
Group differences, explanations for, 46–47
Guided oral reading, 108
Guided reading groups in fifth grade
    literacy stations, 224–226
    proficient but careless readers, 231–232
    skilled readers, 232–234
    struggling readers, 226–230
Guided reading groups in second grade
    beginning readers, 205–206
    developing readers, 201–205
    overview of, 199–201
    proficient readers, 206–207
    schedule for, 200
Guided reading lessons, 58

H

Handheld devices, 189
High-frequency words, 92, 93
Historical factors in achievement gap, 46–47
Historical fiction, genre study of, 221–224
Home language patterns, building on, 13–14
Home–school connections, 12–13, 212,
    241–242. *See also* Family involvement

I

IC. *See* Instructional Conversation
ICTs. *See* Information communication tools
Identity and self-acceptance, books about, 273
Independent reading time, 99–100
Inferring, 122–123, 195–198
Informal reading inventory, 119
Information communication tools (ICTs), 178,
    181
Inquiry searches on Internet, 186–187, 209–210
Instructional Conversation (IC)
    culturally responsive instruction and, 152
    definition of, 135
    examples of, 134–135, 149–152

indicators of, 148
uses of, 147–149
Instructional practices and achievement gap,
    48–51
Integrated learning systems, 181
Interests of students, connecting curriculum to,
    12–13, 212, 241–242
International Children's Digital Library, 191, 196
International Reading Association, 254–255
Internet
    comprehension and, 179–180
    inquiry searches on, 186–187, 209–210
    literacy and, 178
    literature discussions, online, 189
    magazines, online, 162
    resources, online, 274
    uses of in classrooms, 181–182
Interviews for comprehension assessment,
    118–119
Invented spelling
    assessment of phonemic awareness and
        phonics and, 84, 85–86
    as phase in writing development, 35
    phonics instruction and, 89
IPod Touch, 189
IRE sequence, 147

J

Journal writing in second grade, 193–194, 213

K

Kentucky writing rubric, 163
Kidspiration software program, 185
Known words
    reading only, 26–27
    writing, 33–34

L

Language differences, attending to, 70–75,
    80–81, 142
Learning centers or stations
    description of, 59
    in fifth grade, 224–226
    in second grade, 207, 208, 213

Letter strings, nonphonetic, 31–33
Level systems for books, 105
Listening in classrooms, 64–65
Literacy development
    assisted performance and, 37–38
    phases of reading development, 23–28
    phases of writing development, 28–37
    school and community types of, 243
    theories of, 21–23
Literature
    fairytale alternatives, 271–272
    favorite, for reading instruction, 267–271
    multicultural, choosing, 60–62
    multimedia, 181, 187–188
    online discussions of, 189
    by themes, 271–273
    See also Texts
Literature circles, 233–234, 240

M

Magazines, online, 162
Making predictions strategy, 121–122, 201–203
Making Words lessons, 76, 90
Matching texts to readers, 103–105
Materials for writing workshops, 174–175
Mathematics
    instruction in, 59–60
    writing about, 172–173
Mediated SSR, 110, 111
Mediation and literacy development, 21
Memoir genre, 207, 209
Memory, reading text from, 25–26
Mini-lessons, 58, 166–168
Modeling
    fluent reading, 105–106
    interest in words and word consciousness, 140
    writing process, 164–166
Monitoring comprehension strategy, 123
Multiculturalism in reading instruction model, 8
Multicultural literature, choosing, 60–62
Multimedia literature, 181, 187–188

N

Name cups, 194
"Name Game" poem (Roberts), 109–110
Names, using for phonics instruction, 91–92

National Reading Panel (NPR) report, 6, 78–79, 99
National Writing Project (NWP), 156, 157
New literacies
    assessment of, 184
    concerns about, 178–179
    culturally responsive instruction and, 191
    definition of, 178
    in diverse classrooms, 182–183
    overview of, 177–178
    principles for teaching, 183
    research on, 179–183
    strategies, tools, and activities for, 184–191
No Child Left Behind legislation, 44–45, 254
Nonfiction text structures, 131
NPR. *See* National Reading Panel (NPR) report
Numbered Heads Together, 15, 70
NWP. *See* National Writing Project

O

Observation of comprehension, 118, 184
Online literature discussions, 189
Online magazines, 162
Online resources, 274
Open sorts, 89

P

PALS (peer assisted learning strategies), 257, 262–263
Parents/caregivers, literacy levels of, 43–44
Pathway Project, 157–158
PBWiki, 190
Pedagogy, definition of, 8
Peer-mediated instruction, 257, 262–263
Phonemic awareness
    assessment of, 82–86
    instructional strategies for, 86–88
    research on, 77–79
Phonics
    assessment of, 82–86
    instructional strategies for, 88–94
    research on, 77–78, 79–80
Phonics Lessons K–3, 95
Phonological instruction
    culturally responsive instruction and, 96
    linguistic differences and, 80–81

Phonological instruction (*cont.*)
  overview of, 77
  principles for, 81–82
  See also Phonemic awareness; Phonics
Pictures, reading, 24–25
Picture walks, 121, 196
Podcasts, 188–189
Poetry enactments, 109
Positive feedback prompts, 169
Power, English as language of, 71
Predictions, making, 121–122, 201–203
Predictions vocabulary chart, 140, 141, 202
Prewriting activities, 155, 159
Print, access to or experiences with, 42–43
Proficient reading, 27–28
Project Look, 251
Pseudowords, reading, 79
Publishing phase of writing process,
      161–162

Q

Question–Answer Relationships, 124
Questioning
  in comprehension instruction, 124–125
  to invite dialogue, 65–66
Questioning Center forms, 125, 126

R

Racism, subtle, 53
Rainforest unit, books for, 272
Read-alouds, 60, 87, 140–142
Readers' Theatre, 108–109
Reading A–Z program, 249–250
Reading First, 254
Reading instruction, theory and approaches
      to, 2–7. *See also* Comprehension
      instruction; Dialogic instruction; Fifth-
      grade instruction; Fluency instruction;
      Phonological instruction; Reading
      workshops; Second-grade instruction;
      Vocabulary instruction
Reading interventions. *See* Supplemental
      instruction
Reading Recovery, 256, 260–261
Reading wars, 77

Reading workshops
  choosing multicultural literature for,
      60–62
  components of, 57–60
  diversity and, 63
  gradual release of responsibility and,
      62–63
Reciprocal teaching, 114
Repeated readings, 12, 100–101, 107
Research-based reading instruction
  blending with culturally responsive practice,
      10, 12–16
  content of, 7–8
  family involvement and, 252
  in fifth grade, 239–240
  goal of, 17
  overview of, 6–7
  pedagogy of, 8–10, 11
  preparation for, 213–214
  principles for decision making on, 17–28
  purpose of book and, 265–266
  in second grade, 214–215
  supplemental interventions and, 264–265
Research projects in second grade, 209–210,
      211, 212
Respect, communication of, 54, 249–250
Response-to-intervention (RTI) approach,
      255–256
Revising phase of writing process, 160–161
Rhyme Bingo, 94
Rhyme memory, 94
Rhymes, 87, 92
Roles in writing workshops, 175
RTI. *See* Response-to-intervention (RTI)
      approach
Running Records, 102–103
Running starts to books, 106

S

Schedule for writing workshops, 174
Schema theory, 115
School literacy, 243
Science instruction, 59–60
Scribbling, 29
Second-grade instruction
  end-of-day thoughts, 210, 212–214
  greeting time, 194

guided reading groups, 199–207
journal writing time, 193–194
learning centers, 207, 208
morning routine, 192–193
research projects, 209–210, 211, 212
school district information, 192
shared reading time, 195–198
word wall time, 194–195
word work time, 198–199
writing time, 207, 209
Self-fulfilling prophecy, 52–53
Self-questioning strategy, 116
Self-speech, 22
Semantic feature analysis, 146, 147
Semantics, 23
Semantic webs, 144, 145
Series reading, 110
Shared reading
   description of, 57
   in fifth grade, 220–224
   in second grade, 195–198
Shared writing experiences, 237
Sharing time, 60
Sharing with families, 246–248
Sheltered Instruction Observation Protocol
      (SIOP), 74–75, 86
"Show, Don't Tell" mini-lesson, 167–168
Simple view of reading, 40
SIOP. See Sheltered Instruction Observation
      Protocol
Small group instruction
   in fifth grade, 224–234
   phonemic awareness and, 79
   in second grade, 199–207
Social justice, themes of, 232
Sociocultural perspective on literacy
      development, 21, 40–41, 42–44
Software, instructional, 181, 185
Sorting strategies, 86–87, 89–90
Sound dominoes, 198–199
Sound–symbol correspondence, rules for, 80
Southern American English, 71–72
Special education services, 213
Spelling orthography, stages of, 82, 84, 85
SSR. See Sustained silent reading
Stair-step vocabulary, 143–144
"Standard English," 14, 71
Struggling readers, 40–44, 45, 254
Success for All model, 256

Summarizing strategy, 128–130
Supplemental instruction
   description of, 254–255
   principles for, 259–260
   research-based, culturally responsive
      teaching and, 264–265
   research on, 256–259
   strategies for, 260–264
Sustained silent reading (SSR), 99–100, 110,
      111
Syntax, 23
Synthesis comprehension strategy, 12
Synthetic phonics instruction, 80
Systematic instruction, 79

T

Talk triangle activity, 69
Targeted Reading Intervention, 259, 261
Technology, uses of for teaching, 180–182, 196
Texts
   conventions of, 132
   determining important ideas in, 127–128
   electronic, 181, 187–188
   favorite, for reading instruction, 267–271
   level systems for, 105
   matching to readers, 103–105
   structure of, instruction in, 115, 130–132
   by themes, 271–273
   See also Literature
Text-to-speech (TTS) function, 180, 183
Thick and thin questions, 124–125
Think-alouds, 125–127, 140, 221
Think–Pair–Share strategy, 15, 219
Time to Know software program, 185
Tongue twisters, 92
Tools for literacy development, 21–22
Trust, building with families, 246
TTS. See Text-to-speech (TTS) function, 180,
      183
Turn taking in classrooms, 66–67
Tutoring programs, 256
Twitter, 186

U

Use the Words You Know strategy, 90–91

V

Visibility
  of families in classrooms, 248
  of teachers in community, 247
Vocabulary instruction
  culturally responsive instruction and, 152
  principles for, 139
  research on, 137–138
  strategies for, 139–148
Vocabulary learning, 136–139
Vocabulary stair steps, 143–144
Vocabulary teams, 144
Voice–print match, 38
Vowel types, 91

W

Wait time in classrooms, 66–67
"Walking the walk" of students, 247
WebQuests, 187
Web 2.0, 178
Week, questions for, 65
"Where I'm From" (Lyon), 237, 238
Whole-group instruction
  in fifth grade, 220–224, 235–238
  in second grade, 195–199
Whole-language instruction, 3–5
Wikipedia, 189
Wikis, 189–190
Wikispaces, 190
Within-word pattern spelling, 203–205
Word banks, 92–94
Word derivations, 146–148
Word knowledge, continuum of, 135
Word learning. *See* Vocabulary learning
Word prediction chart, 140, 141, 202
Word recognition and fluency, 98
Word sorts, 89–90, 230, 235–236
Words Their Way model, 95
Word study instruction, 77, 94–95

Word walls, 92–94, 194–195
Word work, 58, 198–199, 235–236
World, questioning, 65–66
Writing
  assessment of, 162–163
  developmental phases of, 28–37
  research on, 154–155
  in second grade, 207, 209
  See also Writing process
Writing instruction
  culturally responsive instruction and, 176
  example of, 153–154
  principles for, 158
  research on, 154–158
  See also Writing workshops
Writing process
  explicit teaching of, 166–168
  research on, 156, 157, 158
  stages of, 159–162
Writing process movement, 3, 4
Writing workshops
  conferencing in, 168–170
  in fifth grade, 236–238
  genres and, 170, 171
  managing, 174–176
  mini-lessons in, 166–168
  modeling how to write, 164–166
  reading workshops and, 57
  research on, 156–157, 158
  writing to learn, 170, 172–173

Y

Yopp–Singer Test of Phonemic Segmentation,
  83
YouTube, 185

Z

Zone of proximal development (ZPD), 22–23, 38